W9-DHF-783

THE PRIVATIZATION OF SOCIAL POLICY?

The Privatization of Social Policy?

Occupational Welfare and the Welfare State in America, Scandinavia and Japan

Edited by

Michael Shalev
The Hebrew University of Jerusalem
Israel

First published in Great Britain 1996 by
MACMILLAN PRESS LTD
Houndmills, Basingstoke, Hampshire RG21 6XS
and London
Companies and representatives
throughout the world

A catalogue record for this book is available
from the British Library.

ISBN 0–333–64946–X

First published in the United States of America 1996 by
ST. MARTIN'S PRESS, INC.,
Scholarly and Reference Division,
175 Fifth Avenue,
New York, N.Y. 10010

ISBN 0–312–16437–8

Library of Congress Cataloging-in-Publication Data
The privatization of social policy? : occupational welfare and the
welfare state in America, Scandinavia and Japan / edited by Michael
Shalev.
Includes bibliographical references (p.   ) and indexes.
ISBN 0–312–16437–8 (cloth)
1. Industrial welfare—United States.   2. Industrial welfare–
–Canada.   3. Industrial welfare—Scandinavia.   4. Industrial
welfare—Japan.   I. Shalev, Michael.
HD7654.P75   1996
361.6'5—dc20   96–28751
                                                           CIP

---

11 10   9   8   7   6   5   4
06 05 04 03 02 01 00 99

Printed in Great Britain by
Antony Rowe Ltd, Chippenham, Wiltshire

Contents

Part 1: The United States

Part 2: Scandinavia

Part 3: Canada and Japan

Contributors

Terry Boychuk is an assistant professor in the Center for Health Policy, Research and Education and the Department of Sociology at Duke University (boych001@mc.duke.edu).

Robert Brym is Professor of Sociology and Associate of the Centre for Russian and East European Studies at the University of Toronto (rbrym@epas.utoronto.ca). He is editor of *Current Sociology* and the author of several books on Canadian and Russian societies, including *From Culture to Power: The Sociology of English Canada* (Oxford University Press, 1989).

Frank Dobbin is Associate Professor of Sociology at Princeton University (dobbin@pucc.princeton.edu). He has researched the origins of early personnel administration and the recent evolution of human resource management. He is the author of *Forging Industrial Policy: The United States, Britain, and France In The Railway Age* (Cambridge University Press, 1994).

Gøsta Esping-Andersen is Professor of Comparative Social Systems at the University of Trento, Italy (gesping@risc1.gelso.unitn.it). He has written extensively on social policy and recently directed a project for the UN on welfare states in the new global economic order (to be published as *Welfare States in Transition*).

Melissa A. Hardy is the Director of the Pepper Institute on Aging and Public Policy and Professor of Sociology at Florida State University (mhardy@coss.fsu.edu). Her recent research has explored the retirement decisions of older auto workers, income inequality in old age, and the disproportionate risks of poverty in old age faced by women and minorities in the United States.

Jon Mathias Hippe was until recently Director of Research at FAFO, the Institute for Applied Social Science in Oslo. He is now Director of Public Relations and Research at UNI-Storebrand in Oslo.

Sanford Jacoby is a member of three departments at UCLA: History, Management, and Policy Studies (sanford.jacoby@anderson.ucla.edu). His work examines labor market institutions from historical and comparative perspectives. His most recent book is *Workers of Nations: Industrial Relations in a Global Economy* (Oxford University Press, 1995).

Olli Kangas is Professor of Social Policy at the University of Turku in Finland (Olli.Kangas@utu.fi). His current research deals with links between public opinion, interest mediation and models of social policy. He is the author of *The Politics of Social Rights* (Stockholm University, 1991).

Gregg M. Olsen is an Associate Professor in the Department of Sociology at the University of Manitoba in Winnipeg, Canada (olsen@cc.umanitoba.ca). His areas of research include comparative social policy, social inequality and economic democracy. He is the author of *The Struggle for Economic Democracy in Sweden* (Avebury, 1992).

Einar Øverbye is deputy director of the Institute of Applied Social Research in Oslo (einar.overbye@isaf.no). His published work deals with pension politics and social policy in a comparative context.

Joakim Palme is a researcher at the Swedish Institute for Social Research, and he teaches in the Department of Sociology, both at Stockholm University (joakim@sofi.su.se). His work has been on comparative social policy and income inequality.

Axel West Pedersen is Research Fellow at FAFO, the Institute for Applied Social Science in Oslo (Axel.W.Pedersen@fafo.no). He is currently completing a dissertation on comparative occupational welfare at the European University Institute in Florence (pedersen @datacomm.iue.it or).

T.J. Pempel is Professor of International Studies at the University of Washington (pempel@u.washington.edu). He writes mainly on Japanese politics and economics and comparative politics. He is the editor of *Uncommon Democracies: The One-Party Dominant Democracies* (Cornell University Press, 1990).

Jill Quadagno is Professor of Sociology at Florida State University (jquadagn@garnet.acns.fsu.edu). She is past Vice President of the American Sociological Association and the author of *The Transformation of Old Age Security* (Chicago University Press, 1988) and *The Color of Welfare* (Oxford University Press, 1994).

Martin Rein teaches comparative social policy in the Department of Urban Studies and Planning at MIT (mrein@mit.edu). He has written about the interplay between social science research, social policy and practice. His most recent books are *Social Protection and the Enterprise in Transitional Economies* (with Andreas Worgotter and Barry Friedman, forthcoming from Cambridge University Press) and *Enterprise and the Welfare State in Western Economies* (with Eskil Wadensjö, forthcoming from Edward Elgar Press).

Michael Shalev teaches in the Department of Sociology and the Department of Political Science at the Hebrew University of Jerusalem (shalev@vms.huji.ac.il). He has written on comparative social policy and labor markets, and is the author of *Labour and the Political Economy in Israel* (Oxford University Press, 1992).

Toshimitsu Shinkawa teaches in the Faculty of Law at Hokkaido University, Japan. His research focuses on labor politics and social policy in Japan, and he is the author of *Nihon-gata Fukushi no Seiji Keizaigaku* [The Political Economy of Social Welfare in Japan] (San-ichi Shobo, 1993).

Beth Stevens is Senior Program Officer at the Robert Wood Johnson Foundation in Princeton, New Jersey (bas@rwjf.org). She is the author of several articles on the social implications and historical development of employee benefits in the United States.

Fritz von Nordheim Nielsen is Assistant Professor at Copenhagen Business School and Head of Section in the Danish Ministry of Social Affairs (dpfnn@sm.dk). He has written on comparative welfare states and labor movements, with a particular emphasis on pensions and Scandinavian Social Democracy.

Figures

Tables

Acknowledgements

Most of the participants in this project volunteered their services after I suggested that we convene a session on occupational welfare at the World Congress of Sociology in Madrid in 1990. Their dedication to the cause was apparent even then, in being willing to brave the intolerable heat and chaos of that hapless professional get-together. The process of editing and producing this book took far too long under my heavy hand, and taxed their commitment still further. The authors proved to be a remarkably resilient and loyal bunch, however, and I thank them sincerely for their fortitude. I owe a special debt of gratitude to the outstanding scholars—they know who they are—who joined the project as a personal favor to me, despite having more important things to do. I am also obliged to Marty Rein for initially stimulating my interest in the topic of this book.

No project of this kind can be brought to fruition without substantial institutional support. I have been particularly fortunate in this respect. The Israel Foundations Trustees provided me with a generous grant for research on Israel, which proved to be the stimulus for taking on a comparative project. Our Norwegian contributors—Jon Hippe and Axel Pedersen—subsequently tapped the generosity of FAFO, a research institute affiliated with the Norwegian trade union movement. The result was a seminar in Oslo, where we were able to exchange and discuss first drafts with all the comforts and hospitality one could wish for.

Without wishing to downplay the significance of these contributions to the success of the project, I have decided to dedicate this book to the personal computer and to the remarkable information and communication networks to which it is linked. Insofar as the manuscripts for this volume, written in many different countries and styles, appear coherent and attractive in the finished product it is the result of the synergy between me and my PC, assisted by two awesome but frustrating pieces of software (first *Nota Bene* and then *Word*). The charts and tables were ground many times through the mill of at least one spreadsheet program, and often two (*Excel* and/or *Quattro Pro*). The link between our PC's and the Internet provided a near-instantaneous and virtually costless means for project members to communicate and to exchange electronic documents. The vast resources of the Internet also furnished excellent bibliographic assistance and some of the data that appear in the book. I have to confess to being blown away by these revolutions in the way that information is located, moved and processed, that have occurred entirely within the course of my own professional lifetime.

Introduction

Michael Shalev

Why Occupational Welfare?

Ideological backlash and the severe constraints of fiscal realpolitik have thrown welfare states everywhere into some measure of disrepute. At its fullest, the call for privatization from the political-economic right implies a wholesale shift from collective protection by the state to individual responsibility via the market. Yet to the extent that individual problems of income security, health care and education necessarily demand collective solutions, it is unclear how best to undertake "the private provision of public welfare" (Papadakis and Taylor-Gooby, 1987). Some advocate leaving the job to the more or less spontaneous efforts of families and local communities, while others see voluntary associations and nonprofit organizations as a more practical substitute for the state. Recent years have seen an upsurge in many countries of an alternative which offers collective provision via market mechanisms. That alternative—social protection as part of the employment relationship—falls under the rubric of what is conventionally known as "occupational welfare".

Occupational pensions—which provide supplementary income to retired persons as a benefit embedded in their employment contracts—are the core program of occupational welfare, and hence our principal concern in this book. In principle, however, occupational welfare encompasses not only pensions but other types of income maintenance as well, if they are a condition of employment. In fact the same is true for the complete spectrum of welfare state functions, including health, education, housing, child care and personal counseling.

Under contemporary conditions in the advanced capitalist democracies, the status of occupational welfare as an alternative to provision by government, the market, or the "third sector" has attracted considerable attention from policy actors and their expert advisers. Its appeal is not hard to explain. Governments are looking for ways to divest themselves of fiscal responsibilities. Employers seek methods of attracting, retaining and controlling labor under changing technological and labor-supply conditions. Trade unions are on the defensive in most countries, and correspondingly interested in new ways to buttress their authority and appeal. Finally, entrepreneurs and professionals with a vested interest in occupational programs naturally act to promote their expansion. But while the future of occupational welfare is thus over-determined, our understanding of its comparative history is as yet perfunctory.

Why is such an understanding necessary? First and foremost, because the striking empirical diversity in occupational welfare cries out for explanation. While available data are far from complete (see below), it is evident that there are pronounced national differences in the scope of occupational welfare which are even greater than the far better-known variance among welfare states. For instance, data gathered for around 1980 by Rein and Rainwater (1986c:53) indicate that whereas in France, Germany and England between a fifth and a quarter of overall social expenditure took the form of benefits paid by employers, the corresponding proportions for Sweden and the United States were 6% and 33% respectively! In a review of data on private occupational pensions in 18 OECD countries, Esping-Andersen (1987) uncovered even more remarkable variation. His measure of expenditure as a proportion of national product varied from zero or negligible levels (in Austria, Finland, Ireland, Italy and Norway) to ratios in excess of one or even two percent of GNP (in Australia, France, Switzerland and the US). Where the same indicator could be tracked over time it revealed, in most cases, a trend of rapid expansion throughout the postwar period. There are indications that in many countries growth was even more pronounced during the 1980s, inspired by what one expert described as "the current vogue for turning over state pension responsibilities to the private sector" (Hannah, 1991:11).[1]

Rapid temporal growth in a context of continuing cross-national diversity poses an obvious need to understand the trajectories characteristic of different national settings. Unfortunately, previous scholarship has barely scratched the surface of the problem. Interest in occupational welfare has traditionally been confined mainly to specialists and social policy experts. Because of their strong applied orientation, the former have embraced limited theoretical ambitions, while the latter have been motivated primarily by a deep concern for protecting the welfare state from what are assumed to be inegalitarian inroads by the market. We now know that these fears are not necessarily well-founded. Looked at from a dynamic perspective the relationship between the development of "public" and "occupational" welfare constitutes a dialectic (van Gunsteren and Rein, 1985) which is potentially governed by two quite different dynamics. Knowledgeable observers have identified both a "positive dialectic" of mutually reinforcing growth, and a "negative dialectic" where growth in one arena occurs at the expense of the other.

The need to challenge outworn assumptions about the character of occupational welfare is only one of several weaknesses in past literature which are addressed in this book. In particular, most extant research on occupational welfare is local in orientation, and focuses on the details of specific programs. Consequently, we still do not know enough about how much, and in what ways, national configurations of occupational welfare vary. The last few years have seen a flurry of national studies and also, in Europe, the beginnings of regionally-focused interest in occupational welfare (most notably within Scandinavia and in the framework of the European Union). Nevertheless, the informational base for comparative analysis remains incomplete. Furthermore, although professional associations of providers (such as pension insurers) and international advisory agencies (like the OECD) have stepped up their efforts to describe and compare occupational welfare across different national settings, their emphasis is understandably on the trends and dilemmas of the here-and-now.[2] Without denying the need for such efforts (indeed, that need has motivated much of the work collected in this volume), their utility is sometimes compromised by a lack of historical depth.

Another condition which is essential for understanding the origins of national distinctiveness in occupational welfare and the forces which drive its development, is of course an appropriate theoretical apparatus. Yet, many past studies of the phenomenon have been atheoretical works with a descriptive or normative bent; or else they have been cast in theoretical frameworks (such as the economics of labor markets and employee remuneration) which cannot answer the questions we have posed.[3]

Occupational Welfare and the Welfare State

The contributors to the present volume have steered clear of embracing a single overarching hypothesis. But they do share a common analytical perspective, beginning with the axiom that occupational welfare should not be—indeed cannot be—disentangled from the welfare state. This is not to denigrate the relevance of other perspectives. For instance, as von Nordheim Nielsen (1986) has pointed out, occupational pensions are not only a form of collective immunity from the financial vicissitudes of old age. They are also a means of motivating and compensating employees; and, no less importantly, a mechanism of compulsory savings. Each of these frameworks—social protection, personnel management and capital formation—is best served by a different theoretical apparatus. Is a "multidisciplinary" approach therefore called for?

This volume is premised on a different view. We propose that an emphasis on the social policy dimension of occupational welfare, while undoubtedly incomplete, offers a number of valuable advantages. It forces us to recognize the role of the state in directly or indirectly shaping systems of occupational welfare (whereas the other two perspectives are liable to make the error of treating markets for labor or capital as closed systems). It promotes a relational view of occupational welfare vis-a-vis the welfare state (raising the important question of whether the two function as substitutes or complements). It encourages analysts to seek insights from general theories of public policy and the interplay between politics and markets. In our view, such insights are indispensable to explaining divergence and change in national patterns of occupational welfare.

Before moving to a fuller discussion of the substantive and theoretical axes of our undertaking, we need to dwell in more than the usual detail on how to define its subject-matter. Earlier, occupational welfare was equated with the provision of welfare state functions (income maintenance and social services) as conditions of employment. Unfortunately, merely making such an assertion is not enough to convincingly stake out the terrain for study. The following four issues are particularly important.

Why distinguish state and occupational welfare? A powerful argument can be made to the effect that from the point of view of the life-chances and wellbeing of individuals and groups, occupational welfare is only one component of the overall "welfare economy" or "welfare society" (cf.

Rein, 1982; Rein and Rainwater, 1986a). This argument has particular relevance to the problem of accounting for exceptional "welfare state laggards" (Wilensky, 1975). For example, as Katzenstein (1984) has pointed out, "liberal" Switzerland with its meager public programs, and "social" Sweden with its massive welfare state, offer about as much aggregate social security to their citizens. In a similar vein, Osterman (1990) contends that the sharp contrast usually drawn between the welfare states of Sweden and the United States is in large part illusory. The reason is not only the longstanding role of occupational welfare in the fields of income maintenance and health care, but also a more recent tendency for employers to accept responsibility for providing their employees with a broad range of social services. This is an important insight, but it need not dictate that we study occupational welfare solely from the perspective of overall welfare. That depends on what is to be explained. Our interest here is not in "overall welfare", but in how and why the occupational sector of welfare emerges and grows. For these purposes, what is important in the broader picture is the relationship between occupational and state welfare. That said, however, we must face head-on the issue of whether it is possible to draw a meaningful boundary between the two.

Private versus Public. One seemingly obvious difference between occupational and state welfare is that the former is privately initiated and managed by individual employers or the concerted action of unions and employers, while the latter covers programs that are sponsored and controlled by the state. In fact the private/public distinction is more complicated than this. Occupational pensions for civil servants were often the historic precursor of and model for private sector plans, and they continue to dominate the non-social-security pension sector in a number of countries (e.g. Austria, Italy and Belgium). Are civil service pensions "public" (because paid by the state), or "occupational" (since they derive from employment contracts rather than citizenship)? The public/private boundary is also violated by state regulation of private-sector plans, which has often proved critical in opening or closing windows of opportunity for their proliferation. In some countries (e.g. France and Switzerland) the state has actually made participation in "private" schemes mandatory.

Qualitative "social rights". A second potential basis for differentiating between the two spheres of welfare are qualitative characteristics of the entitlements which they offer, such as their degree of universality or the extent to which they serve to insulate the recipient from market pressures (Korpi, 1983; Esping-Andersen, 1990). An ideal-typical system of occupational pensions (faithful to liberal political economies like the United States) furnishes benefits which are conditioned by individual work histories, and are highly differentiated by both status (occupation) and situs (workplace or sector). The ideal-typical social security pension (especially in social-democratic political economies like Sweden) ought to be the mirror-image: awarded as a citizen's right conditioned only by age, and characterized by comparatively uniform benefits. In practice, no such neat distinction can be drawn in the real world. On the one hand, the custom of making eligibility contingent on individual labor market participation is by no means a monopoly of occupational pensions proper. In countries like Germany and Japan, the generosity of statutory supplementary pensions is almost entirely determined by what Titmuss called "work merit". At the same time, and contrary to prevailing stereotypes, it is not necessarily the case that occupational pensions are either particularistic (varying across occupations and firms) or tenuous (dependent on the worker's attachment to a particular occupation, employer or sector). This is hardly true in Sweden, where the peak associations of blue-collar workers and their employers administer a unified private pension scheme with virtually complete coverage.[4]

Protection or Benefits?   Finally, neither the sponsors nor the beneficiaries of occupational welfare schemes necessarily interpret them—as we do—as a form of collective protection. Indeed, a favorite sport of students of occupational welfare is the debate over where "welfare" ends and "fringe benefits" begin. In principle, the answer is simple enough: income substitutes are benefits, while income maintenance is welfare. But does the Fellow of an Oxbridge college who is entitled to a generous pension and lives in a house owned and maintained by the college regard these arrangements as a way of solving housing and retirement problems, or a means of offsetting an inadequate salary? In all likelihood, both. This type of ambiguity is characteristic of occupational welfare, but hardly unique to it. State welfare, too, has many faces in addition to its role in social protection—among others, it is a work incentive, a macroeconomic de/stabilizer, and a means of structuring classes and political alignments.

Undeniably, occupational welfare is a slippery concept. Despite the analytical advantages of contrasting it to the welfare state, it would clearly be naive to argue that the two domains are distinguishable in any absolute sense. This is true whether the distinction is made in terms of the public/private boundary, the quality of entitlements, or the underlying purpose of the system. Awareness of the conceptually permeable boundaries surrounding occupational welfare may affront one's sense of intellectual tidiness, but for researchers, it is an essential tool for understanding the phenomenon. As this book will show, analysts seeking to comprehend the evolution of occupational pensions cannot ignore the possibility of subtly changing divisions of responsibility and emphasis between employers/unions and the state. Neither can they ignore the complex relationship between pensions as retirement income, as deferred wages, and as forced savings.

The Comparative Dimension

In seeking to address the need for an international perspective, we have taken a middle position between two competing organizing principles. One, the "handbook principle", would have generated a volume of descriptive country studies representing the widest possible range of settings. Alternatively, we might have opted for a fully theoretically-driven approach, selectively contrasting critical cases in order to pinpoint key analytical issues. Instead, recognizing the primacy of gathering and disseminating information in an infant field of study, we have given ample space in the essays which follow to description. But at the same time, in order to keep the analytical focus as sharp as possible, we have also limited the range of countries and issues examined.

Most of the book is set in only two contexts, the United States and Scandinavia. The reasons are twofold. First, these are widely assumed to be polar opposites in terms of the balance between state and occupational welfare. (See the discussion in the next section.) Nevertheless, in recent years the occupational sphere has entered a phase of marked expansion in the Nordic states. In contrast, at least in health care the expense of private schemes has led some large employers in the US to call for their "nationalization". Hence, comparisons between the United States and Scandinavia offer insights into both diversity and potential convergence. The other reason for the particular geographical focus of the studies collected in this volume is a more practical one. The extent of interest in the subject in both Scandinavian and American sociology and related disciplines has created a critical mass of sufficient scholarship to bring to bear a variety of perspectives on a variety of issues.

While one of our major tasks is to convey the facts (not least, to bring the Scandinavian experience to American readers and vice versa), we are also able to move beyond this, to touch upon more general issues of a theoretical nature. These issues are only partly congruent, however. In the course of the mutual explorations by Scandinavian and American authors which were the prelude to this book, it became clear that in each setting occupational welfare has entered the consciousness of scholars in different ways. In the United States, one important lens for viewing occupational welfare has been the new structuralism in the field of social stratification. Given their agenda of "bringing firms and labor markets in", studies in this tradition have inevitably been struck by the unequal distribution of employee benefits and its systematic links to the employment structure on the one hand, and social hierarchies on the other.[5] Other scholars have been fascinated by the historical origins of the distinctive American pattern of modest public protection coexisting with a highly developed occupational system which is decidedly partial in coverage. Not surprisingly, these investigators were drawn into broader debates over the causes of American "exceptionalism" in social and economic policy.[6]

In comparison to the United States, Scandinavian interest in occupational welfare has developed against a very different backdrop. Substantively, it was for long assumed (both inside and outside the Nordic countries) that in Scandinavia the role of the welfare state in constructing systems of social protection dwarfed the contributions of both markets and civil society. The "Scandinavian model" of comprehensive, generous and universal entitlements to public income maintenance and social services suggested that this ought to be the case. So too did the "social democratic model", the dominant version of a class politics perspective among students of Scandinavian social policy. As a result, the priority which ranks highest on the analytical agenda of the Nordic contributors to this volume is to confront this conventional wisdom with the realities of occupational welfare.[7]

Quantifying the Phenomenon

Comparable data on the scope of occupational welfare are very hard to come by, even when the focus is narrowed to the most empirically

tractable subset of the phenomenon: occupational pensions within the
OECD bloc.[8] Population or workplace surveys are the best source of
information on the coverage rate of occupational pensions and their role
in income maintenance for the retired. However, most survey research
has been ad hoc in nature and confined to single nations. Exceptions are
initiatives by the European Union and the Luxembourg Income Study
(LIS). Less comparable but more comprehensive data collections can
only be compiled by eclectic data-gathering. The task of such research is
to bring together various kinds of aggregate data collected by national
statistical agencies and private or public research institutes, attempting in
the process to place them on a more or less common footing.

The most systematic venture of this kind to date was sponsored by the
OECD and the US Department of Labor (Turner and Dailey, 1990;
Dailey and Turner, 1992). Unfortunately this study is limited to only nine
countries, selected because of their comparatively heavy reliance on
nongovernmental group pension plans in the private sector. In the late
1980s the proportion of the private sector labor force participating in
such plans ranged from 20-30% in Britain, Australia and Canada to a
high of more than 90% in Switzerland and France. The United States
was located midway between these two poles with a 46% coverage rate,
its closest neighbors being Germany and the Netherlands.[9]

An earlier attempt to pool diverse national-level data (Esping-
Andersen, 1987) generated estimates of expenditure on private sector
pensions for 18 countries *circa* 1980. I have already cited comparative
data from Esping-Andersen's rich dataset, and will return to it in more
depth shortly.

Finally, a study by Pestieau (1992) using the LIS database yielded a
variety of finely-tuned indicators of the contribution of occupational
pensions to the actual gross income of households headed by retirees.
One such indicator, for around the mid-1980s, focuses on middle-income
households (the second and third quartiles) with heads aged between 65-
74. For this population occupational pensions typically contributed about
a fifth of household income (Canada, Australia, Germany and
Switzerland). The ratio was slightly less in the US (17%) and
significantly more in the UK (27%) and the Netherlands (35%).

Comparing these various indicators it is clear that while variation in
occupational pensions may well have more than one underlying
dimension (e.g. pension fund assets are not necessarily related to pension
expenditure), some of the correlations between indicators are disturbingly
incomplete. Thus the United States appears to have exceptionally high

private pension expenditure, yet its occupational pensions constitute an exceptionally low proportion of retirement income. In the UK, on the other hand, contribution to retirement income is rated high whereas the relative size of both the participating and beneficiary populations is seemingly comparatively low.

Under these circumstances, unless and until better cross-national data become available, the quantitative study of occupational welfare is best carried out using multiple disaggregated indicators for single countries, or limited comparisons between countries with more or less similar systems of welfare. With the exception of Martin Rein's chapter, which builds on a unique data-gathering exercise by the European Union, these two approaches dominate the remainder of this volume. Where data quality is less of an issue is in sketching the broad outlines of cross-national variation, which is the task to which I now turn.

Using Gøsta Esping-Andersen's (1990) well-known classification of welfare state "regimes",[10] this section marshals empirical evidence for our argument that occupational welfare should be studied as part and parcel of cross-national variation in the entire social policy complex, and offers further justification for our selection of country cases. Esping-Andersen's influential study posited that the Western nations can be grouped into three clusters with strikingly different approaches to social protection. In making this argument he referred to a broad spectrum of indicators—employment policy as well as social security; the universality of welfare entitlements and not only how much they cost; and the relative scope of private as well as public provision. His analysis of 18 capitalist democracies that are members of the OECD led Esping-Andersen to the identification of three social policy regimes.

♦ In the *residual* type, welfare guarantees are confined to a stigmatized poor population. Priority is given to market discipline rather than social solidarity. The private sector is seen as the proper place to deal with economic insecurity for all but the least fortunate citizens.

♦ The *institutional* type of social policy regime is the polar opposite of liberalism. It is characterized by social policy universalism (which means that the welfare state includes the middle classes), public income guarantees that effectively "decommodify" wage-earners, and a distinct preference for public over private provision.

♦ Finally, the *corporativist* policy regime is not as favorable to labor as the institutional type, but it also employs state power in order to partially offset insecurities and injustices inherent in the market system. Like the residual type, corporativism is anti-universalistic,

TABLE 1: *Factor Analysis of 14 Social Policy Indicators*

Indicator	Definition	INST	CORP
Poor Relief	Means-tested poor relief as % of total public social spending	-0.78	0.15
Public Employment	Public sector as % of total employment	0.76	-0.14
Social Security	Social security expenditure as % of GDP	0.75	0.09
Social Security Pensions	Expenditure on social security pensions as % of total	0.73	-0.41
Occupational Pensions	Expenditure on occupational pensions as % of total	-0.71	-0.47
Private Health	Private as % of total health spending	-0.68	-0.06
Active Labor Market	"Active labor market" expenditure as % of GDP	0.66	0.07
Pension Spending	Total pension expenditure as % of GDP	0.63	0.19
Individual Pensions	Expenditure on individual annuity pensions as % of total	-0.58	0.28
Benefit Inequality	Gap between basic and maximum benefits (sickness, UI, pensions)	0.58	-0.38
Employment Performance	Longrun index of unemployment and activity rate	-0.29	0.57
Pension Schemes	Number of occupationally distinct public pension schemes	0.09	0.67
Pension Coverage	Automatic citizen's right to pension benefits	-0.01	-0.90
Public Employee Pensions	Expenditure on public employee pensions as % of total	0.06	0.91

but in a different way: it favors differentiated systems of social security for different social groups, with an eye to preserving established status hierarchies.

Table 1 reports the results of an empirical test for the presence of these three subtypes. Factor analysis was applied to almost the entire gamut of social policy indicators collected by Esping-Andersen.[11] Most

usivelyuniversal
income maintenance, emphasizing social security rather than poor relief.
This goes along with high levels of state intervention in the labor market,
and avoidance of private sector solutions to problems of sickness and
retirement. The second factor, labeled CORP, teaches us what it is about
the corporativist policy regime that distinguishes it from the other
models. In some respects corporativism is similar to institutionalism; the
difference is not the scope of the social safety-net, but the prevalence of
differentiated programs for different sectors of the workforce.

Policy and Politics Under Three Regimes

The diverse indicators of pension policy included in this reanalysis of
Esping-Andersen's data help to clarify the varying relationship between
occupational welfare and the welfare state under different policy
regimes. The institutional regime offers generous pensions with a clear
preference for state provision over either occupational or insurance-based
delivery. The residual model presents the mirror-image except that,
surprisingly, the two systems are indistinguishable with respect to the
universality of pension coverage. The corporativist pension regime is a
little above the norm in terms of overall pension spending, despite the
fact that the coverage and significance of universal citizens' pensions are
comparatively restricted. What keeps aggregate expenditure up is the
heterogeneity of benefits, with some groups (notably civil servants)
enjoying more generous entitlements than others. Interestingly,
corporativism shares the institutional regime's aversion to occupational
pensions, albeit not to the same degree. It is in residual systems that
occupational pensions are most prominent.

While Esping-Andersen's notion of regime blurs the difference
between causes (political conditions) and effects (policy preferences and
outcomes), I prefer to differentiate the two. His discussion identified
three distinct political contexts:[13]

♦ *Scandinavian Social Democracy*, characterized by levels of working
  class mobilization almost without peer in other Western nations.[14]

FIGURE 1: *Social Policy Factor Scores for 18 OECD Countries*

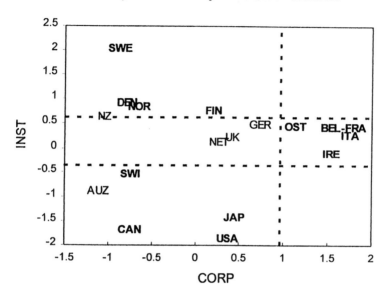

- *Conservative European* nations—Italy, France, Belgium, Austria and Ireland—which share an absolutist past, relatively late-blooming democracy, and a largely Catholic population.
- *Liberal* states—the USA, Canada, Switzerland and Japan—in which working class mobilization is very weak and the conservative heritage is largely or wholly absent.

The remaining five countries in Esping-Andersen's study are more difficult to classify. Their state traditions are either close to the conservative group (Germany and the Netherlands) or liberal in character (the UK, Australia and New Zealand), but they have also experienced moderate levels of working class mobilization.

When the 18 nations are arrayed along the two dimensions of social policy variation uncovered in the factor analysis, the evident linkage between contexts and policies generates an illuminating cross-national mapping of welfare regimes (Figure 1). The countries belonging to each of the three types of political milieu are neatly located inside the three areas of the chart that portray their corresponding policy regimes. As a result, we can see both the strengths and the limitations of the selection of countries for this volume. Our study targets two of the three country clusters—the Scandinavian and the Liberal. It thereby captures both poles of the most important policy dichotomy (Institutional/Residual); that is, the contrast between settings in which individual and group initiative in the market arena loom exceptionally large in social protection, and those in which the state plays the dominant role in providing for retirement and other contingencies. The conservative countries, with their distinctively corporativist policy profile, are left out of our analysis. This omission was a conscious one. The aims of our study were sufficiently ambitious without the additional challenge of interpreting a fundamentally different type of welfare regime. (The same is true for the significant number of countries which are mixed cases with respect to both politics and policy). The tasks of documenting and analyzing the role of occupational welfare in politically conservative Catholic states with corporativist policy profiles clearly ought to be a high priority for future research.

Occupational Welfare in the US

In the United States, the overwhelming majority of the full-time employees of medium and large-scale enterprises in the private sector receive medical care and retirement wages as a fringe benefit. In his contribution to this volume, Martin Rein offers an unusually detailed statistical portrait of the significance of "non-legally required social benefits" in the US and a number of EC member states. He concludes that in the United States "more than 30 percent of total social protection is channeled through the firm in the private sector"—three or four times comparable figures in Europe.

As is well known, despite America's heavy aggregate reliance on occupational welfare, its penetration is very uneven across different types of employers and workers. This is abundantly clear from survey data collected by the Bureau of Labor Statistics (Table 2). As in most other countries, the American civil service is an island of relative privilege so far as occupational welfare is concerned. In the private sector, as theories of economic dualism and segmented labor markets predict, employee benefits are concentrated in larger, more sophisticated firms. But these same firms—historically the cradle of collectively bargained occupational welfare—have also experienced degradation of benefits in recent years (note especially the move towards defined contribution pensions). In fact, not only the quality but also the coverage of

TABLE 2: *Employee Benefit Coverage in the US, by Type of Plan*
(Proportion of full-time employees)

		Defined benefit pension	Defined contribution pension	Any medical care	Generous medical care	Unpaid maternity leave	Life insurance
State & local government	1990	90	9	93	n.a.	51	88
Small private establishments	1990	20	31	69	n.a.	17	64
Medium & large private establishments	1980	84	–	97	n.a.	–	96
	1991	59	48	83	n.a.	37	94
Union		86	33	91	52	41	96
Non-union		50	52	81	18	36	93

Note: A "generous" medical care plan is one that is wholly employer-financed and covers all members of the employee's family.

Sources: Bureau of Labor Statistics, Employee Benefits Surveys (Monthly Labor Review, 1995; Wiatrowski, 1994)

occupational welfare has been shrinking in the US.[15] These trends are usually explained, in part, as a consequence of the decline of trade unionism in the private sector. Indeed, the data show that in 1991 unionized workers continued to enjoy much more attractive medical and retirement benefits.

Union membership is but one example of the many individual-level attributes that are linked to discontinuities in occupational welfare in the United States. To begin with, there is a wide gulf between the economic security and wellbeing of employed persons and those who are unemployed or outside the labor force (although these gaps may be smaller across households than between individuals). There is also substantial inequality between fully and steadily employed workers in comparison with unemployed, part-time, or temporarily employed labor.

And the absence of benefits disproportionately affects those workers (the low-paid, minorities, women and older persons) who are disadvantaged to begin with.[16]

Three familiar approaches have dominated debates over why occupational welfare takes up so much of America's social policy space. Class conflict perspectives portray the private/public mix in the US as a victory for business interests and a symptom of the weakness of organized labor and the left. The welfare state is viewed as the product of sporadic concessions from the state, concessions generated either by pressure from below ("poor peoples' movements") or enlightened self-interest from above ("corporate liberalism").[17] For the last fifteen years the protagonists of both arguments have faced challenges from state-centered perspectives, which deny that class interest and mobilization play a determinate role in social politics and emphasize instead the impact of the policy arena itself. Organizational and political structures and state powers and practices specific to the American context are said to underlie the peculiarity of its public policy profile. The dynamics of policy change (or the lack of it) are seen as rooted in the interests of state managers, the legacy of past policies, and the inner logic of the modalities of policymaking.[18]

The articles assembled here which focus on the American case faithfully reflect this overall agenda and these disputes between competing approaches. The first three papers are all concerned with the historical origins of the mix between state and occupational welfare in the United States. Each favors a variant of one or another of the three master orientations already mentioned, although they also draw in a subsidiary way on the other approaches.

In Chapter 2, Sanford Jacoby deals with the underestimated role of a single corporate figure, Marion B. Folsom, a senior Kodak executive who was instrumental in the thirties in shaping the Social Security Act in ways that were inexpensive for business and left room for a continuing role for occupational welfare. Jacoby's careful micro-historical study supports the view that under American conditions "the vacuum created by a disorganized working class" was filled by the mutually reinforcing efforts of corporate liberals, reformer-experts, and government bureaucrats.

In the following chapter Beth Stevens describes what came close to being a historic departure from this pattern in the late 1940s, following the emergence of mass unionism as a major new force in the American political economy. Had the balance of political and labor market power after World War Two been more favorable, important union leaders might have achieved their nascent strategic goal of (in effect) a corporatist breakthrough to the welfare state. Instead, they were obliged to settle for a narrower postwar settlement, in which substantial new elements of the welfare package were wedded to collective bargaining with management, rather than to political exchange with the state.

However, in Chapter 4 Frank Dobbin and Terry Boychuk point out that even though large employers have traditionally feared that state programs would crowd out occupational welfare, and union leaders accepted the primacy of occupational welfare, the historical record on pensions shows that extensions of public coverage have played a crucial role in stimulating private coverage. The key to this paradox, they suggest, are the feedback effects of changes in public policy on the interests and goals of private actors, especially employers.

The final American contribution is a contemporary case study of retirement provision in a single sector, the automobile industry. Here, changes in government regulation of some of the minutiae of occupational pensions have had the effect of undermining their attractiveness to employers as a means of regulating retirement. In investigating the unanticipated effects of public policy shifts affecting tax and pension rules, Jill Quadagno and Melissa Hardy illustrate once again the complex, dialectical nature of the relationship between occupational welfare and the state.

The Scandinavian Context

According to the social democratic model, the advanced Nordic welfare states—especially those of Sweden and Norway—are the product of strong unions and labor parties committed to public sector solutions to the distributional aspirations of a cohesive working class. One of the most widely cited illustrations of the argument is one which speaks directly to the role of occupational welfare—namely, the celebrated victory of the Swedish labor movement in its struggle in the 1960s to place second-tier pensions firmly within the state arena.[19]

It is indeed true that there is nothing in Scandinavia's institutional welfare states which can compare with the substantial but uneven role of occupational welfare alongside America's residual welfare state. Yet it has also become apparent that occupational welfare plays a far greater role than is usually assumed. In the late 1980s the Norwegian contributors to this volume revealed for the first time that benign neglect on the part of unions and social-democratic politicians, coupled with discreet activism on the part of vendors of group plans, had caused widespread dissemination of enterprise-based occupational welfare in Norway. With increasing effort invested in documenting the occupational domain of welfare, it also became apparent that both its overall extent and its specific forms vary considerably between the different Scandinavian countries. The fiscal and political fallout from earlier welfare state expansion, now belatedly reaching Nordic shores, has thrust occupational welfare still further into the spotlight. By way of illustration, a recent survey of Nordic pension policies speaks the familiar language of "cuts in benefit levels and privatization of pension schemes" (Niemelä and Salminen, 1994:9).

At the theoretical level, the unexpected robustness of occupational welfare inevitably raised questions about the validity of the social democratic model of the welfare state. This was, after all, a model which afforded no status to occupational welfare as a dependent variable, and confined its independent variables primarily to the aims and resources of labor movements, with corresponding neglect of the roles of capital and the state. Additionally, in implying that both the institutions of occupational welfare and the public/private welfare mix could be "read off" from the cohesion and strength of organized labor, the model was bound to encounter difficulties in explaining the intra-Scandinavian variability already remarked upon. For these reasons, explicit or implicit debates with the social democratic model frame all of the Scandinavian contributions to this volume.

In his overview of intra-Nordic variations in the realm of occupational pensions (Chapter 6), Einar Øverbye questions the notion that the Nordic countries share a single, institutional welfare regime. He seeks to show that politics matter for policy in ways more subtle than would be anticipated by a simple class conflict perspective. Based on patterns of union structure and political strength, Sweden and Norway could be expected to have similar policy profiles. Yet in practice, the pension systems of the Scandinavian countries are closer to being polarized between an "east-Nordic" and a "west-Nordic" cluster (Sweden and Finland versus Denmark and Norway). A variety of contextual forces (historical and institutional), as well as strategic political choices, are invoked to explain these differences.

The next Scandinavian contribution, by Jon Hippe and Axel Pedersen, also shows the error of indiscriminately lumping the Norwegian case with the better-known Swedish story. A number of social-democratic premises are found wanting in Norway, including the presumed marginality of the private pension sector, the allegedly more egalitarian impact of public pensions, and the assumption that labor parties and the political arena (rather than labor unions and collective bargaining) hold the explanatory key. Hippe and Pedersen also place current Norwegian trends in longer-term perspective, arguing that the traditional social-democratic dynamic by which national statutes or agreements pushed occupational welfare forward along a broad front and under public sector auspices, has more recently been replaced by a negative interplay which de facto has the state and the unions promoting an expanding tier of company-level sickness and pension schemes.

The remaining two Scandinavian papers also focus on the recent past and the unfolding future of occupational welfare (more specifically, occupational pensions). Echoing a prominent theme of the US studies earlier in the volume, these authors place substantial weight on the second-order consequences of previous policy configurations in shaping contemporary developments. In Chapter 8 Olli Kangas and Joakim Palme trace the ways in which institutional differences in the character and administration of existing supplementary schemes can account for the differing aspirations and strategies of contemporary union and employer leaders in Finland and Sweden. They conclude that program divergence, although not unrelated to differences in class structure and power, will have the effect of further differentiating policy outcomes in what traditional comparisons have presented as broadly similar contexts.

In Chapter 9 Fritz von Nordheim Nielsen also places feedback effects at the center of his analysis, arguing that they not only complicate the tasks faced by social scientists, but also frustrate the intentions of policy activists. In his detailed case study of pension reform in Denmark in the 1980s, von Nordheim Nielsen shows that the growth of occupational programs had the effect of exacerbating emergent structural cleavages within the workforce, and placing the future of these cleavages high on the hidden agendas of key actors in the policymaking drama. In like fashion, the cumulative growth of occupational funds into vast pools of capital led business interests and political elites to redefine their aspirations. A coherent policy consensus thus became virtually impossible to achieve.

Broadening the View

A final pair of country studies has been designed to widen the scope of the book's international coverage, and at the same time to bring out analytically interesting counterpoints to our extended coverage of the US and Scandinavian settings. Like the US, both of the cases in question— Canada and Japan—are liberal states with residual social policies. But there are also significant differences that help place the US experience in perspective.

Canada is of special interest to our comparative inquiry because it is to some extent located in between the Scandinavian and US models, particularly in relation to the organizational and political strength of labor. In Chapter 10 Gregg Olsen and Robert Brym identify an important policy difference between the two North American states, namely the earlier and more comprehensive development of Canada's public pension system. By combining and expanding the theoretical agendas of the Scandinavian and US literatures, Olsen and Brym succeed in pinpointing differences in the political-economic context that are responsible for the partly similar and partly different development of the pension mix in Canada and the US.

The Canadian case throws light on the US experience because in spite of broad contextual similarities between the two, Canada exhibits a significantly different division of labor between occupational and state welfare. The value of our other contrasting case to those who seek to understand the American experience derives from the obverse logic of comparison. For while the form and underlying logic of Japan's public/private welfare mix exhibit striking similarities to the US, there are obvious cultural and political differences between the two contexts.

With its traditionally stunted welfare state and ramified system of occupational welfare confined to the large-enterprise sector, it may be argued that Japan takes the decentralized, dualist logic of American occupational welfare to its logical extreme. Chapter 11, by Toshimitsu Shinkawa and T.J. Pempel, identifies the historical and structural forces which underpin the Japanese system. Shinkawa and Pempel argue that the relative weakness of organized labor in relation to business is the key to the bifurcated division between provision by the state and the large firm in Japan. Yet like the authors of the Canadian chapter, they combine this insight with attention to other important dimensions of the political economic context. Their account offers US observers the possibility of reflecting on what is truly distinctive about the American case, and contemplating a different version of its future.

Theoretical emphases should be sensitive to the context to be explained. This is one of the central themes elaborated by Gøsta Esping-Andersen in his concluding chapter. After revisiting issues raised here and in the body of the book concerning the nature of occupational welfare from a social policy perspective, Esping-Andersen turns to the problem of making sense of the "causal labyrinth" which seems endemic to the study of occupational welfare. Comparing the broad thrust of its evolution in different countries, he suggests that a different developmental dynamic may be discerned in divergent settings, and that this difference may in turn be linked to cross-national disparities in patterns of trade union organization. Applying the same causal logic to a long historical view, Esping-Andersen posits that changing divisions of welfare have been forged by the effects of secular and cyclical trends in politics and the economy—trends that have had a profound impact on both the structure and the relative power of labor and capital. From this perspective, the current dynamism of occupational welfare—including signs of an apparent reversal of long-term trends in both the United States and Scandinavia—may be interpreted as one among many other symptoms of the transition to a "post-fordist" political economy.

Notes

1. As Hannah notes, however (1991:10), employers in some countries have been discouraged from cooperating with this process of devolution by other state interventions, which were designed to improve the reliability of pensions as a form of individual savings. Consequently, in both Britain and North America the proportion of the workforce covered by occupational plans actually fell during the 1980s.

2. Multinational expert studies of private pensions include volumes edited by McGill (1977), International Social Security Association (1987), and Turner and Watanabe (1995). Recent international conferences, all devoted to occupational pensions, have been held under the auspices of the European Community (Bremen, January 1990), the Council of Europe (Lisbon, October 1990), the OECD (Paris, July 1991), and the IRES [Institut de Recherches Economiques et Sociales] (Paris, January 1994). The OECD has published the proceedings of its conference (OECD, 1992) and is sponsoring a series of ongoing country studies of private pension systems.

3. See on this issue Hannah's conclusion that "positive economics" has contributed little so far to explaining national differences in occupational pensions—this in the face of "institutional differences between countries and highly specific legal, tax and cultural variables", not to mention "political accident" (Hannah, 1991:6,4).

4. For further discussion of the variability touched on in this paragraph, see Kangas and Palme, 1989; Schmahl, 1990; and Esping-Andersen, 1987.

5. For illustrations, see O'Rand (1986) and Mosley (1981).

6. Leading studies in this genre are Quadagno (1988) and Stevens (1988).

7. On the Scandinavian or Swedish model (which have usually been treated as synonymous), see Erikson et al. (1987); and on the social-democratic model, Shalev (1983).

8. For some pioneering attempts at data collection, in addition to those I discuss here, see Rein (1982); Kangas and Palme (1989); and von Nordheim Nielsen (1990). I am indebted to Sandy Jacoby for helping me locate data sources.

9. Dailey and Turner also present data for Japan (37% coverage), but this estimate is based on funded plans only.

10. In addition to Esping-Andersen's book *The Three Worlds of Welfare Capitalism* (1990), this discussion also draws on two of his earlier publications (Esping-Andersen, 1985 and 1987). In a few cases data for the secondary analysis performed here were supplied directly to the author.

11. The method of unrotated principal components analysis was used. Two indices on which Esping-Andersen's scaling is questionable (primarily for Australia and New Zealand), which measure the universalism of sickness and unemployment benefits, were dropped from the analysis (cf. Castles and Mitchell, 1991). I also excluded two measures of change (as opposed to level) of social expenditure, which loaded high on a separate factor. All other indicators demonstrated substantial relations to the two factors reported here, which were the only ones with eigenvalues of at least 3. Almost all of the data refer to the period between the late 1970s and the mid-1980s. For additional information on the source data, see the references cited in the previous note.

12. Two findings contradict expectations of the institutional model: the INST factor's comparatively *high* loading on benefit inequality and its weak (actually *negative*) association with employment performance.

13. The proposed classification is again based on Esping-Andersen's original data and was formally confirmed by cluster analysis.

14. The exception is Finland, which scored lower than Austria and Britain on Esping-Andersen's measure of working class mobilization. Nevertheless, other common denominators of the Scandinavian context justify the boundary drawn here.

15. See Bloom and Freeman (1992) on the decline of private pension coverage among male wage-earners. As Woods (1994) points out, however, coverage among women has been rising at the same time as male participation has declined. Similar trends have been noted for health benefits (Olson, 1995).

16. To date, the most comprehensive evidence of these inequalities is provided by a 1986 General Accounting Office survey of a large (n=2,872) and heterogeneous sample of privately-owned corporations. See Maclean (1992).

17. The "corporate liberalism" literature is discussed in Jacoby's chapter in this book. The most important advocates of the pressure-from-below thesis have been Piven and Cloward (1971; 1977)

18. Theda Skocpol and her associates have been prominent advocates of this perspective. For some examples, see Skocpol (1980); Amenta and Skocpol (1986).

19. Consult, for example, Esping-Andersen (1978); Stephens (1979).

Part 1

The United States

1

Is America Exceptional?
The Role of Occupational Welfare
in the United States and the
European Community[1]

Martin Rein

Every country has a range of programs to help people when risks, contingencies and needs arise. This system of "social protection" covers people who are working as well as those who are poor. In each society, social protection is organized in three sectors: a public sector, where government acts directly to administer and finance programs according to some principles of social responsibility; a personal sector where the individual assumes primary responsibility, making use of financial institutions like banks, life insurance or the real estate market; and a mixed sector conventionally referred to as the private sector, where the major actor is the firm in its role of employer but where the state also acts indirectly via its capacity to regulate, stimulate and subsidize civil society. Each society combines these sectors in different ways. In this essay, I examine the firm's social policy within the broader context of social protection in society as a whole.

Over the last decade, the political context for discourse about social policy has changed as themes of privatization and the leveling, or reduction, of public outlays have gained currency. In this new setting, the firm emerges with a new vitality and commitment as an important instrument of social policy (Rein and Wadensjö, forthcoming).

The role of the firm in setting and delivering social policy has been a neglected subject in scholarly writings about private sector social policy.

Data, however, has not been the major limitation.[2] This paper makes use of readily available data for the US and compares it with a unique dataset which has been compiled for EC member states. With the exception of Denmark, the countries covered by the EC survey are not those examined in this volume. But for the purpose of placing the US case in comparative perspective, this is not a serious shortcoming.

If the neglect of social policy at the level of the firm is not the result of a paucity of information, how else can it be explained? The most important reason has been the limited nature of conventional frameworks for interpreting the field of social policy. The traditional focus on the evolution of the welfare state has led to an incomplete, and therefore distorted, picture of the system of social protection. This essay attempts to correct this narrow perspective, in the process throwing a rather unconventional light on the system of social welfare in the United States.

Social protection is more than what the state does. Public and private employers, as well as individuals, also provide social protection. The firm does what the state requires of it, but it also does what it wants to do for its own purposes. Moreover, the firm does more than provide social protection, which may be defined as compensation for the variety of risks that produce loss of income, such as unemployment, disability, sickness, retirement, etc.[3] It also furnishes vocational training, payments in kind, and paid non-work in the form of vacations and holidays which include recreation. When all these activities—whether legally required or not—are combined, they constitute the social policy of the firm. These social benefits channeled through the firm are sometimes referred to as "fringe benefits" or, more technically, "non-wage labor costs".

The social welfare system at the level of the firm is comprised of three parts: (a)"customary" programs that are voluntarily initiated by employers or else contracted with unions; (b)"statutory" benefits that are legally mandated by the state but paid for by the employers; and (c)a range of family-related policies such as child care, parental leave, and elder care. The third of these costs is difficult to quantify, because cash transfers for families are included in the other two categories while services for families are part of what Eurostat calls "other expenditures of a social nature." However, both US and EC data do permit us to make the distinction between statutory and customary benefits.

I draw mainly on two statistical sources in this report: The Survey of Labor Costs and the Employment Cost Index measure the social costs incurred by the firm as a percentage of total labor costs in Europe and the United States respectively.[4] To locate the role of the firm in the broader social context, for the EC countries I use the Social Protection Accounts which provide total societal expenditures. It is possible to construct broadly comparable data for the United States from the National Income Accounts. For Europe, in order to render the social spending of the firm comparable to the EC's Social Protection Accounts, some of the calculations exclude both paid leave and vocational training. I call this measure social welfare spending, and it encompasses statutory programs, customary programs, and "other expenditures of a social nature".

It is difficult in practice to make sharp distinctions between those social activities that are statutory or legally mandated by the state and those that are not governmentally required. This is because many of the voluntary or contractual benefits involve governments directly and indirectly. In some countries, like France, the spending is strongly controlled by government through an elaborate system of rules and regulations which control eligibility and benefit levels. In other countries, they are the outgrowth of contractual agreement with workers, but enforceable by government. For example, in Holland mandated earnings-related private pensions exist only after a contractual agreement has been reached in a specific industry. Although the Dutch government both mandates and regulates, nevertheless many features of private schemes persist and the political efforts to create a uniform national scheme have failed. About 10-20 percent of the employed population are not covered. The value of pensions varies enormously across branches of industry and by company plans. Pensions are not fully vested or portable across firms.

For these reasons, it would be misleading to refer to these non-legally mandated social programs as "private." This paper follows the EC convention of referring to non-statutory programs as "customary". "Occupational welfare" is perhaps a more informative description, implying as it does that benefits depend on the job one holds within a firm.

The Scope of the Firm's Own Social Welfare

In this section I provide new estimates of the size and growth of the non-legally required social welfare obligations of the firm based on the Survey of Labor Costs and the Employment Cost Index. First, the monetary value of non-legally required social welfare spending was

TABLE 1.1: *Customary and Total Social Welfare Costs in EC States*
(Percentages of GDP, 1984)

	UK	FRA	NET	GER	BEL	ITA	DEN
Customary Social Costs							
Manufacturing	2.6	3.6	1.5	1.6	0.6	0.9	0.5
Services	2.0	1.8	2.6	0.6	0.9	0.1	0.6
Total	4.6	5.4	4.1	2.2	1.5	1.0	1.1
Total Social Protection	24.1	28.5	33.7	29.1	29.4	23.3	28.7
Customary as							
percent of Total	19.1	18.9	12.2	7.6	5.1	4.3	3.8

Sources: EC "integrated social protection statistics" (Eurostat, 1988) and labor
costs surveys (Eurostat, 1987 and 1991; see text note 4).

computed from information on employee compensation in manufacturing
and the services. Table 1.1 sets out the main facts.

The United Kingdom, France, and Holland have by far the largest
social welfare spending of the firm, 4-5 percent of GDP in 1984. The
institutional reasons for the differences among the seven EC states are
reasonably clear. Holland does not have a public earnings-related
pension, and has instead relied on a Beveridge-style flat rate pension.
Private firms fill the void through union contracts or their own initiative.
Britain did create a public earnings-related pension, but individuals are
permitted to opt out of the public scheme into occupational or personal
pensions. In France, as noted earlier, the boundary between legally
mandated and occupational benefits is especially fuzzy because
government regulates and mandates so much of what firms provide.

The four countries with comparatively low spending for the firm
exhibit a range of 1-2 percent of GDP. An institutional explanation for
Germany lies in the high replacement rate of public pensions. The
Danish system does not reply on mandatory social insurance financed
directly by the firm. Instead Denmark has an extensive means-tested
program and relies on general government taxation. In Belgium and Italy
the firm's own commitment is low.

What is the contribution of the firm's social welfare outlays to the
total level of public and occupational social protection? In 1984, the
range was very wide—between 4 and 19 percent of total social spending
(Table 1.1). In both Britain and France customary social benefits

accounted for nearly one fifth of the overall cost of social protection. In Denmark, Italy and Belgium excluding these benefits would not significantly affect our estimate of social protection.

Table 1.2 shows the results of an attempt to measure of the role of the welfare state in the US that would be broadly comparable to the data on social protection available for the European Community.[5] Fortunately, the National Income Accounts provide the basis for such an estimate of social spending in the private sector, general government, the military, and the state as employer. The findings indicate that in the United States in 1986 non-legally required benefits were 7.5 percent of GDP (6 percent of GDP in the private sector firms plus 1.5 percent for the civilian public sector). This is the size of spending that is left out in conventional accounts of welfare expenditure.

These findings change our understanding of the role of social protection in the United States. The welfare state literature presents an image of America as a laggard in social development. By focusing on the role of the state as the agent for financing and administering social policy, this conclusion seemed self evident. The United States Department of Health and Human Services reports that in 1984, 18.2 percent of GNP was spent on social welfare of which 4.1 percent was for education (DHSS, 1987:Table 1.1). In other words, 14.1 percent of GNP was dedicated to social welfare—which, according to OECD figures, is about half the proportion spent in European countries. The data presented here challenge this conventional understanding and provide a rather different interpretation of the level of America's social protection. The American laggard position is an artifact arising from a narrow focus on spending by the state as a provider, and corresponding neglect of (a)the state and local government as employer, where government social programs are substitutes for the public social security programs; and (b)the role of the firm as an agent of social policy.

In the United States in 1986, a total of more than 20 percent of GDP was directed to social protection in the public and private sector. Reference to Table 1.1 shows that the US is only 3-4 percentage points behind the UK and Italy, and somewhat further from the mean for all seven EC countries (28 percent). Moreover, data not reproduced here show that social protection in the United States increased between 1978 and 1986 by 23 percent, using this broader definition (cf. Rein and Rainwater, 1986c). By contrast, the level of spending in many European communities rose modestly in this period and stagnated in several countries.

TABLE 1.2: *Social Expenditure in the United States, 1986*

	Percent of GDP	Percent of Total
Government Transfers		
Retirement and disability pensions	4.8	
Public welfare	2.5	
Hospitals	1.8	
Unemployment	0.4	
Total	*9.7*	*47.4*
Government Goods and Services		
Hospitals	1.4	
Welfare	0.6	
Veterans	0.3	
Total	*2.4*	*11.7*
Civilian Public Employment		
Retirement pensions	1.3	
Sick pay	0.3	
Total	*1.5*	*7.4*
Military Public Employment		
Retirement pensions	0.4	
Veterans' benefits	0.4	
Total	*0.8*	*4.1*
Private Sector Benefits		
Health	2.7	
Pensions and group life insurance	2.5	
Sick pay	0.4	
Workers' compensation	0.4	
Total	*6.0*	*29.3*
Grand Total	20.5	100.0

Note: Categories accounting for less than one quarter of a percent of GDP appear only in the subtotals.

Sources: National Income and Product Accounts (Tables 3.11, 3.15, 3.16, 6.13), *Survey of Current Business*, July 1987, 9-21.

This information on the level and rate of growth of social spending in the United States contrasts sharply with the persistent image of America as a laggard welfare society, which allegedly fell even further behind the European community during the welfare cutbacks of the Reagan years. To repeat, what is left out of this picture is the social policy of the firm, distributing benefits which are not legally mandated, and the government as an employer, providing retirement, medical and sick pay to its own employees. In other words, what has been omitted is the social policy of public and private employers—in 1986, 12 and 29 percent respectively of total social expenditure.

The misperception of American social protection as exceptional becomes still clearer when total expenditure (by both the state and the firm) is broken down into its constituent parts. If the findings in Table 1.2 are compared with data on European social protection (Eurostat, 1988), what is most striking for the United States is how little we spend for sick pay compared to the Europeans. The US has no general public program or legally-mandated program for sickness. Nor does it have a developed policy for other forms of paid leave. Discussion about parental leave to care for children or a seriously ill spouse is limited to workers who are on unpaid leave. It is the cost of health care fringe benefits rather than payment of earnings when on leave that is at issue. When the public and private (i.e., non-legally required) spending by the firm for sickness is added together, it amounts to less than 1 percent of GDP in the United States compared to 5 to 8 percent in the European community. Moreover, in the US the scope of sickness among full-time workers declined during the 1980s, whereas in every country in Europe the trend was moving in the opposite direction.

The Public/Private Interplay in Social Protection

We would expect to find that the social provision of the firm is not independent of what government does and that what the firm does is shaped by government action. The interplay between customary and statutory social benefits can be antagonistic or reinforcing. In the first case, if one sector is strong, the other is weak; in the second case, both sectors grow together. We might also expect to find that when the firm plays a large role in the whole social protection system, then some components become more salient than would be the case if the public

TABLE 1.3: *Social Benefits in the Private Sector*
(Percent of Total Labor Costs)

	1966	1975	1984			
	Total	Total	Total	Paid Leave	Statutory Welfare	Customary Welfare
Italy	34	40	44	11	32	1
France	29	34	38	9	19	9
Netherlands	27	36	34	10	16	8
Belgium	29	35	33	9	23	1
Germany	24	31	32	11	16	5
UK	n.a.	21	25	10	8	7
USA	n.a.	n.a.	25	7	9	9
Denmark	n.a.	16	14	8	5	1

Note: Most recent data for the USA is 1988.

Source: EC labor costs survey; unpublished US data provided by the Bureau of Labor Statistics.

statutory system were to dominate. Finally, when the firm plays a large role, it logically follows that work becomes a condition for entitlement; therefore, those who work will be more advantaged than those who are outside the labor market.

The influential approach to social policy represented by Richard Titmuss (e.g. Titmuss, 1959) expresses a clear preference for universal, publicly financed social protection and is opposed to occupational benefits. But actual practice seems to be moving in the opposite direction. Even a country like Sweden, which is supposed to represent the ideal of the social-democratic vision of equality of access and provision, is moving in the direction of extending occupational benefits. The reasons are twofold. First, public schemes have a ceiling above which benefits are not paid. As more blue collar workers earn above the maximum, unions have pressed for firm-based occupational schemes. The second reason is that unions feel the firm provides better security than the state, since political regime shifts could lead to benefit erosion.

The data are not altogether adequate to explore these issues, but they do provide a backdrop for examining some of them. In all countries for which data is available spanning the period 1966-84, we find a declining proportion of total compensation being funneled through direct remuneration (wages and bonuses) and a rise in social welfare costs (both mandated and customary). Table 1.3 shows that with the addition of paid leave, social benefits in 1984 had grown to account for roughly one third of total labor costs in the modal European cases of Belgium, the Netherlands and Germany. The figures for two outlier cases, Italy and Denmark, were 44 and 14 percent respectively.[6] Applying similar calculations to US data yields results almost identical to those for the UK: one quarter of labor costs could be traced to social benefits, with a more or less even split between the three categories (statutory and customary welfare, and paid leave).

These two countries share a distinctive profile in comparative perspective: modest expenditure on paid leave (itself, however, not that variable across countries), among the highest shares of customary welfare costs, and very low statutory welfare expenditure. Clearly, by far the biggest source of variation in the extent of the social benefits provided by firms lies in the realm of government mandating. It is in this respect that the two Anglo-Saxon nations (and even more so, Denmark) stand in striking contrast to Continental Europe.

As noted, the importance of social benefits compared with direct labor costs has everywhere increased over the two-decade period surveyed in Table 1.3. However, this growth seems to have occurred solely, or at least mainly, in the decade preceding 1975, prior to the onset of global economic crisis. Consistent with this general trend, data for the United States indicate that there was considerable stability in the level of benefits as a percentage of total costs during the 1980s. This, of course, does not mean that nothing has changed. Indeed, there have been a number of visible shifts in the structure of spending. Whereas legally-required benefits increased by two percent of total compensation, non-statutory benefits declined slightly. But these aggregate figures mask differences within the non-statutory sector. Health insurance costs grew rapidly (from 3.6 percent to 5.4 percent), while a sharp decline took place in private pensions, largely due to the over-funding of defined benefit plans in the early 1980s in anticipation of increased regulatory pressure to provide an actuarially sound asset pool to draw on for future beneficiaries (Braden, 1988).

Disaggregating the costs of social benefits also yields insight into the underlying dynamics at work in the five Continental countries for which longrun data are available. Expenditure on paid leave as a share of labor costs experienced an almost universal pattern of growth in the first decade (pre-1975) followed by decline in the second (post-1975). In the

TABLE 1.4: *The Components of Private Sector Social Benefits*
(Percent of Total Labor Costs)

	Statutory		Customary	
	USA	Contin-ental EC	USA	Contin-ental EC
Retirement	5.8	10.9	3.6	4.2
Health			5.7	0.3
Unemployment	1.0	0.8		0.7
Other income maintenance		2.0		0.2
Family allowances		3.1		0.1
Accidents	1.8	1.4		
Other	0.3	0.5		0.3
Total	8.9	18.7	9.3	5.8

Notes: Figures for the Continental EC are averages of Germany, France, Belgium and the Netherlands. US data are for 1988; EC data for 1984. US data for customary retirement costs include life insurance and savings schemes.

Sources: EC labor costs survey; *US Department of Labor News*, June 16, 1988, Table 8.

course of the first decade, in all countries except France statutory costs rose substantially while customary spending stagnated. In the second decade, the trends diverge. In countries like Germany and the Netherlands, where expenditure in the statutory system declined, there was growth in voluntary and collectively-bargained schemes. However, where the legally-mandated programs continued to grow, as in Belgium and Italy, the cost of voluntary programs remained unchanged. This suggests the intriguing hypothesis that customary social welfare programs act as offsets to the legally-mandated programs. When the latter decline, the former increase. Of course, it is impossible to tell from these data whether the same services are provided to the same people, as the idea of offsets suggests.

We turn now to a more searching look at the character of the social protection provided by private sector firms in the US and Europe. The comparative data, summarized in Table 1.4, disaggregate both statutory and customary welfare into their component parts. The firm appears to invest its own resources mainly in retirement benefits in most European countries. The pattern in the United States is somewhat different because the firm voluntarily decided to expand health insurance as well as have retirement and savings and thrift programs. So extensive has become the American reliance on private health insurance that some states have proposed legislation which would mandate health insurance to ensure wider coverage. This is because any non-legally required scheme will exclude substantial numbers of workers and thus introduce the kind of inequality that students of social policy have cautioned against. What the public sector fails to undertake, the private sector takes on for a defined part of the population. The private sector acts as a substitute for public sector initiative.

In contrast, from experience in all countries it appears that in the area of pensions, both sectors can grow in tandem. With the exception, again, of health insurance in America, the lion's share of both statutory and customary benefits is everywhere concentrated in pension programs. Nevertheless, the split between obligatory and customary forms of employer contribution to pension schemes is more heavily weighted towards the firm's own efforts in the United States than on the Continent (38 percent versus 28 percent of the total).

Family and child policy may be an example of a programmatic area of dual retreat, i.e. neither sector does very much. The potential demand for child care is very large. In the United States, "the top two future priorities for 'baby boomers' are comparable pay for women and employer-supported day care" (Foster, 1989). Yet the evidence seems to show that the firm has not responded to this potential demand. In Europe as well, programs for maternity, family, and miscellaneous, which are the accounting categories where child care is likely to fall, are very small. Moreover when trends over time are examined, such programs as a percentage of total spending have declined everywhere except in Britain.

In summary, the main themes that emerge from this review of the components of non-governmental social protection are as follows:

♦ There are examples of substitution. When the public sector does not provide a specific social benefit, the private sector may offer it. Health care in the United States and earnings-related pensions in Holland are examples. When firms are not mandated to provide the benefit, many workers are left uncovered.

♦ Over time, as statutory benefits in some countries declined, they were offset by higher contractual outlays of the firm. Again, this makes it important to understand who are the beneficiaries.

♦ There is evidence of dual retreat in benefits for families. In the area of retirement benefits, we see the reverse parallel: both public and private provision have grown in tandem.
♦ Finally, some firm-level programs simply fail to thrive. Very little sick pay is offered in the United States under any auspices (less than 1 percent of GDP). Sick pay is, by and large, voluntary in the United States whereas it is mandated and/or publicly provided in Europe. To some extent this has been part of a conscious policy of offsetting statutory decline by augmenting firm-based systems. For example in both Britain and Germany, there has been crossover from public sickness benefits to private sick pay.

Sources of Variation within the Market Arena

We cannot endorse the widely-held view that the efforts of the state and the firm in the field of social protection necessarily stand in a zero-sum relationship. Cross-national variation in both the scope and the distributional effects of the social policy of the firm cannot be assumed to be simply the residual of what the state does. Factors in the market arena also play a role. I comment on three such factors here: the manual/non-manual division in the workforce; the size of firms; and sectoral differences.

Manual versus Non-Manual Workers

In all countries outlays for statutory programs are a higher proportion of total labor costs for manual than non-manual workers (Table 1.5). The reason is straightforward. As Hart (1980:40) explains, "The vast majority of lower skilled workers receive earnings below statutory ceiling levels so the full impact of statutory payments will pertain." But what Hart failed to realize was that the privileged position of non-manual workers is not always applicable to customary schemes which operate on a voluntary or contractual basis. Table 1.5 demonstrates that in Germany and the United Kingdom, the cost of the customary benefits received by non-manual workers is on average about twice that of the manual workers. In Belgium and Denmark the differentials are far larger, and have been growing over time. On the other hand, in France non-manual

TABLE 1.5: *Social Welfare Costs for Manual and Non-manual Workers*
(Social Welfare as a percentage of Total Labor Costs)

		Manual	**Non-manual**	**Manual**	**Non-manual**
Italy	1984	33.8	28.8	1.5	1.0
Belgium	1984	24.0	20.1	0.3	3.1
France	1978	21.0	16.8	5.5	7.2
Germany	1984	18.3	13.7	3.1	6.8
UK	1981	9.9	8.5	5.2	9.5
USA	1988	9.7	7.3	11.6	10.6
Denmark	1984	5.5	2.8	0.2	2.6

Note: Data pertain to firms with 10 or more employees.

Sources: EC Survey of Labor Costs; "Employer Costs for Employee Compensation," *US Department of Labor News*, June 16, 1988, Table 8.

contractual costs are not very much higher, and in Italy and the United States, manual workers actually do better than non-manuals.

These findings raise more questions than they can answer. For example, why is it that manual workers enjoy comparatively favorable benefits in the United States, where the overall union movement is quite weak, while in Germany, with a relatively strong union movement, they are unable to do better relative to white-collar employees? Part of the explanation may be that the organization of unions is based on industrial sector rather than white or blue-collar membership. Some unions, like the metalworkers, have a mix of highly skilled blue-collar workers and fewer manual and unskilled workers. Similarly, the relatively advantaged position of manual workers in the United States may be due to the degree of unionization inside and outside manufacturing. Historically, industrial unions have been able to get attractive benefit packages for non-legally required benefits. The dollar value of these benefits is equal to those of white collar workers, many of whom are in service industries where contractual fringe benefits are lower. Since white-collar workers earn relatively high salaries, the relative cost of non-obligatory benefits would logically be lower than that of blue-collar workers.

Infrastructural Variables and Social Benefits

It is widely presumed that not all firms can afford to provide social benefits and that perhaps one reason why there is so much variation across countries in the costs incurred for fringe benefits is related to the industry and firm size mix of different countries. Smaller firms cannot take advantage of the economies of scale in financing and administering insurance and pension programs, which as we have seen are the lion's share of social welfare programs. Therefore, smaller firms need to purchase these services from intermediaries because they do not have the capacity to finance and administer these programs from their own resources. Moreover, the profit margins of small firms are smaller and the risk of bankruptcy larger than in the more established and larger firms.

We do have data for EC countries on the distribution of social welfare costs by firm size. Unfortunately, these data do not distinguish between customary and legally-required programs. All that is available is information on total indirect costs (welfare costs, payment for days not worked, and other bonuses and gratuities). What we can learn from this information is that in every country indirect costs increase with firm size, as expected. What is surprising is that the differences are small. The difference in indirect costs between very small firms (10 to 50 workers) and large firms (over 1,000) is only about 10 percent in most countries. It is probable, however, that very large firms (those that employ many thousands of workers) have more extensive social commitments.

Sectoral Differences

We would expect indirect labor costs to vary not only by firm size but also between different sectors of the economy. The American data permit us to compare the experiences of goods-producing and service-producing industries, or manufacturing and non-manufacturing. The only available data in the European survey is within the manufacturing sector. In the United States social benefits in the goods-producing sector constitute 26.9 percent of wages as compared to 23.6 percent in the services. Legally-required benefits cost 9.5 percent of total compensation compared to 8.5 percent in the service sector. Contractual benefits cost firms 17.4 percent in the goods-producing sector and 15.1 percent in the service sector. Clearly, the industry mix is important, but not overwhelmingly so.

The branch-level data available for the EC countries make it possible to examine differences between fundamentally different types of industries. One such source of variation is the division between internationally exposed branches and those that operate primarily in the domestic economy. Another is the contrast within the exposed sector between modern, capital-intensive industries and their more traditional counterparts. An analysis not reproduced here addresses this question by comparing data for four EC countries on the composition of labor costs in the motor vehicle and textile industries. The data show for Germany, France, Italy, and the United Kingdom that in the motor vehicle industry, customary benefits account for a substantially higher share of total labor costs. Nevertheless, the relative cost of total social welfare is about the same, because statutory benefits are a higher share of compensation in the textile industry. The reason is of course that these benefits typically cover only part of the total wage bill, which is considerably lower in textiles than in motor vehicles. This implies that mandatory fringe benefits can play an important role in reducing differentials between industries. Insofar as low-wage industries tend to rely disproportionately on certain kinds of labor, there are implications here for gender and similar types of inequality. Of course, a corollary of the mandating approach is that it makes the provision of social protection work-conditioned, i.e., work is a precondition of entitlement.

It is important here not to lose sight of the fact that by far the weightiest variation in firms' spending for social policy is not within but between countries. To take a conservative example, in both Britain and Germany non-legally required social spending is four percentage points higher (as a share of labor costs) in motor vehicles than textiles. But in both industries, statutory and customary spending together are seven points higher in Germany than the UK.

Conclusions

Evidence has been provided showing that in the US more than 30 percent of all social policy expenditures are channeled through employer-provided, non-legally obligatory social welfare programs. These represent about 7.5 percent of GDP. Over time, employer-related benefits have grown in the United States and some European countries, offsetting declines or leveling in general government spending.

In the past, the social policy of the firm has been neglected as attention was focused on the evolution of the welfare state. But recently a frame shift has taken place, with many political actors turning to the firm as an instrument of social protection, and scholarly inquiry gradually following suit. For students of comparative social policy, this shift in perspective makes possible a new perception of the alleged exceptionalism of the American case. What this paper has shown is that the distinctiveness of the United States lies less in the scope of social protection (with the exception of sick leave), than in the instruments by which it is provided. I hope that the present attempt to shed empirical light on the social policy of the firm will encourage other researchers to undertake more refined investigations, and to seek out data for a wider range of countries.

Notes

1. I am indebted to Michael Shalev for editing that helped bring the tables into sharp focus, and to Lee Rainwater for his thoughtful comments and help in extracting data from the tape made available to us for Eurostat's labor cost surveys.

2. See for example Eurostat, *Digest of Statistics on Social Protection*, Vol. 1: Old Age, Vol. 2: Disability, Vol. 3: Survivors. (Brussels and Luxembourg, 1992). These volumes have extensive statistics on public pensions, complementary or supplementary schemes, and means-tested welfare schemes. The supplementary schemes include benefits provided voluntarily or contractually through the firm.

3. Eurostat defines social protection very broadly as expenditures by a third party designed to meet "costs incurred by individuals or households as the result of certain risks, contingencies, or needs."

4. The Survey of Labor Costs is sponsored by the Statistical Office of the European Community (Eurostat) in Luxembourg. The survey covers all firms with 10 or more employees in all branches of the private sector. Some of the findings have been published (Eurostat, 1987; 1991). We were kindly given access to raw data on microfiche and magnetic tape for further analysis. For the United States we made use of the Employment Cost Index, which measures the rate of change in employee compensation. The data are derived from a survey of 3,600 establishments. This sample is representative of the

entire population of private, non-farm establishments of all sizes. In each establishment, 5 occupations on average are selected on a probability-sample basis to represent all the occupations in the establishment. The 1980 occupational weights have been used for the 1988 data. Insofar as the distribution of occupations changed during this period, the figures are no longer fully representative of all occupations in the economy; but this is unlikely to constitute a significant source of error.

5. The format for this table was developed by Lee Rainwater for an earlier year. Similar data for 1992 focused only on pensions show that public cash transfer programs for households headed by persons aged 55 and older accounted for 5.2% of GDP, private and public supplementary schemes were 4.4% of GDP and the personal sector of life insurance and IRA's was 0.7% of GDP. Thus the enterprise and personal sectors or pillars are the same size as public schemes. Each of them accounted for about half of the 10.3% of GDP spent on pensions in 1992 in the USA. Source: United State Department of Commerce, Bureau of Economic Analysis, *Survey of Current Business*, National Income and Product Accounts Tables 2.1, 3.12 and 6.11c.

6. In order to enhance comparability with the US data, Table 1.3 does not include several types of social benefits available in the original Eurostat data. These are payment in kind, vocational training, "other expenditure of a social nature", and subsidies and taxes. There is only one instance in which inclusion of these categories would significantly alter the impression afforded by the data reproduced here. As a result of rapid growth in benefits under the heading of "subsidies and taxes", in Italy in 1984 this category accounted for an additional 9 per cent of total costs, further highlighting Italy's exceptional position.

2

From Welfare Capitalism to the Welfare State: Marion B. Folsom and the Social Security Act of 1935

Sanford M. Jacoby

During the heyday of modernization theory, sociologists attributed the welfare state to the logic of industrialism: As nations came to have the requisite economic resources, their governments responded to universal social problems (e.g., old-age dependency) by adopting welfare programs. Implicit in this logic was the notion that welfare state formation was an apolitical and automatic process, given rising income levels (Wilensky, 1975). In recent years, scholars have leveled damaging charges against this explanation of the welfare state. For one thing, it does not accord with the statistical facts, which show widely varying lags between national income levels and dates of welfare state formation. (Myles, 1989) Second, it fails to recognize the importance of politics—especially class politics—in the development and subsequent shaping of national welfare programs.

The most coherent political theory of the welfare state in western democracies is what Shalev (1983:319) calls the social democratic model, which emphasizes that "the welfare state is a class issue. Logically and historically, its principal proponents and defenders are movements of the working class." While the social democratic model captures the experiences of a wide range of western democracies, it breaks down in the case of the United States, where unions and other working-class organizations were, at best, barely involved in the enactment of the landmark Social Security Act of 1935. (An omnibus law, the act created national programs for unemployment insurance, old-age pensions, and aid to indigent children and elders.) The CIO's fledgling industrial unions had not yet developed their social agenda, while the AFL's craft unions retained a voluntarist ambivalence toward federal welfare initiatives. To the extent unions focused on legislative issues in the mid-1930s, their main concern was securing passage of a law governing union-management relations.

In the search for social actors to take labor's place, scholars of US welfare history have turned up various candidates. Adherents of the corporate liberal thesis emphasize the role played by employers from large companies. By pushing for a two-tier system, employers ostensibly sought to maintain social order while subsidizing their own private welfare programs (e.g., Berkowitz and McQuaid, 1988; Jenkins and Brents, 1989; Quadagno, 1988). Yet the claim that big business molded features of the Social Security Act has come in for its share of criticism. Most large employers, say the critics, opposed social security because of a laissez-faire antipathy to federal activism. And the corporate liberals who supported social security played only a "marginal role" in passing the act and did not achieve even their limited objectives (Leff, 1987:39; Skocpol and Amenta, 1985).

As an alternative, critics of corporate liberalism point to the importance of government bureaucrats and social reformers, since in the US, federalism and the absence of an effective labor party made state politics and middle-class reform activity especially important. Numerous welfare programs were enacted at the sub-federal level in the 1910s and 1920s that later guided federal efforts (Skocpol and Ikenberry, 1983; Amenta and Parikh, 1991; Gordon, 1991). Reformers and bureaucrats were groups with permeable boundaries. In Wisconsin, for example, students of John R. Commons regularly took jobs in state government and some, most notably Edwin E. Witte, later advised Roosevelt on the Social Security Act. Skocpol argues that the act's drafters "did not get the idea of contributory social insurance from liberal capitalists... They had been arguing alone these lines for two decades" (1990:435).

Skocpol and others do a good job of deflating ultra-instrumentalist versions of the Social Security Act that have a cabal of welfare capitalists pulling all the legislative strings. But they err in drawing too sharp a line between reformers and bureaucrats on the one hand, and welfare capitalists on the other. From the 1910s through the 1930s, these groups regularly mingled at meetings of the American Management Association, the YMCA's Silver Bay Conference, the American Association for Labor Legislation (AALL), and elsewhere. They forged a common solution to the nation's "labor problems," one that idealized technical competence, efficient administration, and expert-led reform. Both in government and industry, they favored the use of science, planning, and professional knowledge as substitutes for rule-of-thumb methods and customary authority. Reformers sought to infuse government with an ethos of efficiency and administrative rationality, while graduates of university engineering and business schools attempted to bring more professionalism to management. (Haber, 1964; Ross, 1991; Wiebe, 1967).

Along with middle-class reformism, the vacuum created by a disorganized working class produced industry's extensive welfare and personnel management programs. The relationships here are complex: Unionism's limited scope gave American managers room to act preemptively whenever they felt threatened by an increase in labor's bargaining power, as during the 1910s. The result, as Commons observed, was that in the US, "the restraints which laborers place on free competition in the interests of fair competition [are being] taken over by employers and administered by their own labor managers." (1924:311) Reformers like Commons were impressed by welfare capitalism and by the use of specialized managers to administer health, retirement, and job stability plans. When proposing public policy in this area, the Commons group incorporated employer initiatives and market principles in their legislative designs.

To further explore these issues, this essay focuses on the ideas and actions of Marion B. Folsom, a self-effacing manager who nevertheless was one of the nation's most prominent welfare capitalists. A graduate of the Harvard Business School, Folsom helped to design Eastman Kodak's elaborate welfare programs during the 1910s and 1920s. The experience brought him to Washington in the early 1930s, where he was one of a handful of employers backing the Social Security Act and lobbying in favor of a mixed public/private approach.

Folsom's Washington experience demonstrates a point missed by critics of the corporate liberal thesis: Precisely because the number of employers opposing social security was large, the few who endorsed the act wielded enormous influence. As a leading spokesperson for that minority, Folsom's opinions carried great weight in Congress and the White House. His support deflected charges levied by other employers that the administration was engaged in a "bungling effort...to regiment

American business" (Ames, 1935:20). Folsom's influence was bolstered by his ties to Labor Secretary Frances Perkins and to the academics who drafted the act. During the 1920s, they had met at conferences on industrial and social problems, while in the early 1930s Folsom served in Albany as one of Governor Roosevelt's experts on unemployment insurance. Because of this shared history, administration officials trusted Folsom and respected his views. Yet Folsom and the bureaucrats did not agree on all issues related to social security. Folsom's primary concern was to keep Kodak's tax costs low while preserving the company's existing unemployment insurance and pension plans. He was largely successful in obtaining these objectives. By lobbying and other means, Folsom kept taxes and benefits minimal while securing tax privileges for private plans.

Thus, this essay supports the corporate liberal and the reformer-bureaucrat theses: Key social actors sprang from the same milieu and shared ideas that shaped the development of the Social Security Act. Yet the essay also provides evidence showing that liberal employers had their own priorities, which they pushed at key junctures in the political process. In other words, whether by direct (political) or indirect (ideological) mechanisms, the Social Security Act owed its features to the elaborate system of welfare capitalism that preceded it and which the act, in turn, preserved.

Kodak and Welfare Corporatism

In contrast to Europe, the industrial landscape in the US during the early 20th century was dotted with giant firms geared to mass production (Chandler, 1990; Haydu, 1988). Although European observers alternately praised or excoriated "Fordism," they agreed that it was an American phenomenon. Mass production technology made these firms less dependent on skilled labor and this, combined with their size and labor's relative weakness, made them resistant to unionism. But employers realized that unions might someday gather strength, especially given the unrest that periodically erupted. So with an eye to the future and a glance overseas, these companies preemptively introduced measures to secure worker loyalty—such things as career employment practices, personnel management, company unions, and welfare benefits.

This amalgam was known as welfare capitalism; a better term is "private welfare corporatism."[1]

At its peak in the 1920s, welfare corporatism was unevenly practiced. It rarely was pursued by small firms (those employing under 250 workers) since most—as in Europe—lacked the resources to bureaucratize employment relations (Melling, 1991). Welfare corporatism was more common in large firms, though exceptions abounded. Among giant concerns (those employing over 5,000 workers), only half had personnel departments in the late 1920s and even fewer had pension plans or company unions. As a result, welfare corporatism was limited to an elite comprising about 20 percent of the industrial labor force in 1929.[2]

Yet the movement's impact was greater than that figure alone would suggest. Welfare corporatism was concentrated among the nation's most visible companies (consumer goods and science-based firms), thus ensuring attention from academia, the press, and other employers. Because these firms were bellwethers when it came to product innovation and management techniques, they endowed welfare corporatism with an aura of social inevitability. Hence despite its obvious limitations—coverage was limited and benefits meager—welfare corporatism came to be seen as America's future. Perception and reality combined to undermine labor solidarity and make it difficult to press for expanded public welfare programs, particularly at the federal level. In this climate, reformers and academic experts came to share business's view that workers were best taken care of by their employers. That welfare corporatism and efficient management were complements, jointly rooted in the logic of mass production, was held to be the American alternative to European welfare statism.

A prominent member of the corporatist elite was the Eastman Kodak Company, a photographic camera and film manufacturer based in Rochester, New York. Founded in the 1880s by George Eastman, Kodak pioneered a mass market for photography by making inexpensive and simple cameras. The source of Kodak's enormous profits was not cameras but film, a market that Kodak dominated around the world. Cameras—no matter who built them—merely created the demand for Kodak's principal product. By the late 1920s, Kodak employed over 14,000 workers in the United States, with the bulk (82 percent) concentrated in Rochester.[3]

Kodak's earliest welfare programs were quite traditional, such things as cafeterias, athletic facilities, and an employee auditorium. But the company was best known for its generous financial benefits. In 1911 Eastman endowed a Welfare Fund with a stock bequest of over one million dollars. The fund gave money to sick and injured workers and made emergency loans to employees in need. It was followed in 1912 by a profit-sharing plan that annually paid workers a bonus of about a month's wages, supplemented in 1919 by a stock ownership plan.

In its early years, welfare work was often intrusively paternalistic, with employers seeking to improve workers by making their lives more wholesome. Kodak's pecuniary approach, however, was relatively impersonal and reticent. This was due to Eastman's reluctance to "put any string" on employees and to his characteristic lack of sentimentality. "You can talk about cooperation and good feeling and friendliness from morn to midnight," he said, "but the thing the worker appreciates is the same thing the man at the helm appreciates—dollars and cents" (New York Times, 1923:1; Ackerman, 1930:10, 235). Kodak's workforce was mostly native-born, with foreign workers coming chiefly from Britain and Germany. Hence there was less of the pressure other firms felt to "Americanize" a mass of recent immigrants (Webber, 1924).

Nor were Kodak's welfare programs a direct response to union pressure. Even during the war years, unions were a distant threat to Kodak, which paid the highest wages in Rochester. Yet the company felt vulnerable to sabotage by disgruntled employees, especially at Kodak Park, the giant factory where photographic film was made. Here workers labored in darkness surrounded by delicate equipment, damageable photosensitive goods, and proprietary products. (Film emulsion formulas were a closely guarded, but not inviolable, secret.) Although the chance of protest—whether individual or organized—was remote, its cost could have been enormous. Hence Kodak managers repeatedly stressed the importance of securing the employees' "cooperation," by which was meant a sense of obligation that would develop from receiving fair treatment, good wages, and generous benefits. But there also was a manipulative element in the company's munificence: By raising the employee's cost of job loss, Kodak could deter employee mischief it could not otherwise control.[4]

Other reasons for welfare work at Kodak had to do with external pressures on the company. With a near monopoly on film, Kodak periodically faced antitrust litigation. Since public opinion could tilt the scales of justice, Kodak heavily advertised its welfare programs; in fact, the Welfare Fund was launched during a major suit. Kodak management also worried about the financial markets, which didn't like George

Eastman holding a large chunk of Kodak's stock. Investors worried that if anything ever happened to him, it might hurt the value of their holdings. Eastman eased these concerns by endowing the Welfare Fund and other programs with his personal stock.[5]

Along with welfare benefits, Kodak had a national reputation for its efforts at employment stabilization. Like other science-based companies, Kodak was imbued with the technocratic ethos that social problems—including those arising in the workplace—were amenable to the same scientific methods used to solve research and production problems. Eastman, a self-taught inventor, never finished high school but had great respect for those who could combine tinkering with scientific knowledge. Even before he opened Kodak's research laboratories in 1913, Eastman regularly picked university science graduates to fill the ranks of Kodak management. This was how Eastman hired his protege, Frank W. Lovejoy, an MIT graduate. In 1903 Lovejoy developed a photographic film with a very long shelf life. By making careful forecasts of demand and by carrying inventory during slack months, he was able to smooth out seasonal irregularities in Kodak's film production. Producing at a steady rate allowed Kodak to economize on expensive film-making equipment while eliminating seasonal employment (Folsom, 1930; 1962:37-39; Metcalf, 1972:51-70; Nelson, 1969:28-46).

An enormous amount of sales data was necessary for Kodak's production planning (and to satisfy Eastman's infatuation with graphs and charts). Eastman turned to the new Harvard Business School to recommend someone capable of managing Kodak's information flows. The school suggested Marion B. Folsom, a Georgia native and recent MBA. honors graduate. Eastman hired the young Folsom (he was 21 at the time), who started at Kodak in the fall of 1914. After war service, Folsom was picked to head Kodak's new Statistical Department, which put out a steady stream of data to use in production planning. He then became Eastman's personal assistant, an association that marked Folsom for rapid promotion. In 1930, at the age of 37, he was named assistant treasurer. Five years later he became treasurer, a position he held for the next twenty years.

Folsom became involved in Kodak's welfare programs during the 1920-1921 depression. That winter he heard a lecture on unemployment given by B. Seebohm Rowntree, the progressive British employer. He was struck by Rowntree's claim that the British unemployment insurance system, "inadequate as it is, has saved us from something like a revolution." Folsom discussed the lecture with Eastman, whose dread of social unrest had been kindled by a wave of strikes in Rochester the preceding year. Folsom proposed that Kodak set up its own unemployment fund, reminding Eastman that "the fear of unemployment is one of the most potent causes of labor unrest." Eastman liked the idea and told Folsom to proceed (Nelson, 1969:23; Folsom, 1967:6; Alsop, 1955:136).

That unemployment could be both relieved and prevented by private efforts was a popular idea that winter. The President's Conference on Unemployment, organized by Commerce Secretary Herbert Hoover, urged businessmen to regularize employment and investment. At the conference, reformers touted Kodak—where employees worked year-round—as an exemplar of statistical controls being used to stabilize employment. Folsom wanted Kodak to maintain its position in the stabilization movement and thought an unemployment fund was the logical next step. Layoffs that winter at the Camera Works had exposed the Achilles heel of the stabilization approach: its inability to shield workers from cyclical, as opposed to seasonal, instability. An unemployment fund could solve the cyclical problem, thought Folsom, by giving laid-off workers an income to tide them through joblessness. Yet Folsom's logic failed to persuade Kodak's powerful plant managers, who opposed the plan. Folsom proposed his plan again in 1927 but without success.[6]

By the late 1920s, Kodak was, if anything, too successful at stabilizing its workforce. Above-average pay, good benefits, and steady work made it a "sticky" company, with turnover rates well below the US average. But in solving one set of problems to do with security and motivation, Kodak managers unwittingly had created another. Older workers, who received the highest relative pay, were reluctant to retire. Not only was this costly for Kodak, but it had the effect of blocking promotions for younger workers. Kodak managers were reluctant to dismiss older workers, even as they privately complained of "privileged senility" and "deadweight." Compounding the problem was the absence of a formal pension plan. Eastman opposed the idea, believing that workers should fend for themselves with funds saved from profit-sharing. Few did so, however. In 1927, Folsom—by now fascinated with welfare issues—investigated corporate pensions and then went to Europe to study social insurance policy. Upon returning, Folsom and an insurance executive designed a pension plan for Kodak, which they persuaded Eastman to adopt. It went into effect in January 1929.[7]

In addition to retirement annuities, Kodak's plan included life insurance and disability benefits. The annuities were the most innovative and costly part of the plan. While pension plan details are not usually of much interest today, matters were different in the 1920s. Of the roughly 400 pension plans then in existence, the vast majority were discretionary, noncontractual, and unfunded. Even before the stock market crash, some firms abandoned their plans because of financial problems (Jacoby, 1985:196-99; Quadagno, 1988:77-96). Kodak, however, caught the industrial world's attention by being the first major manufacturer to adopt a pension that was contractual, non-discretionary, and fully insured. Other features included complex actuarial projections and vesting after 20 years. The plan was analyzed at a special session of the American Management Association (1929) and featured in an article in the New York Times (21 December 1928). Folsom boasted that it secured Kodak's place "in the vanguard of the leading American corporations," although he claimed that it was not intended to win Kodak accolades but simply to "retire workers after they have passed their period of usefulness and replace them with more efficient workers" (1928:23).

The Depression

Kodak's pension plan was one of welfare corporatism's crowning achievements, but it came only months before the movement began to collapse. By mid-1931, even the largest firms had succumbed to the Great Depression. Sharp wage and job cuts were accompanied by drastic reductions in welfare programs. Everything from company unions to company pensions, from personnel departments to paid vacations, was curtailed or cut. With the private sector in disarray, growing numbers of citizens looked to government to relieve the situation. State legislatures held hearings on unemployment insurance, although President Hoover resisted calls for federal intervention (Jacoby, 1985; Epstein, 1933).

Yet welfare corporatism was down but not out. Liberal employers—especially from consumer goods industries least affected by the depression—held fast to their belief that corporations were the logical unit for structuring a welfare system. They backed Hoover's efforts to put businessmen in charge of relief efforts, as with the Share-the-Work movement. But gradually they began to break with Hoover over how large a role the government should play. At a discussion panel sponsored by the US Chamber of Commerce in April 1931, several prominent businessmen, including E.A. Filene and Marion B. Folsom (who headed the Rochester Chamber of Commerce), urged Hoover to relax antitrust laws and promote private unemployment reserve funds. In September, General Electric's president, Gerard Swope, announced a plan calling on the federal government to organize private trade associations to set industrial prices and output. Under standards to be fixed by the government, each association would also administer health, pension, and unemployment reserve plans for firms in the industry (Berkowitz & McQuaid, 1988:90-94; Bernstein, 1987; Himmelberg, 1976; Nelson, 1969:140-3).

The Rochester Plan

Additional proof that welfare corporatism still was very much alive came when the Rochester Unemployment Benefits Plan was announced in February 1931. Sponsored by the city's Industrial Management Council, the plan was designed by Folsom and had its origins in his persistent efforts to initiate an unemployment fund at Kodak. A year earlier Folsom had again raised with Kodak president Frank Lovejoy his idea for a reserves fund. Lovejoy was receptive; General Electric and the Rochester branch of the Clothing Workers union had started unemployment plans that spring. Lovejoy approved the idea but suggested that Folsom get other firms involved. After months of discussion, 14 local companies agreed to a cooperative plan. Each firm would create separate but similar reserve funds to which they would contribute up to 2 percent of their payrolls. An employer's contribution was tied to his layoff history, a practice known as "experience rating." This kept costs down for stable firms like Kodak, while providing an incentive for unstable firms to rationalize their employment practices and reduce layoffs. Because of experience rating, said Folsom, "greater effort is made by the entire company to plan better, to spread work, and to adopt other means to prevent layoffs."[8]

To businessmen worried that the depression would lead to compulsory welfare legislation, the plan appeared a stroke of genius. It covered firms of varying sizes and, because of endorsement by Rochester community groups, came wrapped in the civic virtues of American voluntarism.

Forbes, the business magazine, hailed it as "one of the landmarks of 1931. In these days of confusion and stress, it has the merit of being purposeful, well-planned, well-coordinated, and voluntary" (Hoskins, 1931:28). But this favorable publicity came as no surprise to Folsom. As he told another employer, it was "our intention in drafting the Rochester Plan...to get up a plan which could be recommended generally." That summer, Folsom addressed a gathering of welfare corporatists (the Silver Bay Industrial Relations Conference) and urged them to start similar plans as an alternative to the "compulsory legislation" then being considered by the states. Private experimentation, said Folsom, will "provide experience [from which] it could later be determined what legislation, if any, is necessary."[9]

Folsom did not think much of public welfare programs. Testifying before the Senate in 1931, he said that "any government system [of unemployment insurance] is impractical, because its administration would be under government control" (in Alsop, 1955:135). As for pensions and health insurance, he said that these had been tried "in a number of European countries...and from what I have learned of their experience, I would not be so keen about having them tried here. We may have to someday, but I do not think we are ready yet. It would simply be turning over one more thing to the State which private employers should take of."[10] Yet Folsom, a lifelong Democrat, was drawn into government when Governor Roosevelt appointed him in 1931 to the New York State Legislative Committee on Unemployment. Folsom (1967:9) threw his weight behind a bill requiring employers to create reserve funds. That would permit the Rochester Plan to continue, while forcing other firms to share the burden. As in Wisconsin, which passed a reserves bill in 1932, the AFL in New York initially joined Folsom in backing an employer reserves bill as opposed to a European-style pooled fund (the Ohio plan). While the reserves approach emphasized prevention, the Ohio plan focused on relief; pooling funds permitted payment of larger benefits. By 1933 the unions had switched their support to an Ohio-type bill, partly as a result of the economic situation and partly out of fear that reserve funds would "tie workers to their jobs and promote company unionism" (Nelson, 1969:166, 172).

In these early skirmishes between advocates of the Ohio and Wisconsin models, existence of the Rochester Plan was powerful ammunition in support of the employer-reserves approach. Yet the plan was more impressive on paper than in practice. During 1931 and 1932, the worst years of the depression, it paid no benefits. Under the original guidelines, participating firms were to gradually endow their reserve funds and start payments in 1933. Folsom hoped that by 1933 enough new firms would have joined so that at least half of Rochester's labor force would be covered. But the depression proved this to be overly optimistic. After 1931, the plan shrank instead of growing; promised benefits were cut; and only seven firms remained when the first benefits were paid in 1933. Privately, Folsom admitted that "no one expected [in 1931] that the depression would be so deep or of such long duration."[11]

The plan's poor showing failed to dampen Folsom's enthusiasm for the reserves approach. It did, however, convince him that government was needed to compel reluctant employers to initiate reserve funds. In a 1933 letter to a Procter & Gamble executive, Folsom admitted that,

For some time I have felt that legislation of Unemployment Insurance might be forestalled by volunteer action on the part of employers in setting up their own plans. I now feel that such action is apt to be so slow that it will not forestall legislation. I now feel it is better for employers to cooperate in the enactment of sound legislation rather than have bills written by those who have had no practical experience.[12]

Folsom's change of view also stemmed from a pragmatic recognition that political currents were shifting. The new administration was committed to a major federal effort to combat economic insecurity, something Folsom discovered firsthand in Washington in 1933, where he headed an NRA committee for the photographic industry and served on the Business Advisory Council, created to provide a link between the administration and employers from large companies. Folsom knew that Roosevelt and Perkins wanted to enact permanent measures to deal with unemployment, as they had tried to do in New York, and that they were sensitive to the growing popularity of the Townsend pension clubs.[13]

During the years to come, Folsom devoted himself to ensuring that Congress enacted "sound legislation." His chief concern was to prevent government from displacing private welfare programs, thus ensuring that workers would still look to employers for their security needs. Government, said Folsom, should only provide "basic minimum protection and it should not be intended to cover all the needs of everyone" (US Congress, 1939:1132). Folsom also had positive reasons for supporting the emerging welfare state. In addition to realpolitik considerations, he favored public programs financed by payroll taxes because this narrowed costs between Kodak and those employers who spent little or nothing on welfare benefits. In line with this logic, he favored expanding social security to uncovered sectors like small business and agriculture. To hold costs down, Folsom wanted to tax employees and keep benefits to a "basic" level.

Most Kodak executives were more conservative than Folsom. Yet they supported his efforts to protect Kodak's array of welfare programs by working with, rather than against, the government. Until his death in 1945, chairman Frank Lovejoy stayed in close touch with Folsom and kept abreast of his Washington activities. Like Folsom, Lovejoy believed that Kodak's benefits were a bulwark against the post-1933 surge in union organizing activity. But when it came to politics, the two men politely disagreed and tried to sway each other: Lovejoy, an officer of the National Industrial Conference Board (NICB) and the National Association of Manufacturers (NAM), sent Folsom a copy of The Roots of Liberty, written by NAM president Henning Prentiss; in return, Folsom complained to Lovejoy several times about the NICB's anti-New Deal activities.[14]

Social Security: Unemployment Insurance

In March 1934, Congress opened hearings on the Wagner-Lewis bill, the first piece of New Deal legislation proposing unemployment insurance. Intended as a compromise between the Ohio and Rochester-Wisconsin approaches, the bill utilized a tax-offset funding mechanism that permitted states to craft their own unemployment insurance systems while subject to a uniform federal tax. In her efforts to drum up support, Frances Perkins had difficulty finding employers who would testify on behalf of the bill. Folsom, however, agreed to speak (Nelson, 1969:198-202).

Folsom began his testimony with a description of Kodak's stabilization policies and of the Rochester Plan, which he held out as models for government to promote. He castigated the Ohio approach as "a relief system," an inferior alternative to company reserves that "serve as an incentive for the employer to stabilize his force...and plan production." Folsom stressed the moral virtues of reserve funds, noting that it was better "to have the employees go to the individual employer for their benefits instead of to the State. If the benefits are paid by the State, the people will look to the State for a continuation of the benefits and you are bound to have them looking to the State to carry it all the way through." Yet despite this appeal to voluntarism, Folsom wanted federal legislation to ensure "that employers in one state would not be placed at a disadvantage with competitors in other states" and to compel the involvement of smaller firms, the sort who had dropped out of the Rochester Plan. "Speaking for Kodak and for myself, we are fully convinced of the desirability of the adoption of unemployment reserve plans [but] we realize that legislation will be necessary before such plans are generally adopted" (US Congress, 1934:70-1, 74, 85-86).

Although Folsom favored federal action, he saw the Wagner-Lewis bill as premature and flawed. Worried that additional taxes would hurt recovering businesses, he urged enactment be "delayed until business conditions improve." He also criticized the 5 percent payroll tax and said it should be pared to 2 percent or less. Finally, Folsom asked that the bill exempt from taxation any employer whose reserve plan met state guidelines and paid jobless benefits equal to or better than those required by law. He defended this by claiming that unemployment would increase if "strong companies had to support the weak" (US Congress, 1934:74, 76, 81; Folsom, 1934:66).

Testimony like Folsom's convinced Roosevelt to postpone the Wagner-Lewis bill until business and Congress showed greater enthusiasm. As he had done back in New York, Roosevelt appointed a study group—the Committee on Economic Security (CES)—to draw up model welfare legislation. In charge of the CES was Edwin E. Witte, an economist from the University of Wisconsin. In the summer of 1934 Witte created a technical board and an advisory council to assist the CES. The technical board drew the bulk of its personnel—including Bryce M. Stewart and Murray W. Latimer—from Industrial Relations Counselors, a consulting group financed by the Rockefellers. The Advisory Council on Economic Security (ACES) was made up of ten social welfare experts, five labor leaders, and five employers, including Folsom, Morris E. Leeds (Leeds & Northrup), Sam Lewisohn (Miami Copper), Gerard Swope (General Electric), and Walter C. Teagle (Standard Oil). All were prominent welfare corporatists who had been active in the stabilization movement in the 1920s and early 1930s. All were also members of the Business Advisory Council (BAC), which worked behind the scenes to orchestrate support for the employers' position. That the BAC was willing to do this reflected its increasingly liberal composition, the result of defections that summer by several BAC members (including managers from General Motors and Du Pont), who quit in a rage over the administration's alleged pro-union sympathies.[15]

The ACES labored throughout the fall of 1934 to produce a bill for Congress. Predictably, there was what one participant called "bitter disagreement" between backers of the Ohio and the Rochester-Wisconsin models (Altmeyer, 1968:22). As head of the ACES subcommittee on unemployment insurance, Folsom mustered significant support for the Rochester-Wisconsin approach. His subcommittee recommended that federal law permit experience rating and that it sanction corporate and multiemployer reserve funds. These "house and industrial accounts" could contract out from a state's pooled fund if their reserves were adequately funded. More controversial was Folsom's attempt to gain approval for guaranteed employment plans (employers who promised year-round jobs, as did Procter & Gamble, would not have to pay unemployment taxes) and for interstate reserve funds (companies operating in more than one state, such as Kodak, would be allowed to circumvent state prohibitions on employer reserves).[16]

Folsom also focused the council's attention on fiscal matters. Together with the other ACES employers, he urged a cut in the Wagner-Lewis tax rate from 5 to 3 percent or less, depending on business conditions. A majority of the committee supported the employers' position on taxes. But the employers stood alone when it came to their proposal for employee contributions, which Folsom argued was a way of making workers "more interested in the system."[17]

From Folsom's perspective, the administration bill was shaping up favorably. It left the states free to choose between the pooled and reserve fund models; in either case, firms with stable employment levels would receive "additional credit" to reduce their tax rates. The initial rate was set at 1 percent, scheduled to rise to 3 percent, but only if business conditions improved (Altmeyer, 1968:24; Witte, 1963:89). While the bill precluded employee contributions and interstate employer funds, it contained the most important items sought by Folsom.[18]

Yet when Folsom appeared before Congress in February 1935, giving separate testimony to the House and Senate, he said that the proposed act would seriously discourage states from experimenting along Rochester-Wisconsin lines. What concerned Folsom was a provision—added in at the last minute—requiring employers with reserve accounts to pay 1 percent of their payroll to a pooled state fund. (Arthur Altmeyer had put this in the bill to placate advocates of the pooled approach.) This provision, when combined with a requirement barring experience rating until an employer's reserve stood at 15 percent of payroll, would have the effect of delaying any tax reductions until 1946. "Obviously," said

Folsom, "an employer would not do very much about stabilization in 1936 and 1937 on the chance that he might get a reduction in his rate in 1946." Moreover, the provisions would "practically bar the States from experimenting with a system of separate accounts and will prevent experimentation in the one field which employers who have had experience with unemployment-benefit plans feel is the most promising one" (US Congress, 1935:31-2). To convince Congress that employer reserves were necessary, Folsom explained in great detail Kodak's stabilization techniques and the Rochester Plan. In a nation still recovering from depression, the Plan's results seemed impressive. According to Folsom, layoffs totaled only 337 in 1933 and 140 in 1934, this out of a workforce in those years of about 13,000.[19]

Yet Folsom's testimony had little effect on the House. In March, it stripped from the administration's bill all provisions for experience rating. It also eliminated the section permitting states to have employer reserve accounts. These steps were taken by Republicans opposed to the administration and eager, as one representative put it, to "gum up the works" (Witte, 1963:90). Organizations representing small business— including the NAM and the US Chamber of Commerce—were opposed to unemployment insurance and to Folsom's strategy of 'making the best of the inevitable.' Folsom had no doubt that a bill would eventually pass but was deeply concerned lest it preclude federal support for private actions. With the help of friends on the BAC, he launched a campaign aimed at reversing the damage done in the House. A BAC report on unemployment insurance was sent to the President in April. Widely publicized in the newspapers, it urged Roosevelt to back employer reserves and experience rating (Nelson, 1969:215-18; Altmeyer, 1968:33; Krooss, 1970:183; Wilson, 1962). Later that month the president gave a fireside chat in which he endorsed unemployment insurance and said that any plan should promote stabilization by employers. Folsom told another manager that "I heard the president's address and of course was quite pleased at his statement in regard to providing an incentive to stabilize. I felt all along that he was in favor of this."[20]

Folsom's greatest success was in the Senate. According to Folsom (1962:110), the chairman of the Finance Committee told him he was "the first witness to appear who had practical experience in pension and unemployment benefits. He then asked me if I could indicate specifically the amendments which I would suggest. I had prepared the wording for different amendments and I went over each one of them, which he copied into his personal copy of the bill." Subsequently, the committee asked Folsom whether he would be willing to confer with them during their executive sessions. Although he never was called on (because the chairman was opposed to bringing in outsiders), Witte (1963:89, 141-2) says that "Folsom's testimony was frequently quoted by senators in the executive sessions." The committee followed several of Folsom's suggestions, including elimination of the requirement that reserve-plan employers had to contribute to a pooled fund. And it restored provisions, struck by the House, permitting employer reserve plans and experience-rated tax credits. These changes were contained in the Senate bill passed in June and signed by Roosevelt in August 1935.

In the ensuing years, experience rating became a common practice. By 1939, 40 states allowed employers to pay lower insurance taxes if they had stabilized employment. Few states, however, went very far in the direction of employer reserve plans. Just seven states permitted such plans and of these only Nebraska and Wisconsin actually used an employer reserve system (Folsom, 1939:24; Bernstein, 1985:177; Nelson, 1969:171-3). Most disappointing to Folsom was New York's adoption of an Ohio-style plan, with pooled funds, generous benefits, and no mention of either employer reserves or experience rating. In a bitter letter to Witte, whom he accused of giving ineffectual testimony in Albany, Folsom wrote that "It is unfortunate that, as a result of the [New York] legislation...the one plan which has been developed and which to judge from actual experience does provide greater security to workers— the Rochester Unemployment Plan—will have to be abandoned and the workers who are now covered by it will receive less protection in the future than they are now getting." Indeed, the Rochester Plan ceased operation in 1937. But Folsom continued to lobby for experience rating in New York and eventually was successful.[21]

The only other battle Folsom lost concerned how states and the federal government would divide administration of unemployment insurance. Folsom favored giving the federal government, not the states, authority to determine tax and benefit rates. He hoped that this would keep costs down in liberal northern states where industrial firms like Kodak had the bulk of their operations. Federal control would also have made it easier to operate multistate reserve funds. Ironically, Ohio plan supporters also were in favor of a national system because it meant a larger pool and higher benefit standards in southern states.

Despite these strange bedfellows, the administration's experts decided in favor of a plan (the tax-offset) giving states authority to determine program standards. Witte thought Congress and the Supreme Court were likely to block any legislation seen as taking rights away from the states. In response, the ACES employers pushed hard for a compromise federal-state arrangement known as the subsidy plan, which had been developed by Bryce Stewart's staff. They persuaded William Green of the AFL and three other ACES members to vote in favor of the subsidy plan. Then, one of the employers, probably Teagle, leaked word to the New York Times that a majority of ACES members had voted against the CES's tax-offset plan. The unwanted publicity hardened Witte's determination to recommend the tax-offset plan to the president, which he did. Ultimately, this is what Congress enacted (Altmeyer, 1968:22; Berkowitz & McQuaid, 1988:106-39; Nelson, 1969:198-211; Witte, 1963:58-61).[22]

Others have argued that the choice between the two plans was a "crucial issue" and that the CES's failure to back the subsidy plan proves that "the tiny number of welfare capitalists who actually participated in the formulation of the Social Security Act did not win the support of key executive-branch actors" (Skocpol and Amenta, 1985:572). But this is wrong on both counts. First, rather than being a "crucial issue," differences between the subsidy and tax-offset plans were slight, which is why many individuals (including those on the CES) had a hard time choosing between them. Indeed, before Stewart developed the subsidy method, Folsom had been a tax-offset supporter and testified on its behalf at the 1934 Wagner-Lewis hearings (US Congress, 1934:71-2). At the time, Folsom liked the tax-offset plan because it left the federal government neutral on the pool-versus-reserves issue, while subjecting all employers to a uniform federal tax. Seven months later, Folsom shifted in favor of Stewart's subsidy method (Witte, 1963:116-21). But when the CES refused to endorse it, Folsom readily went back to the tax-offset plan. In his testimony to Congress (1935:4-5,31), he acknowledged that there were "good reasons" for the tax-offset approach and said that "the States should be given the opportunity to experiment with different systems." The things that really mattered to Folsom—employer reserves, experience rating, and uniform but low tax rates—were obtainable through either plan. Folsom pressed for these items and, in the end, his persistence paid off. Thus, and this is my second point, the fact that the Social Security Act ratified Folsom's key objectives shows how successful he was in obtaining support from Congress and the CES. Liberal employers like Folsom did not get every item they asked for, but in politics one never does.

Social Security: Pensions and Health Benefits

Old-age support became a major issue in the early 1930s as a result of the Townsend Plan, a proposal to pay all elderly citizens a flat pension of $200 per month, financed by a federal sales tax. Townsend claimed millions of followers, including several in Congress, a group too large for the administration to ignore (Graebner, 1980; Brinkley, 1982). According to Arthur Altmeyer (1968:10), pressure exerted by the Townsendites and by Huey Long's Share-the-Wealth movement "forced the President to develop some alternative plan" for putting money in the hands of the elderly. Roosevelt's alternative, announced in June 1934, called for pension insurance financed by joint payroll taxes.

Folsom thought pension legislation was inevitable, but wanted federal pensions to be as small and inexpensive as possible. Hence he favored a contributory federal plan over more costly measures like the Townsend proposal, which he believed would cause "a tremendous drain on the Federal treasury."[23] Folsom and the other ACES employers firmly backed the CES in its efforts to obtain contributory federal pensions (this in contrast to their shenanigans on behalf of the subsidy plan). J. Douglas Brown (1969:15), the CES pension expert, says that at a critical point in December 1934, "the support of progressive industrial executives ensured that a national system of contributory old-age pensions would be recommended to the President and the Congress... Their practical understanding of the need for contributory old-age annuities on a broad, national basis carried great weight with those in authority."

Yet Folsom initially favored a pension law that would have permitted firms like Kodak to opt out of the federal system, as with unemployment reserves. "Smaller firms could turn their money over to a state fund," he told Lovejoy in 1934, while other companies would be required "to set up their own plans, which would have to meet certain standards."[24] Folsom's approach would have scored ideological points by allowing big business to compete with government to see who could do a better job of providing pensions. Yet Folsom was less concerned with ideology than with reducing Kodak's relative pension costs. Similarly, the insurance companies—who were the leading proponents of a contracting-out provision known as the Clark amendment—were motivated by a fear that federal pensions would destroy the lucrative private pension-insurance business. When the CES refused to include the Clark amendment in the administration's bill, the insurers furiously lobbied Congress on its behalf. In May 1935, the Senate added an amendment to the social security bill allowing firms to remain outside the federal system if their private plans met minimum standards, precisely what Folsom had suggested to Lovejoy.

During the intervening months, however, Folsom lost his enthusiasm for the Clark amendment. Although Kodak was on record in support of it (Berkowitz & McQuaid, 1988), Folsom came to doubt its wisdom. When he testified to Congress (1935:37), Folsom said that contracting out should be permitted only if found "desirable and feasible" by the agency established to administer social security. The reasons for Folsom's hesitance were spelled out by Craig Cochrane, head of Kodak's personnel department, who warned the American Management Association (1935:20) that the Clark amendment would bring undesirable government scrutiny of private pension standards, including "careful accounting of employee contributions and adjustments in cases of separation." In the worst case, "no modification could be made in such company plans without reference to Federal authority." Kodak was not the only firm harboring these fears. Douglas Brown told Senator Wagner in February that "key industrial executives are not interested in the proposals which the insurance groups are making for contracting out. They see that they have little, if anything, to gain and something to lose" (in Bernstein, 1985:314).[25]

With employers giving only lukewarm support, Roosevelt dug in his heels, telling Congress he would not sign a bill containing the amendment. The Senate, however, insisted on its inclusion. The deadlock was finally broken when the Senate agreed to remove the amendment and have a committee prepare a report on it for the next Congress (Altmeyer, 1968:40-2). The following spring, when Congress reconsidered the issue, Folsom again spoke against it. But now he was less measured in his opposition. In a speech to the US Chamber of Commerce that was reprinted in the Harvard Business Review, Folsom (1936) warned that the Clark amendment would bring "constant supervision" and "regulation" of private pension plans by the Social Security Board. Folsom then offered a different method for "fitting individual company plans into the Government plan." His alternative, which he first described to Congress in 1935, was the "supplemental plan." Under it, private pensions would be restructured so that employers deducted from their annual pension contributions the amount they paid to the government in social security taxes. Workers then would receive pensions from both the government and their employer, while the employer's cost remained the same. While supporters of the Clark amendment claimed that employers would abandon private pension plans if the amendment were not passed, Folsom predicted his alternative would preserve existing pension plans and provide an incentive to start new ones. With the government paying only minimum benefits, he said, "many individual companies will find it desirable to adopt supplementary plans...because the benefits paid to the present older workers are greater than could be obtained for the same contribution made to an insurance company."

Another concern of Folsom's was the financing of federal pensions. Encouraged by its employer advisers, the CES endorsed a plan to finance benefits on a pay-as-you-go basis, which meant low tax rates in the plan's early years with a deficit developing in the mid-1960s (Altmeyer, 1968:28-34). Although Roosevelt went along with most of the CES's recommendations, on this issue he followed the advice of Treasury Secretary Henry Morgenthau, who opposed pay-as-you-go in favor of full reserve financing. Morgenthau ostensibly wanted to prevent deficits in the plan's later years, but the real reason he favored full reserves was a desire to reduce the government's large operating deficit (Leff, 1983). Payroll taxes, as we know from current experience, are an easy way to fund deficits under the guise of meeting future pension obligations. Morgenthau wanted to double the initial tax rate proposed by the CES and bring subsequent rates up to 6 percent by 1951 (versus the CES's plan to bring rates up more slowly—to 5 percent in 1959).

Folsom did his best to convince Congress (1935:22-4, 37) that the Morgenthau plan was a bad idea. But rather than focus on the tax rate issue, which might have appeared self-serving, he criticized the size of Morgenthau's proposed reserve fund, which he estimated would reach 37 billion dollars (at one point he even cited a figure of 75 billion dollars). Using an argument that since has become familiar in other settings (for example, see Nielsen's chapter in this volume), Folsom warned that this money would create an irresistible temptation to raise pension benefits or to tap the fund for other purposes. He also attacked the fund in Keynesian terms for being "deflationary;" it took money out of "regular productive channels" and "sterilized" it. As an alternative, he proposed a small contingency reserve and holding tax rates at 2 percent through 1959, below even the CES's original schedule. Yet Congress went along with the Morgenthau plan, much to Folsom's dismay.

In spite of this, Folsom staunchly supported the act in the first years after its passage. But he tempered his support with repeated calls to revise the financing mechanism, which Folsom (1936:423) called the "major defect in the plan." Republicans also hammered away at this, hoping to weaken support for Roosevelt. Presidential candidate Alf Landon made the reserve fund an issue in his 1936 campaign. And after Landon's loss, Senator Arthur Vandenberg, a Republican from Michigan, convened hearings on the reserve fund and ordered Altmeyer, now social security commissioner, to form a second Advisory Council to look into the issue. Altmeyer asked Folsom to serve on the council and help him choose the other employer representatives. The men picked by Folsom were, like him, critical of the act's fiscal details but in favor of its larger aims (Berkowitz, 1987; Folsom, 1967:87).

Inside the Advisory Council and in 1939 testimony to Congress, Folsom repeatedly called for a return to pay-as-you-go financing, a small contingency fund, and lower tax rates. As before, Folsom argued that a large reserve was deflationary, only now he had support from those economists who blamed the 1937 recession on the Morgenthau plan. Although Folsom was a budding Keynesian, he parted company with other Keynesians, including Witte, who wanted to supplement fixed contributory taxes with general revenue funds that could be raised or lowered to stabilize the business cycle. Folsom opposed any recourse to general revenues, fearing that this would loosen the fiscal constraints imposed by contributory taxes and allow federal pensions to rise above the "basic" level. On all of these issues, the Advisory Council went along with Folsom and this time Congress did too. The 1939 amendments substituted a contingency fund for a full reserve, kept the system on a contributory basis, and postponed scheduled tax increases from 1940 to 1943. Finally, in what would prove to be a prime incentive for the adoption of private pension plans, Folsom lobbied for and obtained explicit language in the 1939 amendments exempting private pensions (and other "fringe" benefits) from social security payroll taxes.[26]

One debate Folsom lost was over survivor's benefits, which Brown proposed as a way to shrink the reserve fund. Folsom opposed survivor's benefits because he thought they too rapidly extended the welfare state. As he told the council, "I think we are trying to get across in one or two or three years what other countries have taken 30 and 35 years to do." But when he testified to Congress a year later, Folsom spoke in favor of the proposal. He said it would reduce reliance on old-age assistance, which was funded out of general revenues, and thus tie survivors' benefits to the fiscal discipline of contributory taxes (Berkowitz, 1987:65, 69; US Congress, 1939:1132-3).

The final programs discussed by the CES were disability and health insurance. The medical profession was passionately opposed, as were the ACES employers, including Folsom. Because Kodak did very little in this area, it had no reason to support a government program. Folsom thought a voluntary approach was preferable and, as if to prove the point, Kodak announced in June 1935 an innovative hospital insurance plan that was a precursor to Blue Cross. Anticipating the future, Folsom in 1937 discussed with Altmeyer the possibility that disability and health insurance might someday be run like unemployment insurance, with employers given the right to contract out or be taxed less if their health "experience" was good. But this was pure speculation. When disability insurance came before the Advisory Council, Folsom spoke against it as did other employers, and, as in 1935, no action was taken by Congress.[27]

Conclusions

The US experience demonstrates how the pursuit of welfare corporatism by large firms like Kodak constrained the subsequent development of the welfare state. In unemployment insurance, the existence of private programs gave rise to a governmental emphasis on prevention and to the employer reserve option (although few firms ever opted out of the federal system). As for old-age pensions, firms with pension plans lobbied to keep public benefits low so as not to displace private efforts while also seeking tax subsidies for private plans. Out of this grew a two-tier social welfare system in which niggardly public programs were (and must be) supplemented by employer-provided benefits.

The failure to enact disability and health insurance raises the question of Folsom's role during the 1930s. After all, his was only one voice among many in opposition; Congress and the administration would have dropped these issues even if Folsom had done nothing. And when it came to unemployment insurance and pensions, Folsom's opinions were often shared by Perkins, Brown, Witte, and Altmeyer. But because Folsom was a businessman, his priorities differed from those of the administration's reformer-bureaucrats. Chief among them was minimizing the cost of social welfare programs. Folsom was consistent and successful in his quest for low tax rates and cost controls such as contributory financing, contingency reserves, and experience rating. Low tax rates and contributory financing kept social benefits at a "basic minimum" level, thus meeting Folsom's other objective—preserving a place for private programs.

Folsom's status as a respected manager from a major corporation also aided the administration's efforts to defeat more radical proposals emanating from reformers like Mary Van Kleeck and Abraham Epstein, influential critics of welfare capitalism who favored the Ohio approach and universal old-age pensions.[28] On another front, Folsom blunted opposition from the business community, whose hostility seemed almost hysterical when compared to Folsom's knowledgeable and measured support. But Folsom was not a liberal ideologue, save for an occasional nod to Keynes. Instead, he was a pragmatic businessman eager to level the playing field between Kodak and New York State on the one hand, and less progressive firms and states on the other.

This essay has not tried to explain why the Social Security Act was passed in the 1930s; liberal employers were, at best, indirectly responsible for the surge in federal activism seen in that tumultuous decade. Folsom did not become a supporter of federal welfare programs until after Roosevelt's election, which suggests that his change of heart was a response to new political realities. But while Folsom made an ideological leap in 1933, the distance between welfare corporatism and welfare statism was small enough to make the leap feasible. Like the reformers in the administration's "brain trust," Folsom was a technocrat, trained to seek rational administrative solutions to human problems, whether in the firm or larger social units. His experience at Kodak, where he designed statistical planning models and insurance programs, prepared him to understand, accept, and ultimately champion social insurance and Keynesian planning, albeit conservative variants of the latter.

Today, however, Keynesianism is on the wane. At present, few US employers share Folsom's Keynesian faith in the macro-stabilization effects of countercyclical jobless benefits or in the micro-stabilization virtues of experience rating. Nor is there any interest amongst employers in privatizing jobless benefits through self-insurance schemes. Aside from organized labor, unemployment insurance has no powerful supporters. As a result, benefits are dwindling in real terms; so is the proportion of unemployed workers receiving them. Although experience rating continues to be practiced, it increasingly appears an anachronism and is under attack in some states (Vroman, 1990).

The crisis of unemployment insurance occurs against a backdrop of broader changes in levels of job security provided by large employers (see the paper by Quadagno and Hardy in this volume.) For example, whereas Kodak was once a paragon of stability—offering an implicit no-layoff policy from the 1940s through the 1960s—the company in the early 1980s laid off large numbers of workers in a series of painful restructurings. Today Kodak management says it is operating in a turbulent international environment that precludes guarantees of employment security. International competition also weakens the link between domestic spending and demand for US-made goods, including Kodak products. Folsom's approach to unemployment insurance leaves an uncertain legacy, at best.

However, the same is not true of Folsom's approach to pensions and health insurance. In his later years, Folsom became a supporter of national health insurance for the elderly. But Folsom never lived to see passage of comprehensive national health insurance, which physicians and insurers fought more strenuously than any other proposal to extend the social security act. Only today, more than twenty years after Folsom's death, does it appear possible that some form of national health insurance might be enacted. In 1990, a group of large corporations banded together to form the National Leadership Coalition for Health Care Reform, which supported a proposal to require every employer in the US either to pay a health insurance tax to the federal government or provide a specified minimum level of private health insurance. The proposal was consistent with the mixed public/private approach that Folsom did so much to establish. Small business opposed the idea, while large firms favored it, including unionized employers like Chrysler and General Electric as well as nonunion firms with generous health plans, chief among these being Eastman Kodak.

Although the Clinton administration bungled its first attempt to pass national health care legislation in 1994, the issue remains on the national policy agenda. Currently an enormous group of workers—chiefly in small firms in construction and personal services—entirely lack health insurance. In California, about 23 percent of the state's residents under 65 are medically uninsured; of these, 90 percent are people who work for a living and their families (Brown, 1991). Possibly during Clinton's second term or under a Republican president, some kind of national health insurance legislation will be enacted. Because of past choices—what economists call "path dependence"—it is likely that such legislation will be a mandatory "mixed" program rather than a universal plan. In this as in other areas, Folsom's legacy lives on.

Notes

1. On Fordism's European observers, including ideological opposites Marinetti and Gramsci, see Maier (1970). Most like the US in this regard was Japan, a nation that also developed large firms and mass production before the emergence of mass unionism. Hence it comes as no surprise that Japan today shares with the US public (private) welfare programs that are relatively small (large) by European standards, a point discussed in Shinkawa and Pempel's contribution to this volume and in Jacoby (1993). By private welfare corporatism I mean an enterprise-oriented employment system with extensive welfare provisions and programs to involve employees in the corporation. In recent years there has been much writing on European-style corporatism, a system under which workers negotiate statutory terms of employment and public welfare provisions via unions and labor parties. The qualifier "private" is intended to distinguish class-wide integration from the vertical, enterprise-level variant seen in the US and Japan (Dore, 1989).

2. In the mid-1920s, the Conference Board could find only 245 firms with active pension plans and 399 with company unions. Excluding the railroads, a special case, this put pension coverage at about 6 percent of the private, nonfarm labor force (NICB, 1925:6; Nelson, 1982:337; Jacoby, 1985).

3. Personnel Data File, Kodak Archives, Eastman Kodak Company (hereafter KA). Also see Forbes (1963).

4. Interview with Ken D. Howard, former Kodak manager, 16 June 1987. Also see Raff (1991).

5. Ackerman (1930:359-360); Blake McKelvey to author, 30 October 1987.

6. Minutes of the Meeting of the Unemployment Committee, 1922, box 39, Folsom Papers, University of Rochester (hereafter FPUR); Metcalf (1972):195-238.

7. Marion B. Folsom, "Proposed Annuity and Insurance Plan for Eastman Kodak," 13 July 1928, Folsom File, KA; "Rochester Employees' Labor Turnover," n.d., box 17, FPUR; Folsom (1967):3-4, 46.

8. Lovejoy to Folsom, 8 July 1930 and Folsom to Lovejoy 19 August 1930, box 18, FPUR; "Rochester Unemployment Benefit Plan," *Industrial Relations* 2 (21 March 1931):121-23; US Senate (1935):30.

9. Folsom to R.F. Evans, 24 September 1931, box 1, FPUR; Folsom, "The Rochester Unemployment Benefit Plan," Address to the Silver Bay Industrial Relations Conference, 27 August 1931, Speeches, vol. 1, FPUR.

10. Folsom to Mark A. Daly, 21 January 1932, box 18, FPUR.

11. Folsom to Lovejoy, 25 Sept. 1933, box 1, FPUR; Whitney (1934):1305-7.

12. Folsom to R.K. Brodie, 13 December 1933, box 1, FPUR.

13. Folsom to Lovejoy, 24 May 1933, box 1, FPUR; Folsom (1967):110; National Recovery Administration, Statement of the Secretary of the Code Committee of the Photographic Industry, Public hearing, Washington, DC, 4 August 1933, box 1, FPUR. Also see McQuaid (1978).

14. Eastman Kodak, F.W. Lovejoy: The Story of a Practical Idealist (Rochester, 1947):28, 33-4; Lovejoy to Folsom, 8 September 1939 and Folsom to Lovejoy, 14 February 1939, box 2; Folsom to Lovejoy, 15 September 1937, box 1, FPUR. Differences of opinion within the Kodak hierarchy show the danger of inferring a company's political orientation from the statements of its managers. As Amenta and Parikh (1991) argue, this problem bedevils the analysis of Jenkins and Brents (1989), who try to infer the common characteristics of companies supporting the New Deal from statements of corporate managers. Amenta and Parikh then go on to attack Jenkins and Brents's conclusion that there existed a liberal capitalist faction which supported the Social Security Act. But Amenta and Parikh themselves go overboard, as in their assertion that "Capitalists had little to do with the programs in the bill which became the Social Security Act" (126). Surely, as the present essay shows, this is a hyperbolic claim.

15. "Information Primer: The Committee on Economic Security", box 20, FPUR; Altmeyer (1968:8); Scheinberg (1966:166-7); Witte (1963:89); Ferguson (1989:19); Berkowitz and McQuaid (1988:78-95). Several defecting BAC members formed the American Liberty League, which worked assiduously to unseat Roosevelt (Wolfskill, 1962:165; Burk, 1990:188-91).

16. Altmeyer (1968:22); Minutes of the Advisory Council on Economic Security, 6, 7, 8 and 15 December 1934; box 20, FPUR; Thomas H. Eliot, "Why Industries and Large Employers Operating in Several States Should Not Be Allowed Special Federal Treatment," 3 December 1934, box 20, FPUR.

17. ACES Minutes 6 December 1934, box 20, FPUR; Nelson (1969:20); US Congress (1935:13).

18. Folsom decided not to press for employee contributions; the "main thing" was to secure employer reserve funds. Folsom (1967:16, 32).

19. Folsom conveniently ignored the fact that Kodak went into a tailspin in 1932, the year before the plan took effect. Bottom was reached early in 1933, just as the Rochester Plan went into effect. Thus, Kodak's low layoff rates in 1933 and 1934 had less to do with the plan than with increased demand for

Kodak products in those years. This was precisely the point made by critics of reserve funds: that experience rating "can only cause seasonal stabilization and is wholly inadequate to cyclical, technological, or stochastic stabilization" (Morton, 1933:403). Also see Folsom to Lovejoy, 2 February 1933, box 18, FPUR; Whitney (1934:1307).

20. Folsom to H.W. Story, 2 May 1935, box 20, FPUR.

21. Folsom to Witte, 19 April 1935 and Witte to Folsom, 23 April 1935, box 20, FPUR. In 1954, when Folsom was an adviser to Eisenhower, the president recommended—and Congress adopted—a provision extending experience rating to new employers (Altmeyer, 1968:250).

22. Gordon (1991) stresses that business support for the Social Security Act was a reaction to proposed state-level pension and unemployment insurance programs. No doubt it is true employers like Folsom saw federal preemption as a way to hold down costs. But surely there is more to the story than that. After all, the states proposed all sorts of social legislation throughout the 1920s, as Gordon demonstrates. Yet Folsom, Swope, and other liberals did not propose a federal role until well into the depression. Gordon's article is also marred by various errors. He confuses the Rochester Plan with ACWA's joint unemployment insurance plan (172) and mistakenly asserts that "merit rating" was a way for firms to opt out of the social security act (187).

23. US Congress (1935:21; 1939:1160). Jerry Cates (1983:138-41) claims that the "contributory-contractual" principle (tying federal pension benefits to contributions built up in a worker's account) was a conservative attempt to block the "radical" flat pension approach—radical, because flat pensions were egalitarian (not based on labor market experience) and had more redistributive potential than contributory pensions. But Cates fails to realize that flat pensions also could be more regressive than contributory pensions. Moreover, liberals of the 1930s, including Roosevelt, were less concerned about the flat pension's "radical" implications than about its fiscal feasibility (especially its effect on the federal deficit) and its vulnerability to constitutional and political challenges. Roosevelt thought that a noncontributory program would be branded a "dole," something the public had an aversion to. And, as he told his adviser Luther Gulick, opponents of social security would have a harder time cutting a program based on individual accounts than one funded out of general revenues, a point amply proved in the 1980s (Leff, 1983; Karl, 1983:141). While these accounts are a semi-fiction (workers pay in less than they ultimately receive), they do create a strong presumption that federal pensions are a legal entitlement—a contractual promise to refund past contributions with interest.

24. Folsom to Lovejoy, 26 October 1934, box 18, FPUR; Altmeyer (1968:40-2); Towers, Perrin, Forster & Crosby, Bulletin on Social Security 29 April 1935, box 18, FPUR.

25. Strict federal supervision of private pension standards did not come until 1974, when Congress passed the Employee Retirement Income Security Act (ERISA).

26. US Congress (1939:1135-8, 1150); US Congress, Senate, "Final Report of the Advisory Council on Social Security," 10 December 1938 (76th Cong, 1st Sess.); Altmeyer (1968:91-109); Folsom (1967:82, 125); Leff (1983:371); Murray Latimer and Karl Tufel, Trends in Industrial Pensions (New York, 1940):40, 84.

27. Altmeyer (1968:27-33, 92-103); W.A. Sawyer to J.D. Brown, 20 May 1936, Labor-Management Documentation Center, Cornell University; Witte (1963:173-88); Folsom (1967:163); Folsom to Altmeyer, 26 March 1935, box 20, FPUR; US Congress (1939:1134).

28. Skocpol and Amenta (1985), among others, downplay splits between the reformers. The point is, given opposing factions, what tipped the balance in favor of one group over the other?

3

Labor Unions and the Privatization of Welfare: The Turning Point in the 1940s[1]

Beth Stevens

Most advanced societies have used both the public and private sectors to provide income security, although each tends to rely more heavily on one sector than the other (Rein and Rainwater, 1986b). However, researchers on social welfare programs have focused the bulk of their attention on the development, content, and consequences of the welfare state. Until recently, there was little recognition of the generally smaller and more fragmented domain of occupational welfare. As scholars turn their attention to private sector social welfare, they are confronted by a series of questions: (1) are the two forms of social welfare alternatives to each other (when one is strong, the other is weak) or do they complement and mutually reinforce one another? (2) Why do some countries depend more heavily on public social welfare than on its private sector version (or vice versa)? (3) Can extant theories for explaining the rise of the welfare state be used to illuminate the development of occupational welfare?

Occupational welfare offers complexities that theories of the welfare state have yet to encompass. Halfway between a reward for work and a social right to security, these programs embody both compensation and social obligation. The study of the development of occupational welfare, therefore, needs to take into account not only the relations between the state and the various forces attempting to influence public action, but also the relations of the marketplace, i.e., the relations between employer and employees (or the unions that represent them). Theories of occupational welfare must focus on the actions of employers and unions who choose between wages and fringe benefits in the context of labor-management conflict and market forces, in addition to more macropolitical concerns.

When American researchers focus on the particular characteristics of occupational welfare, they tend to underrate the role of organized labor in the development of private sector welfare benefits (Berkowitz and McQuaid, 1980; Brandes, 1976; Brody, 1968; Dobbin, 1992; Dobbin and Boychuk, this volume; Edwards, 1979; Fitzgerald, 1988; Harbrecht, 1959; Jacoby, this volume; Jones, 1983). In most of these accounts, occupational welfare is interpreted as the result of employer and state action, whether a creative policy to enrich the varieties of employee compensation, a more sophisticated attempt to control the behavior of workers in large scale organizations, or a reaction to the social welfare activities of the state. There is little focus on the role of unions.

Ironically, most social-democratic theories of the welfare state implicitly encourage this neglect of the labor movement's role in the development of private sector welfare efforts. Proponents of this school of thought argue that labor movements have devoted their energies to building the public welfare system as part of their strategy to redistribute the resources of capitalist societies. By expanding the role of the state in the redistribution of income, the labor movement counteracts corporate power over economic resources and avoids the potential divisiveness inherent in benefits based on the hierarchical workplace (Castles, 1978; Korpi, 1978; Shalev, 1983; Stephens, 1979). Because of this focus on labor's statist efforts, social-democratic theories have obscured the fact, amply demonstrated by the historical record, that unions have played a major role in the development of occupational welfare (Quadagno, 1988; Stevens, 1988; Whiteside, 1980).

The United States is clearly a society in which occupational welfare serves as a major source of social welfare protection. The US relies far more than other societies on the private sector to mount social welfare programs. (See Martin Rein's chapter in this volume; and also Kerns and Glanz, 1988; Waldo, Levit and Lazenby, 1986; Rein and Rainwater, 1986c). Moreover, while the American labor movement supported public social welfare programs, it was nonetheless a major proponent of private sector welfare. American unions went out on strikes, petitioned the state, and actively worked to produce collectively-bargained employee benefits plans that substituted for the welfare state. This paper will focus on the question: what prompted American unions to promote private sector employee social welfare as a substitute for public sector welfare state programs?

A persuasive interpretation of the development of American occupational welfare necessitates remaking the conventional explanation for the development of fringe benefits that has prevailed for the last forty years. The traditional explanation—that the growth of benefits were an unintended consequence of the World War II wage freeze—does not recognize the dual nature of fringe benefits. The conventional view depicts employee benefits as a supplementary form of wage compensation and union efforts to win employee benefits as a willingness to take the only available form of increases in pay. This view, however, ignores the fact that employee benefits have another side; they are also an alternative to public welfare programs. Union decisions to press for private health insurance and private pension plans were made within the context of decisions regarding the prospects for national health insurance and the expansion of the Social Security program. In short, we must place the development of employee benefits in the context of both labor/management relations and social welfare policies in order to understand the forces that produced the strategies of American unions.

In this paper I will argue that American unions took their distinctive path in response to a particular concatenation of events that occurred in the second half of the 1940s. This brief period, I will argue, was a critical turning point in the development of both public and private sector welfare systems. During these five years, the forward surge of corporatist political arrangements that had begun in the 1930s and had reached their zenith during the war was beaten back (Brody, 1980; Lichtenstein, 1989; Stein, 1957). The progressive wave of reforms also stretching from the New Deal through the war was similarly stopped as the efforts for legislation guaranteeing full employment, national health insurance, and disability pensions failed again and again (Starr, 1982).

Against this background, the American labor movement turned toward private sector welfare benefits. The drive for employee benefits was, first of all, a result of the decline in the political power of unions in the late 1940s. During this period, labor's rights to engage in political action were being limited, union access to federal decision-making was shrinking, and the support of both Congress and the public for union-sponsored policy goals was deteriorating. The turn to employee benefits was a reaction to the decreasing ability of the labor movement to influence public sector decisions about social programs. The second factor that led to union adoption of a private sector strategy was the worsening climate in labor relations. During the late 1940s, unions were losing ground within the collective bargaining arena as various labor-sponsored initiatives to expand the scope of bargaining were rebuffed by employers. Anti-labor legislation and court decisions inspired by the strong postwar anti-union drive from business, reduced labor's contractual rights that had been in effect since the 1937 Wagner Act. Employee benefits were part of a counter-drive by unions to consolidate their disintegrating collective bargaining rights. Third, and finally, labor's drive for employee benefits was a response to federal encouragement. The federal government supported the negotiation of employee benefits in order to dampen the raging labor disputes of the postwar years and as part of a move by the Democratic executive branch to contest conservative Congressional efforts to both restrict the scope of collective bargaining and to block further development of public social welfare programs.

These three factors—restrictions on political activity, worsening labor relations, and the support of employee benefits by parts of the federal government—prompted many American unions to seek to bargain for private welfare benefits, rather than to place all their efforts towards expanding public social welfare programs. The labor movement's turn towards private sector welfare benefits, I will ultimately demonstrate, was a turn away from the political arena and back towards the traditional turf of American unions—collective bargaining. Unions did not so much unilaterally abandon the public sphere, as much as they were encouraged to turn their attention elsewhere.

Traditional Union Approaches to Social Welfare

In comparison with Europe, American unions' support for public social welfare programs—social security, national health insurance and disability pensions—was both ambivalent and tardy. Strongly adhering to the position that the workers' own organizations could meet the needs of workers, the national federation of unions (the American Federation of Labor, or the "AFL") hesitated to support the development of government welfare programs. It endorsed need-based pensions only in 1909, and until the late 1920s, refused to back government unemployment and health insurance. Only in the 1930s—much later than in Europe—did most American unions wholeheartedly back government programs. They celebrated the passage of the Social Security Act of 1935 and steadily supported the expansion of the system (Orloff and Skocpol,

1984; Quadagno, 1984; Robertson, 1989; Horowitz, 1978; Skocpol and Ikenberry, 1983; and Witte, 1963).[2]

Notwithstanding this limited willingness to expand the welfare state, by the late 1930s various unions had begun to negotiate with employers for private sector equivalents to public programs. These negotiations both continued and departed from traditional union attitudes about private welfare benefits.[3]

AFL unions had a long history of providing their own welfare benefits because they boosted solidarity, aided in organizing new members and helped members in times of stress (such as strikes). National labor leaders tolerated such programs, but often worried about the financial and administrative drain that such welfare funds placed on individual unions (Baker and Dahl, 1945; Kennedy, 1908; Munts, 1967; Slavick, 1953; Stevens, 1988; Bureau of Labor Statistics, 1928).[4] Until the early 1940s most labor leaders were strongly opposed to employer-provided welfare plans, particularly pensions, even if they were a product of collective bargaining (Bureau of Labor Statistics, 1948:1929; Munts, 1967).[5] In 1930 the American Federationist argued that workers should be able to fund retirement or disability out of their wages, if the wages were adequate:

The mere fact that these concerns establish funds is a confession on their part that the wages they pay and expect to pay are not and will not be sufficient for the workers to save any money to care for themselves in old age (McGrady, 1930).

By 1936, labor leaders accepted the necessity for disability and retirement benefits, but insisted that public, rather than employer, welfare programs were appropriate. Employee benefits plans were opposed because they were an attempt by employers to divert the worker's loyalty from his union to his boss.[6]

Organized labor has found from experience that the establishment and maintenance of private unemployment or old age pension funds is used to control the economic power and activities of working people. We believe that the establishment and administration of pension funds is a proper function of government.[7]

But by the late 1930s labor's position had begun to change. Scattered unions had succeeded in obtaining employer contributions towards social welfare programs in the 1920s. The Fur Workers, the Cloth Hat, Cap and Millinery Workers, and other unions in the garment trades negotiated for unemployment benefits as early as 1923. Sickness benefits were won by a local of the Street and Electric Railway Employees in 1926. In

1939, the Amalgamated Clothing Workers succeeded in transforming their collectively-bargained unemployment fund into a social welfare plan. By 1940 some international unions, particularly those from the Congress of Industrial Organizations (CIO), decided to endorse private nonprofit insurance plans.[8] In 1941, Local 3 of the Electrical Workers (IBEW) won a pension plan. The pace quickened further during the war. By 1945 many large industrial unions, including the Mineworkers and the Steelworkers, began to press for pension benefits from employers. Finally in 1946, the annual conventions of both the AFL and the CIO formally announced drives to win private sector welfare benefits from employers (Dobbin, 1988; Slavick, 1953; Dvorsky, 1956; Tilove, 1960).[9]

Between those declarations and 1950, unions were overwhelmingly successful in their demands for fringe benefits. In a mere five years practically every major union in the country had negotiated pension or health and welfare programs. In 1945, thirty-two million Americans were covered for hospitalization insurance; by 1950 this figure had more than doubled. In the same period, the pension coverage of American workers increased by one half, rising from 6.4 to 9.2 million. By 1952 the surge subsided. Unions settled down to debating quality standards for existing programs and fleshing out the cope of coverage. Private sector welfare benefits were safely harbored within America's social welfare system (Rowe, 1951; Skolnik, 1976a)[10]

Explaining the Drive for Employee Benefits

Most historical discussions of modern fringe benefits serve as introductions to contemporary policy concerns (Bernstein, 1965; Greenough and King, 1976; Harbrecht, 1954; Munnell, 1982; and Dearing, 1954).[11] The common, almost hackneyed, explanation offered in these accounts, depicts occupational welfare benefits as the outgrowth of labor and managerial creativity in the face of World War II economic controls. In brief, these accounts suggest that in 1942 the Federal government, through the National War Labor Board (NWLB), placed strict controls on wages. To mollify unions, who sought their first pay raises since the Depression, and to aid employers desperate to retain employees in the competitive war economy, the NWLB ruled that employer contributions to insurance and pension plans would not be counted as "wages." This loophole opened the way to employee benefits programs as unions won wage increases under the guise of these new forms of compensation (Bureau of Labor Statistics, 1950).

This focus on the wage freeze as the reason for the development of employee benefits is technically correct but too narrow in scope. It centers on the wrong time period and ignores the historical patterns of adoption. While the wage freeze provided unions with the opportunity to incorporate private sector benefits into their bargaining demands, the movement toward benefits had begun before the freeze. Moreover, the freeze does not explain the even larger burst of labor pressure for employer benefits that erupted after wage controls were lifted in 1946. Third, the wage freeze explanation places too much emphasis on the impact of wartime policies. If labor and management had so clearly agreed on the advantages of employee benefits during the wage freeze, there would have been no objection to their further expansion after the war. Yet corporations resisted negotiations over benefits quite strenuously. Traditional explanations acknowledge some of the postwar federal actions that supported labor demands for benefits, but depict such actions as the formal confirmation of an established trend in labor negotiations rather than as actions that were necessary for the very survival of fringe benefits. Without the legal support given by federal decisions, collective-bargaining over employee benefits would have ceased in the mid-1940s. Clearly then, we must look at the events during this later period to fully explain the union drive for private benefits.

This paper advances the view that the private sector alternative was a function of interrelated conditions of political and economic adversity which affected the labor movement's bargaining power and political tactics during the late 1940s. The following sections will explore these factors in greater detail.

Restrictions on the Political Options of Labor

The growing restriction of labor's ability to maneuver in the political arena of the postwar era accelerated the shift toward collectively-bargained welfare plans by key labor leaders, such as Walter Reuther and Philip Murray of the CIO (and the UAW and Steelworkers, respectively), William Green and George Meany of the AFL hierarchy, and John L. Lewis of the UMW. The latter half of the 1940s was a period of widespread change in labor's relations with the federal government and the American public. These changes took three forms. First, labor was shut out of the access to federal policy-making that had been extended in the form of representation in the planning agencies that ran the economy during the war. Second, the capacity of labor to organize voters and back candidates was increasingly restricted as new campaign laws redefined electoral rules. And finally, labor was confronted with an increasingly hostile political environment that made it difficult for unions to succeed in winning legislation in their interests. In response to these political setbacks, unions turned toward collectively-bargained benefits in part as a reaction to frustration with the waning of their influence in the public sector.

During the war, labor took part in the development of wartime economic regulation through its membership on such agencies as the National War Labor Board, and the Office of Price Administration. In a series of events that has been called "the breakdown of American corporatism," the OPA, NWLB, and other agencies that had set wages, prices, and production, were terminated—along with the formal participation of the labor movement in government. Thus, the small, but still significant, access to policy-making that labor had during the war, had now shut down (Lichtenstein, 1989; Harris, 1982; Lichtenstein, 1982; Stein, 1957).[12]

Unions were also facing deteriorating political fortunes because of drastically changed rules that governed their role in political life. In 1943 Congress passed the War Labor Disputes Act (better known as the Smith-Connally Act). Southern conservatives designed the act to reduce the power of labor by playing on public annoyance at disruption of the war effort by unions. Among its provisions was a ban on direct union contributions to political candidates. Labor no longer could punish its enemies and reward it friends. Unions, further, were forced to collect political contributions from each member rather than donate from general funds. This proved a difficult task. Even more damaging was the provision that limited union financing to political activities that registered voters and educated the public about general political issues. Direct contributions to actual candidates were illegal. This prohibition weakened union capacity to support friendly candidates. In the long run it made it difficult for any pro-labor political organization that backed political candidates to win financial support from labor. The Machinists, for example, regretfully refused to contribute to the Americans for Democratic Action (ADA), since it supported specific candidates. In effect then, the Smith-Connally Act set up barriers between unions and other progressive political forces. Labor was forced to be nonpartisan regardless of inclination. The Taft-Hartley Act of 1947 reinforced these restrictions; and unions found it increasingly difficult to play an active role in political campaigns.[13]

Finally, unions were forced to adapt their political activities to cope with an ever more hostile political environment. Despite a tremendous wartime rise in membership, political support for labor actually diminished during the second half of the 1940s. General approval of labor unions was high, but public opinion on specific labor issues was increasingly negative. Near the top of the public's list of issues that needed government attention was expansion of regulation of labor unions. In 1945, 58 percent of those in a Gallup Poll favored either the elimination of unions or increased restrictions on their behavior. And in 1946, over half of the public attributed motives of social responsibility to management, but only 7 percent gave labor leaders credit for similar sentiments. In 1946 and 1947, unions began to lose larger numbers of NLRB-sponsored elections for worker representation, while the anti-union voting in those elections began to grow (Gallup, 1972; Mills, 1971; Brown, 1949).[14]

This antagonism stemmed from the blame carried by labor for the turbulent economic conditions that developed during the transition from a war to a peace-time economy. Between December 1943 and June 1947 retail prices rose 26 percent. At the same time, unemployment was fluctuating as war plants closed for reconversion. Both union members, and Americans in general, reeled under the effects of rising prices, escalating layoffs, and increasing competition for jobs as ex-soldiers re-entered the labor force. Not surprisingly, this was a period of labor unrest: 1945 and 1946 were the most strike-filled years in American history, with 8 and 10 percent of workers taking part in strikes (Epstein and Snyder, 1949; Bureau of the Census, 1975).

As the strikes increased, so did public hostility. Labor felt scapegoated as the source of rising prices and social disorder. Unions were attacked as a "special interest" and a "danger to the political system" (Kroll, 1946). They were accused by the Council of Economic Advisers of encouraging "restrictive practices" and fomenting monopolies.[15] According to the Gallup Poll, the public believed that strikes were the "most important problem the US Government must solve in 1946" (Gallup, 1972).

In response the American Federationist lamented, "it is fashionable these days to blame everything on labor" and "there are those who allege that labor ...[is] responsible for the high cost of housing. Over and over again the charge is made that housing costs the consumer so much because the wages paid construction workers are too high."[16] The CIO spelled it out more harshly:

monopoly interests, not content with the highest profits in their history, have had the crowning arrogance to mobilize their vast propaganda machinery to persuade the American People...that "labor" is to blame for inflationary prices, shortages, and production delays.[17]

Unions also felt unfairly blamed for industrial unrest. "Currently, strikes are crowding all other news off the front pages. The public is being warned of the great social cost of this and that strike. You don't see the same treatment accorded unemployment."[18]

Compounding the decline in public support, was a Congress that was increasingly conservative. Beginning in 1946, the pace of anti-labor activity in Congress quickened. The elections of that year brought in a conservative Republican Congress, with many members determined to dismantle the New Deal. In just its first two weeks, members of the 1946 Congress introduced more than one hundred bills to reduce the legal rights of labor unions (Goldman, 1960; Seidman, 1953; Tomlins, 1985).

Between the growing disapproval of the public and the manifest hostility of much of Congress, labor began to lose the political influence it had painfully acquired during the New Deal and the war. AFL and CIO views on the causes and solutions to postwar economic problems were repeatedly ignored or contradicted. Labor leaders were unable to prevent the Truman Administration from removing price controls, despite their contention that inflation would result. They could not stop the repeal of the wartime excess profits tax, despite the fact that corporate profits were the highest they had ever been. Nor could they deter the federal government from selling war production facilities to corporations for a fraction of their value. In short, labor leaders were unable to convince policy-makers of the validity of their views. Unions were cut off from decisions, and increasingly subject to the belief that business was increasing its influence at their expense (Foster, 1975; Harris, 1982; Seidman, 1953).[19]

Ineffectiveness in influencing economic policy-making was only part of the postwar deterioration of labor strength. The political weakness of unions was evident in its inability to win social welfare reforms. As the decade wore on the labor movement became increasingly distressed and frustrated about the failure of Congress to improve and expand social welfare legislation.[20]

This frustration was due to the key strategic position social welfare legislation played in labor's prescriptions for a healthy economy. Labor leaders saw the postwar expansion of social insurance as a way to prevent the massive economic breakdown that they feared would arise with the termination of war production. As part of this strategy, labor urged Congress to improve unemployment assistance (an AFL demand) and create a guaranteed annual wage (a CIO demand). Unions also campaigned for government health insurance and disability pensions, as well as the expansion of existing Social Security and Workmen's Compensation systems. These government programs, union leaders believed, were vital to workers who were unable to save enough to cover the accidents, illnesses, and aging that occur in the average worker's lifetime (Starr, 1982; Quadagno, 1988; Derthick, 1979).[21]

As part of this campaign, the national labor federations and key unions such as the UAW, Textile Workers, Machinists, and Clothing Workers, joined with medical personnel, occupational health and safety experts, economists, and corporate liberals to win social welfare programs (Berkowitz and Fox, 1989; Quadagno, 1988; Starr, 1982).[22] Despite these strong allies and massive organizing efforts, that included letter campaigns, rallies, Congressional testimony, and petition drives, labor saw both the proposals for new programs and the pleas for the expansion of existing programs defeated several years in a row. Unions could not generate the strength to win public sector social welfare programs. Nathan Cowan, the Legislative Director of the CIO, complained "Congress is on a sit-down strike... (It) has turned its back on the needs of the workers."[23]

Employee Benefits As a Response to the Loss of Power

The decline of labor in public opinion, the loss of access to policy-making positions, and the increasingly hostile Congress promoted labor's resort to employee benefits. The labor movement's shift emerged from its perception that the public saw unions as the source of the country's economic dislocations. In an effort to avoid being tagged as the villains behind inflation, unions decided to negotiate for employee benefits rather than demand high wage increases. Thus in 1946, at the height of the strike wave and during the period of most vociferous complaints about labor and inflation, the UAW decided to negotiate for a retirement plan rather than a wage increase because it was less likely to raise hostility. When wage increases again became difficult to win in 1949, unions again placed priority on winning fringe benefits, rather than alienating public opinion by pressing for higher wages. Thus, employee benefits were a means to manage the reputation of the labor movement during periods of public dissatisfaction.[24]

An even more critical factor in the determination of labor to turn to collectively-bargained employee benefits was the inability of labor to overcome Congressional resistance to both unionism and welfare state programs. By the mid-1940s, unions had grown restive about the stagnation in Social Security benefits levels. Walter Reuther, for example, complained that living costs spiraled while benefits stood still:

Social Security payments, which were niggardly on the basis of the 1937 price level that prevailed at the time they were determined, today provide men and women sixty-five and over with only a purse of pennies for their living expenses at a time when living costs are measured in dollars.[25]

Unions were also frustrated at the failure of several attempts to win a federal health insurance program.[26]

Despairing of gaining social welfare programs through the government, labor's frustration grew into discontent. Unions turned to private sector benefits. The CIO justified its drive for employee benefits in blunt terms:

The CIO has unequivocally stated that it is the responsibility of the federal government to provide all these types of benefits... However, political pressures over the past dozen or so years by the CIO and other groups interested in improving federal legislation in this field have not been successful... The American worker was, therefore, faced with the question of awaiting Congressional action or attempting to win some of these benefits through collective bargaining.[27]

Similarly, the AFL argued "the failure of Congress to act has not prevented many of our unions from providing some protection through collective bargaining. While this method is the best available at this time, we recognize that it is not as sound nor as practical as the comprehensive program envisaged in the Wagner-Murray-Dingell Bill" [for National Health Insurance].[28] Fringe benefits were to be no more than temporary substitutes for public programs.

The problem of discouraging government action through private measures was thus finessed by labor. Collectively-bargained welfare benefits were seen as "priming the pump". They were to awaken the taste of both the public and welfare providers (such as physicians) for public programs. To reinforce the point, many unions made sure to draw up clauses in their contracts that would allow private benefits to be converted into public benefits once legislation was passed (Goldmann, 1948).[29]

But the labor view soon shifted—fringe benefits were to be a permanent substitute for the still nonexistent public benefits. Union strategists justified their shift in tactics along two parallel paths. One path sought to change the political conditions for public social welfare programs. Unions (particularly the CIO unions) reasoned that if they were successful in forcing employers to finance fringe benefits programs, employers would be willing to join with labor to push the public sector to provide benefits in order to avoid the costs of fringe benefits plans. Unions asserted the coincidence of union interest and superior public policy:

One of the basic contributions, therefore, which the trade union movement has made in this whole social security field may well be the stimulation of employer groups to fight for improved old age pension programs...not because they believe in them, as such, but because they are interested in reducing their own costs.[30]

The other path led unions to endorse collectively-bargained benefits as not just a stop-gap measure, but instead as a permanent supplement to public programs.[31] The UAW, for example, argued that as a matter of political strategy, union benefits should exist in order to turn adequate public benefits into comfortable standards of living for union members:

The demands formulated by our union are part of a fight on two fronts. While we move toward pensions and social security through collective bargaining, we shall, at the same time be working for national legislation covering retirement and health and medical care. On the legislative front we can expect to win only basic national minimums for all our citizens. These minimums will not be high enough to meet the needs of our members. They will require supplementation through collective bargaining.[32]

Both of these paths represented reactions to criticism and doubts expressed by both unionists and other reform groups about the potentially destructive impact of private benefits on other labor goals. Evelyne Burns, the noted Social Security expert, complained that union programs will inevitably weaken the interest of those workers covered by welfare plans negotiated by unions, in pressing for extensions and liberalization of our public programs. The growth of union welfare plans will also weaken public support... [It will] foster the belief that workers can take care of themselves.[33]

Some unionists worried that the focus on employee benefits would sap labor's drive for a federal health insurance program and expanded Social Security:

There may be a danger that organized labor is doing a disservice to the working people of this country by demanding pension, health, and welfare plans for their members who are employed in a particular company or industry, instead of pressing vigorously for improved social security benefits and a national health program.[34]

But most unions defended employee benefits as either a temporary measure or as a "second tier" to the basic benefits they hoped to win from the public sector.[35] Union leaders seemed resigned to the fact that they would be attacked whatever approach they advocated:

the same interests who cry "communism" when a National Health Insurance plan is proposed, cry "private taxation" when an effort is made to obtain an industry fund through the good old "free enterprise" method of collective bargaining.[36]

The roadblock to the expansion of public sector social welfare programs was a necessary, but not sufficient reason for the labor movement's turn to private sector substitutes. Confronted by such a blockage, unions might have redoubled their efforts to win new legislation. Or they might have temporarily suspended further attempts to expand the welfare state, resolving to win public programs at a later date. But the unions did neither. Instead they turned to collective bargaining with management to win an alternative. To understand this choice, we need to add two factors to our explanation—the changing climate of labor relations and federal encouragement to focus the drive for security onto the private sector.

Changes in Labor-Management Relations

The second factor that contributed to the shift of unions towards private sector welfare benefits were new limitations on union activities in the collective bargaining arena. Thus, while the labor movement was facing limits on its activities in the political arena, it was also confronted with newly aggressive opponents determined to restrict union maneuverability within the labor relations arena as well. These simultaneous pressures—on both political options and collective bargaining rights—led labor to shift much of its energies into pressing for private welfare benefits.

Critical changes in labor relations in the 1940s took two forms. First, labor was continuously rebuffed in its attempt to broaden the scope of collective bargaining. Whether labor sought to unionize supervisory personnel, bargain on an industry-wide basis, or influence corporate production and pricing decisions, it was unable to force management to accede to its demands. Management consistently resisted any enlargement of collective bargaining; and even succeeded in reducing the scope of negotiations. The second change in labor relations during the postwar era, was the dramatic set of anti-labor laws that made it more difficult to organize and retain members. The Taft-Hartley Act of 1947, along with several other pieces of legislation and judicial decisions, struck at some of the most basic union techniques for winning strong bargaining positions. By prohibiting the closed shop and secondary boycotts and establishing fines for union leaders who failed to control sudden strikes, the legislation set severe limitations on union organizing activities.

Given these two setbacks, labor needed some successes. Employee benefits were regarded as a likely victory in a period otherwise filled with defeats, and so were enthusiastically taken up by unions.

Labor's first attempt to expand the scope of collective bargaining began during the war when the Foremen's Association of America was organized. This began a drive to unionize supervisory personnel as a means of expanding unionization into the lower ranks of management and permitting unions to participate in the organization of the production process. Corporations protested the association, arguing that foremen were part of management because they gave orders to workers. As such, they should not be unionized because they were in a position to undermine discipline. The NLRB at first disagreed with management, eventually permitting the organization of foremen into unions separate from those of the rank and file. Management, not accepting this defeat, lobbied Congress for legislation invalidating the NLRB decision. The issue was finally settled by prohibition against the unionization of foremen by the Taft-Hartley Act of 1947. Unions thus lost on two counts. They could not expand upward in the organization, and they lost one potential linchpin in their efforts to have a say in the organization of the production process. The prohibition against the unionization of foremen, in short, reduced union capacity to organize large and critically-situated parts of the workforce and thus establish stronger bargaining positions (Gross, 1981; Brody, 1980)[37]

The second attempt to broaden collective bargaining was an effort to increase the types of issues that could be subjected to negotiation. Unions sought to include such issues as job content, production rates, and guidelines for contracting out (Brody, 1980). One of the key demands centered on union access to information on employer finances. Beginning in the mid-1940s, unions demanded larger amounts of financial information from employers in order to assess the employer's ability to pay wage increases. In 1945, for example, the Research Directors of CIO unions planned a campaign to get the Securities and Exchange Commission and the Treasury Department to compel corporations to report information on investment capital. In another action, AFL leaders demanded the rights to greater information on production capacities (Bernstein, 1965).[38]

The drive for better accounting culminated in its most dramatic form in the UAW's strike against General Motors In 1946. The UAW demanded that the company pay a wage increase without raising the price of cars. When management pleaded lack of funds, the union demanded that it open its books to prove it. The union was demanding a voice in the pricing policy of the company, heretofore an exclusive privilege of management. It sought to publicly link wages with profits and prices and the union's fortunes with the fortunes of the public. Union wage increases were no longer to be the impetus for increased public hardship in terms of higher prices for goods. The company refused to open its books, arguing that the market, not a corporation's ability to pay, was the determining factor. It continued to refuse even when a federal fact-finding board supported the union. Truman declined to force the issue, and other unions undermined the strike by settling for wage increases without financial proof that prices need not increase. The UAW was forced to settle for similar terms; its attempt to sever the link between higher wages and higher prices was unsuccessful. No labor union tried Reuther's tactic again. Yet another attempt to broaden the scope of collective bargaining was rebuffed (Barnard, 1983; Brody, 1980; Seidman, 1953).[39]

But the setbacks in the drive to expand collective bargaining were minor compared to the defeats labor underwent with the passage of the Taft-Hartley Act and related anti-labor legislation. Labor had anticipated an anti-union campaign by employers once the war ended. Union leaders reasoned that with corporations flush with war profits and thus financially able to withstand strikes, management would try to force unions out of the workplace. Various events in 1945 and 1946 seemed to confirm union fears. Intensifying anti-union campaigns within the workplace, a quickening rate of anti-union court injunctions, and the passage of anti-labor legislation on the state level, inspired worry (Lichtenstein, 1982; Bernstein, 1965).[40]

Even before the passage of the Taft-Hartley Act in May 1947, the threat of such legislation encouraged the NLRB to tighten its regulation of unions. Strikes that violated contractual commitments or that sought to force the modification of an existing contract, for example, were made illegal in 1946. Both the AFL and the CIO increasingly complained of heightened evidentiary demands from the NLRB for both documentation of employer interference with union activities and for more stringent proof of worker support for organizing efforts (Gross, 1981; Tomlins, 1985).[41]

The actual passage of Taft-Hartley reduced labor's legal options even further. In addition to placing restrictions on the scope of collective bargaining, this legislation made it more difficult for unions to recruit new members. Taft-Hartley made it easier for small units of workers to petition for separate or different union representation, thus increasing "raiding" by both AFL and CIO unions against each other. Unions were forced to spend large amounts of time and energy in retaining ground previously gained, rather than organizing in new areas. CIO unions increasingly complained that the NLRB was favoring craft unions in disputes between competing AFL and CIO unions. Units of skilled CIO workers within the larger industrial unions became targets for organization by AFL unions. Meanwhile, AFL unions complained that Taft-Hartley increased the raiding between craft unions.[42]

Secondly, both the CIO and the AFL complained that the various provisions of the legislation made it more difficult to organize new units. Among the most onerous provisions were a prohibition of secondary boycotts in support of organizing campaigns and allowing employers to hold meetings to speak against the union. Taft-Hartley restricted union rights to force members to pay assessments for strike funds and prohibited automatic check-offs for union dues; unions would now have to secure individual workers' agreement to pay dues. In short, employers had greater power to discourage and hinder union activities while unions had fewer tools to force employer recognition and maintain internal solidarity to mount successful strikes (Harris, 1982; Witte, 1948).[43]

Fringe Benefits Negotiations as Labor's Response

All of this added to labor's need to win new and generous settlements. Unions had to show that they could be successful despite the new restrictions. They had to appear successful to unorganized workers, who they were trying to bring into the labor movement, and to their business and political critics, who might see labor failures as encouragement to restrict the unions even further.

Fringe benefits provided the possibility for a renewed demonstration of union effectiveness. First, benefits were a likely success because they were desired by the rank and file. By deciding to mount massive drives for fringe benefits, both the national unions and the national labor federations were responding to growing call for private benefits on the part of local unions. Labor leaders could therefore count on strong rank and file support for a pro-benefits drive. This would, of course, increase the likelihood that labor could succeed in winning at least one significant battle with management.[44]

Second, fringe benefits represented a new tool for organizing—one sorely needed given the disruptive effects of Taft-Hartley. Union leaders had begun to realize that employer-sponsored fringe benefits were a strong weapon against union organizers. More and more, labor organizers found that workers were either indifferent to unionization because employers were providing them with fringe benefits or frightened that benefits plans would be scuttled if the union became the bargaining agent (Allen, 1969; Minkoff, 1948).[45]

In sum, demands for fringe benefits became a reasonable approach to the difficult times brought on by Taft-Hartley. Such demands provided a likely success against employers, fended off employer anti-union campaigns, and helped to moderate the difficulties in organizing. As the AFL realized, fringe benefits had tactical advantages:

the union gains new prestige in the eyes of old members, prospective new members, and rival union members. Thus loyalty is secure from within, expansion made easier, and raiding by dual unions made difficult.[46]

Federal Encouragement of Collectively-Bargained Benefits

The final factor that led American unions to turn to collective bargaining for social welfare protection consisted of a series of actions by segments of the federal government that intentionally encouraged the labor movement's campaign for fringe benefits. These actions ranged from the defeat of Congressional conservatives who wanted to prohibit bargaining over benefits, to active help given to unions by federal social security experts, and finally to a virtual endorsement of collective bargaining over employee benefits through a series of decisions by the National Labor Relations Board and fact-finding boards appointed by President Truman to settle national labor disputes.

Federal support of union demands for fringe benefits began with the defense of labor's right to negotiate for benefits, This defense took place within the debate over the Taft-Hartley Act, as Congressional conservatives sought to outlaw collective bargaining over employee benefits as part of their general program to more stringently regulate labor unions (National Labor Relations Board (hereafter NLRB) 1948). Fringe benefits became a target for conservative lawmakers as a result of the 1946 Mineworkers' strike. That strike, called to win employer-financed but union-managed employee benefits, had paralyzed the economy. The conservatives were opposed by a coalition of Congressional liberals and other conservatives who preferred to permit employers and labor to decide whether to negotiate. These Congressional supporters were not able to secure an endorsement of employee benefits as appropriate subjects of collective bargaining, but they were able to block the clear prohibition desired by conservatives. Without this critical Congressional support, therefore, labor would have not had the options to pursue their drive for fringe benefits.

In contrast to the determined opposition by parts of Congress, federal experts on social insurance within Executive Branch agencies, had helped unions develop their fringe benefit demands from the very beginning of labor interest in the subject. Throughout the concentrated campaign of bargaining for employee benefits in 1946 and 1947, federal experts from the Social Security Administration and the Department of Labor met with labor policy planners to give advice and even design exploratory surveys.[47]

More explicit federal support of labor claims for employee benefits came out of the labor relations agencies that were empowered to reduce the labor turmoil of the period. In most of these cases, federal arbitration resulted in some type of endorsement of collectively-bargained benefits. These successive interventions gradually solidified support for employee benefits and institutionalized private sector social welfare programs.

Disputes over employee benefits played a distinct role in the tumultuous labor relations of the postwar era. Beginning in 1946, the number of disagreements over the inclusion of fringe benefits in collective bargaining steadily rose, peaking in 1949 and 1950. Fully fifty-five percent of the strikes in 1949 and seventy percent of the strikes in the first half of 1950 were over health and welfare issues in labor contracts (Bureau of Labor Statistics, 1951).

Explicit federal endorsement of collective bargaining over employee benefits first took the form of the inclusion of benefits in contracts negotiated under the aegis of federal arbitrators. Again, the 1946 Mineworkers' strike was a catalyst. Responding to the adamant refusal of coal mine operators to fund fringe benefits funds, the Truman-appointed managers of the mines worked with the union to fashion a compromise. The result was a federal mandate to establish a welfare and retirement funds to be jointly administered by the union and the mine owners (Seidman, 1953).

The government again endorsed bargaining over benefits in 1948, when the Steelworkers sought to bargain with the Inland Steel Company over its policy of compulsory retirement at age sixty-five. The company refused to bargain, arguing that such issues were not subject to negotiation under federal law. The union appealed to the NLRB. The federal agency sided with the union, arguing that fringe benefits were under the jurisdiction of federal labor law.[48]

Despite the seemingly clear federal endorsement of the legality of negotiations over fringe benefits, employers delayed compliance. In the same year as the landmark Inland Steel decision, the federal government had to again intervene in the coal industry to force recalcitrant employers to implement the pension plan it had first ordered in 1946. Then in 1949, the NLRB had to reiterate its decisions on benefits by siding with the Autoworkers to force General Motors to consult with the union before it instituted a health insurance plan (Warne, 1949; Slavick, 1953).

The labor dispute that finally cemented federal support for labor's demands for collectively-bargained benefits was a 1949 steel dispute that centered on the United Steelworkers demand for a pension plan. Again, employers refused to consider benefits as subject to negotiation. In an effort to avoid another crippling strike, the Truman administration appointed a fact-finding board to settle the dispute. Once more, a federal board generally supported the union. It not only affirmed that pensions were indeed subject to negotiation, but also supported the union position that industry had an obligation "to provide insurance against the economic hazards of modern life...as supplementary to the amount furnished by government (Dearing, 1954)."[49] The steel industry rejected the Board's findings, but with the endorsement of employee benefits by the fact-finding board, the union went out on strike. After two months the industry conceded and negotiated a pension plan. Employer resistance effectively disappeared with this settlement. The federal government had thrown its weight behind the unions and employers retreated.

Explaining Federal Support for Fringe Benefits Negotiations

Why should the federal government have supported the inclusion of fringe benefits in negotiations? Two disparate motives served to generate such support. First, Democratic frustration with the lack of expansion of public social programs, and the consequent desire to ease the political pressure coming from pro-expansion groups such as labor, led to their support for benefits. Federal support of union claims to employee benefits, in short, was motivated by the desire to support and supplement the stagnating public social security system. The second motive grew out of the acrimonious labor relations of the period. Government insistence that employers reverse their opposition and negotiate over fringe benefits was the result of federal desire to stifle the labor unrest that was disrupting the economy.

Federal support for fringe benefits can be tied to the Democratic frustration with the difficulties of expanding the stagnating Social Security system. In 1946, I.S. Falk, of the Social Security Administration, argued that private benefits could supplement public social programs:

The social security program is designed to provide basic security for employed persons and their families. Even under a comprehensive program with more adequate benefits than those now paid...there would still be room for important supplementations of the social security benefits. [It] might take the form of additional amounts which would bring the retirement income or the income of the permanently disabled closer to their previous income from employment.[50]

Secretary of Labor Schwellenbach observed in 1947 that health and welfare fund clauses in labor contracts were "an effective and flexible means of providing greater social security through collective bargaining." Some administration sources went further, asserting that the

Federal system should be a basis for retirement security but "supplemental plans, voluntarily arrived at, are to be applauded."[51]

Key members of Congress favored employee benefits for similar reasons. During the debate over the Taft-Hartley Act, several congressmen favored benefits because they wanted to minimize the possibility that unions would redouble their efforts to expand the welfare state if negotiations over private benefits were not made legal. Arguing against the exclusion of benefits from a list of negotiable topics, Congressman Ray Madden said,

The alternative—presented by this bill—is just one more step toward making the worker the ward of the State and toward increasing the demand for public support when the State refuses to private industry the power and right to help itself (NLRB, 1948:800).

Senator James Murray echoed these sentiments, pointing out that "these plans decrease the responsibility and burdens of the State (NLRB, 1948:1050)."

In fact, federal support extended beyond the desire to take pressure off the public system. Fringe benefits were also a means to curb labor unrest in the form of inflation, strikes, and attacks on the Taft-Hartley Act. Just as unions sought fringe benefits in order to avoid being tagged for adding to inflation, federal officials promoted benefits plans because they were not as inflationary as wage increases. Labor could be satisfied at a smaller cost. The Steel Industry Fact-Finding Board, for example, felt that an increase in wage rates "might well cause price dislocations, with adverse effects on the general economy," while "social insurance and pensions—especially pensions—involve long range considerations" (NLRB, 1948:60,61). In the debate over Taft-Hartley, some Congressmen argued that the failure to allow bargaining over employee benefits would result in wage demands that would be inflated in compensation (NLRB, 1948:313). By supporting benefits, the government could satisfy labor in the short run and worry about the costs in the long term.

But inflation was only one of the federal concerns about labor unrest. A long wave of strikes, often related to the drive for employee benefits, was crippling the economy. The strike wave of 1946 alone cost the nation 119.8 million person-days of lost production (Brody, 1980). The Mineworkers walkout, for example, was settled by the federal government because it had to get coal back into the factories before the economy collapsed for lack of fuel. This labor turmoil clearly stimulated government support for employee benefits. Congressional supporters of employee benefits argued that such plans would help restore labor peace and that the refusal to allow bargaining would lead to further labor unrest (NLRB, 1948:798, 800, 369). The Steel Fact-Finding Board took the view that fringe benefits negotiations were essential to reduce labor disaffection, and the attendant social dislocation:

> the board must try to make recommendations that are consonant with the economic welfare of the country. Second—and a matter which may or may not, be in conflict with the first, the board must endeavor to eliminate the threat of a work stoppage. That is perhaps its main function."[52]

Finally, federal support of fringes was directly connected to its drive to win labor acquiescence to the Taft-Hartley Act, Such acquiescence was far from assured. Taft-Hartley was despised by most labor unions. The CIO Executive Board considered a proposal to use work-stoppages to protest the Act. The Steelworkers reacted by refusing to deal with the NLRB; while the Typographers refused to enter into contracts with employers, believing that this would exempt them from Taft-Hartley regulations. But perhaps the most deeply-held objection to Taft-Hartley was to its requirement that union leaders sign affidavits testifying that they were not Communists. These loyalty oaths were widely attacked as a violation of free speech; John L. Lewis, President of the Mineworkers, and other major leaders categorically refused to sign the affidavits (DeVyver, 1949; Burns, 1949; Warne, 1949).[53]

Federal support for employee benefits was seen by administration officials as a partial solution to this crisis. According to Arthur Goldberg, then on the legal staff of the Steelworkers Union, "the NLRB has decided the Inland Steel Case in labor's favor—but that it is conditional upon our [the Steelworkers] compliance with the filing provisions of the Taft-Hartley Act."[54] In short, the NLRB decision in the Inland Steel dispute was decided in favor of the unions as part of a federal effort to win labor cooperation with the controversial Taft-Hartley Act.

Conclusions

The American labor movement has traditionally been characterized as the most conservative and politically quiescent of all labor movements in Western advanced industrialized nations. And indeed, when one contemplates the actions of the American unions in terms of their support of occupational welfare, they have followed a strategy that fits this portrayal. Their shift in target, from the public welfare state to private sector employee benefits programs, was an action that was more politically timid than the strategies followed by their European counterparts. The peculiarity of the American labor movement, however, was not an automatic expression of inbred ideological conservatism or an idiosyncratic strategy brought about by unusual conditions. Rather, it was a realistic response to pressures from the state, the corporate sector, and their own members, to withdraw from the political arena and concentrate on exerting pressure within collective bargaining.

The development of occupational welfare in the US, therefore, fits neither the European social-democratic approach, predicting that the labor movement would disparage private sector strategies in favor of an all-out drive for public sector programs, nor the conventional historical explanation of the American experience, that concentrates on employee benefits as a function of employer strategies. This is not to say, however, that neither the dynamics of welfare state politics nor the actions of the business sector were unimportant. Rather, it is to say that explanations of the development of private sector welfare benefits must also include consideration of the actions of labor unions. The rapid expansion of occupational welfare in the 1940s was the outgrowth of both the stagnation in public sector programs and the postwar settlement, under which labor won large wage and benefit increases but paid the price of abandoning its claims to negotiate the division of labor in the workplace and to link increases in compensation to the profits of the corporation.

Explanations of occupational welfare, in short, must include the dynamics of labor relations as well as the political forces that focus on the state, if they are to fully reflect the hybrid nature of occupational welfare, where compensation for work is combined with social rights to protection against economic insecurity.

Notes

1. This paper is a revised version of "Labor Unions, Employee Benefits, and the Privatization of the American Welfare State". The original version was published in the *Journal of Policy History*, 3(2), November 1990, 233-260,

and is drawn upon here by permission of The Pennsylvania State University Press.

2. State and local federations often broke with their national unions, and the national federation to back some programs (Orloff and Skocpol, 1984). Wm. Green to Henry Morgenthau, 5 November 1941 and Wm. Green to Congressman R. Doughton, 23 January 1942, Florence Thorne Files, State Historical Society of Wisconsin, Madison, WI. (hereafter SHSW).

3. Minutes of the International Executive Board, United Automobile Workers (hereafter the UAW), 13 June 1938, George Addes Papers, Walter P. Reuther Library, Detroit, Michigan, (hereafter WPRL); Wm. Green to C.O. Van Horne, 20 November 1939, Florence Thorne Files, SHSW; Wm. Green to Claude Hawley, 25 October 1940, Florence Thorne Files, SHSW; Minutes of Meeting of Viscose Advisory Council, 17 August 1940, Textile Workers Union of American Papers (hereafter TWUA Papers), SHSW; W.G. Flinn to E. Leach 17 December 1943, International Association of Machinists Papers (hereafter IAM Papers), SHSW.

4. Most union plans did not survive the Depression. See Greenough and King (1976); and Bureau of Labor Statistics (1933).

5. Harvey Brown to B. Jewell, 24 August 1939, IAM Papers, SHSW.

6. Minutes of Meeting of Staff and Business Agents, 15 May 1943, TWUA Papers, SHSW; Emil Rieve, "Proposed Programs For a Union Conference on Health Insurance," 24 May 1945, TWUA Papers, SHSW.

7. Wm. Green to C.F. Brewster, 23 March 1936, William Green Papers, George Meany Archives, Silver Spring, Maryland.

8. Surprisingly, the more left-wing CIO unions were the pioneers in demanding fringe benefits, while the more conservative AFL unions tended to cling to the expansion of public plans. This issue is beyond the scope of this paper. See Quadagno (1988) and Stevens (1988).

9. "The Textile Industry in the Post-War Era.", n.d., TWUA Papers, SHSW; American Federation of Labor, Convention Proceedings, 44th Annual Convention (Washington, DC: The Federation, 1946); Congress of Industrial Organizations, Daily Proceedings of the 8th Constitutional Convention of the CIO (Atlantic City, NJ, November 1946).

10. These last statistics refer to covered individuals only, some of which are covered by collective-bargained plans. See Reed (1967) and Skolnik (1976).

11. There are two additional literatures that discuss the history of employee benefits that are not directly relevant here. The first is a history of modern employee benefits from the perspective of corporations; see Dobbin, 1988. The second literature focuses on predecessors of fringe benefits, the company-sponsored plans known as "Welfare Capitalism" that flourished in

the first decades of this century. See Berkowitz and McQuaid, 1980; Brandes, 1976; Brody, 1968.

12. E. Rieve to All Locals, 17 July 1946, TWUA Papers, SHSW; Grand Lodge Representative Dameron to A.J. Hayes, 9 February 1948, IAM Papers, SHSW; Walter Reuther, UAW President's Report 1946-1951, (Detroit: UAW), 8.

13. This discussion does not imply that labor was shut out of politics entirely. The labor federations did maneuver around some of these restrictions by setting up political organizations that were legally separate from the unions. The campaign law sapped labor strength, however, by forcing the construction of elaborate countermeasures that complicated the task. Congressional committees investigated union activities in political campaigns on several occasions thus ensuring that the labor movement did obey. See Josephson (1952); Memorandum from William Pollock to Staff, 17 May 1944, 10 July 1944, 21 August 1944, TWUA Papers, SHSW; Harvey Brown to David Dubinsky, 6 February 1946, IAM Papers, SHSW; Carl Huhndorff to Harvey Brown, 7 October 1946; IAM Papers, SHSW; H. Brown to All Lodges, 3 March 1948, IAM Papers, SHSW.

14. Americans consistently gave relatively positive approval to labor from 1936 to 1981 when measured by the only continuous source of data, the Gallup Poll. The Gallup question tapped opinions on the general social value of unions, however, rather than feelings about the behavior of actual unions. Once specific union behaviors were mentioned, public opinion was more negative. See Lipset and Schneider (1983).

15. Minutes of the Meeting of the AFL and the CIO to Discuss Unity on Taft-Hartley, 1 May 1947, Katherine Pollack Ellison Papers (hereafter KPE Papers), WPRL.

16. Richard Gray, "The Truth About Building Wages," *American Federationist* 54(1947):6; Boris Shishkin, "Don't Blame Labor," *American Federationist* 53(1946):7; International Typographical Union (hereafter ITU), *Monthly Bulletin* 50 (1948):11.

17. Philip Murray, "Report to the Council of Economic Advisers," *Economic Outlook* 9(1948):1; "Recommendations of the Executive Officers to the Meeting of the CIO Executive Board," 30 August 1948, Walter Reuther Papers, WPRL.

18. CIO, *Economic Outlook* 6(1945) :1.

19. Resolutions of the National Executive Council - TWUA, 24 August 1945, TWUA Papers, SHSW; Report by CIO Wage Research Committee, 10 October 1945, Philip Murray papers, Catholic University, Washington, DC; CIO, *Economic Outlook* 7(1946):2; Recommendations of the Executive Officers to the Meeting of the CIO Executive Board, 30 August 1948, Walter Reuther papers, WPRL; R.J. Thomas, "Report Submitted to the 1946

Convention of the UAW-CIO," 23 March 1946, Atlantic City, NJ; Testimony of Emil Rieve Before the Joint Committee of the Economic Report, 26 June 1947, Walter Reuther Papers, WPRL; Joseph Gaer, "The Road to Freedom.," CIO Political Action Pamphlet #5, 1 January 1946, Murray Papers, Catholic University Archives; Elizabeth Paschal, "The Place of Social Security in the Post-War Period," Report Prepared for the Post-War Planning Committee of the AFL, 6 October 1944, George Meany Files, SHSW; Memorandum by Philip Murray, "Labor and the Postwar World," 27 July 1944, KPE Papers, WPRL; Sol Barkin to E. Rieve, 16 August 1946, TWUA Papers, SHSW.

20. *Economic Outlook* VI(6)(1945); "Statement of William Green to Special Subcommittee of Labor, US House of Representatives," 1 July 1946; AFL Papers - Office of the President, SHSW; Nelson Cruikshank, "Issues in Social Security" *American Federationist* 54(2)(1947):26-28; "Testimony of Emil Rieve Before Joint Committee of the Economic Report," 26 June 1947, Walter Reuther Papers, WPRL; "Statement by Van A. Bittner, CIO, to Senate Appropriations Committee," 12 May 1948, KPE papers, WPRL; "Legislative Program Recommended to CIO Executive Board by CIO Executive Officers," 30 August 1948, Walter Reuther Papers, WPRL; "Statement of Philip Murray to House Ways and Means Committee," 12 April 1949, XPE Papers, WPRL; "Statement by William Green to Senate Finance Committee in Support of HR 6000, A Bill to Improve the Social Security System," 1 March 1950, William Green Papers, Series 11, SHSW.

21. "Speech by Philip Murray Over Radio KQV," 24 December 1943, KPE Papers, WPRL; United Auto Workers, Proceedings of the 8th UAW-CIO Convention, (Buffalo, NY: UAW, 1943); R. Schrank to H. Brown, 8 November 1944, IAM Papers, SHSW; "Statement of Executive Council," 7 February 1945, 6 August 1945, George Meany Archives; "Postwar Planning Committee, Interim Report on Social Security," 12 May 1944, KPE Papers, WPRL; "Interim Report on Social Security"; "The AFL Post-War Program" presented at the Post-War Forum, New York City, 12 April 1944, William Green Papers, George Meany Archives; Speech by Clinton Golden, "Labor's Views on American Economic Policies," 29 April 1943, KPE Papers, WPRL; 21st Convention of the International Association of Machinists, 29 October 1945, New York City, NY, IAM Papers, SHSW; Speech by John Brophy, to the National Conference of Social Work, 24 May 1946, KPE Papers, WPRL; Memorandum to All CIO Unions from Philip Murray, 18 August 1945, Murray Papers, Catholic University Archives; American Federation of Labor Convention 1943, Boston, Florence Thorne Files, SHSW; "Statement by Philip Murray to House Ways and Means"; "Statement by James Carey to the Democratic Convention Resolutions Committee," 8 July 1948, KPE Papers, WPRL; *Economic Outlook* IV(1),(5)(1943),V(12)(1944),VII(4)(1946); G. Addes, "Statement Before

Senate Committee on Labor and Education on Wagner-Murray-Dingell National Health Bill," 23 May 1946, UAW Research Department Papers, WPRL; "Reference Memorandum for Dr. W. Sawyer on the Activities of the International Association of Machinists in Health and Rehabilitation Programs, n.d. (approx. 1952), IAM Papers, SHSW.

22. National Planning Association, "Joint Statement on Social Security," 6 January 1944, Florence Thorne Files, SHSW; Minutes of the Meeting of the Health Program Steering Group, 18 April 1946, Florence Thorne Files, SHSW; J. Voorhls to H. Brown, 3 July 1948, IAM Papers, SHSW.

23. N. Cowan, "Report of the Legislative Committee," 1 November 1945, CIO Executive Board Meetings, Reel 3, WPRL.

24. Minutes of the Meeting of Top GM Negotiating Committee, 8 October 1946, Walter Reuther Papers, WPRL; "How New Union Demands On Pension Plan Differ From Industry Practice" Collective Bargaining Bulletin, Report #128, 30 October 1947; Elmer Walker to E. Broeker, 1949, IAM Papers, SHSW; Labor Trends and Policies, Issue #35, 24 January 1949, Toledo, Ohio; "Welfare Benefits: 1949 Goal" *Business Week* 15 January 1949.

25. Walter Reuther to All UAW-CIO Local Union Presidents, 15 November 1946, Walter Reuther Papers, WPRL.

26. "Statement by Wm. Green to Special Subcommittee of House Labor Committee," 1 July 1946, AFL Papers - Office of the President, SHSW; "Fringe Issues Are Basic" *Economic Outlook* 7(2) (1947); John Edelman, "Your TWUA Memo From Washington," 2 January 1948, TWUA Papers, SHSW; Statement by Van A Bittner to Sub-committee of Senate Appropriations Committee, 12 May 1948, KPE Papers, WPRL; Nelson Cruikshank, "Issues in Social Security"; "AFL Day of Social Security" *American Federationist* 56(5) (1949):20; *Economic Outlook* 9(8) (1948); "Welfare Plans for Workers" *American Federationist* 56(10) (1949); "Statement by Philip Murray to House Ways and Means"; "Statement by William Green to Senate Finance Committee, 1 March 1950, AFL Papers - Office of the President, SHSW; ITU, Proceedings of the 88th Session of the ITU, 47.

27. Congress of Industrial Organizations, "CIO Pension Gains Mean Victory for All," *Economic Outlook* 9(12) (1949).

28. Nelson Cruikshank, "Report on Developments in Social Insurance," Executive Council Reports, 30 July 1948, Florence Thorne Files, SHSW.

29. Nelson Cruikshank, "Issues in Social Security"; W. Rulon Williamson to Walter Reuther, 27 July 1945, George Addes Papers, WPRL; John Edelman, "Your TWUA Memo From Washington", 10 October 1947, TWUA Papers, SHSW; AFL Committee for Social Security Bulletin #8, "Hospitalization Insurance", 1943, Pamphlet File, George Meany Archives; Executive Council Minutes (AFL), 1 October 1946, Files of the Office of the President,

AFL Papers, SHSW; S. Stetin to I. Katz, 23 October 1946, TWUA Papers, SHSW.

30. "Pension Gains Mean Victory For All", emphasis added.

31. "Memorandum on NHI Act, 1947 (S.1320)," AFL Legislative Files, George Meany Archives; Memorandum from S. Barkin to E. Rieve, 2 December 1949, TWUA Papers, SHSW; "The Two-Way Drive for Social Security." *Economic Outlook* 9(12).

32. "Economic Program for 1949", UAW Convention Proceedings (Detroit: The Union, 1949).

33. *New York Times*, 2 December 1949.

34. C. Huhndorff to Executive Council, 18 July 1949, IAM Papers, SHSW. The AFL's expert on social welfare also expressed an awareness of this problem. See N. Cruikshank to Wm. Green, "Draft of Executive Council Report on Developments in Social Security", 20 July 1950.

35. Resolution #15 "Old Age, Survivors and Disability Insurance and Public Assistance", Report of the Resolutions Committee, 11th Constitutional Convention of CIO, Cleveland, OH. 10/31 to 11/4/49, Murray Papers, Catholic University; E. Rieve, Testimony to Senate Finance Committee, 27 February 1950, KPE Papers, WPRL.

36. G. Addes, "Statement Before Senate Committee on Labor," 8.

37. Some in fact argue that the desire to block the unionization of supervisory personnel was one of the main spurs to the Taft-Hartley Act (Harris, 1982; Lichtenstein, 1982; Seidman, 1953; Tomlins, 1985).

38. Minutes of the CIO Research Directors Meeting, 2 March 1945, KPE Papers, WPRL; Matthew Woll to Joint Committee on the Economic Report, 8 July 1947, Florence Thorne Files, SHSW.

39. "The Case for Maintaining Take-Home Pay Without Increasing Prices," Economic Brief Part II, Presented to the General Motors Corporation, 24 October 1945, Philip Murray Papers, Catholic University Archives; UAW President's Report 1946-1951, Detroit: The Union.

40. Memorandum by Philip Murray, "Labor and the Postwar World," 27 July 1944, KPE Papers, WPRL; CIO, *Economic Outlook*, Vol.6 (1945) (all issues); E. Rieve to All Staff, 9 January 1946, TWUA Papers, SHSW.

41. C. Huhndorff to All IAM Representatives Attending V.P. Walter's Staff Conference, 29 October 1946, IAM Papers, SHSW.

42. Lee Pressman, Current Legal Reports #46 and 48, 1 December 1946 and 1 February 1947, Philip Murray Papers, Catholic University Archives; International Typographical Union (ITU), *Monthly Bulletin* 49 (1947):14; Report of the President, Submitted to the 12th Convention of the UAW, Milwaukee, WI. 10 July 1948, WPRL; *The Labor Trend*, 19 August 1947;

Brown, "The NLRB"; Confidential Memorandum from Matthew Woll, "Experience of A.F. of L. Unions Under the Taft-Hartley Act," 8 December 1952, IAM Papers, SHSW.

43. E. Rieve, Speech to New York State Industrial Union Council, 1947; Woll, "Confidential Memorandum"; Testimony of William Green before Senate Committee on Labor and Public Welfare, 18 February 1947, George Meany Archives.

44. Wm. Green to C. Hawley, 25 October 1940, Florence Thorne Files, SHSW; Minutes of the Meeting of the Viscose Advisory Council, 17 August 1940, Washington, DC TWUA Papers, SHSW; Minutes of the UAW Executive Board, 15-22 March, 1942, George Addes Papers, WPRL; United Brotherhood of Carpenters and Joiners, Indianapolis to AFL Research Department, 30 August 1946; United Cement, Lime and Gypsum Workers, District 5 to AFL Research Department, 17 December 1946, Boris Shishkin Files, AFL Papers, SHSW.

45. Ironically, by the 1960s, fringe benefits might have lead to the decline of unionization. See Cornfield (1986).

46. AFL, Collective Bargaining Series #1.

47. I.S. Falk to Wm. Green, 30 November 1939, Florence Thorne Files, SHSW; Ewan Clague to Walter Reuther, 7 January 1947, UAW Research Department Papers, WPRL; Katherine Pollack Ellickson to All CIO Research Directors, 23 December 1946, KPE Papers, WPRL; Sol Barkin to E. Rieve, 5 November 1947, TWUA Papers, SHSW.

48. Inland Steel Company v. United Steelworkers of America (CIO), 77 NLRB 4 (1948). The NLRB was upheld in 1949 by the US Supreme Court, see "Inland Steel Company v. NLRB et al., C.A. 7th Cir. Certiorari denied."

49. The Steel Industry Board, Report to the President of the United States On the Labor Dispute in the Basic Steel Industry (Washington, DC: Government Printing Office, 1949); Quotation from the Report was cited by Dearing, Industrial Pensions, 61.

50. Draft Memorandum by I.S. Falk, "Health and Welfare Plans in Industry," Social Security Administration, 4 December 1946, William Leiserson Papers, SHSW.

51. "Labor `Aids' Asked By Schwellenbach," *New York Times*, 17 June 1947; "Summary of Discussion of Union-Management Welfare Plans and Their Relationship to Social Security at a Meeting Between Members of the Social Security Administration Staff and Region 4 Commissioners of the Federal Mediation and Conciliation Service," 10 November 1949, Edwin Witte Papers, SHSW.

52. Quoted in Dearing, Industrial Pensions, 63.

53. Minutes of the CIO Executive Board, 16 May 1947, WPRL.

54. Arthur Goldberg to Philip Murray, 13 April 1948, Murray Papers, Catholic University Archives.

4

Public Policy and the Rise of Private Pensions: The US Experience since 1930[1]

Frank Dobbin and Terry Boychuk

The American system for providing retirement income allocates an unusually important role to private employment-related pension insurance. In the US private sources provide over twice the share of the pension pie that they provide in the average Western European country (Esping-Andersen, 1990:85). A comparative perspective on the public/private mix of pension coverage in the US suggests that private insurance corresponds to the inadequacy of public coverage—it operates as a functional substitute. However, the historical record shows that private coverage appears to grow in response to the establishment and expansion of public coverage. The growth of Social Security coverage between 1939 and 1955 increased the popularity of private plans, and the rapid growth of Social Security benefits after 1975 was followed by another surge in private pensions. The rise of private pension coverage in the United States highlights important questions about the relationship between public and private coverage. In the literature there has been an increasing tendency to view these forms of coverage as codeterminate (Rein, 1982; Rein and Rainwater, 1986c; Shalev, 1988), however we know relatively little about how public policy initiatives influence private sector action.

In this chapter we explore the growth of private pensions in broad historical perspective. We present time-series data that span a period of six decades, beginning in the late 1920s. The data demonstrate that public policy has had important, and often unintended, effects on the rise of private pensions. Public policy has influenced the preference for private pensions among affected groups, and brought new social groups into the historical stage. In short, public policy has caused diverse interest groups to advocate private pensions at different points in time, and has helped to create two important groups: the personnel profession and the insurance industry. Whereas most studies draw arrows directly from policy to occupational welfare outcomes, or from group interests to outcomes, we focus on the role of public policies in shaping the goals and behavior of interest groups, which in turn affect the incidence of private pensions.

Public Policy versus Interest-Based Arguments

By and large, students of policy have identified the growth of private employment-related old age insurance with the paucity of public coverage and the absence of broad congressional support for the expansion of Social Security. Analysts have linked the growth of pensions in the pre-war years to tax changes in 1916 and 1926 that offered tax advantages to companies that provided guaranteed pension programs, and to the meager pension benefits offered by Social Security (Graebner, 1980:134; Quadagno, 1984:637; Schieber, 1982; Macaulay, 1959:24). Wartime pension growth has been tied to "wage stabilization policies, which stimulated a search for non-wage forms of remuneration...[in addition to]...excess profits taxes, and tax exemptions for health and welfare contributions, which reduced the additional cost of insurance and pension programs" (Munts, 1967:9).

During the 1950s legislation expanding Social Security benefits and public regulation of pension schemes were expected to reduce the demand for private insurance and to cause employers to terminate weak schemes (Institute of Life Insurance, 1974). New Social Security increases of the 1960s and 1970s promised to lessen the need for employer-provided coverage, and the Employee Retirement Income Security Act (ERISA) of 1974, which established strict ground rules for pension funds, pledged to make employers more wary of offering pensions (Achenbaum, 1986). Whereas most of these arguments privilege the intended effects of policy as explanatory variables, we argue that the most important policy stimuli to the growth of private pensions have come as the unintended consequences of policies: as policy shifts have led business, labor, personnel management, and insurance industry groups to advocate private coverage at different times.

Explanations focusing on the conflicting interests of business and labor have figured prominently in interpretations of the predominance of occupational welfare in the United States. Most analysts suggest that American unions were too weak to win broad-ranging social insurance coverage, and succeeded at winning employer-provided pensions primarily because employers saw them as the lesser of two evils. Interest-based arguments explain the growth of early pensions associated with welfare capitalism, which employers touted as union-avoidance devices (Brandes, 1976; Slichter, 1929; Jacoby, 1985). Union agitation for fringe benefits stimulated the growth of employer-provided pensions after the late 1930s (Bernstein, 1970; Quadagno, 1988; Stevens, this volume). While the immutable objective interests of stable social groups determine outcomes from this perspective, we argue instead that group interests vary significantly over time as a result of shifting public policy incentives. Our historical approach makes it clear that business groups, for instance, could favor social insurance in one year and then back private pensions in the next.

The Data

To assess arguments about factors that influenced the growth of private pensions we examine data on private pension insurance from two sources. (This information is presented in six charts that can be found at the end of the chapter.) First, we examine time-series data on the number, and proportion, of American workers covered by private pension plans. The federal government compiled these data from public and private sources, notably the Institute of Life Insurance. The data cover pensions purchased through life insurance companies and pension schemes directly organized by employers. Figure 4.1 reports the proportion of the total labor force covered by a private pension plan annually between 1935 and 1987. The data compensate for duplication, so that employees who have earned pension benefits from two firms, or who have vested pensions and have invested in IRAs, are not counted more than once.

Second, we examine over-time data collected in a series of industrial surveys on personnel practices conducted by the National Industrial

Conference Board, a business research group. **Figure 4.2** reports the percentage of large employers reporting formal group pension plans for their employees in 1928, 1935, 1946, 1953, 1963, 1972, and 1979. The Board's surveys provide the most consistent over-time evidence of organizational pension practices available. One drawback is that the surveys are biased toward large, publicly-held firms (see Baron, Jennings, and Dobbin, 1988). Because some of the surveys neglected firms with fewer than 250 employees, in Figure 4.2 we report data only from firms with 250 or more employees. These sub-samples consist of 1,676 firms in 1928, 1,644 in 1935, 1,839 in 1939, 2,631 in 1946, 375 in 1954, 275 in 1963, 1794 in 1973, and 1,308 in 1979 (NICB, 1929; 1936; 1940; 1947; 1955; 1964; Meyer and Fox, 1974; Meyer, 1981). This series of studies is particularly useful because the Board used consistent sampling procedures for their personnel surveys. Thus, while the sample sizes may vary the sampling frame does not, making the surveys comparable over time.

The remainder of the paper, apart from our closing remarks, is organized chronologically. For a series of successive watershed events or discrete sub-periods, we examine arguments about processes at work in the light of the time-series data on pension growth. We are particularly interested in how public policy shifts influenced interest group strategies.

The Tax Code Change of 1926

Analysts suggest that the tax code changes of 1926 provided one of the first incentives to firms to establish insured pension plans, which would thereafter receive preferential tax treatment. The tax code changes should have increased the incidence of insured pension plans after 1926, particularly in such technologically-advanced industries as iron and steel, the railroads, machinery, and the utilities (Schieber, 1982). Evidence is hard to come by in these early years, in part because the aggregate data on private pensions reported in Figure 4.1 are estimated for 1930, and interpolated between 1930 and 1935, and thus may not be reliable. It is clear from Figure 4.2, however, that the incidence of formal pension coverage does rise between 1928 and 1935, despite the economy's decline. The NICB conducted a 1925 study covering every informal and formal pension plan the Board could locate. The returns suggest that informal pensions were most common in iron and steel, the railroads, and the utilities even before the tax code changes. The formal plans, singled out to receive preferential tax treatment in 1926, were still rare: they constituted only 28 of the 239 plans studied (NICB, 1925:14). Follow-up studies support arguments about the effects of the tax code changes. The NICB studies show that informal pensions stagnated between 1928 (26.4% of large firms) and 1935 (27.4%) while formal group pensions, which took advantage of the tax code changes, grew substantially (from 1.9% to 13.4%). The tax code change evidently encouraged firms that were considering installing pensions to install the insured group plans.

The Depression Years

We begin this section by providing evidence that contradicts the received wisdom that the depression led to the demise of pension programs associated with industrial "welfare work." We then discuss the public policies that caused pension coverage to flourish even during the depression. A number of analysts argue that the Great Depression dealt a blow to company pension programs. David Brody (1980:78) suggests that it put an end to informal "welfare work" forms of pension coverage; employers had no obligation to honor those pension promises and could ill afford to. Andrew Achenbaum argues that the depression caused employers to cancel all kinds of pension programs, "Bankrupt firms obviously could not honor their pension obligations to superannuated workers: Forty-five plans covering 100,000 employees were discontinued between 1929 and 1932 alone" (1986:17).

The evidence presented in Figures 4.1 and 4.2 contradicts the suggestion that occupational pensions declined during the early 1930s: between 1930 and 1935 federal estimates of total pension coverage do not decline, and in the NICB studies of 1928 and 1935 the incidence of company pension programs increases substantially. The discrepancy between the aggregate trend figures and the figures from the NICB samples, moreover, doubtless results from the fact that between 1928 and 1935 many firms failed or fired large numbers of workers: thus even if the percentage of firms offering plans increased during the early thirties, the number of workers covered may have stagnated. The most telling evidence of the trends during these years comes from an NICB study: many firms added pension programs during the early 1930s, but few surviving firms canceled them. The 1935 study reported that discontinued informal pensions amounted to only 4.7% of operating plans in 1935, and discontinued formal pension plans amounted to only 7.2% of operating plans (NICB, 1936:11). Similarly a study published in Factory Management and Maintenance found that between 1929 and 1936 only 4.8% of surveyed firms had abandoned a pension plan of any kind (Parks, 1936:39).

This evidence counters the widely-held belief that welfarism came to an end in the early thirties, and that private pension coverage dipped between the onset of the depression and the war years, rising again during the war. It supports Sanford Jacoby's (1985) contention that the depression coincided with the disappearance of some forms of welfarism, but not pension welfarism. But why did the use of pension insurance increase during the worst years of the depression when firms were least able to shoulder new labor costs? Historical evidence suggests that pension coverage expanded for two reasons. America's notoriously weak government income protection programs compounded the insecurity of Americans during the depression. This coincided with the insurance industry's massive effort to market new forms of income insurance).

The life insurance industry had done little business in pension coverage before the 1930s, however two changes in public policy contributed to a decision on the part on large insurers to market pension insurance to companies more aggressively (Dobbin, 1992). On the one hand the 1926 tax code changes favored contributions to pension trusts, and on the other hand federal taxes increased during the 1930s. As a result of these changes, each dollar contributed by an employer to a pension trust for an employee, which neither the employer nor the employee paid current taxes on, represented significantly more than a dollar in increased income. These tax code shifts made pensions attractive to business groups and convinced insurers to put more energy into selling pension insurance, particularly as they saw their other sources of revenue decline.

More broadly, the life insurance industry diversified into pension insurance and other non-life forms of coverage in the early 1930s as a result of public policy, namely American social insurance exceptionalism. The absence of public income protections when the depression hit led labor and business groups to back private forms of income protection offered by the insurance industry—by contrast throughout most of Europe labor groups first called for the reinforcement of the existing social insurance net. The absence of public protections also contributed indirectly to the rise of the insurance industry's new strategy of diversification. Because the public sector provided no protections against income loss, employees and employers took advantage of the disability coverage attached to life insurance, to offset income loss during the economic crisis. Disability claims more than doubled between 1926 and 1934 (NICB, 1934:36; Bureau of Labor Statistics, 1935:54). Most insurers responded by disentangling death and disability insurance, and offering employers inexpensive insurance packages, bundling together separate life, disability, accident, and pension policies (NICB, 1934:37). Of course, poor business conditions stimulated insurers to try to sell new forms of coverage. When it came to life insurance policies, "New business was definitely hard to get," and in response Mutual Benefit Life, for example, extended the age limit for life insurance down to age 10 in 1931 and introduced a retirement income bond as well as a contract combining life insurance and a group annuity form of pension in 1932 (Stone, 1957:154). The popularity of pension insurance increased markedly in response to these new insurance industry strategies (Bureau of Labor Statistics, 1935:53).

In brief, American social welfare exceptionalism had contributed to the growth of the life insurance industry since the nineteenth century. Without recourse in the public sector, labor and business leaders backed private forms of income protection during the 1930s, helping to shield the industry from the shock of the depression. If American had already had a social insurance scheme before this time, labor and business groups might have behaved like their European counterparts and called for the expansion of public coverage.

The Wagner and Social Security Acts

In this section we demonstrate that the Wagner and Social Security acts did not have the expected effects on the incidence of occupational pensions, and concentrate on the unanticipated effects of public policy during the late 1930s. The Wagner Act (1935), and the subsequent Supreme Court decision confirming its constitutionality (NLRB v. Jones & Laughlin Steel Corp., 1937), bolstered union legitimacy and led to a massive increase in collective bargaining in American industry (Bernstein, 1985). In the NICB samples the percentage of unionized firms rose from 12% in 1935 to 43% in 1939, and there are a number of reasons to believe that these two samples were nearly identical (see Baron, Dobbin, and Jennings, 1986). Analysts expected these legislatively-fortified unions to win wage increases along with new fringe benefit packages. However, between 1935 and 1940 the proportion of American workers with pension plans remained fairly stagnant (see Figure 4.1), and between 1935 and 1939 the number of firms with formal pensions increased more slowly than it had in the previous period (see Figure 4.2). In the realm of fringe benefits, the Wagner Act may have had little effect because subsequent court decisions denied unions the right to bargain over benefits. Those decisions would have an important effect on union strategy during the forties.

As envisioned by some of its proponents, and equally by some of its opponents, the Social Security Act night have rendered private pension programs obsolete: When social security was proposed, some people raised the alarm that it would kill the sale of life insurance and cut off the growth of pensions. That did not happen. In fact, social security may have helped to stimulate the subsequent growth of those benefits by making economic provision for the future appear no longer to be hopeless (Tilove, 1968:187). Indeed, while the data do not show an increase in pension coverage associated with the Wagner Act, neither do they show the dismantling of private pension programs as a consequence of Social Security. Pension coverage increased gradually in the last half of the thirties. In a 1939 study of the effect of the Act on private pensions, over twice as many firms reported installing private pension plans in response to the Social Security Act (25%) as reported canceling them (10%) (NICB, 1939). Why would the adoption of public coverage have caused firms to adopt private pensions?

Social Security paid an inadequate retirement wage, but it did provide a foundation that made supplementary pensions relatively inexpensive. However uncertainty over the future of Social Security slowed the growth of pension coverage in the late 1930s. Fiscal conservatives opposed Roosevelt's plan for benefit expansion, which might have relieved firms of the need to offer supplementary coverage. Roosevelt's most ardent critics hoped the supreme court would declare the legislation unconstitutional. As a result the NICB's 1939 study found that many firms awaited further legislative action to see which way Congress would swing:

This delay [by firms] in making necessary adjustments may be explained by the constant agitation for certain fundamental changes in the law which began almost as soon as it became effective. Inasmuch as government pension payments were not scheduled to begin until 1942, the company could afford to wait for further congressional action as it was not considered a wise policy to change the company pension plan frequently. (p. 24)

Many companies neither installed pension plans nor canceled them for the time being. In the late thirties, then, the uncertain future of one federal program caused the business community to hold off. But why hadn't Roosevelt passed social insurance legislation that would provide a living wage in the first place?

Roosevelt compromised on Social Security legislation to get the bill through Congress. Unions had generally supported Social Security after 1932. Most business interests wanted a low-cost program offering benefit levels below the minimum wage so that they would not drive wages up (Quadagno, 1984; Witte, 1963:89). The business community temporized on the issue of public old age pensions in the mid-thirties, forcing Roosevelt into concessions to placate adequate numbers of tax-wary industrialists. The major business groups were of two minds; Henry Harriman, President of the US Chamber of Commerce, testified in favor of the bill yet the National Association of Manufacturers attacked it in the congressional hearings (Witte, 1963:89).

The insurance industry had opposed public pension coverage. When public coverage appeared inevitable they promoted the unsuccessful Clark Amendment to the Social Security Act which would have exempted from participation in Social Security those employers who carried private insurance. H. Walters Forster and executives of Equitable Life had lobbied hard for the amendment (Witte, 1963:161). Suffering this loss, they petitioned to keep benefits low, so that supplemental private pensions would be needed. In brief, once the tide of public opinion seemed to be behind Social Security the insurance industry made the best of the situation and lobbied for forms of coverage that would help to expand the popularity of private pensions. In subsequent years they would come to see Social Security as the greatest boon to private pensions in history.

OAS's inadequate benefit levels, in turn, would stimulate agitation on the part of labor for supplementary private pensions and elicit action from personnel professionals who recognized in pension insurance some of the same labor-control advantages they had seen in welfare work. The 1935 compromise set in motion a series of events that would enhance the growth of private pensions. The first of those events was the passage in 1939 of amendments to the Social Security Act. Roosevelt and his supporters won amendments initiating pension payments in 1940, two years ahead of schedule. They successfully expanded benefits for participants who had not spent a lifetime paying into Social Security, and extended benefits to family members and survivors. However they compromised with fiscal conservatives in Congress on one key issue; Social Security taxes would not rise accordingly. This made the program a zero-sum game. Expanded coverage would make it impossible to significantly increase benefit payments.

This decision dispelled the uncertainties that mediated collective bargaining over pension benefits. Social Security would not—at least anytime in the near future—provide an adequate retirement wage. CIO unions renewed the fight for the expansion of fringe benefits, and employers who had delayed action due to uncertainty over the future of the 1935 legislation began to install pension programs.

The changes in Social Security had palpable effects on leading business and personnel management groups, who responded rapidly by advocating supplemental private pensions. By the end of the year a group of banks had established the New York Savings Banks Retirement System to supplement Social Security. They argued that "this system is designed to afford a means whereby supplemental benefits may be provided so that the benefits of the Social Security Act may be increased to amounts which afford adequate retirement allowances" (quoted in Baker, 1940:38). In December of 1939 the NICB published a report in its series for personnel directors examining reactions to the 1935 legislation and the 1939 amendments. The thrust of this report, and of other contemporary publications aimed at management, was that "for a very small outlay a firm could earn its employees' gratitude by supplementing the inadequate pension provided by the government" (Jacoby, 1985:254). The base retirement wage provided by Social Security lowered the financial barriers to private pension plans. The report argued that supplemental pensions plans had a number of positive effects. These plans could invigorate operations, because the retirement of older workers; "makes room for younger ones to advance, and ambition throughout the company is stimulated" (1939:6). Moreover; "production costs are lowered through the removal of aged workers whose lagging productivity may hamper the efficiency of all working in cooperation with them" (1939:29). More generally, 74% of the firms with pension plans reported that the improved morale of the workforce offset the costs of their plans (1939:29).

If business organizations had mixed feelings about company pension plans before the passage of Social Security, after its passage and particularly after the 1939 amendments they promoted supplemental pensions as an inexpensive solution to employment problems brought about by the growth of unionism (Jacoby, 1985). The fledgling personnel profession bolstered this trend by identifying pensions as a means to quell union activism and, at the same time, build their own ranks.

The War Years

Pension coverage rose precipitously after 1939. Figure 4.1 reports that the proportion of the labor force covered by private pensions doubled in the forties, and Figure 4.2 shows that the incidence of pension plans rose from less than 20% to over 70% among large firms over a 14-year period. We contend that the wage freeze and tax code changes of the war years did not cause this increase. Rather, the inadequacy of Social Security benefits combined with court rulings on the Wagner Act favoring employers to incite unions to fight for expanded fringe benefits. Thus we find unions struggling for fringe benefits prior to the period which Beth Stevens discusses in Chapter 3. First we review the arguments commonly made about the effects of wartime policies, and demonstrate that the timing of the growth of fringe benefits qualifies those arguments.

The new Revenue Act of 1942 altered the 1926 tax exemptions for corporate pensions. The law required pension plans to cover at least 70 percent of employees, and to equalize eligibility and benefits for high and low income employees. These provisions withdrew tax concession from pension trusts created for executives to dodge corporate taxes, and favored the expansion of coverage (Macaulay, 1959). Moreover the enactment in 1940 of a corporate excess profits tax, which would tax profits exceeding pre-war levels at up to 90%, is thought to have created an added incentive for firms to expand tax-exempt pension payments (Ilse, 1953:297). These changes may have encouraged employers to adopt broad-based tax-exempt pension plans, and to expand their expenditures on private pension plans in order to reduce their taxable income. Beth Stevens (1988) reports a five-fold increase in employer contributions to pension trusts, from $171 million in 1941 to $857 million in 1945.

The wage freeze came from Roosevelt's newly-founded National Labor Relations Board (1942). In adjudicating the Little Steel case, a wage dispute between Bethlehem, Republic, Inland, and Youngstown steel works and their unions, the NWLB ruled that wages could increase to reflect inflation, but not more than that (Seidman, 1953; Civilian Production Administration 1947; Kerry, 1980). The Little Steel formula was soon applied to all American industry. In 1943 the NWLB exempted fringe benefits from the wage freeze, allowing them to expand to "reasonable" levels. After 1943 the tight labor market, the wage freeze which limited employers to attract and retain workers with fringe benefits, and the excess profits tax are thought to have caused employers to install private pension plans and other fringe benefits.

However data suggest that annual increases in pension coverage stabilized throughout the period, and did not respond to either the Revenue Act of 1942 or the NWLB's pension exemptions. Figure 4.3 charts the number of group annuity certificates—then the most popular form of pension insurance—in the United States between 1939 and 1951. These data, collected yearly by Equitable Life and by the Life Insurance Association of America, show a consistent increase throughout the period, with no discernible deviation between 1942 or 1943 and the end of the war in 1945.[2]

If these public policies do not account for the increase in pension coverage during the forties, what does? In what follows we seek to adjudicate between two competing explanations. One argument has it that court decisions regarding the Wagner Act stimulated unions to fight for pension coverage. The 1935 legislation recognized collective bargaining over "wages and conditions of employment," which unions took to include pensions and other fringe benefits but which employers interpreted more narrowly (Munts, 1967:10; Bernstein, 1970). Until 1948, when the National Labor Relations Board and then the Supreme Court sided with unions, the courts had offered a conservative interpretation of the Act which did not require employers to bargain over pensions. Between 1935 and 1948 unions fought to win the right to negotiate over pension plans without legal backing. While they rarely convinced employers to include pension coverage in union contracts, it has been argued that union agitation had indirect effects. Unionized firms may have offered pensions unilaterally to dampen union activity, and non-union firms may have installed them to forestall organizing efforts. These arguments suggest that we should see a significant growth in the coverage of wage workers, both unionized and not.

A second argument expands on a point made above. To wit, the 1939 Social Security amendments sent industry the signal that public coverage would not provide fully for retired workers, and in particular would replace a very small proportion of working income for highly-paid employees. On the one hand, "it was ordinarily believed that the benefits set up [under Social Security] would relieve the employer of the necessity of providing a retirement income for workers earning under $3,000 per year" (Ilse, 1953:296). On the other hand, it was believed that the legislation would stimulate the growth of pension plans for high-wage employees. If pension growth responded to projected benefits in the 1939 legislation, rather than to union agitation, then we should find significant growth in specific coverage for high-wage managerial classes not subject to unionization.

The NICB data illuminate the merits of both interpretations. Figure 4.2, which reports the proportion of firms with pension plans for wage earners between 1946 and 1972, shows that 47% of sampled firms had pension plans in 1946, but only 34% of firms had plans that covered wage workers.[3] The difference between these two figures approximates the percentage of firms that had plans exclusively for salaried or high-income employees, because virtually no firms had plans exclusively for wage workers (NICB, 1954). It should be noted that these figures include white collar firms, where low-income salaried positions were common. When we limit the sample to the newly-unionized manufacturing sector where the wage-salary distinction is more meaningful the discrepancy is more striking: 37.5% of firms had pension plans but only 22.6% offered pensions to wage earners (NICB, 1947).[4] Thus despite the fact that the tax code had rendered pension plans that did not cover 70% of employees taxable since 1943, in 1946 many firms had plans which did not cover wage workers. This evidence appears to support our argument about the effect of the 1939 Social Security amendments; it had clearly stimulated a number of firms to install supplementary pensions for non-union managerial employees who would receive only a small proportion of their working income in Social Security benefits.

On the other hand, pension plans for wage workers, who were normally subject to unionization, did rise sharply between 1939 and 1946. While the NICB did not distinguish between wage and salary pension plans in 1939, the overall figure for that year was 16% for large firms, and the figure for wage-earner-only plans in 1946 was 34%; pension plans for wage earners at least doubled in this period. Union agitation doubtless induced the growth of pensions during these years as well.

Pensions for wage workers grew in part because of the indirect effects of the Wagner Act and of wartime federal controls on labor turnover. As Sanford Jacoby (1985) has argued, the Wagner Act motivated the rapid growth of the field of personnel management, as firms across the country installed personnel departments to deal with industrial relations problems. Then during the early 1940s the War Labor Board, the War Production Board, and other arms of the federal government instituted labor turnover controls that required firms to document their labor needs, prompting many firms to initiate personnel departments (Baron, Dobbin and Jennings, 1986). We would not expect significant growth in the popularity of personnel departments prior to the Supreme Court's confirmation of the Wagner Act in 1937. However, between the NICB's 1939 and 1946 surveys, the percentage of large firms with personnel departments increased from 47% to 75% and the percentage of small firms (<250 employees) increased from 7% to 30% (Baron, Dobbin and Jennings, 1986:354). This growth is significant because fringe benefits programs were one of the principal tools advocated by personnel professionals to win workers' gratitude and to undermine unionism. Thus policies that propelled the diffusion of personnel departments also stimulated the diffusion of pension programs.

In sum, during the war the inadequacy of Social Security benefits convinced businesses to install new supplementary pension programs, particularly for high-wage and managerial employees. Moreover, the Wagner Act accelerated the growth of the personnel management profession. Personnel managers advocated liberal fringe benefit programs, including supplementary pensions, to counteract protections afforded in the Wagner Act. In particular, the Supreme Court's unwillingness to acknowledge collective bargaining over fringe benefits offered business groups an opportunity to secure worker loyalty and preempt pro-union sentiment with unilateral pension programs. Had the Court gone the other way, employers might have favored the expansion of Social Security benefits, in part because the cost of Social Security was divided between the employee and employer while the cost of supplemental pensions was usually borne entirely by the employer. As we shall see, that is what happened when the court reversed its position.

After the War

Many historiographies date the wide diffusion of pension plans to the 1950s. Figure 4.1 shows a steady growth of private pensions from the mid-forties through the late fifties, and Figure 4.4 shows high annual percentage increases in pension coverage from the mid-thirties through the late fifties. Between 1950 and 1960 the proportion of the private wage and salary labor force with private retirement plans rose from 22 to 37 percent (Skolnik, 1976b:4).[5] While the rate of growth was steady throughout the forties and fifties, there is wide agreement that the processes underlying growth differed during and after the war. We have offered some evidence which dispels the notion that war-related federal policies account for the growth of private pensions in the first half of the forties. We have suggested, instead, that the inadequate retirement wage promised under the Social Security Act of 1939 conspired with the conservative judicial interpretation of the Wagner Act by the courts, inciting unions to battle for the right to bargain over pension benefits. This fueled the rise of pension plans. Unions did not win pension plans during negotiations; instead employers responded to the threat of unionization and union strife by unilaterally installing pensions.

Labor's position changed significantly after the war, as Beth Stevens argues in greater depth in the preceding chapter. First, in 1945 and 1946 the CIO and the AFL shifted more of their energies from endorsing public pension expansion to winning private pensions, largely as a result of congressional inaction on Social Security and the increasing viability of private pension programs. During the early 1940s, with Democrats in firm control of Congress, AFL unions had almost exclusively backed public pensions and CIO unions had fought for both public and private pension coverage. In 1945 the CIO's United Mine Workers, United Auto Workers, and Amalgamated Clothing Workers each began a campaign to win pensions from employers, and the AFL passed a resolution in favor of private pensions at its annual convention in 1946 (Stevens, 1988:135). Second, in 1947 the Taft-Hartley Act cut back the gains associated with the Wagner Act, and like Wagner remained vague on the negotiability of retirement plans. Third, in 1948 the National Labor Relations Board finally legitimized negotiations over pension benefits in a case brought against the Inland Steel Company, arguing; "The term 'wages' as used in Section 9 (a) [of Taft-Hartley] must be construed to include emoluments of value, like pension and insurance benefits," and in 1949 the Supreme

Court upheld that decision (Ilse, 1953:319). In the aftermath of the Steel Industry Fact-Finding Board's report in 1949, which favored the introduction of fringe benefits to settle a wage dispute, negotiated pension plans appeared in steel, autos, rubber, and other sectors (Goldner, 1950:5). By 1950 such major unions as the United Mine Workers, the United Auto Workers, the United Steel Workers, and the International Brotherhood of Electrical Workers had negotiated pension plans (Goldner, 1950:38). In short order virtually every unilateral pension plan in a unionized firm was transformed into a negotiated plan.

In brief, Taft-Hartley had bolstered union support for negotiated pension plans, because when the 1947 legislation cut back union powers, industrial unions fought particularly hard to win pension plans in order to demonstrate their efficacy to members and prospective members. In addition to enabling unions to negotiate over pensions, the 1948 NLRB ruling also removed all union opposition to employer-financed pension plans. A number of unions had favored pension programs which incorporated employee contributions on the premise that such plans would be non-forfeitable, however unions could now negotiate non-forfeitable employer-financed pensions (Ture, 1976:35).

Figures 4.1 and 4.2 show significant post-war increases in pension plans, and taken together they support the traditional wisdom about when and where pension plans thrived. First, among the large firms represented in Figure 4.2 pension plans grew most between 1946 and 1953, doubtless in part as a result of the Inland Steel decision. Second, there were substantial post-war gains in pensions for wage workers, who were subject to unionization. This is evident in Figure 4.3, which shows that among large firms the gap between the total number of firms with pensions and those with wage earner pensions narrowed from 13 points to 3 points. Similarly, the Bankers Trust Company found that in 1943-45 only 63% of company pension plans surveyed covered virtually all employees, and the remaining 37% were usually targeted to managers, whereas by 1953-55 about 90% covered virtually all employees (Bankers Trust Company, 1960:7). Third, throughout the economy as a whole, and particularly in smaller firms, pension coverage grew steadily until the late fifties, as we see in Figure 4.1. Figure 4.4, which reports the annual change in the percentage of the labor force covered by private pensions, also supports that conclusion. These data suggest that many large firms had already installed pensions by the early fifties, but that pension coverage diffused to small firms in the mid- and late fifties. The total number of company pension plans in operation grew rapidly in those years, as small firms installed pensions.

Social Security Benefit Increases of the Fifties

Private pensions grew during the 1950s as a result of the effects of public policy on both business and labor strategies. For labor, as Jill Quadagno (1984) has argued, the prevalence of "offset" private pensions made it futile to lobby for Social Security increases, which would not result in a net pension income gain for members, hence many unions continued to advocate the growth of private pensions. Of course, federal policy permitting the deductibility of "offset" pensions had made that pension form viable in the first place. After 1945 CIO leaders had deliberately fought for private pension plans as a way to get employers to back the growth of social insurance (Stevens, 1988:137), and the strategy eventually paid off. For business, what happened was more complex. In brief, the Inland Steel decision meant that firms could no longer quell unionism by offering unilateral fringe benefit plans. Instead large-scale businesses backed the expansion of Social Security benefits, to reduce their pension expenditures. In the aftermath of legislation increasing Social Security benefits, which reduced the cost of supplemental pension plans, small and medium-sized businesses moved to adopt private pensions. In other words, new federal policy vis-a-vis the union negotiation of pensions changed the incentive structure for large scale industry, which then successfully backed Social Security increases, which in turn made private pension programs more attractive to small businesses.

Business support for Social Security increases

Business came to support more generous public benefits in part as a result of the Inland Steel decision in 1949. The AFL and CIO had long backed the expansion of Social Security benefits, but they had also fought for employer-provided pensions (Stevens this volume). On the other hand, the business community in general had opposed Social Security increases, because they preferred to keep wage taxes down and because they believed that unilateral fringe benefit programs helped to undermine unionism. In the aftermath of Inland Steel industrialists in large unionized firms no longer saw fringe benefits as a potential means to undermine unionism; on the contrary unions were claiming credit for successfully negotiating generous fringe benefit packages.

Meanwhile the structure of the popular "offset" or "envelope" pension plans created a financial incentive that caused employers to favor Social Security increases. Those plans guarantee the employee retirement benefits based upon Social Security payments, typically reducing the monthly retirement benefit by either fifty cents or a dollar for every dollar of Social Security income. Once pension plans lost their labor-control allure, business leaders realized that their expenditures for offset pensions would be reduced every time Social Security benefits rose. Within months of the 1949 Inland Steel decision many of the major steel producers had signed offset pension agreements tied directly to Social Security payments, and most of the negotiated agreements made over the next few years took this form (Ilse, 1953:321). From the perspective of the employee,

One problem with the offset plans was that when social security increased, the worker had to pay a higher contribution but he did not realize any increase in benefits, and the employer plan got a 'windfall' because of the increased offset to the benefits which it had to pay. (Tilove, 1968:189)

By contrast, every increase in public benefits would preface declining employer outlays, and this helped to garner support among industrialists for the growth of Social Security—as CIO leaders had calculated that it would when they accepted offset pensions (Quadagno, 1988:169). As many private pension plans were fully financed by employers—42% of those in a 1948 survey—whereas employees and employers divided the cost of Social Security payments, the expansion of Social Security benefits transferred more of the total cost of pension insurance to the employee (NICB, 1950). The Inland Steel decision thus brought business support for the expansion of Social Security, and in turn the expansion of Social Security helped to popularize private pension plans with newly reduced rates.

The effects on small firms

Between 1950 and 1954 Congress adjusted Social Security benefits three times, in the first increases since 1939. The growth of pensions among small firms between 1952 and 1959 evidenced by the overall growth of pension coverage shown in Figures 4.1 and 4.4, coupled with the stagnation among large firms shown in Figure 4.2, may be traced in part to these benefit increases. Between 1939 and 1950 wages rose dramatically but Social Security benefits did not follow, making supplemental pension benefits increasingly expensive for employers. The problem was simple; in 1939 Social Security benefits were set at 40% of the first $600 in annual wages, plus 10% of the next $1200, plus a 1% increase for every year of covered service (NICB, 1939). Average wages doubled during the war (Bureau of Economic Analysis, 1986), which meant that if an employer wanted to provide workers with a retirement wage equal to 40% of working income, in 1939 she would not have to purchase supplemental insurance for a worker with an annual income of $600. However by 1946 when inflation had increased that employees' wages to $1200, she would have to provide $240 in supplementary pension benefits (Ilse, 1953).

The Social Security increases between 1950 and 1954 reversed that trend, and once again made it relatively inexpensive for employers to install pensions. Now retirees would receive benefits equal to 55% of the first $1320 in average annual wages, plus 20% of the next $2880 (NICB, 1954:16). For retirees currently receiving the minimum monthly benefit of $10, benefits rose to $20 in 1950 and to $25 in 1952 (Ilse, 1953:329). These benefit increases stimulated the growth of private pensions in small firms.

The effects of the subsequent decrease in the cost of supplemental pension insurance were evidently strongest among small firms. As Figure 4.1 demonstrates, the proportion of the labor force covered by private pensions nearly doubles during the 1950s. Yet the number of company retirement plans in operation increases nearly fourfold between mid-1950 (12,925) and the end of 1958 (47,520) (Macaulay, 1959:191). In other words, most new plans were to be found in firms with relatively small workforces. By one estimate the number of workers covered by the average company pension plan declined from 231 in 1950 to 94 in 1965 as a result of the adoption of company pensions by a large number of small firms (Ture, 1976:28). Figure 4.2 also suggests that little of the increase in pension coverage during the 1950s occurred in large firms.

Stagnation in the 1960s

Figures 4.1, 4.2, and 4.4 suggest that pension growth slowed significantly after 1958. Annual growth had proceeded at an average rate above 8% between the mid-thirties and the late fifties, and it dropped to about 3% during the sixties (see Figure 4.4). We contend that pension growth slowed during this period in part because no intermediate group advocated the expansion of pensions, and also because federal activity of two sorts tended to discourage pension adoption. By the mid-1950s virtually all unionized employees were covered by private pensions. Having won pension programs, unions turned their attentions to other issues. By late in the 1950s most of the major large and middle-sized employers offered private pension programs; the segment of the business community that had used pensions to quell labor conflict was largely saturated.

Thus the remaining sectors without private pension coverage constituted a "hard core of resistance," where employment conditions made pension coverage unlikely. For instance, in the construction industry jobs are typically of short duration, and with the exception of unionized segments of that industry, which fell under industry-wide pension agreements, workers had no pension coverage. Likewise agricultural work is frequently seasonal, thus employers virtually never offer pension plans. In industries characterized by high turnover, as well, workers may not remain with a single employer for long enough to gain pension coverage, even when the employer offers a pension plan (Tilove, 1968:192). The remaining uncovered sectors consisted of peripheral industries that offered low wages, little in the way of fringe benefits, and no employment stability (Gordon, Edwards and Reich, 1982). By some accounts fully 65% of non-agricultural, non-young, full time workers were covered by private pensions by 1960 (Murray, 1968:29).

Two federal activities tended to discourage the adoption of new pension programs. The Federal Welfare and Pension Plan Disclosure Act of 1957 tightened federal regulation of pension funds and made it more costly to establish, and sustain, viable schemes (Life Insurance Institute, 1974). The legislation's framework for preventing pension insolvency increased the cost of pension plans, discouraging their adoption in the low-wage peripheral sectors that made up the "hard core of resistance." That is, the legislation made private pension schemes particularly unattractive to the kinds of firms that did not already offer them.

Then in the late 1960s and early 1970s a series of Congressional studies and legislative proposals apparently delayed private action on pension plans. After a 13% increase in Social Security benefits in 1968, Congress closely studied the problem of pension coverage. Legislators made it clear that they would undertake significant changes in Social Security and in pension regulation. Between then and the passage of the Employee Retirement Income Security Act (ERISA) in 1974, employers again waited to see what direction federal legislation would take. In the early seventies in particular; "The imminent passage of Federal pension reform legislation introduced an element of uncertainty into the picture" which led to caution on the part of employers (Skolnik, 1976b:3). After the mid-seventies, however, the die was cast and employers began installing pension programs once again.

Finally, despite the slow aggregate growth of pensions during the sixties, the trend of growth among small firms that began during the 1950s continued during the '60s, and apparently spread to even smaller firms. Figure 4.1 shows growth in the proportion of Americans covered by private pensions did increase slowly during the 1960s, but growth in the number of plans skyrocketed; from 32,340 in 1960 to 289,510 in 1970, or nearly 900% (Ture, 1976:28). Taken together, these figures suggest that only the smallest of firms were adopting plans in these years.

The Seventies and Beyond

In this section we argue that the growth of private pensions after about 1975 was not the predicted outcome of the increase in Social Security benefits, which was expected to obviate the need for many pension programs, and was not primarily the result of other public policy shifts it has been tied to, such as the liberalization of Individual Retirement Account rules. We argue that these increases resulted in large measure from the unintended effects of Social Security increases, which made supplemental pensions cheaper and thus more attractive to employers, and ERISA regulations, which made many more Americans eligible under existing pension programs. Once again, federal policy changed the incentive structure for businesses.

Concerned about the inadequacy of benefits, Congress increased them 58% in five separate raises between 1968 and 1974, and in 1975 the automatic COLA increases went into effect (Bixby, 1986). Congress had also signalled that it would expand private pension regulation in 1968, but it was not clear what form the new regulations would take. Combined with this uncertainty was the effect of a high rate of inflation, which discouraged employers from adopting pensions. Pension costs rose notably as a result of inflation. Between 1970 and 1974, when the Consumer Price Index rose 27%, total employer-employee contributions to private retirement plans rose 79%; by contrast, in the previous four-year period, when the CPI rose 16%, retirement plan contributions rose only 51% (Skolnik, 1976b:8; Bixby, 1986:13).

The economy-wide figures presented in Figure 4.1 show a huge increase in private pension coverage during the latter half of the 1970s. Unfortunately there is a gap between 1975 and 1980 in the federal series that reports the number of Americans covered by private pension plans, so we have had to interpolate the rate of growth across this period. Pension coverage grew by over 50% during these years, increasing by 18 million persons. Several shifts in public policy appear to have been important.

Individual Retirement Accounts

Did these increases result from the liberalization of IRA rules? ERISA made it possible for employees without employer-provided pension plans to create IRAs beginning in 1974, and over a million people took advantage of this in the first year of the scheme. Yet these retirement schemes account for a small fraction of the growth in private pensions. According to the Internal Revenue Service, in 1980 only 2.6 million people claimed deductions for IRAs on their income tax returns, yet the overall increase in private pension coverage between 1975 and 1980 was some 18 million. The 1981 Economic Recovery Tax Act allowed anyone to establish an IRA, beginning in 1982, and as a result by 1983 13.6 million Americans were investing in IRAs (American Council of Life Insurance, 1988:10). However the utilization of IRAs by some 10 million people who already had employer-provided pension plans after 1982 is not reflected in Figure 4.1, because the data are adjusted for the duplication of pension coverage. In short, the introduction of IRAs for some 2 to 3 million people not already covered by private pensions accounts for little of the 1975-1980 growth in coverage.

ERISA vesting and funding requirements

In addition to creating IRAs, ERISA imposed stricter fiduciary requirements for private pension plans, insured them through the new Pension Benefit Guaranty Corporation, and liberalized vesting standards. These regulations required a significant infusion of capital into underfunded schemes and wider eligibility for employees. The legislation prefaced a "flurry of pension plan terminations" (Achenbaum, 1986:149). A Conference Board report found that thousands of small firms had abandoned pension programs; "the stricter standards and additional administrative and cost burdens imposed by ERISA have caused the abandonment of a multitude of small-company pension plans" (Davey, 1978:4). By some estimates the cost of an average pension plan would rise by over 15% in response to the new federal requirements (Hakala and Huggins, 1976). However, on the whole pension coverage increased in the years following passage of ERISA. Why?

While the legislation caused some employers to terminate weak pension plans, its vesting requirements would have a positive effect on pension coverage. Vesting refers to the point at which accrued pension benefits become non-forfeitable in the event of the termination of employment, and the new law set three alternative standards. Under two of these standards benefits vest, at least partially, after five years of service. Under the third, benefits vest fully after ten years. In the NICB's 1972 study of pension programs the modal time to vesting was 15 years. Seven years later every surveyed firm adhered to the new ERISA regulations; 82% of firms used the 10 year standard, and 18% used one of the graduated vesting schedules that began after 5 years. In short, the new vesting requirements brought millions of employees, with over 5 years of service, under pension coverage.

Beyond this, the legislation caused firms to restructure their pension plans. Over 300,000 company pension plans were rewritten in accordance with the new federal guidelines (Klein and Moses, 1974), giving personnel professionals an opportunity to rethink their pension plans. Most important, it gave them an opportunity to extend coverage to uninsured groups of workers, usually in occupations characterized by high levels of labor mobility or turnover. The new legislation sought to encourage pension portability via schemes allowing employees to change jobs without losing their pension benefits. Personnel professionals responded with schemes that would facilitate portability for affected groups of workers (Phillips and Fletcher, 1977).

Social Security COLAs

The negative effects of the new ERISA guidelines might have been much more devastating but for increasing Social Security benefits. The expansion of benefit levels between 1968 and 1975 and the implementation of automatic cost of living increases in 1975 vastly improved the lot of social security recipients. Social Security benefits averaged 16% of full time wages in 1971, but rose to 26% in 1983 despite rapid inflation (Figure 4.5). In absolute terms, annual benefits rose from just over $1000 in 1970 to over $6000 in 1990 (Figure 4.6). For employers without pension programs, it became much cheaper to provide supplemental pensions that would guarantee an adequate retirement wage.

Other companies switched from flat-rate plans to offset plans. In 1972 40% of the pension plans surveyed by the NICB (Meyer and Fox, 1974:53) were of the offset variety, yet in response to the ERISA legislation of 1974, by 1979 64% of the surveyed plans were offset plans.

Data from the 1980s suggest that private pension growth has slowed and that the percentage of the labor force covered by private pensions may have declined for the first time in history (see Figure 4.1). Structural changes in the economy have been linked to this switch. In the 1980s most job growth occurred in the service sector in small non-union firms. Many of the new jobs were poorly paid and/or part-time. This sector, and these sorts of jobs, were among the least likely to carry pension and other fringe benefits before the 1980s (Bernstein, 1990; Harrington and Levinson, 1988). On the other hand, Quadagno and Hardy offer compelling evidence in Chapter 5 that ERISA and subsequent federal pension regulations may have a negative impact on the prevalence of employer-provided pensions in the longrun by undermining employer support for pensions. They show that employer support for pensions had been fostered by lax public controls over private pensions, which had enabled employers to use pension policies to manage labor flows. In the absence of this incentive to install supplementary pensions, employers may be more reluctant to do so in the future.

At this writing (Spring, 1995) the 1990s have not produced any new shocks in pension law on the order of ERISA. Consequently, the organizational battle lines in the realm of pensions have not been redrawn. Instead, all three branches of government have been occupied with unexpected consequences of ERISA. In 1992 and 1993, the administration focused on the unexpected shortfall of the federal Pension Benefit Guaranty Corporation, resulting from both a rise in business failures and the discovery of an unusual number of underfunded plans (Vise, 1994). Meanwhile, states found that by preempting state-level regulation, ERISA had the unintended consequence of preventing them from adopting more stringent pension regulations than the federal government enforces (Rich, 1994). In 1994 and 1995, the main focus of judicial and legislative activity surrounding ERISA was its health insurance provisions, and in particular the status of novel health care options such as managed care plans (Causey, 1995). As there has been little change in the law, there has been little change in the politics of pension coverage.

Perhaps the most significant development to affect the field of pensions during the 1990s has been the growth rate of temporary workers. Preliminary evidence suggests that the high cost of such fringe benefits as pension insurance has led many employers to substitute temporary employees, who have little or no fringe benefits rights, for permanent employees. It is too early to tell whether pension costs are indeed a cause of the rise in temporary employment. If they are, we are witnessing a dramatic new employer response to ERISA that will affect the nature of work and retirement for years to come.

Conclusion

We have argued that interest groups influenced the development of private pension insurance, but key interest groups altered their goals and strategies over time and we contend that they did so largely in response to public policy changes. Broadly speaking, unions have favored the expansion of pension coverage, however public policy shifts caused them to back, alternately, public and private coverage. Broadly speaking, employers opposed the growth of pension expenditures, however public policy caused them to favor, alternately, no pensions, private pensions, and public pensions. Broadly speaking, the insurance industry favored the growth of private coverage, but policy caused them to promote private coverage in certain periods and caused them to support public coverage at times. Broadly speaking, personnel professionals favored the growth of private benefits, as a means to enlargement of the profession, however certain public policies shifts enabled them to talk employers into adopting private plans. While interest groups may have identifiable long-term interests, their specific goals and strategies have been highly contingent on public policy. Our contention is that to understand the effects of public policy one must look beyond the outcomes intended by the proponents of policies to the concrete effects those policies have on the behavior of affected groups.

Chapters 2 and 3 of this book have sketched out some of the ways in which interest groups influenced the development of federal legislation, and we have focused on the return arrow—the effects public policies then had on interest group goals. Our findings suggest a number of corrections to current thinking. First, the wartime wage freeze and excess profits tax had little effect on private pension growth in the data, however the passage of the Social Security Act apparently spurred the growth of private pensions by providing weak coverage for highly paid employees. Second, between 1944 and 1950 private pensions grew largely because unions put their energies into expanding private rather than public coverage in response to several federal policies, as well as to Congress' resistance to expand public benefits. In particular, vagaries of the Wagner Act caused unions to struggle for the right to bargain for private pensions, and when unions lost power as a result of the Taft-Hartley Act they sought to demonstrate their efficacy by exercising their newfound right to negotiate for pensions. Third, both the Wagner Act and wartime labor controls had indirect effects by boosting the growth of the personnel profession—the one group in industry pushing hardest for private pensions, with the rhetoric that pensions could improve morale, solve a crucial moral dilemma, and quell labor conflict. Fourth, the expansion of Social Security benefits in the 1950s and again in the 1970s had a surprising effect on private coverage; by reducing the cost of providing supplemental private coverage these changes in Social Security stimulated more employers to offer pension insurance. Economists have suggested that Social Security expansion stimulates the growth of private pensions because it lessens the worker's cost of establishing full retirement coverage (see Ture, 1976:36-42), but we are suggesting that Social Security has primarily increased the popularity of pension insurance by influencing employer strategies. Fifth, uncertainty over the future of public action delayed private sector action, both in the late 1930s when it was unclear whether Social Security would be expanded or eliminated and in the early 1970s when it looked as if Congress would restructure the program. Finally, public policies contributed to the rise of the insurance industry, and caused industry leaders to effectively market pension insurance in the 1930s: each federal policy that made private insurance attractive to firms gave the industry a wider entrée into the business sector.

Our findings have interesting implications for students of comparative policy. We argue that timing was vital, for instance Congress's late adoption of old age insurance contributed to the growth of various private forms before 1935, which helped to build constituencies for private pension programs among industrialists, insurance industry leaders, and personnel professionals (Dobbin, 1992). One implication is that if Social Security had been passed earlier—in the Progressive Era for instance—private pensions might never have come to play an important role in American retirement coverage. In fact, there were many critical conjunctures at which forces converged to favor private pensions. In many cases things could have turned out quite differently, which suggests that the argument that the strength of the American business community vis-a-vis labor groups overdetermined US pension exceptionalism fails to take the complexity of history into account. We hope to have shown that the historical relationship between social welfare and occupational welfare is not simple, in large measure because the unintended effects of public policies are often the most important effects and because interest group strategies, far from being predetermined by objective interests, swing back and forth wildly over time.

Finally, our approach is supported, we believe, by the findings of Chapters 2, 3, and 5 in this volume. Sanford Jacoby provides evidence that personnel managers saw distinct advantages to private pension coverage once they had experimented with it, and that they played an important role in the popularization of employment-related pensions. Beth Stevens shows that contrary to standard interest group accounts, public policy in America led labor unions to put their energies into private, more than public, pension coverage in key periods. Jill Quadagno and Melissa Hardy show that lax regulatory policies led employers to favor private pensions as a tool for labor market management, but that more stringent regulations may take away that option and hence may undermine the support of employer groups for private pensions.

Notes

1. Financial support from Princeton's Committee on Research in the Financial support from Princeton's Committee on Research in the Humanities and Social Science is gratefully acknowledged. We thank Michael Shalev and the other contributors to this volume for helpful comments on an early draft.

2. Data in Figure 4.3 are from Ilse (1953:315) and from the Institute of Life Insurance (1951:29). Figures for 1939 and 1940 were collected by Equitable Life and covered both the US and Canada, whereas figures for the later years were collected by the Institute and covered only the US Thus we have recalculated the figures for 1939 and 1940 to reflect the number of annuities in force in the United States by calculating the average proportion of total policies that were in effect in Canada between 1941 and 1944, when the two series overlap, and deflating the 1939 and 1940 figures by that proportion.

3. Note that the NICB did not publish figures for wage workers before 1946 or in 1979, thus wage worker pensions are not shown in Figure 4.2 for those years.

4. Manufacturing sector figures include firms of all sizes, because the 1947 report does not break down the use of pension plans by sector and size simultaneously.

5. Note that these numbers, unlike those presented in Figure 4.1, include only the employed, private-sector labor force. Figure 4.1 includes in the denominator public sector workers and the unemployed.

Data Appendix

Sources: The data presented in Figures 4.1, 4.4, 4.5, and 4.6 were compiled from Bureau of the Census (1975) and various issues of the *Statistical Abstract of the United States*. The data in Figure 4.2 come from the National Industrial Conference Board (1929, 1937, 1940, 1947, 1954 and 1964), Meyer and Fox (1974) and Meyer (1981). The data in Figure 4.3 are compiled from Ilse (1953) and other sources (see note 2).

FIGURE 4.1: *Pension Coverage of the Labor Force*

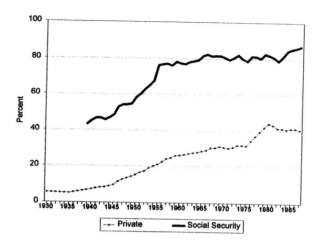

FIGURE 4.2: *Large Firms with Pensions*

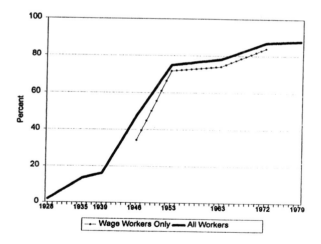

FIGURE 4.3: *Group Annuities*

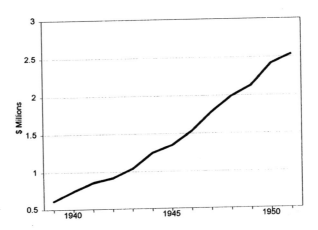

FIGURE 4.4: *Annual Changes in Pension Coverage*

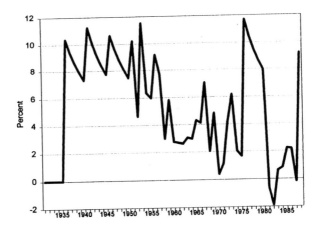

FIGURE 4.5: *Social Security Benefits as a Proportion of Mean FTE Wages*

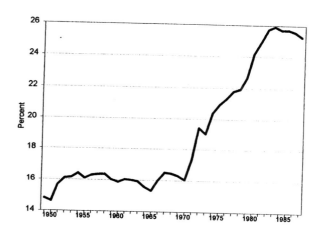

FIGURE 4.6: *Average Annual Social Security Benefits*

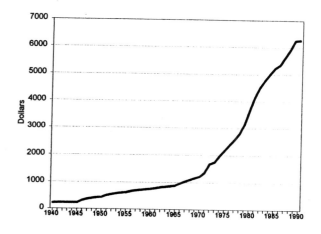

5

Private Pensions, State Regulation and Income Security for Older Workers: The US Auto Industry[1]

Jill Quadagno and Melissa Hardy

Theories of the welfare state have explored the impact of the state on public policies but have largely ignored the connection between state policies and occupational welfare programs in the private sector. The goals of social welfare can be achieved directly through state sponsored programs of income replacement and service delivery; but the state can also work indirectly through structures of incentives designed to promote private programs that are responsive to social needs. The American welfare state has developed as a corporate welfare state that sustains capital production not only through public programs of income maintenance directed toward workers as beneficiaries but also by shaping corporate policy. The influence of the state can be seen in two arenas: regulatory policy and tax policy. Regulatory policy can require adherence to certain principles of distribution, whereas favorable tax treatment can serve to subsidize the adoption and development of occupational welfare programs.

During the first three decades of this century, state policy left private sector programs virtually unregulated. In the absence of regulation, employers devised their own welfare policies as an integrated part of their general labor management strategies. A central component of corporate benefits structures were the employer-controlled pension systems established during the late 1800s and early 1900s (Olsen, 1982). Company pensions became a useful tool of labor control. Pensions reduced labor turnover, dampened labor unrest and provided a framework for employers to remove less productive older workers. In addition, costs to employers were low, since few workers reached retirement age. Indeed, employers had no obligation to pay pensions at all, and many eligible workers received no benefits when they retired (Graebner, 1980; Quadagno, 1988; Jacoby, this volume).

Beginning in the 1930s, federal regulation of pension funds gave workers some rights to pensions, and in the 1940s pensions became part of the wage package negotiated in collective bargaining agreements (Stevens, this volume; Dobbin, this volume). Since the 1950s the American private pension system has evolved around this dual purpose of labor control and deferred compensation. It has continued to serve employers as a tool of labor market management but has also become part of the "retirement wage," an increasingly stable benefit that, combined with Social Security, provides income security in retirement. Ironically, state regulations that have made private pensions more secure have also reduced their use to employers as a mechanism of labor control.

In this paper we summarize the historical development of private pensions, evaluate the transformation of public policy that has reduced their utility to employers and then use the case of the auto industry to demonstrate the tension between the dual functions of pensions both as a tool to regulate the flow of labor and as a retirement wage providing income security to retired workers.

Private Pensions in the Wage Package

During the 1930s private pensions primarily functioned to regulate the labor force, but workers' claims to benefits remained largely at the discretion of the employer. In this period the Townsend movement, a social movement of older people seeking support from the federal government in old age, increased public awareness of the plight of the elderly and pressured federal officials to legislate a national program of old age pensions (Amenta and Zylan, 1991). The Social Security Act of 1935 initiated a program of Old Age Insurance for industrial workers. Instead of increasing the income of pensioners, however, many companies simply reduced the amount the company contributed to the retirement benefit. "Pension integration," that is, defining a set benefit and then subtracting Social Security from it, allowed firms to retire older workers while reducing their costs (Dyer, 1977a:38).

The Role of the Tax System

The tax code encouraged firms to initiate pension plans by allowing them to accumulate deferred contributions tax free but forcing them to pay corporate taxes on accumulations outside the plan. By recognizing contributions to pension plans as a non-taxable business expense, the tax laws benefited employers and encouraged the growth of private pensions.

Under the Revenue Act of 1938 the state began regulating pensions. The Act prohibited the exemption of company pension funds from federal income taxation unless the funds were placed in an irrevocable trust for employee benefits. This law closed the tax loopholes that had allowed employers to contribute to pension funds during years of high earnings and then recapture the earnings in poor years by revoking the trust.

Subsequent amendments to the Internal Revenue Code set further conditions for qualifying a plan for tax exemption, forcing businesses to stabilize pension funds. The Revenue Act of 1942 allowed employers to deduct contributions to a pension plan only if the pension was incorporated into a written contract guaranteeing a permanent program for the exclusive benefit of employees and their beneficiaries (Quadagno, 1988:159).

The 1942 Act also established rules for integrating pensions with Social Security. To prevent pension plans from being used as devices to mitigate top bracket taxes of high wage employees, the act limited benefits on earnings over those covered by Social Security. This regulation established a new form of pension integration. In practice it meant that workers could receive a certain percent of wages in pension benefits up to the Social Security ceiling and then a higher percent above the ceiling (Dyer, 1977b). In interpreting what discrimination in favor of highly paid employees involved, however, the IRS agreed that a plan could exclude employees earning under the Social Security wage limit and not be disqualified from tax exemption. In essence, this interpretation meant that companies had the right to deny pensions to low-wage workers by allowing the state to pay their benefits through Social Security (Dyer, 1977a).

TABLE 5.1: *Marginal Federal Tax Rates and Pension Assets 1920-1980*

Year	Noninsured Pension Assets (Book value in 1980 dollars, per capita)	Marginal Corporate Tax Rate Paid by Large Firms (Percent)
1920	2	10.0
1925	8	13.0
1930	35	12.0
1935	60	13.7
1940	82	24.0
1945	124	40.0
1950	209	42.0
1955	444	52.0
1960	773	52.0
1965	1,203	48.0
1970	1,478	49.2
1975	1,435	48.0
1980	1,517	46.0

Source: Ippolito (1986a:25).

Thus, federal regulations allowed firms to avoid providing income security to the working class and reinforced a two-tiered system. This dual system placed responsibility for the income maintenance of lower-income workers on the state, yet preserved the option of rewarding upper-income workers through tax subsidized private pension programs.

A sharp increase in corporate income taxes in 1940 stimulated employers' interest in pension plans by making the preferential tax treatment associated with pensions more attractive. Table 5.1 illustrates marginal federal tax rates on firms from 1920 to 1980 and pension assets in 1980 dollars. In 1940 the marginal tax rate paid by firms was 24 percent; by 1945 it had increased to 40 percent. The increase in the corporate tax rate encouraged firms to place corporate funds in pension plans. In subsequent years, further amendments in the Internal Revenue Code provided tax advantages both on money paid into pension funds and on interest generated by those funds (Quadagno, 1988:118). Initially, then, tax incentives—combined with the ability of private firms to "integrate" their pensions with Social Security benefits—encouraged the expansion of private benefits that did more for firms than for workers.

Building a Retirement Wage

In 1948 the National Labor Relations Board ruled that pensions were a negotiable item in collective bargaining agreements. Immediately, the large industrial unions began demanding private pensions as part of the wage package (see Stevens, this volume). In 1949 the Ford Motor Company agreed to provide company-financed pensions of $100 a month to retired workers at age sixty-five who had acquired thirty years of service. Yet the $100 was only partly financed by the auto company, since the pension was integrated with Social Security. The program became a pattern setter in the industry, and soon all Big Three auto companies had similar pensions for their workers (Quadagno, 1988:163-64). The concept spread to other industries, and by the late 1950s, over half of all unionized employees were covered by integrated pension plans. Workers had won the right to income security in old age. Employers could provide it at little additional cost and considerable tax savings.

In the early 1960s a separate tier of pension income was added to the existing retirement wage. "Early" retirement benefits allowed workers to retire before they became eligible for Social Security. Early retirement was pushed by organized labor, which had experienced severe setbacks in the postwar period, and sought more protection for older workers. When plants closed or relocated, older workers had to choose between moving from their homes or trying to find new employment at age 50 or older. Further, technological changes in the industry disproportionately threatened older workers (Gordus, 1980).

The first early retirement provisions were added to the collective bargaining agreement of the United Auto Workers and the Big Three—General Motors, Chrysler and Ford—in 1964. The new provisions allowed auto workers to retire with reduced benefits at age 60 if they had at least 10 years of service and at age 55 if they had at least 30 years of service.[2] The key to early retirement provisions was the availability of "supplemental" benefits, an additional benefit paid until the worker was eligible for Social Security at age 62. To qualify for the supplemental benefit, the worker had to agree to limit earnings in retirement. The early retirement program outlined in the UAW contract was therefore aimed not only at early retirement from the auto industry itself, but early retirement from the labor force, in general (Barfield and Morgan, 1969:166).

When the option had been in effect for 6 months, Barfield and Morgan surveyed auto workers between the ages of 58-61 regarding their response to the liberalized plan. They found that auto workers took advantage of the early retirement provisions rather quickly, thereby establishing the effectiveness of pension incentives for pulling older workers out of the labor force. Of those interviewed, two-thirds either had retired before age 65 or were planning to take early retirement. In fact, fully one-third of their original sample had retired before age 62, the age of eligibility for reduced Social Security benefits. Thus, the early retirement provisions benefited workers and companies. Older workers could retire early and still receive benefits. Firms could use pensions to weed out less productive workers who could not keep up the pace on the assembly line.

During the 1973-74 recession and again during the 1981-82 recession, many companies added "sweeteners" to the usual early retirement benefits. These sweeteners, or early retirement incentive programs (ERIPs), developed as a variant of severance pay by allowing firms to offer monetary bonuses to workers meeting specified criteria. Because they were available for a defined "window" of time and restricted to a portion of the firm's labor force, the additional cost to the employer was limited.

"Windows" extend retirement opportunities to otherwise ineligible workers as a means of increasing the rate of retirement when a company is eager to reduce the size of its workforce. For example, in 1986 when oil prices were declining, Exxon Corporation, the nation's largest oil company, offered immediate retirement to its employees aged 50 and over who had more than 15 years of service. The offer was open for a short window period, from April 22 to May 30, and granted credit for an extra three years of service in calculating retirement benefits (Meier, 1986:5).

Like "windows," "mutuals" represent an agreement between a worker and the firm or union in which a similar suspension of the rules occur. While "mutuals" may accompany a window, they have also been offered more informally to individual workers. Until recently "mutuals" allowed companies to retire inefficient older workers and also provided health-impaired workers who failed to meet the eligibility criteria for regular disability retirement the chance to retire under a special agreement. Thus, they represented an additional source of flexibility for companies in managing the labor force and for workers in opting to retire when they did not qualify under other types of provisions. "Windows" and "mutuals" provided firms additional flexibility in regulating the flow of workers beyond that afforded by regular early retirement schemes. They allowed firms to define special terms for retirement when they needed to reduce the labor force without liberalizing the regular pension plan.

The early retirement option was a boon to workers in heavy industry, who often "wore out" before they became eligible for full benefits. But these early retirement benefits also provided employers with a new tool for managing the labor force. While national data on the availability of early retirement plans is difficult to obtain, a 1984 survey of executives of 363 companies found that nearly two-thirds had early retirement provisions. These either took the form of unreduced pension benefits, usually at age 62, for employees who met age and service requirements, or reductions that were more generous than if they had been based on actuarial projections, usually at age 55. One-third also had "windows," which offered additional financial incentives for older workers to leave (Quinn and Burkhauser, 1990:314).

Regulating the Retirement Wage

Expansions in the availability and level of private pension benefits coincided with growing national concern over the adequacy of retirement benefits to the general population of retired workers and the high rate of poverty among the elderly. Congress responded to this concern by adjusting the benefits provided by Social Security. Real benefit levels were gradually increased and then indexed to the cost of living.[3] During roughly the same period, new federal regulations were enacted to provide protection to workers covered by private pension plans. In other words, rather than expand the public pension system to address both adequacy and equity issues, the state reinforced the two-tiered system. Public benefits were to provide minimally adequate income to lower-income workers with some provision for graduated benefits based on tax contributions; but the general structure of Social Security benefits was to be redistributive. The equity provision—the provision that reproduces the stratification of pre-retirement income in post-retirement income replacement—was strengthened by regulating the delivery of private pensions. One consequence of that regulatory intervention has been a shift in the balance of tax incentives relative to regulatory requirements.

Beginning in the early 1970s the spread of private pensions virtually ceased (Quinn and Burkhauser, 1990:321). A decline in the unionized manufacturing sector and increase in service employment, where coverage is sparse, was partially responsible for this trend.[4] Reductions in corporate tax rates also reduced incentives for firms. But other factors played an important role. During the 1960s demands for equal opportunity in employment emanating from blacks and then women became a stimulus for protecting older workers as well (Burstein, 1985). By the 1980s increased state regulation of tax laws regarding private pensions to improve the quality of the retirement wage reduced the ability of firms to use pensions to manage the labor force. Increased governmental regulation has reduced the attractiveness of pensions for firms. The regulations include ERISA, tax policy and equal employment opportunity legislation.

Reducing Flexibility through ERISA

Although earlier legislation had forced companies to protect the pension rights of older workers to a limited degree, through the 1960s protection remained minimal. In 1963 the Studebaker Corporation, a small automobile producer, went out of business. Fourteen years earlier the company had established a pension plan that ultimately covered about 11,000 employees. When the company closed its plant in South Bend, Indiana, the assets were insufficient to meet all the pension rights that workers had accumulated. Because of the number of workers affected and the prominence of the industry, the Studebaker case became an example cited by those favoring pension reform.

The move for pension reform culminated in 1974 when the Employee Retirement Income Security Act (ERISA) initiated a series of new regulations governing pension plans. These regulations were particularly important for defined benefit plans like those negotiated in manufacturing industries (Ippolito, 1986b). By requiring minimum vesting standards, more stringent funding requirements, pension insurance fees, and improved reporting of plan benefits and finances, the regulations increased the costs of these plans (Schulz, 1985). The regulations also reduced the ability of employers to use pensions to target specific workers for retirement through "mutuals." ERISA prohibited a firm from offering to one worker a benefit not offered to an entire class of workers (Jackson, 1977; Clark, 1990:393). However, the use of "carrots" such as ERIPs to entice older workers into retirement has been upheld, so long as eligibility for the retirement bonus was viewed as nondiscriminatory.[5]

Reducing Flexibility through the Tax Code

Since 1974, federal legislation has placed further restrictions on how pension benefits can be structured and limited particularistic terms of eligibility. Changes in the tax code have forced modifications in the treatment of higher wage relative to lower wage workers by restricting pension integration.

The Tax Reform Act of 1986 prohibited firms from offsetting pension benefits with Social Security by narrowing the permitted integration spread and eliminating plans based solely on pay in excess of Social Security wages (Jackson, 1977:21).[6] According to Schulz, Borowski and Crown (1991:136):

This was accomplished (in principle) through the expansion of Internal Revenue Code section 401(1), which essentially provides an exception for integrated plans to the general nondiscrimination rules that prohibit plans from providing highly compensated employees benefits that are greater, as a percentage of pay, than benefits provided to less highly compensated employees.

Amendments to the tax code have also reinforced the decision that eligibility for special early retirement plans must be made categorically rather than individually. These amendments have eroded the discretionary power of employers to target individual workers through early retirement programs, specifically the "windows" offered in periods of downsizing the labor force. The legal objection to these "windows" is that they are unfavorable to employees who are too old to receive them and that while voluntary, individuals may be subject to direct or indirect pressure to retire (Bessey and Ananda, 1991). By forcing companies to offer these benefits on a class basis (making any employee within a certain category eligible for the benefit), employers were prevented from targeting particular workers.

The tax code now also limits pre-retirement lump-sum distributions, early withdrawals by workers, and asset acquisition from plan terminations. Tax law has also been used to limit maximum benefits payable under defined benefit plans as well as maximum contributions payable under defined contribution plans (Clark and McDermed, 1991). Introducing these regulations as amendments to the tax code provided an effective enforcement mechanism, since firms must adhere to the IRS regulations to maintain a tax exempt status for their pension funds.

Reducing Flexibility through ADEA

In 1964 when Congress held hearings to draft legislation banning discrimination in the workplace, the discussion focused on protection for minorities and to a lesser extent, women (Burstein, 1985). However, some testimony also considered the plight of older workers, who were susceptible to displacement because of automation. Rather than risk possible delay of the passage of Title VII of the Civil Rights Act of 1964, which was a response to demands from the civil rights movement to reduce job discrimination on the basis of race, Congress decided to add a section to Title VII directing the Secretary of Labor to study the factors that might result in age discrimination and to report recommendations for legislation to prevent arbitrary discrimination on the basis of age (Bessey and Ananda, 1991).

The Department of Labor discovered widespread use of arbitrary age cutoffs in hiring and employment termination and suggested that federal policy was needed to combat age discrimination. In 1967 the Age Discrimination in Employment Act (ADEA) was passed. ADEA prohibited employers from firing, demoting or reducing the salary of older workers on the basis of age.[7] Because workers older than age 65 were not defined as part of the protected group (the protected age range spanned 40 to 65), mandatory retirement beyond age 65 was still legal. Also, since the act excluded "bona fide" employee benefit plans, firms could continue to reduce pension benefits after the retirement age of 65 (Clark, 1990:392). Thus, ADEA maintained reduced employer flexibility in managing the labor force through early retirement.

Amendments to ADEA in 1978 required firms to change the terms of their pension programs, making it more difficult for employers to penalize older workers who chose not to retire at the normal age. The application of ADEA to the specification of differential conditions of employment or benefits was triggered by concerns that employers were using early retirement programs selectively to get rid of workers perceived as less able. Thus, while ADEA still allowed age to be a factor in a bona fide employee benefit plan, it prohibited corporations from using the age structure of benefits as a subterfuge for discrimination.

The Omnibus Budget Reconciliation Act (OBRA) of 1986 also targeted the penalty provision in private pension plans that discouraged delayed retirement. Before the act was passed, employers could stop older workers who remained beyond the normal retirement age from accruing higher benefits. This increased the financial pressure on older workers to leave the labor force. OBRA allowed workers to continue accruing pension credits for service beyond "normal" retirement age (Bessey and Ananda 1991).[8]

As the age group protected under ADEA expanded to include all workers over age 40, the ability of firms to incorporate work disincentives into their pension schemes has been reduced to situations in which "costs" can justify the differential. Further, given that eligibility for early retirement incentives must now be defined categorically, employers face the additional problem of losing through early retirement the older workers they prefer to keep, and retaining through the combined loss of disincentives and enhanced provisions for job protection, the older workers they would prefer to remove. It is not that the new regulations prohibit firms from using pensions to induce early retirement but rather that the regulations prevent them from retiring specific individuals. As a result, if the workforce needs to be thinned, the firm has less control over who leaves and who stays.

The changes in vesting requirements, the elimination of mandatory retirement policies, the regulations governing eligibility, the restrictions on penalties, and the decision to uphold the use of pension incentives accomplished through the combined impact of ERISA, the tax code, and ADEA have made private pensions a more cumbersome, more expensive, and less adaptable strategy for labor market management. These same regulations have granted workers more secure pension rights and have reduced the arbitrary or discriminatory use of early retirement incentives. Ironically, then, the regulations that have made pensions less useful in regulating the labor force are those that have enhanced the quality of the retirement wage and brought greater income security to retired workers.

The Case of the Auto Industry

The auto industry has long been considered an innovator within US labor relations because many features of US collective bargaining agreements that were introduced in the auto industry later became common in other industries. For example, the 1948 General Motors-UAW agreement was the first major industrial agreement to include a cost-of-living escalator for wages as part of a multiyear contract; in 1955, supplementary unemployment benefits were adopted; and by 1976, the auto industry had agreed to paid personal holidays (Katz, 1985). In 1989, a pilot program addressing workers' growing concern over their need to care for family members (young children, elderly parents, disabled family members) was also adopted in the auto industry (Ruben, 1990).[9] The auto industry provides an exemplar of how increasing federal regulation of pensions has made it more costly and more cumbersome for firms to manage their labor forces through retirement while increasing the bargaining power of unions to improve benefits for retiring workers.

Pensions and the Decline in Production

In 1950, the US produced 80 percent of the world's cars (Feldman and Betzold, 1988). By 1960 the US share of world automobile production dropped to 52 percent, by 1988 to 14.6 percent. In a 1982 report, the Commerce Department identified several trends that had affected the long-term competitiveness of the US auto industry: a shift in consumer demand to smaller, fuel-efficient vehicles, an expansion of world trade in motor vehicles due to increased Japanese exports, and growing competitive pressures on domestic manufacturers to improve quality (Secretary of Commerce, 1984:1). These trends emerged in the 1970s but did not present serious challenges to US auto manufacturers until "a second round of oil price shocks in 1979 fundamentally altered the competitive environment of the world vehicle motor industry" (Secretary of Commerce, 1984:1).

These losses not only reflected a decline of market share, but also a reduction in actual units produced (Ward's, 1989).[10] One of the sharpest drops occurred between 1978 and 1982, when US production of motor vehicles dropped 45 percent. In 1984, however, the auto industry experienced a turnaround with General Motors reporting profits of $5.3

billion, Ford $2.5 billion and Chrysler $1.5 billion (*Solidarity*, Feb., 1984:5). Since 1984 the industry has rebounded from the lows of the early 1980s, but has failed to fully return to the level of production achieved in the late 1970s.

The decline in US production was reflected in employment trends. Between 1978 and 1983 employment in the motor vehicle industry declined from 1,004,900 to 753,700 workers, a reduction of 25 percent. From 1980 to 1983 between 150,000 and 269,000 workers were on indefinite layoff with the number peaking in January, 1983 (Bureau of Labor Statistics, 1985). Employment rebounded somewhat in the early-1980s, but rather than simply recalling laid-off workers, the industry increased overtime for presently employed workers.[11] As a result more than 100,000 UAW members in auto plants were not called back to work and "tens of thousands more...lost recall rights" (*Solidarity*, Feb., 1984:5).[12]

The case of General Motors provides an illustration of these trends. During the 1980s, General Motors had a steadily declining share of the US market—from 44.3 percent in 1984 to 34.7 percent in 1989. In 1987, average employment at GM was 583,000 workers; by 1988, average employment had dropped to 538,000 and by 1989, to 531,000—a loss of 52,000 workers over a three-year period (Ward's, 1989).

Attempts to return to profitability involved labor force reductions. One mechanism for reducing the labor force was to increase pension benefits and encourage early retirement (*Solidarity*, July-Aug., 1984:5). During the 1984 contract negotiations with GM and Ford, the UAW won significant increases in pension benefits. Basic benefits increased $3.85 per month per year of service, reaching $22.30; a $270 per month increase for 30-and-out retirees raised their total monthly pension benefits to $1,205, a move the union hoped would encourage "more workers...to retire earlier" (*Solidarity*, Dec., 1984:5). The 1987 contract increased basic benefits to $26.50 per month per year of service and "30 and out" pensions to $1500 a month (*Solidarity*, Sept., 1987:19). These incentives helped reduce the labor force. In 1984 only 7,000 workers retired. In 1986, 13,000 retired and in 1987, 14,000.

The strategy adopted by General Motors demonstrates the dual functions of pensions. As GM sought to use pensions to downsize the labor force, federal regulations limited management's discretion in accomplishing the downsizing move. During this period, the UAW took advantage of pressures to reduce the labor force to improve the quality of worker pensions.

The GM Retirement Plan

The General Motors retirement plan covers workers from the day they are hired with the company paying the full cost of benefits. The cornerstone of eligibility in these plans is years of credited service, which are accumulated according to the number of hours worked each year.[13] In addition, workers who have at least five years of seniority can earn service credit for absences caused by layoff or (under certain circumstances) while on sick leave.

The GM contract defines four types of retirement: normal retirement (at age 65 or older); regular early retirement (based either on "30 and Out" or a combination of age and years of service); special early retirement ("windows" or "mutuals"); and disability retirement (available to disabled workers younger than 65 with 10 years of service). The special early retirement plan increases the flexibility of early retirement programs by allowing older workers caught in a move to downsize the labor force to take early retirement even though they may not qualify for pensions under the conventional regular early retirement program.

Table 5.2 describes the eligibility criteria for these three types of retirement (regular early, mutual, and "normal" retirement at age 65). Lifetime income benefits are calculated as the product of the lifetime income benefit rate (established through collective bargaining) and the years of credited service. Workers who retire under the regular early retirement plan before reaching age 62 or before "30 and Out" have their benefits reduced on average about 5-6% for each year prior to age 62. For example, a worker retiring at age 61 would receive 93.35 percent of the life income benefit; at age 55, 57.9%. This benefit reduction only applies to the regular early retirement plan, not to the special early retirement plan.

TABLE 5.2: *Retirement Options for GM Employees*

Type of Retirement	Eligibility Requirements
Normal Retirement	Age 65 or over
Regular Early Retirement	Age 55-60 with at least 10 years creditable service *or* Any age with 30 or more years creditable service *or* Has seniority when age and service requirements first met
Special Early Retirement	Age 55-65 with at least 10 years creditable service, *and* retires at Company option or under mutually satisfactory conditions, *and* has seniority immediately before retirement *or* Age 50 or over with at least 10 years creditable service, *and* laid off due to plant closings, *and* no other plant in same labor market
Disability Retirement	Age under 65 with at least 10 years creditable service, *and* has seniority, *and* totally and permanently disabled for at least 5 months

TABLE 5.3: *Projected Pension Benefits for Different Retirement Options*

	Regular	**Early**	**Special**	**Early**	**'Normal'**
Years of service	30	<30	30	<30	30
Mean age	56.7	59.9	58.9	58.7	[65]
Mean service	32.8	22.0	36.2	22.0	[30]
Under Age 62					
LIB[a]	$603	$506	$959	$583	n.a.
Early Ret.	$897	$447	$642	$471	n.a.
Supplement					
Monthly Benefit	$1,500	$952	$1,500	$1,054	n.a.
Yearly Benefit	$18,000	$11,425	$18,000	$12,646	n.a.
Age 62					
Monthly Benefit	$869	$506	$959	$583	n.a.
Yearly Benefit	$10,430	$6,066	$11,512	$6,996	n.a.
Age 65+					
Monthly Benefit[b]	$897	$534	$987	$611	$823
Yearly Benefit	$10,766	$6,402	$11,848	$7,332	$9,876
Life Exp. at mean age	20.8	17.9	18.6	18.6	14.5
Projected Lifetime Benefits[c] (000)	$192.9	$96.5	$183.6	$117.7	$115.3
Projected Lifetime Supplement[d] (000)	$49.5	$10.5	$22.1	$16.2	n.a.

Notes:
a. Lifetime Income Benefit level from private pension.
b. Differs from benefit at age 62 because of the special age 65 benefit.
c. "Projected lifetime benefits" is the present value of the benefits that could be expected to accrue over the lifetime of a retiree. It is calculated as the summation of expected yearly benefits from the first year of retirement through successive years, weighted by the probability of survival, and discounted by a real discount rate of 0.0275. Survival rates are based on the mean age for the retirement category. The calculation does not include survival benefits to a surviving spouse, and it assumes that as in the past, the real value of pensions will be maintained through benefit adjustments.
d. The "projected lifetime supplement" is the present value of the early retirement supplement over the lifetime of a retiree. It is calculated as described in the previous note, except that the summation begins from the average age of retirement and continues up to (but not including) age 62.

Table 5.3 provides an estimation of actual benefit rates for workers retiring in 1989. It demonstrates the importance of years of service and type of retirement in determining monthly benefits at various ages.[14] Retirees with 30 years of service receive significantly higher benefits than other retirees. The "average" 30-and-out retiree could expect an annual income of more than $17,000 upon retirement. At age 62, he loses his UAW supplement but begins to receive Social Security. For regular early retirees with 30 years of service, the supplemental benefits are substantial. They provide a reasonable level of retirement income instead of a level close to the poverty line. Thus, the supplements provide "30 and Outers" with a true "retirement wage." Once Social Security benefits begin, the average 30-and-out retiree will continue to collect more than $800 a month in private pension benefits, or almost $10,000 a year. Benefits at age 65 are increased by an amount designed to cover Medicare premiums, which raises yearly benefits by something over $300.

The Growing Importance of Mutuals

In addition to incentives, decisions to close plants and eliminate jobs in the auto industry has forced GM to increasingly rely on "mutuals" to trim the labor force in economic downturns. In 1979 only 2.3 percent of retirement occurred through "mutuals." During the 1986-89 contact period, by contrast, 40 percent of the more than 14,000 early retirees retired under a "mutual."

Despite the use of incentives and "mutuals," the number of early retirees who take these options regularly falls short of the target level for reductions of the labor force. In 1988, for example, the goal of the "mutual" plan offered by General Motors was 7,500 workers. Instead only 3,600 chose to retire. The value of the early retirement plan for accomplishing labor force reductions has increasingly been limited to situations in which the incentive structure of the program (coupled, in some cases, with the uncertainty of continued employment in the industry) is sufficient to entice older workers into retirement. Yet the general worker characteristics that serve to define both the terms of eligibility and the level of benefit entitlement do not always parse well management's goals for labor force reduction. But more specific targeting of workers would violate ERISA, and mandatory retirement, as well as other types of disincentives that penalize older workers for delaying retirement, would violate ADEA.

Conclusion

The concept of social welfare policy has generally referred to explicit income transfer programs, training programs, or health care programs in which government funds are redistributed either through dollar or in-kind benefits to people in need. However, programs consistent with the goals of social welfare can also be funded through government subsidies that operate through the intricacies of tax legislation. Through the tax structure, the government can invest in the development of private sector programs through the mechanism of tax relief. The other side of tax subsidies, however, are government regulations put in place to ensure that these private programs remain true to the original intent. As the development of private pensions was encouraged through tax policy, government regulation of these programs was gradually increased. The overall effect of these regulations has been to shift the emphasis of defined benefit pension plans from programs that emphasize the management objectives of employers toward compensation programs directed toward the income security concerns of workers. Entitlement to private pensions came to be defined more in terms of workers' rights and less as a management option. Where workers' rights to jobs and replacement income are protected, the cost of reducing productive capacity must include the burden that will be placed on workers who have, in the past, demonstrated their loyalty to the firm.

In absolute terms employment in the manufacturing sector was stable until the 1970s, providing young males (but rarely females) who lacked higher education with access to high-paying jobs on assembly lines. Still, manufacturing was in relative decline from the late 1940s in the sense that manufacturing employment was not increasing as rapidly as employment in services (Levy, 1988). Sector decline was accompanied by changes in state policies that have made private pensions less useful to firms. The irony of American welfare policy is that these regulations, which improved private pensions by extending workers rights and increasing the security of pension funds, have jeopardized the system that had provided income security in retirement to the working class.

As the cost of pensions in private industry is escalating, public retirement policy is gradually shifting toward later retirement. In 1983 Social Security amendments included four measures (to be phased in gradually) that either directly or indirectly discouraged early retirement. They included: (1) a greater penalty for retiring at age 62; (2) a gradual increase in the age of entitlement to full benefits from 65 to 67; (3) an increased incentive to defer retirement; and (4) a lower penalty for continuing to work on a reduced basis while in receipt of retired worker benefits (Sheppard, 1991).

Even though economists estimate that work incentives within Social Security are likely to have a minimal effect on early retirement behavior (Boaz, 1989:154), to the extent that the policy shifts in the public pension system signal a more general disaffection with early retirement and its related costs, the availability of early retirement may be increasingly restricted. These changes in Social Security shift the financial burden of early retirement more in the direction of private pension plans. They reduce the advantages of providing pension plans while changing the dynamics of pension integration. To the extent that workers respond to a certain threshold of retirement income in making their retirement decisions, private pension plans will have to bear more of the financial burden in providing that level of retirement income. Whether firms can absorb the additional financial liability and continue to view early retirement as a cost effective plan will determine whether "early" retirement remains an option for the future.

Notes

1. This research was supported by a grant from the AARP Andrus Foundation. We appreciate the assistance of Mindy Stombler in preparing the data for analysis and the comments of Einar Øverbye, Michael Shalev, Olli Kangas, John Myles and James Schulz. We thank William Hoffman, Director of the UAW Social Security Department, for his assistance in carrying out the survey and for his support and advice.

2. Long service workers with fewer than 30 years could retire as early as age 55 if their age and service totaled at least 85.

3. For example, in 1972 Congress enacted a 20-percent increase in benefits and provided for future annual cost-of-living adjustments indexed to changes in the Consumer Price Index. The goal of these adjustments were to increase and then stabilize the replacement rates provided through Social Security. In

fact, concern over the failure of Social Security benefits to supply adequate retirement income led to a temporary over-adjustment of the benefit formula. Under the 1972 amendments, replacement rates depended on the performance of the economy. During periods of high inflation and small increases in real earnings (conditions which existed in the 1970s), the cost-of-living adjustments also led to rising replacement rates. The 1977 amendments revised the technically flawed benefit formula to ensure stable replacement rates over time (Schwartz and Grundmann, 1991).

4. In 1983, for instance, 82 percent of unionized workers were covered by pension plans as opposed to only 44 percent of non-unionized workers (Clark, 1990:390).

5. In a 1981 case (Henn v. National Geographic Society, 819 F. 2d 824 7th Cir. 1987), an employee protested the firm's use of an ERIP. All employees older than age 55 were offered a bonus if they retired within 2 months after the offer was made. In that case, the court reasoned that there was no discrimination within the group eligible for early retirement and that "no one suffered because of his age except employees under 55." Further, the court argued that, although the protected age range begins at age 40, by allowing workers within the 40-54 age range to protest their exclusion, "early retirement plans would effectively be outlawed and that was not the intent of the framers of the Age Discrimination in Employment Act" (Bessey and Ananda 1991:318).

6. Until 1989 sponsors of pension plans had no guidelines on procedures they had to follow to comply with the new methods of integrating private plans with social security and still maintain their tax exempt status. In November, 1988 and June of 1989, the Internal Revenue Service proposed regulations specifying that an employer had to take into account three key elements in the design of any integrated plan. The first, the integration level, referred to a threshold that would determine which participants could receive benefits in excess of the basic rate. The second, the maximum offset or spread, placed a limit on the difference that could exist between the accruals or contributions of employees who earn more than the integration level and those who earn less. Finally, the "two-for-one" constraint prevented employers from integrating a plan to avoid paying pension benefits to lower-paid employees (Schulz, Borowski and Crown, 1991:137).

7. Equal opportunity in employment legislation was first adopted in 1964 as part of the Civil Rights Act. Title VII prohibited discrimination in employment on the basis of race, religion, national origin or sex by private employers with fifteen or more employees, by employment agencies and by local, state and federal governments (Burstein, 1985:37). Although two early bills included age, age discrimination was not prohibited by the Civil Rights Act.

8. Although the effective date was January 1, 1988, some collective bargaining agreements were not affected until 1990.

9. Even though the auto industry has historically functioned as a pattern setter in labor/management relations, collective bargaining in the auto industry is different from some other industries because the auto industry is both highly unionized and dominated by a single union. Compared to other industries where growth in nonunion firms has interfered with union strategies, the bargaining structure of the auto industry has been relatively centralized. However, during the 1980s, the auto industry (as well as the steel industry) was faced with continuing problems stemming from foreign competition and from expanding operations of foreign-owned facilities in the US In 1989, the UAW was unsuccessful in organizing a Nissan Motors Manufacturing plant and later established a Transnational and Joint Ventures Department to aid its efforts to organize foreign-owned plants (Ruben, 1990).

10. The US share of world passenger automobile production in 1960 represented 52 percent of 14.6 million vehicles, or 7.6 million units. In 1988, the US share was 12.8 percent of 48.628 million vehicles, or 6.2 million units (Stark, 1989).

11. In 1982, production workers in the motor vehicle industry averaged 2.5 hours of overtime per week; by 1985, the average had more than doubled to 5.4 hours of overtime per worker per week. Average overtime hours was maintained at 4 to 5 hours per worker per week through the late 1980s (Bureau of Labor Statistics, 1984; 1989).

12. In spite of these difficulties, the UAW continued to protect the favorable wages earned by auto workers. In 1988, for example, the average weekly earnings for production workers in the motor vehicle industry (SIC 371) was $609 compared to $419 for production workers in manufacturing industries, in general, and $322 for production and related workers across all industries. Compared to 1980 average earnings, production workers in the motor vehicle industry experienced a 55% increase in current dollars, whereas average weekly earnings increased 45% for production workers in manufacturing and 37% for production workers across all industries. This translates into constant dollar increase of 9.8% in the motor vehicle industry, 3% in manufacturing industries, and a decrease of 3% across all industries (*Statistical Abstract of the US. 1991*, p.413).

13. Credited service is accumulated according to the number of hours of paid employment in a calendar year; in addition, workers who have at lest 5 years of seniority can earn service credit for absences caused by layoff or (under certain circumstances) while on sick leave.

14. These figures were calculated from a survey of retired male auto workers conducted by the authors.

Part 2

Scandinavia

6

Public and Occupational Pensions in the Nordic Countries[1]

Einar Øverbye

The Nordic countries are often regarded as sharing a distinctive welfare state "regime". One influential formulation (Esping-Andersen, 1990) has contrasted the Scandinavian pattern with the Anglo-American (liberal) and Continental-European (conservative-corporatist) models of social policy. This type of comparative mapping has definite limitations with regard to pensions. In this domain the only common denominator among the Nordic countries is their emphasis on generous minimum pensions (Kangas & Palme, 1989). Beyond that, there is marked internal diversity within Scandinavia. A case can be made for distinguishing between a west-Nordic (Denmark, Norway) and an east-Nordic (Sweden, Finland) pension-political structure. The west-Nordic pattern resembles the liberal (Beveridge-style) regime in the sense that public pension systems focus mainly on minimum protection. The east-Nordic countries are closer to the corporatist (Bismarckian) tradition in the sense that their public pension systems to a larger degree emphasize income maintenance as well as minimum protection.

The difference between the east-Nordic and west-Nordic countries is not a clear dichotomy but rather a sliding scale with Finland and Denmark emerging as almost polar opposites. Denmark never introduced any earnings-related public pension scheme and its occupational pension structure is more diverse than in any of the other Nordic countries. In Finland earnings-related semi-public pensions almost completely crowd out regular occupational pensions. Most of the remaining occupational schemes will disappear when the semi-public schemes are fully developed. Sweden combines generous earnings-related pensions with extremely standardized occupational pensions. Norway combines earnings-related pensions (on a less generous level than Sweden) with an occupational pension structure more fragmented than the Swedish but less fragmented than the Danish structure.

How can the differences between the Nordic countries be accounted for? Some would point to differences in the geo-political position of these countries. Denmark and Norway are "sea-states" traditionally oriented toward the Atlantic ocean (and the Anglo-American world). Sweden and Finland are to a much larger extent "land-states" looking inward toward the central-European mainland (Rokkan, 1981). This is especially true for Finland, historically located at the intersection between the Swedish, Russian and German sphere of influence. Norway's position "in between" the Swedish and Danish pension structure might also be derived from the country's past history: Norway has been part of/in union with both of these older Nordic nation-states.

Such observations may serve as fruitful starting points, but they do not take us far in locating the actual social mechanisms that have shaped the pension structure (including the structure of occupational pensions) in the Nordic countries. These mechanisms must be sought in the shaping of the policy preferences of pension consumers, and the workings of the institutions that mediate these preferences and engage in the struggle over policy choices. In the latter context, while many factors have contributed to shaping the present-day variation among the pension structures of the Nordic countries, among the most important of these are the different degrees of cohesion within the trade union movement and among parties on the left and right side of the political cleavage. Different degrees of cohesion are not only relevant to explaining the public/occupational pension mix. They also shed light on the very wide institutional variation to be found within the occupational pension sector.

Historic Choices in Pension Policy

In Scandinavia as in Europe more generally two basic questions have dominated (and to some extent still dominate) the pension-political debate. 1) Should public pensions be based on an insurance principle ("to each according to merit") or on a taxation principle ("to each according to need")? 2) Should public pensions be reserved for segments of the population or should every citizen be included? The first German pension system was reserved for industrial workers only (Alber, 1987). By contrast, the first British scheme made every citizen a potential recipient of public pension benefits. The Nordic states (unlike most countries on the European continent) made the same choice as Britain. They did however differ in their attitude toward the insurance principle. The first Danish system (1891) consisted solely of tax-financed means-tested benefits (Vesterø-Jensen, 1984:41).[2] The first Finnish system (1937) by contrast relied on a "people's insurance principle" linking benefits to contributions (Kangas, 1988:16). Sweden (1913) and Norway (1936) chose the middle road, combining "people's insurance" with means-tested supplements (Rasmussen, 1985:20, Hatland, 1986).[3]

In the course of time the Nordic pension systems converged. The insurance principle was gradually abolished. Tax-financed means-tested pensions became dominant.[4] After 1945 means-testing was gradually softened and was finally replaced by a system of flat-rate pensions financed out of general revenues ("basic pensions"). Sweden pioneered (1948) followed by Norway (1956) Finland (1957) and Denmark (1970).

Supporters of tax-financed public pensions defeated those who wanted an insurance-based (Beveridge-style) minimum pension system. However, the debate reemerged as the demand for earnings-related pensions came onto the political agenda during the 1950s. Three of the four Nordic countries (Sweden, Finland and Norway) introduced earnings-related pensions. Again, Sweden pioneered (1959) followed by Finland (1960) and Norway (1966). By introducing earnings-related public pensions these Nordic countries have moved towards an insurance-based public pension system.[5]

The Interplay between Occupational Pensions and Public Superannuation

Occupational pensions were widespread before the introduction of earnings-related public pensions, especially in the public sector and among salaried staff. Employees with access to occupational pensions have no immediate self-interest in supporting a demand for public superannuation schemes. A large occupational pension sector might therefore reduce the political support for public earnings-related pensions. However, a different situational logic is also at work: Occupational schemes may serve as points of reference for other occupational groups, showing them "the promised land". If occupational pensions become more widespread, and if membership is limited to some employees in each company, an ever larger segment of the labor force is confronted with the gap between their pension level and the pension level of their more fortunate colleagues/comrades. In this fashion occupational pensions for salaried staff fuelled the demand for earnings-related pensions among (blue-collar) workers.

Central government civil servants were among the first to get access to occupational pensions.[6] The pension level was approximately two-thirds of final salary given a service record of at least 30 years. The demand for similar occupational pensions soon spread to local government civil servants and to salaried staff in the private sector. As larger segments of white-collar employees acquired occupational pensions, the demand spread even further to manual workers. After the war the unions of blue-collar workers in all the Nordic countries began demanding equal pensions for white-collar and blue-collar workers (Heclo, 1974:233, Vesterø-Jensen, 1984:117, Pedersen, 1990:51-55, Kangas, 1988:32).[7]

The demand for earnings-related pensions thus resembles a diffusion process. Civil servants were the first to receive this type of pension, and the demand then spread like circles in the water to ever larger segments of the work force. Reference group theory may explain the social mechanism behind this process. People have a drive to evaluate their outcomes or rewards. To accomplish this evaluation they select others similar in "inputs" (defined as the contributions an individual brings to the job). The greater the (perceived) similarity in inputs and the greater the (perceived) difference in "input/output" ratio, the greater the urge to reduce it.[8] Local government civil servants are used to comparing their salaries with central government civil servants and were quick to demand similar pension arrangements.[9] As these employees gained access to occupational pensions, the demand spread further to groups less inclined to compare themselves directly with central government civil servants. In the end almost the whole labor force had internalized the pension level of central government civil servants as a "natural" point of reference.

The choice of strategies

Wage-earners demanded access to supplementary pensions similar to those enjoyed by salaried staff. The trade unions could respond to this demand by making occupational pensions a high priority goal in collective bargaining, or by lobbying for public schemes. It is sometimes regarded as self-evident that trade unions prefer public (political) welfare solutions rather than private solutions whenever possible (e.g. Korpi, 1983). Political solutions have some obvious advantages from a trade union point of view, the most important being that public arrangements shift the visible costs from those without coverage to the employers or taxpayers in general (if the schemes are financed through taxes or employer's contributions).[10] By contrast, in a collective bargaining situation the employers will normally demand wage restraint in order to establish an occupational pension plan. However, this need not be a sufficient reason for trade unions to prefer public earnings-related pensions. Unions organizing low-paid workers might choose to lobby for higher minimum pensions rather than earnings-related pensions. Strong unions might choose to use their bargaining power to negotiate a pension settlement with their employers rather than to pursue a time-consuming and uncertain political strategy together with weaker unions.

There must be a large degree of cohesion in a trade union movement in order to pursue a common strategy. It must be hierarchically organized and local unions must be willing to submit to decisions made at the central level. Even if the central level in the confederation is strong it might prefer a bargained solution if the employers are willing to deny unorganized workers access to the scheme. Last but not least, the strategies pursued by the trade unions will of course depend on how likely an attempted political solution is to succeed.

Sweden probably has the most coherent trade union movement among the Nordic countries (Rasmussen, 1985:37). The Swedish LO (blue-collar confederation of labor) demanded public earnings-related pensions as early as the 1940s.[11] The trade union movement had strong ties to the Social Democratic party which was by then the ruling party, thus a public solution seemed within reach.[12]

When earnings-related pensions came onto the political agenda in Finland, the diffusion of occupational pensions had been more limited than in Sweden. Occupational pensions were rare outside the public sector. In Finland the confederation of white-collar workers was first to demand public earnings-related pensions, although it was soon followed by the confederation of blue-collar workers (Kangas, 1988:67).

While the Swedish and Finnish unions sought public solutions at an early stage, the Norwegian and Danish unions were originally somewhat more inclined to follow a collective bargaining strategy. In 1960 the Norwegian Confederation of Trade Unions (LO) and the Norwegian employers' association agreed to introduce an occupational pension scheme (FTP) covering all employees in the private sector. This scheme only provided flat-rate benefits. In 1964 the Danish (social democratic) government introduced a similar scheme as part of a larger tripartite collective-bargaining agreement. The purpose of the scheme was primarily to offer compensation for compulsory wage restraint (see von Nordheim Nielsen's chapter in this volume).

Unorganized workers are provided with a strong selective incentive to join unions if only organized workers have access to occupational pensions. However, neither the Norwegian nor the Danish LO succeeded in denying unorganized workers access to the negotiated pension scheme. Neither did the schemes provide the workers with pensions as generous as the occupational schemes enjoyed by salaried staff. Not surprisingly therefore, in the years that followed the unions became more interested in a political solution.[13]

In order to understand why the trade unions in all the Nordic countries eventually decided to use political lobbying rather than collective bargaining as their main strategy, the institutional set-up of the traditional occupational pension schemes must also be brought into the picture. Occupational pensions for white-collar employees were usually regarded as "gratification pay" rather than "deferred wages" (Hyman & Schuller, 1984). They were as a general rule not introduced through collective bargaining (in the public sector these schemes were even introduced through legislation). The lack of institutional links between occupational pensions and wage negotiations made it possible for workers and their unions to interpret these schemes as privileges given to salaried staff. To fight privileges and give workers and salaried staff "equal rights" to supplementary pensions are clearly political issues (while finding the optimal balance between current and deferred wages is more likely to be seen as belonging to the collective bargaining-arena). Thus occupational pensions not only fuelled the demand for supplementary pensions among workers: Their institutional set-up (lack of formal links to wage negotiations) also influenced the choice of strategies pursued by trade unions, by making it easier for proponents of political lobbying to get acceptance for a politicized frame of reference within the labor movement.

The response of the political parties

The Nordic left parties responded to the demand for earnings-related public pensions in different ways. Some were sympathetic, arguing that such pensions would equalize the benefits of blue-collar and white-collar workers and/or that "income maintenance" was a more adequate pension-political goal than minimum protection. Others argued that public pensions ought to counteract inequalities created in the labor market rather than to preserve them. They wanted to stick to flat-rate or means-tested minimum pensions. Thus two different concepts of "equality" collided: Equality between blue and white-collar workers versus equality between citizens regardless of labor market performance.

Different points of view were also voiced from the other side of the left-right divide. Some economic liberals argued that the state ought to limit public pension provision to those who were unable to buy private insurance ("bad risks"). Thus flat-rate or means-tested minimum pensions were to be preferred. On the other hand, it is easier to forge a link between taxes/contributions and benefits in an earnings-related pension system ("to each according to their merit"). Besides, earnings-related pensions preserve status differentials and thus enhances the stability of the social order.

The Social Democrats ended up supporting the demand for earnings-related pensions, although in Denmark the internal opposition was strong enough to prevent the social-democratic government from actually bringing a proposal to the vote (Vesterø-Jensen, 1984:143). Communist parties opposed the demand for earnings-related pensions in all the Nordic countries except Sweden.[14]

The Swedish non-socialist parties opposed the proposal advocated by the Social Democrats (SAP) but they were unable to agree on an alternative. In 1959 SAP's proposal was passed by a one-vote majority. In Finland the Conservative Party supported the demand for earnings-related pensions but the powerful Agrarian Party (which controlled the government) originally opposed the idea (Kangas, 1988:36). However, the Agrarians later changed their minds and the proposal was passed in 1960 by a "broad coalition". In Norway two small center parties (the

Liberals and the "Christian People's Party") supported the demand for public earnings-related pensions even before the Social Democrats had made up their minds. The Conservatives and Agrarians opposed the idea but later accepted it. The non-socialist parties won a parliamentary majority in the 1965 election and the resulting non-socialist coalition government introduced Swedish-style earnings-related pensions in 1966. In Denmark some conservative delegates inspired by the Swedish example suggested introducing a similar pension system in Denmark (Nelson, 1984:70). However, when the social-democratic minority government finally made a half-hearted attempt to pursue the issue, all the non-socialist parties opposed it.

The different and sometimes changing opinions expressed by the parties reveal not only the lack of clear ideological guidelines, but also differences in the economic interests of their voters. As Molin (1965:187) points out, earnings-related pensions might be in the interest of high-income earners (who tend to vote conservative) while many low-income earners (who traditionally vote for the Social Democrats, Communists or Agrarians) would be better served by increases in the minimum pension.[15]

How can the different attitudes of the political parties be accounted for? Why did the non-socialist parties unite in opposition to demands for earnings-related pensions in Sweden and Denmark, while their Norwegian and Finnish sister parties ended up supporting such schemes? The major political controversy in the Nordic countries turned out to be how the schemes were to be financed rather than the pension issue itself.

The Swedish Social Democrats wanted to finance the public earnings-related pension scheme (ATP) through large government-controlled pension funds. This evoked the fear of "pension fund socialism" and united the non-socialist parties against the proposal.

Proponents of earnings-related pensions inside the Danish Social Democratic Party also argued that the pension issue could be used as a vehicle to increase the government's control of capital. (This was one of the main reasons why the supporters of earnings-related public pensions were able to carry the day within the party.) This argument united the Danish non-socialist parties against the proposal as in Sweden. Faced with opposition not only from the non-socialist parties but from the small parties to the left of the Social Democrats as well, coupled with persistent opposition from within the party, the social democratic minority government in the end abstained from putting forward a formal proposal to introduce earnings-related pensions.

The Finnish employer's organization was advised by its Swedish sister organization not to oppose earnings-related pensions, but rather to channel the demand into schemes that the employers felt more comfortable with (Pentikainen, 1987:27). The employers declared their willingness to support earnings-related pension schemes provided that the administration of the pension funds was decentralized and in the hand of private financial institutions. The trade unions accepted this idea.[16] The Conservative Party sided with the employer's organization. The Agrarian government grudgingly accepted the proposal when the Social Democrats suggested introducing a pension scheme for seasonal and part-time workers (LEL) alongside the main pension plan (TEL). The end result was the introduction of earnings-related pensions in 1960. However, although membership is compulsory the government is not formally responsible for the payment of benefits. The schemes may in principle go broke. For this reason they must be regarded as semi-public rather than fully developed public systems. (The National Accounting system actually categorizes Finland's private sector superannuation schemes as private pensions.)

Initially, influential members of the Norwegian Social Democratic party were reluctant to adopt the policy of its Swedish counterpart (Hatland, 1986). Nonetheless, in 1962 a government committee was appointed to work out a proposal for a Norwegian earnings-related pension scheme (Pedersen, 1990). Before the committee had finished its work a mining accident in a state-owned pit in 1963 caused the downfall of the social-democratic government.[17] For the first time since the war a non-socialist coalition government came to power. A few days after the new government was installed the Social Democratic Party announced its intention to introduce Swedish-style earnings-related public pensions. The motive was probably to drive a wedge between the parties in the new non-socialist coalition government (Hatland, 1986; Ringen, 1987; Skånland, 1989). The Liberals and the Christian People's Party wanted to introduce earnings-related pensions, the Conservatives and Agrarians did not. However, the Swedish experience had taught Norway's non-socialist parties not to let the Social use the pension issue to enhance cleavages in the non-socialist camp. Rather than opposing the proposal, both the Agrarians and Conservatives announced that they too supported earnings-related pensions. The non-socialist parties gained the Parliamentary majority in the following 1965 elections and introduced earnings-related public pensions in 1966.[18] The Norwegian scheme was modelled on the Swedish system, with one important exception: To a

TABLE 6.1: *Public Pensions as a Percentage of Average Male Wages in Industry (After Tax). Single Pensioner, 1990.*

	Denmark	**Norway**	**Sweden**	**Finland**
Minimum pension only	51	45	43	34
Including public supplementary pension	56	70	71	58

Source: *Nordisk Socialstatistisk Komite (1992:118-9)*

much larger extent it was financed on a pay-as-you-go basis. In this way, the non-socialist coalition government avoided accumulating a large public pension fund.

To sum up, supporters of earnings-related public pensions won the internal power struggle inside the social-democratic parties (despite opposition from within the parties, especially in Denmark and Norway). Thanks to the dominant role of the socialist parties, disagreements were more or less "kept within the family" on the left but were played out openly on the political scene by the many competing parties on the fragmented right. This created a divide-and-rule situation which ultimately led to the introduction of earnings-related public or semi-public pension schemes in all the Nordic countries except Denmark. Due to the larger degree of cohesion on the left, supporters of earnings-related pensions within the social-democratic parties were able to win the game.

The Danish case is an exception to these generalizations. Denmark has kept the flat-rate supplementary public pension (ATP) introduced in 1964, but as can be seen from Table 6.1 this pension supplement has much less impact than the supplementary pension systems of the other Nordic countries on the overall pension level.

The role of occupational pensions in the political process

An employee covered by an occupational pension scheme has no immediate self-interest in a public superannuation scheme, especially if the public scheme is supposed to marginalize (crowd out) existing occupational schemes. As von Nordheim Nielsen argues (this volume), lack of enthusiasm on the part of workers already covered explains some of the difficulties of Danish LO in keeping the unions united behind the demand for public superannuation. There are however ways to win the support (or at least prevent opposition) from those already covered by occupational pensions, as suggested by the experience in Finland, Norway and Sweden.

In Finland occupational pension coverage was not widespread outside the public sector. Membership in the new earnings-related pension schemes (TEL and LEL) was simply limited to private sector employees, thus bypassing the problem of how existing occupational pensions should be integrated in the new public schemes.

The Swedish 1959 proposal aimed at introducing an earnings-related scheme covering everybody, including members of existing occupational pensions. Opposition from public employees was countered in two ways: They were granted an overall pension level higher than the level they enjoyed before the public scheme existed, and they received wage compensation. In the private sector it was made possible to "contract out" of the new public scheme during a limited time period, given certain conditions (Molin, 1965).[19]

Norwegian employees covered by occupational pensions were not given wage compensations or increases in their overall pension level when the new public superannuation scheme was introduced in 1966. This difference between Norway and Sweden can be explained with reference to the bargaining position of employees covered by occupational pensions. In Sweden the pension question created one of the most intense political conflicts in postwar Swedish history. An advisory referendum, dissolution of Parliament and new elections were necessary before the Social Democrats were able to squeeze their proposal through Parliament with a one-vote majority (a renegade from the Liberal Party secured the majority). Hence it was of utmost importance for the Social Democrats to gain the consent of as many voters as possible. By contrast, in Norway all the major parties in the end agreed to introduce earnings-related public pensions. There was no need to "buy" support from members of occupational pension schemes since they had nowhere to go with their frustration.

The packaging of second-tier reforms has been of relevance not only to their acceptance by those with a vested interest in occupational schemes, but also to the wider struggle to use social policy as an instrument for shaping the political allegiances of the mass public. In this context, Esping-Andersen (1985) has argued that the social-democratic parties used the pension issue as a vehicle to forge a new alliance between manual workers and the rising middle class. This is correct, but only up to a point. The Social Democrats were primarily interested in granting their traditional core constituency earnings-related pensions, rather than forging a new cross-class alliance.

These two motives did move in tandem to some extent, but both the Swedish and Norwegian parties proposed upper limits on the income that would "earn" supplementary pensions. Low-income groups were given more generous pensions (expressed as a percentage of their wages) than high-income earners.[20] In Norway the income ceiling fixed by the 1966 pension Act was raised substantially in 1971 by a non-socialist coalition government against the votes of the Social Democrats (Hatland, 1982). In 1990 the Norwegian Parliament (led by a social democratic government) lowered the income ceiling, thus reducing the pension level of high-income earners. This strengthens the hypothesis that the primary aim of the Social Democrats was and is to grant their traditional core constituency earnings-related pensions. However, the public superannuation schemes undoubtedly maintained an appeal also to lower-to-middle income groups among salaried staff. To some extent, then, they also served to enhance the popularity of social democratic parties among new segments of voters.

Esping-Andersen's thesis carries more explanatory weight in relation to the problem of cohesion within the traditional labor movement. A single earnings-related public pension scheme limits tensions between different labor unions and between the unions and their traditional alliance partners (small-scale farmers and fishermen). This argument was indeed utilized by core actors inside the unions and the social-democratic parties, at least in some of the Nordic countries (Pedersen, 1990).

Parties on the left thus opted for income ceilings in the earnings-related pension system, while their counterparts on the right preferred to emphasize linkage between contributions and benefits. This probably explains the absence of an income ceiling in the Finnish earnings-related pension system. The Social Democratic Party in Finland was weaker than in Norway and Sweden and had to join forces with the Conservative Party to squeeze the proposal through Parliament. If the motive behind the introduction of earnings-related pensions is to forge a link between contributions and benefits and/or to stabilize status differentials, then income ceilings should be avoided. Thus as far as the Nordic experience goes, the stronger the political position of the Conservative Party, the less likely it is that the earnings-related scheme has an upper income limit.[21]

The Growth of Occupational Pensions: Four Variations on a Basic Theme

Imitative demands for pension coverage have not been limited to the quest for parity with public pensions. Depending on the outcome of the struggle for public earnings-related pensions, the demand for similar coverage took new forms (Finland, Sweden and Norway) or stayed within the same framework (Denmark).

The Finnish TEL and LEL schemes provided private sector employees with pensions almost as generous as the schemes benefiting public employees. In Sweden and Norway however the income ceilings in the earnings-related schemes prevented high-income earners from reaching a pension level equal to the level enjoyed by those with access to additional occupational pensions. This was even more so in Denmark: The Danish flat-rate supplementary scheme left even middle-income earners with low replacement rates. Hence in Denmark the unions did for many years continue to lobby for a public earnings-related pension scheme. In Sweden and Norway the unions were more inclined to use collective bargaining to close the remaining gap between employees with and without additional (occupational) pension coverage, while in Finland the lack of an income ceiling in the public superannuation schemes left private sector employees with few incentives to try to "top off" their public pension coverage with additional occupational schemes. In Finland pressure for new pension reforms mainly came from those excluded from the TEL and LEL schemes: public employees and the self-employed.

Finland: The bandwagon effect

Workers covered by earnings-related pensions (be they public or private) have no self-interest in supporting other groups demanding similar pension schemes. However, the success of some groups can also trigger a bandwagon effect. Public employees liked the unified structure of the new TEL and LEL schemes (compared to the patchwork of different schemes to be found in the public sector at that time). In 1964 the existing pension arrangements benefiting local government employees were replaced by a new unified scheme (KVTEL). In 1967 the pension arrangements of central government employees were similarly reconstructed (VEL). Finally, farmers and other self-employed acquired their own earnings-related pension schemes (MYEL and YEL) in 1969.[22] Through these six legislated pension schemes almost the entire work force got access to earnings-related schemes.

The remaining role for regular occupational schemes (schemes not introduced through legislation) is limited to providing pensions to birth cohorts born too early in the century to earn full pension rights in the new legislated systems. In 1985 only 15 percent of Finnish employees were members of occupational pension plans (Kangas & Palme, 1989:72). The number of such plans has declined and occupational pensions will almost disappear completely if the public earnings-related schemes are allowed to fully mature.

Sweden & Norway: The art of leapfrogging

In the aftermath of the 1959 legislation the employers and the Swedish confederation of private sector white-collar unions (TCO-P) agreed to set up an integrated occupational pension scheme (ITP).[23] Manual workers soon discovered that despite the introduction of earnings-related public pensions they still lagged behind their white-collar colleagues. This led the blue-collar confederation (LO) to negotiate a pension settlement with their employers in 1972. This scheme (STP) covers manual workers in the private sector.[24]

In 1974 central government employees renegotiated their occupational pension arrangements. The new scheme (SPV) covers workers as well as salaried staff and part-time as well as full time workers. Local governments operate their own scheme (KPA) which is fairly similar to SPV.[25] As a result of these collectively bargained arrangements, Sweden has the highest coverage of occupational pensions in the world (von Nordheim Nielsen, 1990). Almost all employees are members of one of the four major schemes.

The occupational pension arrangements covering Norwegian central government employees (SPK) resemble the Swedish scheme. The local government sector is in principle more fragmented. A local government may administer its own scheme. However, a private insurance company

(KLP) has almost monopolized the provision of local government occupational pensions. This has resulted in standardized pension schemes imitating SPK.

In the private sector the situation is very different from Sweden. Nothing similar to ITP or STP exists. Approximately 1/3 of the employees are covered by company-based occupational pension plans. In 1988 59 percent of white collar employees and 24 percent of blue collar employees reported that they were covered by such plans (Hippe & Pedersen, 1988). Almost every scheme has been introduced by employers without formal negotiations between the employees and the trade unions.[26] The schemes are earnings-related and provide a pension level of between 60 and 70 percent of final salary.

In the absence of negotiated settlements a genuine market for occupational pensions exists in Norway. This market is however tightly regulated. Employers who refuse to adopt the regulations are denied tax privileges otherwise granted to occupational pension arrangements.

The different occupational pension structure in Sweden and Norway cannot be explained by looking at differences between the public pension systems. The Norwegian earnings-related scheme is less generous than the Swedish.[27] If the crowding-out thesis is correct, the lesser generosity of the Norwegian scheme should coincide with a larger occupational pension sector. The opposite is true. Why?

The main explanation is to be found in the different trade union structure of Sweden and Norway. In 1960 the TCO-LO axis almost monopolized the organization of Swedish workers. TCO-P organizes white collar workers in the private sector while LO organizes blue collar workers. This division of labor enabled TCO-P and the employers to set up the ITP scheme without having to include blue-collar workers in the deal. It also made it easier for LO to negotiate a similar deal for manual workers some years later. Since manual workers were altogether excluded from ITP no tensions emerged between LO members with and without occupational pension coverage.

Norwegian trade unions lack a clear division between blue-collar and white-collar unions. The main confederation of trade unions consists of unions organizing both salaried staff and manual workers. Nothing similar to TCO exists. This makes it almost impossible to reach a central agreement covering only white collar or only blue-collar workers.

The structure of the insurance market is a second factor explaining the differences between Norway and Sweden. Sweden never had a free market for occupational pensions. Prior to the introduction of ITP almost all occupational pension arrangements were administered by the SPP insurance company. In Norway the administration of occupational pension schemes was divided between several competing companies. Sweden could move from many different schemes administered by one insurance company to one scheme administered by the same company. Norway would have had the much more difficult task of shifting from a free market situation to a unified scheme.

In the absence of a negotiated settlement the Norwegian trade unions retorted to political lobbying in order to influence regulatory policies directed toward the occupational pension sector. In response, the (mainly social-democratic) governments of Norway have utilized these policies as a means of fulfilling union aspirations, acting for instance to increase occupational pension coverage among manual workers.[28]

The very different types of occupational pensions now in place in Sweden and Norway show that institutional variation within the occupational pension sector can be as large as the variation between the public and occupational pension sectors. The Swedish and Norwegian stories also show that the structure of the public pension system is only one among several factors influencing the scope and structure of occupational pensions. Equally important is the structure of the trade union movement and the structure of the insurance market The Norwegian case further illustrates that political lobbying is not necessarily limited to demands for public pensions: Trade unions may lobby for favorable regulatory policies in conjunction with and/or as an alternative to lobbying for public pension protection. Finally, the Swedish experience demonstrates that private savings are not the only alternative to public (pay-as-you-go) pension schemes. None of the Swedish occupational pension schemes (the SPV, KPA, ITP and STP) are fully funded in an actuarial sense.[29] Thus the alternative to a pay-as-you-go public scheme may very well turn out to be occupational schemes also based on a pay-as-you-go basis. This is a point almost totally overlooked by the economists in their debate concerning the effects of public pensions on national savings.[30]

Denmark: Multiple role models

Denmark deviates from Norway and Sweden not only with respect to public pension arrangements but also in the set-up of occupational pensions. First, no integrated occupational pension scheme exists either in the public or the private sector. A segment of government civil servants have access to earnings-related occupational pension plans similar to the pension arrangements of their Norwegian, Swedish and Finnish colleagues. These schemes do not however cover all state employees as is the case in the other Nordic countries. Second, defined benefit schemes do not dominate the occupational pension sector to the same extent as in Sweden, Norway and Finland. (A defined benefit scheme defines the pension level as a percentage of earnings. By contrast, a large segment of the Danish market consists of defined contribution schemes. In a defined contribution scheme pension contributions are defined as a percentage of annual earnings. The resulting pension level depends on the size of the contributions and the interest rate.)

Defined benefit schemes did predominate in Denmark until the 1960s. Occupational pensions in the private sector were company-based schemes copying the old civil service plan. Following a reorganization of the public sector during the 1960s many public employees were allowed to opt for new defined contribution schemes and they chose to do so.[31] By 1990 almost all public employees not covered by the old-style defined benefit scheme had gained access to defined contribution schemes through collective bargaining.

The Danish LO tried to keep the unions organizing private sector workers united behind a proposal to introduce public earnings-related pensions. The confederation was internally strong enough to prevent separate unions from breaking away and negotiating their own pension settlements with the employers, but not politically strong enough to get the political parties to introduce a public earnings-related scheme. For many years this stalemate produced a situation in which workers in the private sector gained neither public superannuation nor occupational pensions. However, the ability of the Danish LO to keep the unions in line diminished during the 1980s as the balance of power in Parliament shifted toward the non-socialist parties.[32] In 1990 the powerful Metalworkers' Union finally decided to go its own way. Other unions immediately followed and by the end of 1991 most major unions had negotiated separate pension settlements with the employers. The new schemes were based on the defined contribution principle.[33]

As in the other Nordic countries, the development in the Danish private sector seems to mirror earlier development inside the public sector. However, since the diffusion process inside the Danish

TABLE 6.2: *Share of Total Pension Expenditure by Pension Type, 1985* (percentages).

	Denmark	Norway	Sweden	Finland
Public pensions				
Minimum	76	64	45	39
Supplementary	2	25	42	56
Occupational pensions				
Public sector	10	7	7	0
Private sector	5	3	4	4
Personal pensions	8	1	2	1
Total	101	100	100	100

Source: von Nordheim Nielsen (1990:82)

Note: With respect to Finland, von Nordheim Nielsen argues that the semi-public schemes benefiting public employees must be regarded in part as occupational schemes because they provide more generous benefits than similar schemes in the private sector. A good theoretical case can be made for this view, but public sector schemes have not (until very recently) been perceived that way in the Finnish debate. This table observes the traditional distinction, and all the Finnish legislated schemes have been categorized as "public" pensions.

government sector resulted in two occupational pension designs rather than one, the private sector was in a position to choose between two role models.

After the 1960s, pension negotiations in the private sector resulted in defined contribution rather than defined benefit schemes. However, the long period without either public superannuation or occupational pension coverage among large segments of the labor force has also led to a much larger market for personal pension schemes in Denmark than in any of the other Nordic countries, as illustrated in Table 6.2.

Feedback Effects from Earnings-Related Pensions to the Minimum Pension System

A major argument in favor of public superannuation rather than occupational pensions has been the supposedly positive feedback effect of an "institutional" (all-encompassing) pension structure on the minimum pension level, as compared to a "residual" public pension structure (Korpi, 1983). It is assumed that "institutional" public pension systems (such as the Swedish and Norwegian systems) motivate the middle classes to consent to high basic pensions for the poor. In contrast, a "residual" system like the Danish is said to encourage the better-off to care for themselves through occupational or personal pensions.

The Swedish and Norwegian basic pension is defined as the value of one "base amount". This base amount serves a dual purpose: it both determines the basic pension level and enters into the calculation of the earnings-related public pension. It has thus been argued that since the working population has a self-interest in a high basic amount, they also have a self-interest in providing the poor with high basic pensions (Hagen, 1988). Thus it may seem as if these pension systems are better able to unite the pension-political interests of mainstream and marginal groups, securing the latter a better deal in comparison with a country like Denmark that focuses on minimum pension protection.

This hypothesis implies that the Swedish and Norwegian politicians who introduced earnings-related pensions acted as "Machiavellian altruists", deliberately constructing their public superannuation schemes so as to provide marginal groups with strong alliance partners. Unfortunately, this interpretation is not consistent with the facts.

First, Denmark has a minimum pension level at least as high as the other Nordic countries, despite the fact that occupational (and personal) pensions play a much larger role.[34] Equally important: when Sweden introduced public superannuation in 1959 the Swedish parliament decided to link the adjustment of the base amount to a price index rather than a wage index. Provided that real wages continued to grow, in the long run this would shrink the basic pension.[35] By linking the adjustment of the base amount to a price index the social democratic government actually induced a slow transformation of the Swedish pension system toward a system in which the working population receive earnings-related pensions and the non-working population (marginal groups) become increasingly dependent on means-tested benefits.

Thus Sweden's 1959 pension reform did not create an "institutional" pension structure linking the interests of marginal groups and the working population (including salaried staff); rather it marked the beginning of a shift away from a (Beveridge-inspired) flat-rate minimum protection system toward a (Bismarckian) dual system. This however is not the whole picture: The upper income limit that will "earn" pension points is also linked to the base amount. If real wages continue to grow, a larger percentage of the working population will in the course of time hit this income ceiling (7.5 times the base amount), and in the very long run the Swedish earnings-related pension system will be transformed back toward a (contribution-based) flat-rate system!. These rather schizophrenic attributes of the Swedish system must be regarded as the outcomes of compromises struck at the time of the 1959 reform.[36]

Norway has a Swedish-style system but the base amount is in principle linked to a wage index, not a price index. Thus Norway may at first glance seem closer to an ideal-typical "institutional" pension system. However, adjustments to the base amount are not automatic. They are determined each year by Parliament after consultations with organizations representing different groups of social security recipients. In these consultations adjustments in the base amount have often been pitted against adjustments in different types of means-tested benefits (Hem, 1991). The tension between income maintenance and minimum protection has thus been institutionalized within the system.

As far as Finland is concerned, bitter conflicts prevail between the National Pension Institute (in charge of the minimum pension system) and the Pension Security Institute (coordinating the earnings-related systems). Accordingly, it is mistaken to describe the Nordic pension systems (including the occupational schemes) as stable, "institutional" pension regimes. These systems should rather be perceived as institutional outcomes of conflicts and struggles between supporters of different pension-policy visions (within and between different parties and interest organizations), as well as institutional settings for the continuation of these struggles. Their stability is a matter of degree. This is not to say that the characteristics of minimum pension systems are totally uncorrelated to the choice between public superannuation or occupational pensions. The structure of the minimum pension system varies significantly between the Nordic countries even though the level is somewhat the same. In all the Nordic countries the minimum pension is made up of two elements: a flat-rate basic pension plus a pension supplement granted only to those who do not receive income from public superannuation.[37] As can be seen from Table 6.3 the basic pension is of decreasing importance in all the Nordic countries. However, the tendency is most pronounced in Finland and less so in Denmark. How can this be explained?

TABLE 6.3: *Maximum Pension Supplement as a Share of the Basic Pension*

	Denmark	Norway	Sweden	Finland
1970	0.22	0.08	0.06	2.66
1972	0.22	0.16	0.12	3.38
1982	0.18	0.49	0.46	4.18
1987	0.19	0.54	0.48	4.67
1991	0.26	0.58	0.54	4.67

Note: Data are for a single pensioner.

Sources: St.meld.12 (1988-89) (Norway); Socialforsäkringsfakta RTV (Sweden); Statistical yearbook of the Social Insurance Institution (Finland); internal statistics from the Department of Social Affairs (Denmark).

First, it must be noted that the shift from means-tested toward flat-rate minimum pensions during the 1940s and 1950s was a controversial issue among all the political parties (including the Social Democrats). On the left, some argued that means-tested benefits had the highest redistributive potential and were preferable to flat-rate benefits. The trade unions however lobbied for abolishing means-testing, because means-testing served as a disincentive for employers and unions in their efforts to set up occupational pensions. Some further argued that a minimum pension should be regarded as a "citizenship right" and be given to everybody regardless of previous income.[38]

Social-democratic governments more or less grudgingly yielded to the pressure by limiting and ultimately abolishing means-testing (Hatland, 1986; Kangas, 1988:21; Olson, 1991:102; Baldwin, 1989).[39] However, most parties (including the Social Democrats) have always had factions calling for a return to means-tested minimum pensions. Second, and more important in this context, the introduction of earnings-related public pensions changed the balance of power in favor of those preferring means-tested minimum pensions. The trade unions no longer had any reason to lobby for flat-rate pensions in order to encourage the employers to set up occupational pensions. Besides, in order to increase the pension level of the worst off without simultaneously increasing the pension level of those covered by earnings-related pensions, it became necessary to introduce benefits that were at least tested against income from earnings-related public pensions. This explains why Denmark remains the only country maintaining a high basic pension.[40]

The high basic pension in Denmark is not however due only to the lack of an earnings-related public pension scheme: It also reflects the fact that Danish LO for more than two decades successfully prevented its unions from setting up separate occupational pension schemes. In the long period without either public superannuation or occupational pensions, the only (remaining) strategy for the unions was to lobby for increases in the minimum pension. However, this was bound to change, and the unions in 1990/91 finally decided to opt for separate occupational pension schemes. In 1992 the major Danish unions were finally on their way to securing their members earnings-related supplementary pensions (although by very different institutional means than their Norwegian, Swedish and Finnish colleagues). This created momentum for a scaling back of the basic pension and increased reliance on the pension supplement.[41] Beginning in January 1994, the basic benefit is now income-tested (Ploug and Kvist, 1994:36). Thus in one stroke, Denmark has moved from providing the least means-tested to providing the most means-tested minimum benefit of all the Scandinavian countries.

To sum up, public superannuation and occupational pensions have fairly similar feedback effects on the minimum pension system. The introduction of earnings-related supplementary benefits, whether by legislation or collective bargaining, leads to a scaling back of the basic pension and increased reliance on pension supplements. Employees covered by earnings-related pensions, be they public or occupational, have no economic self-interest in generous pension supplements. Hence in the long run, the level of the minimum pension in all the Nordic countries will depend increasingly on the altruism of the working population rather than their self-interest.

Conclusions

The original "gratification pay" type of occupational pension schemes served as a point of reference for the pension-political demands of other groups. A process of "bandwagon" and "leapfrogging" effects followed. The way these effects occurred depended on a number of factors, two of the most important being the degree of cohesion within the trade union movement and the degree of cohesion on the left and right ends of the political spectrum.

The bandwagon effect also occurred across countries: The success of the Swedish trade unions and Social Democrats in introducing earnings-related public pensions, and their humiliating defeat of the non-socialist parties, shaped the political preferences of trade unions and political parties in the other Nordic countries (although not always in the same fashion). As soon as earnings-related systems were established (through legislation, collective bargaining or both), a feedback effect took place, leading to more extensive means-testing in the minimum pension scheme.

Old political tensions are built into the pension policy designs of the Nordic countries and will probably keep reemerging in the future. Increased competition in the world market and gloomy demographic forecasts have led all of the Scandinavian countries to consider changes and/or cutbacks in their public pension schemes. The increased influx of women into the labor force, as well as into politics, point in the same direction: Women seem to prefer spending on welfare services (such as kindergartens and nursing homes), and minimum income protection, rather than earnings-related benefits. Already at this stage, the Scandinavian welfare states are sometimes referred to as "welfare service states" as opposed to the "welfare transfer states" prevailing on the Continent (Kohl, 1981:312-14). The ever-stronger presence of feminist factions in most political parties might further the tendency away from transfers towards services, implying that a further scaling back of superannuation benefits might be expected in the future. However, if this should happen it will not necessarily increase the importance of voluntary-based occupational pensions.

Recent changes in taxation policies indicate that other types of private savings might increase faster than occupational pensions: During the 1980s the Nordic countries reduced tax subsidies to occupational pensions in an attempt to broaden the tax base while bringing down the tax on all (other) types of capital. This is likely to stimulate the demand for alternatives to occupational pensions. There has also been a trend towards deregulating the occupational pension sector. Fewer regulations will probably result in increased "product differentiation". This may also happen if a free market for annuities and life insurance is established within the European Economic Area (EEA). To sum up, a more diversified, but not necessarily larger, occupational pension sector is likely to emerge in the Nordic countries in the future.

Notes

1. The author wishes to thank Olli Kangas, Axel Pedersen, Karii Salminen, Michael Shalev, Toshimitsu Shinkawa and Fritz von Nordheim Nielsen for valuable comments on earlier drafts.
2. The first British pension system was introduced in 1908. Hence it has been argued that the Danish system influenced the British pension-political approach rather than the other way around (Petersen, 1990). In 1925 Britain moved away from a tax-financed towards a contribution-financed minimum pension system, but the legacy of (mainly) tax-financed minimum pension systems lives on in the immigrant Commonwealth nations (Australia, Canada and New Zealand).
3. In the Norwegian case it can be argued that the pension system only paid lip service to the insurance principle. An earmarked tax financed the pension benefits but no attempt was made to forge a link between contributions and the benefit amount (Hatland,1984). It is interesting to note that already at this early stage in the pension-political process Denmark and Finland emerged as polar opposites with Sweden and Norway in between.
4. Means-tested supplements were made more generous and the link between contributions and benefits was broken, converting contributions into earmarked taxes.
5. However, an earnings-related pension system is not necessarily financed through contributions, any more than a minimum pension system is necessarily financed through taxes. The Finnish earnings-related pension system is financed through contributions only while the Norwegian system to an ever larger extent is financed through general taxes. Thus the conflict between proponents of contribution-financed and tax-financed public pensions can also be found within an earnings-related pension structure.
6. The origins of these pension schemes dates back to a period even prior to the formation of the present Nordic nation states (to the days of the Swedo-Finnish and Dano-Norwegian kingdoms). In the beginning of the 20th century these pension arrangements were codified through legislation following the introduction of formal retirement ages. Sweden pioneered (1907) followed by Norway (1917) Denmark (1919) and Finland (1926).
7. Parallel to this development the demand for pensions spread from full-time to part-time employees and from permanently to temporarily employed personnel inside each segment of the labor market.
8. This prediction is taken from Goodman (1977) and refers to Leon Festinger's dissonance theory.
9. Actually, many local government employees were included in the central government scheme. This fuelled the demand from the remaining groups of

local government employees to have similar schemes of their own. See Thulin (1945); Vesterø-Jensen (1984); Bastiansen (1988).

10. From an economic point of view it is necessary to take into consideration the possibility of cost-shifting through the elasticities of supply and demand in different markets. From a political perspective this objection is of limited importance. Not actual costs but perceived costs matter in the political decision-making process.

11. Even the Swedish confederation had some initial problems in keeping the construction and metalworkers' unions in line with the other unions (Molin, 1965:15-16).

12. Still, the Swedish Confederation also entered preliminary negotiations with the employers in the 1940s (Molin, 1965).

13. The Norwegian LO made an (unsuccessful) attempt to get Parliament to investigate the question of public earnings-related pensions before they started negotiations with the employers (Pedersen, 1990). Confederations of trade unions are not monolithic organizations and different opinions no doubt existed—and continue to exist—within them. This may to some extent have led to the pursuit of multiple strategies. This makes it difficult to reconstruct an exact chronology of positions taken by the trade unions at different points in time.

14. By the time the pension issue came onto the political agenda (late 1950s) the Communist parties were small and marginalized in all the Nordic countries except in Finland.

15. A survey conducted in Norway in November 1990 shows that attitudes toward earnings-related pensions also cut across the left-right dimension at the mass level (Øverbye, 1991).

16. The Finnish left was split between the Social Democrats and the Communists (who opposed earnings-related pensions), and the trade unions had little reason to believe that they could get earnings-related pensions implemented unless they made this concession to the employers. Actually, they were not that interested in large public pension funds in the first place. The National Pension Institute (which controlled the funds for the minimum pension scheme) was lead by the leader of the Agrarian Party. Larger pension funds controlled by the National Pension Institute were likely to imply larger investments in the rural parts of Finland benefiting farmers rather than workers (Kangas, 1988:34).

17. The Social Democratic government controlled the Parliamentary majority only through the support by the two MPs from a small Socialist Party. In 1963 these MPs joined the non-Socialist parties in a vote of no confidence.

18. The Social Democrats supported the proposal. Premiums paid to the collectively-bargained FTP scheme were stopped the same year.

19. It turned out that nobody contracted out; instead the employers and the confederation organizing private sector salaried staff (TCO-P) agreed to set up a new national pension scheme (ITP) on top of the public superannuation scheme.

20. Molin (1965) argues that the Swedish Social Democrats increased the pension level for high-income earners as the conflict with the non-socialist parties escalated. Hence the motive to "buy" support from higher income groups was brought into play at a late stage of the decision-making process. It was not part of a pre-designed long-term strategy.

21. The fact that the Norwegian scheme has a more liberal upper limit than the Swedish system further confirms this hypothesis.

22. Although not without a fight: The Agrarians wanted to attend to the interests of the self-employed through increases in the minimum pension. They lost.

23. ITP covers white collar employees in the private sector from the second up to and including the eight level in the Swedish nomenclature of assignments. It is in some respects even more generous than the scheme covering civil servants.

24. It is however less generous than the ITP scheme.

25. The state scheme was renegotiated once again in 1991 introducing some new elements that have not yet been adopted in the local government scheme.

26. With one exception: In 1988 LO and the employers agreed to set up an early retirement scheme (AFP) covering private sector employees only.

27. The Norwegian scheme demands an employment record of 40 years to achieve full pension rights, whereas 30 years is required in the Swedish system. Pension benefits are calculated on the basis of average earnings in the "20 best years" in Norway as compared to the "15 best years" in Sweden. The so-called "pension-percentage" that enters the final pension calculation is 60 in the Swedish system and 42 in the Norwegian. On the other hand the Norwegian system has an upper income limit equal to 12 times the base amount compared to only 7.5 times the base amount in Sweden. Besides, the Norwegian base amount is regulated according to both wage and price increases while the Swedish base amount is linked to a price index only. Nonetheless the Swedish system is more generous than the Norwegian at least for low and middle-income groups and provided that wages do not grow faster than prices.

28. As early as 1952 the government introduced regulations stating that an employer must include all employees in the occupational scheme regardless of their occupational status if the scheme is to enjoy tax privileges.

29. SPV and KPA are full-fledged pay-as-you-go schemes. STP has only accumulated funds large enough to secure the pension promise of those already retired. ITP is in principle a fully funded system, but the 2000 largest

firms are members of the FPG/PRI arrangement (a "plan within a plan"). They pay pensions on a pay as you go basis but have to buy insurance against bankruptcy from the SPP insurance company.

30. I am referring to the debate initiated by Feldstein's (1974) seminal article and still going on in most international and national economic journals around the world.

31. These schemes were easier to integrate in a collective bargaining-framework. Besides, the funds were to be controlled by the unions without interference from the employers.

32. Incidentally, the Danish confederation is generally regarded as weak (low degree of cohesion) as compared to the confederations of the other Nordic countries. Danish LO may resemble the British TUC rather than Sweden's LO or TCO (Scheuer, 1990).

33. For further discussion of these developments, see von Nordheim Nielsen's chapter in this volume.

34. This is the case both if the minimum pension is measured as a percentage of the average industrial wage (Kangas & Palme, 1989:7), or by using purchasing power parities (Øverbye, 1991:13).

35. In 1959 everybody assumed that real wages would continue to grow. The architects of the pension system expected annual growth rates of at least 3% (Eriksen & Palmer, 1992:28). Actually, during the 1980s Sweden experienced a period when real wages declined. This unexpected development has slowed down the marginalization of the basic pension.

36. A recent proposal for a new Swedish superannuation scheme eliminates this indexation rule. It also removes the linkage between the minimum and superannuation system, as the "base amount" is no longer to enter into the calculation of the superannuation benefit (Könberg, 1994).

37. In Denmark the pension supplement is also reduced if the pensioner receives income from other sources.

38. This argument was also utilized outside of the left, especially by the Agrarian parties. Most Conservatives preferred means-tested benefits, but some supporters of flat-rate benefits were also to be found. They argued that flat-rate benefits did not discourage private savings to the same extent as means-tested benefits, echoing old Conservative concerns that the incentive effects of different welfare arrangements should be given more emphasis than their redistributive effects.

39. In Finland means-testing was abolished by an Agrarian Party government.

40. The minimum pension level in Table 6.3 is defined as basic pension plus general income-tested supplements. In Table 6.1, municipal income-tested housing allowances were also included in the minimum pension definition. This change in definition does not affect the general tendency in Table 6.3.

41. Table 6.3 indicates that this process has already gained momentum—note the increased importance of the pension supplement in Denmark between 1987 and 1989.

7

The Labor Movement, Social Policy and Occupational Welfare in Norway

Jon Mathias Hippe and Axel West Pedersen

The Scandinavian welfare states are often associated with inclusive and generous public social security programs and a correspondingly marginal role played by occupational welfare. This image of public predominance in the provision of welfare is central to the interpretation of Scandinavian welfare politics offered by the "social democratic model". According to this model, strong labor movements in Scandinavia succeeded in creating "institutional welfare states" which leave little room for private supplements:

The traditional boundaries of the welfare state have been trespassed to a greater extent than is typical, and public responsibilities have marginalized and even superseded private provision... (Esping-Andersen and Korpi, 1987)

The underlying assumption is that the relationship between public and occupational welfare is inherently competitive and antagonistic. Because of its ability to crowd out occupational provision, the ideal-type Scandinavian welfare state should contribute to a more egalitarian distribution of welfare (Titmuss, 1958) and higher and more stable support for the welfare state, since all segments of the labor force rely on public programs for income replacement (Esping-Andersen, 1990).

In this paper we shall address both historical and present developments in the public/private mix of welfare in Norway, and based on the Norwegian experience we shall argue that the interplay between public and occupational welfare is far more complex than conventionally assumed. Moreover, closer attention to the changing interplay between public and occupational welfare raises new questions as to the causes and political dynamics underlying the postwar development in Norwegian welfare policies.

Within the "social democratic model" there is a tendency to treat the labor movement as one coherent actor. The key explanatory factor is the parliamentary strength of social-democratic parties, while the impact of trade unions is considered to be more secondary in nature: the role of helping to mobilize votes for the party. In the Norwegian context this seems to be an undue simplification. Even though the Norwegian Confederation of Trade Unions (LO) is closely related to the Labor Party, these two "branches" of the labor movement should be treated as separate actors in the study of social politics. Firstly unions have special strategic concerns, e.g. their need to recruit members. Secondly, the policies of the Labor Party have to a varying degree been modelled by the necessity to attract voters among groups outside the ranks of unionized workers (Rokkan, 1966). Thirdly, unions have alternative means at their disposal to achieve social policy ends for their members— namely mutual insurance and collective bargaining.

In the following section we describe how the balance between public and occupational welfare has developed in the postwar period, and we present data on the character, coverage, and distribution of current occupational welfare arrangements. After this descriptive exercise we shall turn to historical analyses of the political forces behind the observed changes in the mixed economy of welfare in two important areas: pensions and sickness benefits.

Occupational Welfare in the Postwar Period

In this section we shall see how the balance between public and occupational welfare has developed over recent decades in Norway. How was employers' expenditure on occupational welfare schemes affected by the rise of an institutional welfare state during the 1960s and 1970s, and what is the benefit structure and coverage of contemporary company-based welfare?

Labor costs statistics are a useful source of information on the historical development of occupational welfare (cf. Martin Rein's chapter in this volume). Since 1954 the Norwegian Employer Confederation has registered the size and composition of total labor costs in mining and manufacturing companies. Since the late seventies similar data have been collected for other important segments of the labor market.

To describe the present benefit structure and the coverage of occupational schemes we shall rely on survey data. It was not until the late eighties that survey data on the coverage of occupational pensions, and in some cases a wider range of benefits, became available.

Marginalization of occupational provision?

The early fifties could be characterized as the golden age of occupational welfare in Norway. Many private companies were voluntarily engaged in a wide range of social welfare activities for their workforces: from housing, canteen and sports facilities to income maintenance in case of sickness, disability, and old age. The company welfare of the time was, however, marked by a distinct dualism between white-collar staff and blue-collar workers.

Generous pension schemes and the right to paid sick leave were traditionally build into the employment contract of civil servants and the salaried staff in private companies. Together with special guarantees for job security, they gave an impression of permanent (lifelong) commitment to the welfare of the salaried staff, which was intended to stimulate loyalty (Øverbye, 1988).

During the sixties and seventies high standards of social security were extended to all wage-earners through general legislation. Table 7.1 presents an account of the resulting changes in the composition of labor costs from 1954 to 1983 in mining and manufacturing industries. Total labor costs are divided into direct pay and indirect labor costs. The latter include paid leave,[1] statutory social security contributions, "customary" social expenditure based on voluntary or contractual arrangements, and other costs connected to the use of labor power[2]. We refer to indirect labor costs as the "social" component of total remuneration for wage-earners, and we treat expenditure on customary social security as a proxy for occupational welfare spending.

TABLE 7.1: *Indirect Labor Costs as a Percentage of Direct Labor Costs*

	Blue collar			White collar		
	1954	1968	1983	1954	1968	1983
Pay for days not worked	8.2	13.6	14.1	10.1	13.8	13.7
Statutory social costs	2.4	12.9	23.5	1.3	11.4	20.8
Customary labor costs	8.3	5.7	9.0	23.5	12.8	10.3
Pension schemes	3.0	1.3	2.6	16.3	7.0	5.5
Paid sick leave	0.3	0.2	0	1.9	2.0	0
Total indirect costs	18.9	32.2	46.6	34.9	38.0	44.8
Gross wages (1954=100)	100	140	190	100	153	192

Source: Norwegian Employers Confederation.

Note: Data for mining and manufacturing companies with more than 50 employees.

The statistics on labor costs in mining and manufacturing collected in Table 7.1 reflect tendencies over three postwar decades which are relevant for all segments of the Norwegian labor market.

First of all there has been a dramatic growth in statutory social security contributions levied on employers. In this period employer contributions were increased to cover the rapidly rising costs of public social security. In 1983 statutory expenditure by employers amounted to 23.5 and 20.8 percent of direct pay for blue and white-collar workers respectively[3].

Secondly, customary social expenditure has declined—especially occupational expenditure on behalf of white-collar employees. In 1954 customary spending accounted for a substantial part of total compensation for white-collar employees. But by 1983 it had dropped from 23.5 to 10.3 of direct pay. In the field of sickness benefits the crowding out of occupational provision was virtually complete. However, expenditure on occupational pension schemes was still quite significant in 1983, and it had even increased for blue-collar workers since the mid-seventies. On average, customary expenditure was 9 and 10 percent of direct pay for workers and salaried staff respectively.

Thirdly, total indirect labor costs have increased far more rapidly than gross wages. In 1954 social labor costs for blue-collar workers

TABLE 7.2: *Non-statutory Social Costs as a Percentage of Direct Labor Costs*

	1978/79	1983	1988
Wholesale and retail trade	5.7	n.a.	7.7
Private insurance	20.1	n.a.	32.3
Banking/finance	15.4	n.a.	22.3
Manufacturing industries	8.7	9.7	n.a.
Electro-chemical		18.3	
Petroleum		16.7	
Metal		8.3	
Wood and timber		4.2	
Textiles		2.6	

Source: Non-manufacturing: Central Bureau of Statistics; Manufacturing: N.A.F.

accounted for 18.9% of direct pay. By 1983 the figure had increased to 46.6%. While the average gross wage for blue-collar workers almost doubled from 1954 to 1983, the "social" component of labor costs quadrupled. For white-collar workers the development has been less dramatic.

Finally, the formerly marked difference in the relative size of the social wage component between white and blue-collar workers had disappeared by 1983. The growth in statutory social security almost eradicated the previous division between of welfare between white and blue-collar workers, which was to a large extent embedded in occupational sickness benefits and pension insurance. While in 1954 expenditure on pensions was on average five times higher for white-collar staff than for blue-collar workers (16.3 versus 3.0 percent of direct pay), it was only twice as high in 1983 (5.5 versus 2.6 percent of direct pay).

These findings lend some support to the thesis that the establishment of statutory social security tends to crowd out occupational provision, and that this in turn has an equalizing effect on welfare distribution between wage-earners. It is also interesting to note that the leveling out of indirect labor costs between manual and non-manual labor took place without a corresponding widening of differences in gross wages.

Thus, welfare state expansion in the sixties and seventies did lead to a partial marginalization of occupational provision. Nevertheless, occupational welfare was still quite significant in 1983, both as a component of total labor costs and as a source of income security among wage-earners. Furthermore, the average figures for blue and white-collar employees conceal substantial differences between industries, companies, and individual employees within each company.

So far we have concentrated on mining and manufacturing industries. Table 7.2 presents the latest available data on non-statutory welfare expenditure in selected industries. It displays a picture of rising expenditure rates with wide and increasing differences between different segments of the labor market.

In typical low-paying industries like wholesale and retail trade, voluntary social expenditure was relatively modest both in 1979 and 1988. Banking and insurance companies, on the other hand, score extremely high on customary social expenditure, and expenditure levels in this sector have been rising throughout the eighties. Occupational pension schemes account for a substantial part of the labor costs in these industries. In 1988 average contribution rates to pension and life insurance schemes amounted to 6.9 percent of direct pay in banking and 14.8 in insurance companies.

The latest available data on social labor costs for manufacturing industries are from 1983. There is, however, strong reason to believe that on average expenditure increased throughout the eighties. The aggregate figures for manufacturing companies conceal wide differences between individual branches. In highly capital-intensive branches, like the electro-chemical and petroleum industries, customary labor costs amounted to 18.3 and 16.7 percent of direct pay in 1983. At the other extreme we find the wood and textile industries where the figures were 4.2 and 2.6 respectively. Throughout the eighties occupational welfare has expanded despite comparatively high standards in statutory social security schemes. The former discrimination between white and blue-collar workers has disappeared, while differences between industries and sectors in the labor market persist.

Benefit structure and coverage

To get a picture of the types of occupational benefits responsible for high and rising expenditure rates we must turn to survey data. The

TABLE 7.3: *Coverage of Selected Occupational Benefits in Private Companies with more than 10 Employees (1990)*

	Percent of companies	Percent of employees
Supplementary pensions	55	77
Accident/life insurance	85	87
Supplementary sickness benefits	55	77
Early retirement pension	9	21
Health insurance	9	7
Extended maternal leave	6	9
Child care	2	13
	(n=403)	(n=94,000)

Source: Hippe and Pedersen (1992)

results of a representative survey in 1990 of companies with more than 10 employees show that many private employers offer a wide range of welfare benefits to their employees. Table 7.3 gives an overview of selected welfare schemes and their coverage in the private sector labor market.

More than half of the private companies in this survey had established supplementary pension schemes for their employees. These companies were responsible for more than ¾ of all employees covered in the survey. Employer-financed life insurance and supplementary sickness benefits for high-income earners were also among the more widespread benefits.

Early retirement schemes, extended maternal leave, child care facilities, and health insurance schemes were relatively rare among private companies. For instance, only two percent of them organized child care facilities for their employees. These were, however, mostly large companies and they accounted for 13 percent of the workforce. Similarly, early retirement schemes are almost exclusively found in large companies. This trend to provide opportunities for exit from the labor market prior to the general retirement age at 67 is a fairly recent phenomena. Often schemes of this type serve as managerial instruments for rationalization and flexibilization without leaving a real choice to elderly employees (Hippe and Pedersen, 1991).

These types of occupational welfare have been established outside the framework of centralized wage bargaining—either unilaterally by employers or through bargaining at the company level. The range of occupational welfare schemes offered by private companies is, however, systematically related to firm size, industry, composition of the workforce (educational background and sex), wage level, and union density (Hippe and Pedersen, 1992). These differences at the company level in turn translate themselves into systematic differences between different categories of wage-earners.

This survey covers only the private sector. There is, however, a long tradition of occupational welfare in the public sector. All employees in central and local government are covered by supplementary occupational pensions (Hippe and Pedersen, 1988; Øverbye, 1990). Public employees also enjoy special welfare arrangements like extended maternal leave and the right to full pay during sickness for income above the ceiling compensated by the statutory scheme.

Among the occupational benefits offered by both private and public employers, supplementary pensions are the most important—whether measured in costs to the employer or in economic significance to the employees. In both the public and the private sectors occupational pensions are of the defined benefits type aimed at supplementing the statutory pension scheme. As shown in Table 7.4, coverage by an occupational pension schemes strongly improves compensation rates—especially for high-income earners.

We may conclude that occupational welfare schemes are more widespread and significant in Norway than has usually been assumed. Despite high standards of public welfare, occupational provision has by no means been completely marginalized. During the last decade expenditure rates and coverage under occupational schemes have been growing, creating systematic differences in the social wage among different segments of the labor market.

In the following sections we shall look more closely at the political process behind historical changes in the social division of welfare in two selected areas: pensions and sickness benefits. We suggest that the structure of trade unionism and wage bargaining is an important factor shaping the mixed economy of welfare, and specifically that the Norwegian trade union movement has been an influential actor in the development of social security throughout the postwar period.

TABLE 7.4: *Rates of Net Pension Compensation for Employees With and Without Occupational Schemes (1988)*

Pre-retirement income	100	150	200	250	300	350	400
No scheme	76	68	64	62	56	52	48
Public sector	90	88	90	91	84	78	72
Private sector	90	88	90	91	90	89	84

Source: Hippe and Hagen (1989)

Notes: The figures are calculated for single pensioners with a full contribution record who retired in 1988. Private sector figures are for a typical scheme.

Case I: The Politics of Public and Occupational Pensions

Norway's first public old-age pension scheme became operative in 1937. It shared the same principal features that characterized contemporary pension legislation in all the Scandinavian countries. Coverage was universal. Benefits were flat-rate and subject to a means test which only excluded a small minority of the relevant population. Finally, the necessary funds were raised partly through general taxation and partly through a premium levied proportionally on all income-earners (Pettersen, 1982).

In the aftermath of World War II there was broad political consensus behind a universalist approach to pension policy. In influential policy documents drawn up by the trade union movement and political parties[4], the existing flat-rate system of old age pensions was proposed as a model for a future comprehensive system of income security.

The flat-rate public pensions gave way to a rapid expansion of occupational schemes. In the early fifties coverage by income-related occupational pension schemes was high among white-collar workers in central and local government, as well as in private companies. A generous pension scheme for civil servants served as a model for the establishment of regular pension schemes covering white-collar employees in local government and in private companies. In the interwar period traditional gratuity pensions for salaried staff were replaced by funded pension schemes organized either through insurance companies or through company-based pension funds. The introduction of funded pension schemes in private companies was stimulated by favorable tax regulations (Øverbye, 1990).

Since the late thirties company-based pension schemes also gained ground among manual workers, especially in large industrial enterprises. However, those employers who chose to include all employees maintained a dual system of pension plans for white and blue-collar workers. While the pension plans for white-collar workers were directly related to salary upon retirement, the schemes covering blue-collar workers aimed at modest flat-rate supplements to the state pension.

Despite the rapid expansion of occupational pension schemes among public employees and core groups in the private sector, almost two-thirds of the total labor force was still without coverage in the mid fifties (Pedersen, 1990).

Pensions as part of centralized bargaining

This growth of occupational pension schemes took place in an industrial relations setting in which a highly centralized LO played a dominating role as representative of wage-earners.

As coverage under occupational pensions increased among some segments of the membership, and wage levels and living standards rose, the demand for a general scheme of supplementary pensions was put on the trade union agenda.

Although LO was never directly hostile to the expansion of occupational pensions, the highly fragmented and employer-dominated system of occupational pensions was deemed unsatisfactory by the LO leadership. First of all, LO could not in the long run accept that a significant part of total compensation was determined outside established bargaining routines. Welfare arrangements at the company level tended to strengthen company loyalties at the expense of broader union solidarity. Secondly, LO estimated that only between 30 and 40% of its active members were covered by occupational pensions in 1958 (Holler, 1958). As long as the question of supplementary pensions was left to individual employers or to local bargaining, the weaker segments of the labor organization's membership were not likely to be covered. Thirdly, the existing occupational pension schemes served to tie employees to their present employer, thus restricting the mobility of elderly workers in particular[5]. Last, but not least, the discrimination practiced by employers between blue and white-collar workers created strong resentment. It served as a focal point for the mobilization of pension demands among unionized workers.

In light of these developments, union strategies changed. The exclusive commitment to flat-rate public pensions from the early postwar period, was replaced by a demand for equal pension rights among all wage-earners. This new approach to pension policy was spelled out at the Trade Union Congress in 1957:

> Our ultimate goal is to secure all wage-earners in this country the same pension rights, whether they are employed in the private sector, or in central or local government.[6]

The focus on equity among wage-earners implied that LO was prepared to accept that benefits in excess of the universal minimum standard should reflect previous earnings. The traditional commitment to a redistributive system of flat-rate pensions gave way to the demand for income-related benefits. The new policy departure also implied an attempt to improve future pension claims for the active population without automatically raising benefit levels for the already retired.

LO considered two alternative strategies to achieve a more comprehensive system of supplementary pensions. One was to follow the example of the Swedish LO (Molin, 1965; Heclo, 1974) and demand a legislated supplementary pension scheme covering all wage-earners. Since the Labor Party had an absolute majority in the Norwegian parliament the conditions for progress by political means seemed favorable. Even so, LO opted for the alternative of placing the demand for supplementary pensions onto its bargaining agenda with the Norwegian Employers' Confederation (NAF).

The decision to take the question of supplementary pensions to the bargaining table was influenced by strategic considerations. In the late fifties LO faced stagnation and even decline in membership. A negotiated pension scheme would allow LO to take the credit for a major improvement in the social standards of wage-earners. Furthermore LO hoped to be able to exclude non-members from the scheme and thereby create a positive incentive to boost membership. It was important to the LO, however, that the scheme should include all unionized workers, and would not encourage division between unions in different branches of the economy.

In the round of centralized wage bargaining that took place in 1958, LO and NAF agreed to establish a supplementary pension scheme (FTP) covering workers in the unionized sector. Details of the scheme were finally agreed in 1960. The new scheme did not satisfy LO's original ambitions. From the outset, benefits were modest and LO failed to achieve a system of automatic indexation. Consequently the FTP scheme could not match the generosity of the income-related schemes for public employees and white-collar workers in private companies. The fact that the NAF insisted on including non-unionized employees in the scheme implied that the potential for boosting recruitment was reduced.

Furthermore, the costs of the bargaining strategy turned out to be high. The centralized bargaining in 1958 involved considerable wage restraint, which created dangerous tensions within LO. Core groups of relatively well paid manufacturing workers were already covered by company-based pension schemes. For these groups the FTP agreement only led to marginal improvements. Unions organizing workers in low-wage industries, however, felt that the costs of the FTP scheme were high in terms of wage restraint and member premiums.

Even before FTP became operational in 1962, the bargaining route to higher pension standards for blue-collar workers seemed to have come to a dead end. However, the FTP agreement helped trigger off a political process which, within a few years, led to the establishment of a statutory supplementary pension scheme.

From bargaining to politics

The introduction of FTP left a significant part of the labor force, and hence the voters, without supplementary pensions. Prior to the 1961 parliamentary election both the Labor Party and the Liberal Party signalled their commitment to extend coverage by supplementary pensions to wage-earners outside LO and NAF and to the self-employed. For both parties electoral support from these segments of the gainfully employed were of strategic importance. Both the Conservatives and the Agrarian Center adhered to the flat-rate principle but advocated a substantial rise in benefit levels. Of course, the unprecedented economic growth of the early sixties helped to put an expansive pension reform on the political agenda.

The 1961 election left the governing Labor Party without a stable majority in Parliament and the pension issue became an object of party tactics (Rokkan, 1966). After a government crisis in 1963 the Labor Party announced plans to establish a statutory pension scheme for all the gainfully employed targeted at two-thirds of prior income. The opposition parties that had originally opposed supplementary pensions, the Conservative Party and the Agrarian Center, decided to give way. As a result, a broad political consensus was achieved for a radical new pensions policy. The new policy departure was welcomed by LO, since the heaviest financial burden was to be carried by the employers and since the reform promised to fulfill the goal of equal pension standards for all wage-earners, as fixed by LO in 1957.

The main features of this new National Insurance (NI) scheme were elaborated by the Labor government in a green paper presented in 1964, and the scheme was finally implemented in 1966 by the non-socialist coalition government elected in 1965. From the outset, NI included old age, disability, survivors and single mothers pensions. The system combined universal basic pensions with statutory supplementary benefits related to contribution record and income level. The supplementary pension was to compensate income up to a ceiling fixed at 2.5 times the average annual wage of industrial workers.

Disagreement on the merits of funding was the only significant flaw in the much celebrated consensus behind the NI reform (Hatland, 1986). The consequences of pension reform for the capital market and aggregate savings was clearly the most controversial issue.

Originally, the Labor Party wanted to build up a large public pension fund while the system matured, in order to stimulate economic growth and to level out the financial burden between generations. However, the idea of a public pension fund, which could become an influential actor in the capital market, met with strong opposition from the Norwegian Employers Confederation and the non-socialist parties. Consequently, the role of funding was deliberately played down by the non-socialist government when the scheme was implemented in 1966.

Later Labor cabinets in the seventies were not prepared to meet the demand for fiscal discipline which would be required to revitalize the NI fund. Instead, expensive social security reforms[7] were carried out without a corresponding increase in premiums. In the same period reductions in employer contributions and member premiums were used as part of incomes-policy packages aimed at reducing growth in labor costs (Kolberg, 1983). Currently the NI system is financed exclusively on a pay-as-you-go basis.

Erosion of state dominance?

At the time of its implementation, the NI system was expected to marginalize occupational provision of pensions. Both proponents and adversaries saw the reform as an attempt to "nationalize" pension insurance. The negotiated FTP scheme was immediately closed down, but occupational pension schemes for public employees and company-based schemes in the private sector were converted to a third tier of pension provision, which aimed to complement basic and income-related pensions from the statutory scheme.

Measured both in financial terms and in terms of the proportion of the labor force covered, occupational pension schemes have expanded—especially since the eighties. By 1993 more than 60% of all wage-earners were covered by occupational pensions. As Figure 7.1 shows, the 20-point overall growth in coverage since the end of the 1970s has encompassed both the public and private sectors.

The steady accretion in coverage by occupational pensions is related to several factors. First of all, the favorable tax regulations for occupational pension schemes were upheld after the introduction of NI in 1967. Growing marginal tax rates have increased the comparative advantages of deferred as opposed to direct wages. Secondly, due to defective indexation the NI scheme has not reached the compensation levels originally envisaged. Thirdly, structural changes in the labor market have increased employment in industries with a long tradition of occupational pensions (public sector, banking and insurance).

Until recently this development was hardly noticed by the public and central policy makers. The growth in occupational pensions has been overshadowed by an accelerating political concern for the financial soundness of NI and the possibilities for meeting the future obligations which are built into the system of income-related pensions. In 1989 a broad coalition in the Norwegian Parliament agreed to substantial cuts in the statutory NI scheme. Concrete measures to reduce compensation rates were carried through parliament in 1990, effective from 1992. These cuts in the public system have of course widened the scope for occupational provision. Many private companies with occupational

FIGURE 7.1: *Percent of Wage-earners Enrolled in Occupational Pension Schemes*

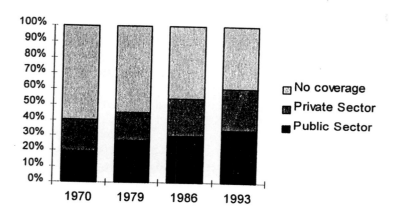

Sources: Hippe and Pedersen (1991) and additional unpublished data.

pension plans have decided to fully compensate their employees for cuts in the public system, while others have left their plans unchanged. The latter option was strongly recommended by the Norwegian Employers Association, but only with very limited success. Similarly, the occupational pension schemes for public sector employees have built-in provisions to automatically compensate for lower replacement rates in the general public pensions.

LO has officially denounced reductions in NI, but without putting too much political muscle into the matter. The LO congress in 1989 actually signalled a new policy on pensions. For the first time since the late sixties LO now opened for the possibility of once again taking pension demands to the bargaining table. A complex mixture of motives has led LO to redefine its policy platform. The existing occupational pension schemes in the private sector are developing outside the centralized system of wage bargaining and without union control. As is turns out, coverage by occupational pensions is lower among LO members than among wage-earners belonging to competing organizations (Hippe and Pedersen, 1988). In this context a centrally negotiated pension scheme for the core membership groups of the LO could become a strategic asset. Finally the potential of a negotiated pension scheme to increase savings and to develop new institutional investors has recently drawn attention both from the LO and the Labor Party.

Interestingly enough the decentralized growth in company-based occupational pensions has also been watched with some suspicion by the Norwegian Employers Association, mostly because of its inflationary effect on labor costs.

As a concrete result of this new orientation towards occupational welfare, LO and the Norwegian Employers Association have set up a general contractual scheme for early retirement covering LO workers in the private sector. The establishment and improvement of this schemes has been a core item in nation-wide wage negotiations in the late eighties and the early nineties. However, except for early retirement the complex of occupational pension schemes has remained completely decentralized in the private sector, and there are no immediate signs that the peak organizations will agree to establish more general schemes or attempt to coordinate the existing structure of company plans.

Case II: The Politics of Public and Occupational Sickness Insurance

The first state-organized system of sickness insurance was agreed upon by parliament in 1909, and became operative three years later. From the outset statutory sickness insurance covered only industrial workers in the lower income brackets. In the following decades the scheme was gradually extended to cover new groups of wage-earners.

In the late thirties a parliamentary committee proposed that sickness insurance should be made compulsory for all residents above the age of 16 (Epland, 1990). By this time a universal approach to sickness insurance was supported by all political parties. In 1953 all wage-earners were included in the statutory sickness benefit scheme and a fully universal scheme was finally reached in 1956 when the self-employed were also included.

The level of compensation was modest, however, and benefits could only be obtained after a waiting period of three days. In early policy documents the political intention had been to secure 60% wage compensation for workers with average incomes. In the early fifties the actual level of compensation for industrial workers was just in excess of one third of the normal wage and, due to a fixed maximum benefit, compensation levels decreased with higher incomes.

The public sickness benefit scheme coexisted with a host of occupational and mutual benefit programs. Public employees enjoyed full income protection by way of legislation (central government) or through wage agreements (local government). For civil servants the right to maintain full salaries during periods of sickness had been ensured by law in 1918. Full pay could be upheld for a period of three months with a possibility for further extension. This generous income protection for public employees served as a point of reference for other occupational groups trying to improve their claim to sick pay.

By and large, the salaried employees in private companies were covered by voluntary sickness benefit schemes which allowed them to uphold full wage compensation for a maximum period of at least one month. The public scheme reimbursed benefits paid by the employers.

Even among manual workers a small but growing minority were covered by occupational sickness benefit schemes. The level of compensation varied from 60-100%. These schemes normally entitled the employees to cash benefits for three months per year after a waiting period of three days.

For workers without occupational coverage, mutual benefit schemes were a widespread alternative. Many trade unions operated their own sickness benefit schemes offering limited supplements to the public scheme. The waiting period in these schemes varied from three days to several weeks.

The complicated mix of sickness benefit arrangements presented a political challenge to the trade union movement. The privileged position of white-collar employees compared to the majority of blue-collar workers had a strong mobilizing effect. At the same time the quality of income protection varied considerably within the blue-collar trade union movement. In the early fifties a substantial minority of LO members (approximately 40 percent) were covered by supplementary sickness benefit arrangements—either occupational or mutual-benefit schemes— while the majority of members were without any form of supplementary income protection.

A higher and more even distribution of benefit levels was considered necessary in order to maintain solidarity across unions. This could be achieved either through a centrally-negotiated scheme covering the core member groups, or through substantial improvements of the universalistic public scheme.

Sickness benefits in centralized bargaining

Prior to the Trade Union Congress in 1953, the LO leadership proposed that the question of incorporating sick pay into the general wage agreement be thoroughly reviewed by an internal committee.

As a long-term objective the committee called for equal treatment of blue and white-collar workers in field of sickness insurance. Its recommendations confirmed that the choice between political solutions and solutions achieved through centralized bargaining was to be decided by practical considerations. The chosen strategy should depend on "which solution gives the greatest chance of rapid and positive results"[8]. The committee drew the conclusion that it was very unlikely to achieve full pay during sickness by political means alone.

During the centralized wage negotiations in 1954, LO and the NAF agreed to build up a fund to finance a future sick pay arrangement. In 1956, the parties agreed to incorporate a supplementary sick pay arrangement into the wage agreement. However, the employers refused to accept the demand by LO that the scheme should cover only union members.

On the basis of this agreement LO succeeded in substantially increasing compensation levels for the majority of wage-earners. Still, the total level of compensation did not exceed 50% for a single worker with average earnings. Another shortcoming was that the negotiated scheme operated with a waiting period of six days, in contrast to a waiting period of three days in the public scheme.

The fact that employers and employees alike recommended that the negotiated scheme be administered by the state and adapted to the public sickness benefit scheme illustrates the close integration of the two schemes. This intermixing of statutory and bargained benefits is a remarkable example of pragmatic and harmonious co-existence of public and private institutions.

It turned out, however, that the practical operation of the negotiated scheme caused considerable friction. After the introduction of scheme, absence increased dramatically. The guarantee fund build into the LO-NAF scheme was rapidly depleted[9]. Therefore LO and NAF decided to curb expenditure by slightly reducing the level of compensation and by increasing the waiting period from six to fourteen days.

As a result of these measures the negotiated scheme eventually started to balance, and it was possible to make minor improvements. In the early sixties the two parties to the agreement cautiously decided to give priority to increasing the maximum period a person could receive sick pay, while compensation levels and the waiting period were maintained.

In 1966 LO and NAF agreed to a declaration of principle that "there was no social justification for maintaining different levels of sickness benefits for blue and white-collar workers" (Petersen, 1975). This meant that NAF was ready to accept the long-term objective of LO to approach full wage compensation for blue-collar workers.

In order to harmonize benefit levels, it was decided to gradually raise the level of compensation in the LO-NAF scheme. As of 1 April 1969, total sick pay for members of the scheme reached 90% of net income. Since the late sixties the waiting period was gradually reduced, and in 1974 it was finally reduced to one day.

From occupational welfare to state responsibility

In spite of the success of the occupational sickness benefit program, an important shift in trade union opinion on sick pay took place in 1970. LO proposed that the occupational scheme be incorporated into a statutory arrangement covering all employees (Petersen, 1975).

The main argument for this proposal was that, in spite of the negotiated scheme, 20% of all employees were without access to supplementary sick pay. The new policy departure on the part of LO was also motivated by the fact that the negotiated scheme suffered from financial troubles. Time and again LO and NAF were forced to take emergency measures, agreed by negotiation, in order to maintain the economic foundation of the scheme.

At the political level the time was now ripe to propose an extension of the public scheme. The broad but still not universal coverage of occupational schemes invited more extended political involvement. In the political debate on sickness insurance even the Conservative Party referred to defects in the existing occupational schemes, and emphasized the need to ensure for the remaining 20% of the working population full compensation for loss of income during illness.

In 1976 a public committee, dominated by representatives of LO and NAF, proposed to extend the state scheme to provide 90% wage compensation from the first day of illness. In minority statements NAF recommended to maintain a waiting period of one day as in the previous negotiated scheme, whereas LO argued in favor of full wage compensation. In the political process following on the committee's recommendations, LO succeeded in persuading the Labor government to support its preference for full wage compensation as from the first day of illness.

A renaissance for occupational provision?

The statutory sickness insurance program became operative in 1978. It completely replaced the previous occupational programs by offering full income protection from the first day of absence. Full compensation was mandated for income below a ceiling which affected only a tiny proportion of wage-earners. By its inclusiveness and its ability to crowd out the former occupational schemes, the Norwegian sickness insurance scheme from 1978 conforms to the ideal-type of the inclusive Scandinavian welfare state.

However, the system had only been in operation for a few years when proposals to curb expenditure were raised on the political agenda. The Conservative government lowered the income ceiling in 1983 and again in 1985 (Hippe, 1988). As from 1985, only income up to just above average wages is compensated by the statutory scheme. The reduced income ceiling in the statutory scheme has reintroduced the need for occupational sickness benefits, and many employers choose to neglect the ceiling and continue to give full wage compensation to all or some of their employees.

The Labor government that took power in 1986 also focused on the need for reductions in spending on sickness benefits. Further direct reduction in benefits levels was not proposed. As a first step a public committee was appointed with an explicit mandate of proposing measures to lowering absence and thereby reducing expenditure. The general elections of 1989 led to a new non-socialist government. In the budget for 1990 it was proposed to reduce wage compensation from 100 to 90 per cent. However, a majority in parliament voted for a withdrawal of the proposal and called on the government to negotiate with the trade unions and the employer organizations to initiate concrete actions to reduce absenteeism. In 1990 LO and NHO (the former NAF) came to an agreement on a joint project that should reduce absence by 10 per cent by the end of 1991.

Absence actually fell quite significantly from 1991 to 1994 and, given the commitments made by both employers and parts of the political establishment, cuts in the public schemes were removed from the political agenda—at least temporarily. Moreover, the non-socialist government coalition broke down because of internal disagreement over the EU issue. This opened the way for a new social-democratic government, strongly committed to support centralized wage determination as a means to keep Norway well in line with a low-inflation international environment. Attempts to reduce public sickness benefits could harm the delicate tri-partite cooperation, and thus threaten the prospects for moderate wage agreements.

Even though a reduction of sickness benefits is not on the immediate political agenda, the issue could well reappear. Inspired by the reductions in sickness benefits undertaken by the Social Democratic government in Sweden, the Conservative Party has committed it self to a proposal for reduced wage compensation. Norway's generous sickness benefits have also been criticized by social-democratic MP's. If the present tendency of declining absenteeism should be reversed a new debate is inevitable. In the event of an eventual political move to reduce compensation levels, LO is already now contemplating the re-establishment of mutual benefit systems and occupational schemes.

Lessons from the Past and Prospects for the Future

The development of public and occupational welfare in Norway is not entirely consistent with a "social-democratic" interpretation of Scandinavian welfare politics.

First of all we have found that occupational welfare plays a more important role than conventionally assumed. Despite the introduction of high standards of public welfare in the sixties and seventies, occupational provision was never completely marginalized. Since the late seventies a rapid growth in occupational pension schemes has further modified the predominance of public pensions. Recent cuts in public pensions will leave even wider scope for occupational provision. In the field of sickness insurance public provision is still predominant, but future reductions in the public scheme could lead in the same direction.

Secondly, the postwar development of pension and sickness benefit schemes was characterized by a positive interplay of public and occupational provision.[10] In the fifties and sixties wide coverage by occupational schemes stimulated rather than blocked attempts to improve public social security standards. In our view this was mainly due to the ability of LO to integrate occupational pensions and sickness insurance into the centralized system of wage bargaining. The political consensus which evolved around proposals to reform public pension and sickness insurance in 1966 and 1978, must be understood in light of the existing public/private mix which had to a large extent been shaped by LO's bargaining efforts. The subsequent parliamentary action was justified on the grounds that wage-earners and self employed outside the LO-NAF bargaining system should share the same standards of income security.

This leads us to the final point: Trade unions have in their own right been important actors in Norwegian welfare politics, and their strategies have not always pointed towards public provision. In the fifties LO decided to rely on the centralized system of wage bargaining in order to establish supplementary income security schemes for unionized workers. This choice was influenced by strategic considerations. LO hoped that negotiated social security schemes would help to strengthen the recruitment potential of its affiliated unions. In the eighties this kind of strategic motivation has once again become manifest.

From a positive dialectic to institutional competition?

While occupational welfare schemes helped to trigger the development of public welfare in the favorable economic and political climate of the fifties and sixties, the logic has now been turned around. Reductions in public welfare standards can further stimulate the growth of a decentralized system of occupational provision.

It appears that the kind of mutually reinforcing interplay between occupational and public welfare of the fifties and sixties was contingent upon a set of crucial conditions that have changed profoundly in the last decades.

Firstly, the "social division of welfare" caused by the present growth in occupational provision does not follow the same visible and clearcut lines as the former dualism between white and blue-collar workers. Differences in occupational pension coverage exist within unions, thereby making it difficult to mobilize for collective solutions.

Secondly, LO no longer commands the same predominant position as representative of wage-earners. In 1956 LO organized almost 50 percent of all employees, while only 10 percent belonged to unions and professional associations outside LO. By 1993 the proportion of wage-earners organized by LO had shrunk to 31 percent, and competing organizations had increased their share of the total labor force to 26 percent (Stokke, 1994). The growing fragmentation of labor organizations creates problems for centralized wage bargaining, and it can force unions to give priority to narrow strategic concerns at the expense of broader solidarity. On the other hand, in contrast with recent developments in Sweden and other European countries, centralized bargaining has so far survived in Norway. So long as this system continues to deliver very low wage inflation, not even the employers see their short-term interests as being served by experiments in decentralization.

Thirdly, reduced economic growth and demographic developments have sharpened distributional conflicts both within and between generations. In the fifties, sixties and seventies improvements in social standards could be achieved without threatening the continuous growth of disposable incomes for wage-earners. In the years to come this will become much more of a zero-sum game. Even under optimistic assumptions about economic growth, the projected rise in social security expenditures over the next decades will leave little room for increasing wage-earners' take-home pay.[11]

Fourthly, increased international economic integration sets new conditions for national welfare policies. Even as a non-member of EU, Norway may be forced to modify her tax structure in order to maintain competitiveness in the European Single Market. Moreover, increasing international competition might create pressure to reduce statutory welfare expenditure, and at the same time block attempts by LO to compensate the loss through centralized collective bargaining.

Norwegian labor organizations increasingly face a dilemma between defending standards in the public schemes and trying to build or improve occupational schemes for their constituencies. If the latter strategy should gain ground or if occupational welfare continues to develop outside the framework of centralized wage bargaining, it could profoundly change the balance between public and occupational welfare.

Notes

1. The category "pay for days not worked" includes vacations and holidays.

2. These could include anything from benefits in kind like subsidized meals and company cars to training and safety measures, some of which are actually mandated.

3. In 1954 blue-collar workers accounted for 81% of total employment in manufacturing industries. The figure had dropped to 64% in 1983.

4. See, respectively, Framtidens Norge (the postwar Labor Party program published by LO in 1944) and the so-called "Joint Program" shared by all political parties in 1945 (Kuhnle and Solheim, 1981).

5. The point was elaborated by a committee appointed by the Trade Union Congress in 1957.

6. *Protokoll fra LO-kongressen 1957.*

7. The age of retirement was reduced from 70 to 67 years and a special supplement for pensioners with a short contribution record was introduced.

8. See the report of the LO "Committee on Pay during periods of Sickness" (published in 1954), page 19.

9. Norwegian Official Report, No. 23, 1976, page 11.

10. The idea of a positive dialectic between public and private pensions was developed by van Gunsteren and Rein (1985).

11. See *Stortingsmelding*, No. 12, 1988-89, page 27.

8

The Development of Occupational Pensions in Finland and Sweden: Class Politics and Institutional Feedbacks

Olli Kangas and Joakim Palme

There are striking commonalities between Finland and Sweden in the provision of old-age pensions. Both countries are exemplars of the ideal-typical "Scandinavian model", where pensions are universal in their coverage, basic pensions are high by international standards, legislated earnings-related pensions guarantee high income security, and finally, the role of occupational pensions is limited. In a wider international perspective, they also appear to be "most similar" cases in several other respects. For historical reasons, the Swedish and Finnish legislatures are rather alike. The similarities of these cases are also obvious when it comes to societal class cleavages and how these are reflected in political party systems. Yet the two countries differ in other respects—namely, the structure of legislated pensions and the division of labor between national pensions and earnings-related benefits, the control of pension funds, and the coordination and role of occupational schemes versus statutory programs.

The purpose of this paper is to examine past, present, and possible future trends in the development of occupational pensions in Finland and Sweden. Our aim is to identify historical and currently emerging interactions between political coalitions, institutional arrangements, and demands for reforms. For the analysis of class politics and institutional feedbacks, Finland and Sweden offer particularly interesting material.

Even though they share common characteristics in terms of social and political structures, the different paths followed by the two countries show how, on the one hand, political actors with the same basic social interests have chosen divergent strategies in the different countries, and how, on the other hand, similar political reforms have been backed by different combinations of political forces.

Class interests are always mediated in the context of existing welfare institutions. But these institutions, in turn, reflect prior investments of power resources and earlier legacies of political coalition-building. Moreover, the structure of social security programs has secondary consequences for both class formation and the legitimacy of the welfare state (Esping-Andersen, 1985; Esping-Andersen and Korpi, 1987). Therefore, the structure and quality of pension schemes, legislated or contractual, is likely to affect the interests of different social classes as regards subsequent policy initiatives in this field. By contrasting and focusing on two country cases we will try to illustrate these dialectics between class politics and institutional feedbacks. For evaluating current program trends and future prospects, institutional differences in the pension programs under study are of great importance.

Structural and Political Characteristics

From a West European perspective, both Finland and Sweden were latecomers to the process of modernization (Flora and Alber, 1981; Kuhnle, 1983). In terms of GDP per capita, Sweden caught up with the leading industrialized countries only after World War II, and Finland's ranking among the world's richest nations is of even more recent vintage. As late as 1950, almost one half of Finland's labor force was still engaged in agricultural production (Alestalo, 1986:26). Finland and Sweden also share a common heritage with the other Scandinavian countries in that their pre-industrial production systems were primarily based on independent family farming. With the advent of industrialization, a tripolar class structure evolved which included capital, labor, and the farmers (Valen and Rokkan, 1974; Alestalo and Kuhnle, 1987). This has meant that in Scandinavian societies, in addition to the two traditional classes in capitalist economies, employers and workers, a third class of independent farmers has continued to play an influential role, not least in the political arena. However, there are and have been remarkable intra-Scandinavian differences as to the relative importance of these three social classes which, in turn, affected choices made in pension policy.

In Sweden, capital and labor organized rather early. The two organizations formalized their relationships in 1906 when they officially recognized each other's right to organize. Collective bargaining was established in the second decade of the century, and the first central agreement was made in 1938 (Kjellberg, 1983:98, 213-221; Elmstedt, 1985). In Finland, relationships between capital and labor were more conflictual and biased in favor of the employers. They were well organized already after the Civil War in 1918, whereas the activities of trade unions were highly circumscribed and periodically even forbidden. Trade unions were accepted as legitimate partners in labor market negotiations only after World War II (Kangas, 1991:143-144).

In Sweden, as well as in Denmark and Norway, the postwar period can be characterized as a time of Social Democratic hegemony (at least until the mid-1970s). In Finland, given its later industrialization and splits within the socialist bloc between the Social Democrats and Communists, the political representation of agrarian interests continued to be very influential until the mid-1960s. During this period, the Agrarian Party came to exercise much of the same kind of hegemonic power as the SAP did in Sweden[1]. The Swedish Social Democrats took advantage of cleavages between the non-socialist parties (Castles, 1978), whereas in Finland, the Agrarian Party could, in a similar fashion, made use of internal disputes both within and between the socialist and bourgeois blocs.

The relative power resources of the Finnish working class improved considerably from the mid-sixties onwards. In 1966 the socialist parties gained an absolute majority in Parliament, and thereafter all but a few cabinets were headed by Social Democrats. The Communists also participated in governments periodically. In the labor market, the interest representation of Finnish workers improved rather dramatically. Due to the extraordinarily rapid structural transformation of the economy, Finland has almost reached the Swedish level of development, although a larger share of the population is still engaged in agricultural production. The size of the non-agricultural labor force has greatly increased, and the relative importance of employees as a social group has grown correspondingly (Alestalo, 1986). In addition the trade union movement, previously divided into bitterly competing Social Democratic and Communist fractions, was unified in 1969. Consequently, union membership density rapidly increased from 31% of the non-agricultural labor force in 1965 to 83% in 1985 (SSIB-data[2]). By comparison, Swedish union density was about 2/3 of the non-agricultural labor force already by 1960 but just below the Finnish figures by 1985 (SSIB-data).

In both countries, there is a single central union confederation for blue-collar workers—SAK in Finland, LO in Sweden. In addition, both have separate union federations for upper- and lower white-collar workers. AKAVA represents the Finnish upper white-collar workers, while SACO plays the same role in Sweden. Lower white-collar workers are represented by the TVK[3] and TCO in Finland and Sweden respectively. Employers have a more centralized representation in Sweden through one organization (SAF), whereas in Finland there are two main federations: one for the industrial sector (STK) and one for banks and commerce (LTK). The former clearly has been the most important in formulating employers' social policy strategies.

Undeniably, these similarities are important for how the present challenges and constraints to welfare programs are perceived. It would, however, be a mistake to try to reduce the sources of current policy outcomes between the two countries to their present configurations of class political power. There are two reasons for this. First, formative policy differences emerged at a time when these power configurations were quite dissimilar. But secondly, yesterday's political conflicts are "frozen" into present-day institutions (see, Korpi, 1985 and 1989). Our working hypothesis is that once different institutional complexes were in place, they began to constrain subsequent policy choices. They have continued to structure the incentives faced by the contending societal actors differently, despite the fact that the countries converged considerably in their political and structural properties. Differences between the two countries with regard to the political backing of pension reforms had important ramifications for the public-private mix in pension policy. We therefore expect that, despite the continuing similarities between the two societies, institutional differences are likely to have crucial repercussions when future challenges and constraints are discussed.

The Legacy of Institutions and Political Coalitions

In both Sweden and Finland, the first pension rights were extended to civil servants. In both cases, the origin of these privileges goes back to Swedish legislation passed in 1778. Later, the public sector schemes were reformed and codified, with a common feature of these programs being that benefits were fixed at a certain share of previous salary, usually two-thirds. Public employees' schemes often served as a point of reference for employees in the private sector (see Øverbye in this volume).

From a comparative perspective, the Scandinavian countries legislated old-age pensions for employees beyond the civil service at an early stage of industrialization. Yet, it was hardly the existence of rather limited occupational programs that triggered the early legislation of pensions in Scandinavia. The causes have to be sought in other circumstances. One important factor was that the growth of the elderly population, the principal user of the poor-relief systems, had strained the budgets of local governments. Therefore, the representatives of municipalities were more than willing to support reforms that promised to shift the burden to the central government (Kuhnle, 1981). Limiting the coverage of welfare programs to the urban working class could not be accepted by the political representatives of the rural population. Only those measures that would also guarantee benefits to farmers were politically feasible (Alestalo, Flora, and Uusitalo, 1985; Baldwin, 1990; Kangas, 1992). Hence, the agrarian structure of society was an important factor behind the universalism of the Scandinavian Model (see Baldwin, 1990). But the timing of the legislation is also important for the development of private pensions, individual as well as occupational. Since the development of occupational programs was fragmented before the introduction of public programs, statutory insurance schemes soon became the most important basis of social security.

Sweden's first pension scheme was implemented in 1913, while Finland's was formed in only in 1937 (Palme, 1990:43). Though these early schemes were called national pensions the actual coverage was not complete due to qualifying conditions. After World War II the national pension schemes were reformed in both countries, and full universalism in terms of complete coverage was accomplished. Social Democrats usually get the credit for the emergence of social policy universalism in Sweden. However, the picture has to be somewhat nuanced. In fact, the balance of attitudes among Swedish Social Democrats vacillated between support for universal flat-rate pensions versus income-tested supplements, but they ultimately adopted positions in favor of the flat-rate principle (Elmér, 1960:85-95). Earners of high incomes who were excluded from means-tested national pensions due to their individual or occupational pensions, also were in favor of abolishing means-testing in order to become eligible. They had to pay for the means-tested benefits via the tax system in any case. Thus it was also in the interests of the upper strata to support the abolition of means-testing (Baldwin, 1990:114).

During the early postwar years, SAF and LO discussed income-related pensions based on collective agreements. Although no agreements were achieved, the discussions revealed that high national pensions without means-testing formed the best platform for the future development of second-tier pensions, since means-testing would reduce the basic pension if the claimant benefited from an occupational pension program (Elmstedt, 1985:196). Therefore, both LO and SAF recommended the most expensive alternative in the national pension debate of 1946. Occupational pensions thus played an indirect role for the legislation by forming the opinions held by the leadership of SAF and LO. The Social Democratic cabinet finally introduced the plan that was approved in 1948 by a large parliamentary majority, making Sweden the first Scandinavian country with flat-rate benefits without means-testing (Olsson, 1990).

In postwar discussions of pension reforms in Finland, the Agrarian-Social Democratic coalition government outlined a scheme which would have included both a basic pension and income-related supplements. However in the Parliamentary debate the Agrarians changed their minds, rejecting the income-related part of the plan. Following agrarian interests, the National Pension Act of 1956 extended universal flat-rate pensions to all citizens. The basic flat-rate payments were improved by income-tested supplements. The scheme was a disappointment to the trade unions and the Social Democrats. Since the previous 1937 scheme was based on funds mainly accumulated by employees' and employers' contributions, the representatives of both sides of the labor market felt that the Agrarians and the National Pension Institute had confiscated pension funds to favor the rural population. This political experience made employee-representatives very suspicious of the publicly controlled National Social Insurance Institution, and produced a search for other institutional solutions when the legislation of second-tier pensions was at stake (Salminen, 1993; Ahtokari, 1988:215).

To summarize, the historical record shows that the political backing of the national pension schemes was different in the two countries. In Sweden basic pensions were instituted rather consensually without sharp cleavages between political parties or socio-economic groups. In Finland the reform was carried through in accordance with Agrarian plans, whereas the representatives of both white- and blue-collar workers were not that satisfied with the legislation.

The institutional setup of national pension schemes also came to differ between the two countries. In Sweden, the national pension was paid out at an equal level to all, from beggar to king, whereas in Finland, national pension provision was divided into a rather low universal basic amount and income-tested supplements. As a result of these differences in the institutional setup and the political coalitions supporting them, the reforms (in spite of similar income replacement rates) came to form different platforms for the subsequent development of other types of pensions, legislated as well as occupational.

The Struggle for Earnings-Related Pensions

Even though basic pensions were universal in both countries and provided a level of economic security which was high by international standards, needs and demands for income replacement were not adequately met by the national pension programs. Moreover there were occupational groups, within both the public and the private sectors, that could count on better compensation for loss of income at retirement. As argued by Øverbye elsewhere in this volume, this is an important mechanism underlying attempts to provide income security via legislation.

In Sweden, the first collective pension fund for white-collar workers in the private sector was founded as early as in 1916. Ten years later, employers and salaried employees established a mutual insurance institution (SPP) that was financed jointly by premiums from both partners. Old age pensions for blue-collar workers were less homogeneous. With few exceptions, they were company-based and not regulated by collective agreements. After World War II, SAF expressed its willingness to expand voluntary insurance schemes in order to solve the pension question through collective agreements, but LO preferred to wait and see what the Social Democrats' plans for a legislated and compulsory pension scheme would offer to blue-collar employees (Molin, 1965; Elmstedt, 1985). The implementation of legislated earnings-related pensions in 1959 followed a social democratic formula. The SAP aimed at a fully "public" solution, a legislated scheme for all employees with pension funds under state control. Although ideologically unanimous in their resistance to the Social Democratic proposal, the bourgeois parties were unable to find a uniform strategy to combat it. Instead, they put forward two separate alternatives. The Agrarian alternative was based on higher basic pensions to be supplemented by voluntary individual insurance provisions. The Conservatives and Liberals also rejected legislated pensions, but instead of individual insurance they advocated pensions contracted collectively by employers and employees. SAF favored the latter model, since it was in accordance with the proposals it developed on occupational schemes in the 1940s and early 1950s.

After an advisory referendum, a governmental crisis, a dissolution of Parliament, new elections, and highly dramatic struggles in Parliament, the ATP (national supplementary pension scheme) was finally passed with a one-vote majority, in precisely the same form in which the Social Democrats had originally proposed it (Esping-Andersen and Korpi, 1987; Olsson, 1990).

In Finland, individual employers also provided some forms of pensions for their elderly workers as signs of gratitude for long and faithful service. But due to the weaker position of employees relative to employers, the Finnish schemes were more scattered and rudimentary than the Swedish ones. Despite the rapid growth of occupational schemes towards the end of the 1950s, the actual coverage of these programs remained limited to only about 20% of private sector employees, mainly white-collar workers in big companies. In order to guarantee portability of benefit entitlements and to extend coverage also to blue-collar workers, the trade unions preferred a legislated and compulsory scheme. At first, such a scheme was decisively rejected by the employers, but their attitudes gradually became more approving. Sweden's SAF advised Finnish employers to accept a legislated scheme if it was possible to make it decentralized, with the funds based in private insurance institutions (Ahtokari, 1988:240). In fact, the Finnish TEL scheme established in 1961 has much in common with proposals favored by the Swedish Employer's Federation in the ATP-struggle.

Why were the representatives of the Finnish trade unions willing to accept such a decentralized model? The most urgent issue for them was adequate income security, so that the question of organizational form was of correspondingly lesser importance. In addition, a centralized scheme would have been channeled through the National Pension Institute, which the employees' organizations held to be unreliable because of its "confiscation" of previous pension funds and its domination by the Agrarians (Salminen, 1993; Ahtokari, 1988:236-238). The Finnish superannuation scheme for private sector employees[4] (TEL) was, hence, a result of a deal between employees and employers. The former got their statutory pensions financed through employer contributions, the latter got a decentralized system, mainly organized through private pension insurance companies.

As with the basic pension scheme, the political coalitions behind the legislation on earnings-related programs were different in the two neighboring countries. In Sweden, parties to the debate were clearly aligned on the left or the right, with the bourgeois parties and SAF all opposing the reform. In Finland the relevant cleavages ran along rural/urban lines, with the Agrarians and Communists opposing the scheme and the Social Democrats[5], Conservatives, the largest trade unions and the employers supporting it (Salminen, 1993). It is interesting to note that the strategies pursued by the Swedish and Finnish Social Democrats diverged with regard to determining the funding and administration of the schemes. This reflects differences in the political context and the distribution of power resources between societal actors. In Sweden, the Social Democrats had a stronger position in the political arena and favored public administration of pension funds, whereas in Finland, due to the political hegemony of the Agrarian Party, the labor movement was not willing to subordinate the funds directly to political decision-making but was willing to keep income-related pensions at least in part a labor market issue. In neither of the two countries were the preexisting occupational programs wide enough in coverage to provide the basis for a 'resistance coalition' of the Danish type (Esping-Andersen, 1985).

The benefit structure of the Swedish and Finnish pension schemes is depicted in Figure 8.1. The Swedish earnings-related benefits are added on top of the basic pensions (which include, since 1969, a supplement paid out to those pensioners with low or non-existent ATP benefits). However, only earnings up to a certain level are taken into account for calculating the ATP benefits, while contributions are levied on the basis

FIGURE 8.1: *The Structure of Pension Benefits in Finland and Sweden*

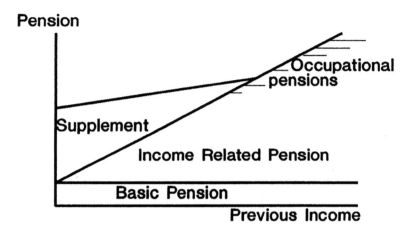

Finland

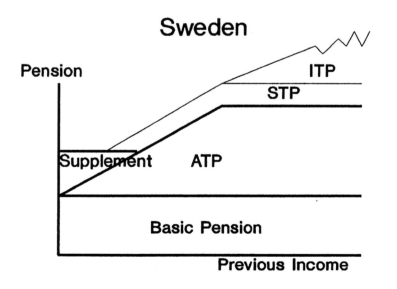

Sweden

of the entire wage. This leaves high-income earners, currently about one tenth of the labor force, without full compensation.

The organization of the Finnish scheme deviates from that in Sweden in several respects. Firstly, the "base amount" of the national pension is much smaller in Finland. Secondly, the receipt of earnings-related pension benefits, whether statutory or occupational, reduces the supplement. In consequence, the maturation of TEL will crowd out national pensions to a much greater extent than will ATP, or occupational pensions for that matter, in Sweden. The pension-income test in the national pension scheme has also reduced the marginal utility of occupational benefits, which partly explains why they play a smaller role in Finland than in Sweden. Finally, there is no income ceiling for benefits purposes, which may have important implications for the legitimacy of the scheme among high-income earners.

ATP as well as TEL benefits have been entirely financed by employer contributions that by now equal 20% and 14%, respectively, of the payroll. As of the beginning of 1993, employees will also participate in the financing of TEL, with gradually increasing rates of contribution.

In both countries the financial construction of these schemes is a mixture of pay-as-you-go and funding methods. Yet, when it comes to funding important differences are to be found, especially in how the accumulated funds are administered and invested. The Swedish scheme substantially increased public control of credit markets and ATP assets were mainly used to finance public housing construction (Esping-Andersen and Korpi, 1987:67-68). The financial form of the ATP-pensions and the use of the assets did not satisfy the employers.

Finland's TEL-funds constitute a very important source of investment capital. In 1990 TEL institutions accounted 14% of the total credit stock—second only to commercial banks (Kommittébetänkande, 1991b:96). The investment of TEL assets can take place in two ways: they can be channeled into the credit market either through relending or investment loans. Relending means that employers can borrow back up to 65% of their contributions[6]. The funds that remain after pension payments and relending are invested according to recommendations made by the TEL Advisory Committee, which consists of representatives from the pension institutions and from labor market organizations. Hence, the employers' desire for access to and control over investment capital was satisfied via the legislated scheme. As the providers of TEL pensions, insurance companies profited too, which muted their resistance to the legislated and compulsory scheme. They placed more emphasis on consolidating ranks in the campaign for legislated pension assets than on trying to promote alternative insurance based policies.

Occupational Pensions

In order to comprehend occupational pension arrangements in the two countries under consideration, it is essential to draw a distinction between the public and private sectors.

Public Employees

The implementation of general supplementary programs gave rise to some changes in other schemes. In Sweden, pensions for public sector employees were integrated into the ATP scheme. The amount of the state pension was to be calculated as the difference between the target replacement level and what was paid out as ATP benefits. As a result, the maturation of the ATP program has gradually eroded the relative importance of public sector occupational benefits. The share of public employees' pension expenditure in total pension outlays has decreased from 22% in 1965 to only 6% in 1990, as can be seen in Table 8.1. Another factor working in the same direction was the lowering of the normal retirement age in general public programs in the mid-1970s. This decreased the costs for the public employee scheme, which traditionally had a lower retirement age. Even though in both countries most state employees can still retire younger than their private sector colleagues, they are in both countries losing their relative privileges.

In Finland existing arrangements for public employees' schemes were neither financially nor administratively merged with TEL[7]. The benefits have been somewhat more generous: they have replaced 66% of the final salary after 30 years of employment compared to 60% after 40 years in the private sector; the normal retirement age has been 63 years compared to 65 for employees covered by TEL. Thus the occupational "bonus" was built into the legislated scheme for the public sector employees, rather than being paid through additional and separate arrangements as in Sweden. However, the primary function of the Finnish public sector employees' schemes was to provide income-related pensions in the same way as the TEL program.

TABLE 8.1. *Occupational Pensions in Finland and Sweden 1960-1990.*

	Coverage (% of all employees)						Premiums (% of payroll)		Share of Total Pension Expenditures (%)						
	Public		Private		Total				Public			Private		Total	
	Fin	Swe	Fin	Swe	Fin	Swe	Fin	Swe	Fin1	Fin2	Swe	Fin	Swe	Fin	Swe
1960	23	n.a.	15	16	38	n.a.	2.1	2.2	24.4	2.4	17.0	4.3	4.6	n.a.	21.6
1965	23	22	13	23	36	45	1-2	3.0	23.7	2.4	22.0	4.7	4.4	7.1	26.4
1970	23	20	18	28	41	48	1-2	3.8	26.4	2.6	18.6	4.3	4.6	6.9	23.2
1975	24	24	19	61	43	85	1-2	6.8	24.4	2.4	12.8	3.9	7.5	6.3	20.3
1980	29	28	18	66	47	94	1-2	8.3	24.3	2.4	8.6	4.1	5.5	6.5	14.1
1985	34	36	15	73	49	100	1-2	7.7	22.5	2.3	7.1	3.9	6.8	6.2	13.9
1990	35	35	14	74	49	100	1-2	6.9	24.4	2.4	6.2	3.7	5.8	6.1	12.0

Notes: "Public" refers to public sector employees' schemes; "Private" refers to private sector employees' schemes. In the coverage figures for the public sector schemes in Finland there is some overlapping which exaggerates the actual coverage. 'Fin1' refers to total pension expenditures in the public schemes. 'Fin2' refers to the "purely" occupational part of the public scheme. Since the replacement level in the public employees' schemes has been ten percent higher than in the statutory program which covers the private sector, ten percent of the total expenditure of the Finnish public sector schemes was estimated to be "purely" occupational.

Sources: Kangas & Palme (1989); *Statistical Yearbook of the Social Insurance Institution of Finland* 1985 and 1990; Olsson (1990); *Statistical Yearbook of Sweden* 1992, p. 222; Swedish Employers' Federation (1991); OECD *Quarterly Labour Force Statistics*, No. 4, 1991.

224   *Olli Kangas and Joakim Palme*

The different character of Finnish and Swedish arrangements for public employees is also reflected in pension expenditures. In Sweden, only 6% of pension expenditures go to the public employees, while the corresponding share in Finland is as high as 24%. As Table 8.1 shows, when estimating cross-national differences in the privileges enjoyed by public vs. private employees, the distribution of pension expenditures is not a sufficient measure. Expenditures tell more about the functional division of labor between different schemes than about the actual status differences between various employment categories.

Private Sector Employees

When the debates on legislated pensions first began, Sweden and Finland did not differ dramatically in the extent of coverage or the economic importance of the occupational schemes (Table 8.1). However the Swedish occupational schemes (for example SPP) were nation-wide, while Finland's were company-based. Therefore, the schemes had different ramifications for the division of labor between legislated and occupational benefits. The institutional solutions adopted, in turn, conditioned the subsequent development in the public-private mix and the two countries took partially different paths.

When the ATP struggle began, a network of union-based white-collar schemes already existed, as shown above. In the ATP issue one of the most crucial questions for salaried employees was how to coordinate the existing SPP scheme with ATP. The issue was solved through the implementation of an additional program, ITP, based on an agreement between SAF and salaried employees in the private sector (Molin, 1965:115-118).

The ATP scheme can be seen as an attempt by LO to extend white-collar privileges to its blue-collar constituency. But due to the implementation of ITP, this maneuver became as tricky as shooting at a moving target. After the implementation of legislated benefits LO changed its views on occupational pensions, and to bridge the benefits gap between ordinary workers and salaried staff it insisted on an occupational scheme for the former. The bargaining on this issue with SAF resulted in a special supplementary pension-scheme (STP) for blue-collar workers in the private sector (Elmstedt, 1985:202). Because of Sweden's highly centralized labor market organizations and bargaining structure, in contrast to other OECD countries, Swedish occupational pensions came to cover all private sector employees (Table 8.1).

Because of labor's relative weakness, all forms of occupational welfare in Finland were undeveloped at the end of World War II. After the war, cooperation in the labor market rapidly increased. With respect to pensions, this expanding activity was formalized in 1955 by an act on voluntary pension foundations. As a consequence, the number of foundations increased from 65 in 1955 to 445 in 1962 (Ahtokari, 1988:230). Against this background it is obvious that if the legislated pension scheme had not been accepted, the foundation alternative would have been the most probable option to meet the growing need for income security. Although for reasons already described this scenario did not materialize, the act had two important consequences for the structure of the TEL scheme. First, the replacement level was fixed at 60% of previous earnings, precisely as in the voluntary schemes. Second, the funded premiums not needed for current outlays were partially directed back to employers in the form of loans from the pension foundations. The feature was replicated in the structure of the TEL system. This exemplifies how "private" programs may affect the formation of "public" schemes.

There are also obvious feedback loops in the coordination of occupational and legislated benefits. In Sweden, coordination mainly follows the "floating" principle—that is, occupational benefits are added on top of the ATP pensions. In principle, both STP and ITP now provide an extra pension corresponding to 10-15% of pensionable income. Thus, the total gross replacement rate is 70-75% of previous earnings. However, there are differences between the two schemes having to do with how benefits are calculated and with the normal retirement age, which render ITP benefits more valuable (Elmér, 1986:132). The relative importance of occupational pensions also varies between income groups. Because of the ceiling built into ATP, a move upwards on the income ladder decreases the compensation level. Consequently, ITP benefits have acquired additional importance.

In Finland, occupational systems were closely integrated into the TEL system. First, the existing pension institutes could acquire responsibility of the TEL scheme together with the private insurance companies. Secondly, these institutes were given the option of guaranteeing additional TEL benefits for those interim cohorts that, due to their advanced age, had no possibility to accumulate full pension 'percentages'. In principle entry to these schemes is voluntary, but after entrance benefits are completely regulated by TEL legislation. In practice this means that the portability, indexation, and target benefit levels in occupational schemes are the same as in TEL, but a full pension can be accumulated in less than 40 years. Thus, the coordination of second- and third-tier pensions in Finland follows the "difference" principle—that is, the amount of the occupational benefit is determined as a difference between the targeted 60% level and the actual TEL level. The closer the gradually-maturing TEL pension comes to the target level, the less room is left for occupational benefits. Indeed, since the late 1970s occupational pensions have lost their relative importance. This declining trend in coverage is likely to continue, since the influx of new members is gradually ebbing away.

Different institutional solutions have also led to somewhat different trends in expenditures. In Sweden the maturation of ATP has eroded the importance of occupational schemes, except in the public sector. In the private sector the significance of collective programs has increased, but not linearly (Table 8.1). In 1990 occupational pensions accounted for 5.8% of total pension expenditures[8]. The corresponding figure for Finland was 3.7%. The cost shares of Finnish occupational pension premiums have been rather constant, accounting for 1-2% of the payroll. In Sweden occupational pension premiums as a percentage of total remuneration increased until the early eighties, but have since then been on the decline. However, closer inspection shows that the expenditure share of premiums to occupational benefits for blue-collar workers have increased rather linearly from 0.6% in 1960 to 6.3% in 1991, while the share going to reimbursements increased continuously to 11% in 1980, thereafter declining to 6.8% in 1991 (SAF, 1991). Lowering of the normal age of retirement in the statutory schemes in the mid-1970s from 67 to 65 years of age has contributed to cutting costs. Previously, white-collar employees could retire at 65 with a full scale occupational pension being paid for two years until the normal retirement age of the statutory schemes was reached. Then the payment of the occupational benefit continued, but now on top of the statutory pension.

These trends are also reflected in the macroeconomic importance of occupational pension funds. In Finland, the size of these funds has decreased with declining coverage. The opposite is true for Sweden, where the degree of funding is higher in the private sector employees' occupational programs than ATP. As a consequence of the maturation of the occupational schemes, their size relative to the ATP fund has increased from 20% in 1975 to 42% in 1990.[9]

One may wonder why SAF accepted costly occupational schemes on the top of the generous ATP benefits. First, there was the institutional issue. The white-collar worker's ITP emerged as a solution to problems with coordinating existing occupational schemes with legislated pensions. The implementation of STP was a result of the pressure from LO to guarantee blue-collar workers comparable benefits. Once instituted, these schemes have more or less automatically expanded due gradual maturation and coordination with legislated pensions. Secondly, from the employers' point of view it is more advantageous in certain cases to pay insurance premiums for job-related benefits rather than the corresponding sum in wages, provided that the employers can use the funded assets. Such an arrangement may be preferable—from both the employer's and employees' points of view—if there is little scope to secure real wage increases due to inflationary pressure and high marginal tax rates (Esping-Andersen, Rainwater and Rein, 1988:344). All these requirements were fulfilled in the Swedish situation. In addition, compared to company-based schemes, universal collective insurance offered advantages to the employers: SAF could coordinate occupational pensions more effectively, facilitate labor mobility, and equalize the conditions of competition between companies (Edebalk and Wadensjö, 1988). However, the Employer Federation is willing to abandon centralized wage negotiations that have been a corner stone in the traditional "Swedish model". In consequence, branch and company level negotiations on wages and occupational fringe benefits will be more important (Lewin, 1992). This may diminish the relative role of the centralized ITP and STP schemes. In this context it should be noted that the tax reform of 1991 has considerably curtailed the advantages of paying out occupational pensions rather than ordinary wages, which may decrease employers' interest in further developing the occupational schemes.

In many respects the Finnish TEL scheme qualifies as an "ideal" pension scheme according to the standards of Swedish employers during the ATP struggle: a decentralized scheme administered by private insurance companies, with guaranteed employer access to pension funds. The marginal utility of occupational schemes would by contrast have been rather limited. In addition, since there has always been a surplus of labor in Finland employers have had no acute need to try to attract employees with extra welfare arrangements. In this respect STK's policy has been very restrictive. In its circulars the employers' association cautioned its members against using occupational pensions as tools for personnel management, which is held to be a slippery and costly method.

Challenges and Constraints

The most significant expansion of the Scandinavian welfare states began in the early 1960s. Characteristic of this period was that, following the lines of Keynesian doctrine it was believed that social policy promoted growth and balanced fluctuation in economic cycles. Today, the golden age of economic growth has apparently passed. The positive Keynesian link between social policy and the macro economy has been called into question, and it is often maintained that the public sector has became an obstacle to economic growth. Sweden, in particular, has been used as an example of this postulated state of affairs, yet neo-liberal thinking of this type has also come to dominate political rhetoric in the other Scandinavian countries.

In addition to the challenges posed by lower growth rates, both countries face increases in the proportion of elderly in their populations, a trend which will accelerate rapidly over the next few decades (OECD, 1988). Moreover, the trend towards early retirement will in a the long run inevitably lead to booming pension expenditures which will increase the rates of employers' contributions.[10] When both countries are trying to acclimatize to the European Common Market, the problem will be accentuated. Therefore, various ways to lessen the burden upon employers and the public sector dominate the public debate.

A common problem in Finland and Sweden, as well as most other countries with generous public pensions, is the low rate of household saving (Ståhlberg, 1988). Pension funding, collective or individual, is held to be one solution to the resultant problems of financing capital investment.

In Sweden, a further challenge is posed by the pension ceiling in ATP. Because this is indexed to the development of consumer prices it has not kept pace with recent wage developments. More and more Swedes have therefore reached above the maximum limit. It has been calculated that in a few decades, over half of all wage-earners may have incomes exceeding the ceiling. According to this projection, ATP will gradually be transformed into an extended basic pension. The more rapid the rate of economic growth, the quicker this process will be.

Hence, the Swedish and Finnish pension schemes are facing challenges which show both commonality and variation, but the differences in institutional solutions are likely to condition the responses of the actors involved. In order to gauge these responses, we conducted a series of interviews during the fall of 1991 with representatives of the major interest organizations and political parties in Finland and Sweden. The interviews were open-ended but structured around a set of pre-determined issues; perceived challenges and constraints for the future, the relative role of occupational programs in the public/private pension mix, early retirement, costs, and funding. In addition to these interviews, we have been able to scrutinize the views of the central actors via official documents. In the Swedish case, the major interest organizations submitted comments to the review of the pension system carried out by a parliamentary pension committee in October of 1991. In Finland, two parliamentary reports on the retirement issue were recently released (Kommittébetänkande 1991a and 1991b).

The Relative Role of Occupational Programs

One of the most crucial questions for the future of the Swedish pension system is treatment of the ATP income ceiling. In the 1991 report of the parliamentary pension committee the problem was recognized and outlined in detail, but the committee did not provide any recommendations. In its response to the report, the National Social Insurance Board (RFV)—responsible for running the public programs—insisted that the income ceiling should be raised immediately in order to secure future pensions.[11]

The strongest support for reforming the ATP scheme, by tying the pension ceiling to changes in the wage level, is found among the leaders of the white-collar TCO unions. Yet the TCO is also anxious to protect the role of occupational pensions. They are well aware that in the private sector it would be very difficult to negotiate with the employers for full compensation if a very large proportion of their members' incomes exceeded the ATP ceiling and if the replacement levels of ATP benefits were substantially decreased. According to the TCO, well-functioning occupational welfare requires a well-functioning public sector. Therefore, the present division of labor between public and occupational pensions is preferred.

The blue-collar union confederation (LO) also advocates an increase in the ATP ceiling, but does not regard the task to be as urgent as TCO. So far, rather few LO members have earnings above the ATP ceiling. With the recent change of government, LO has also had to confront the issue of which strategy is best for securing future pensions. It might be that, if the political commitment to public welfare programs diminishes, it is better to negotiate on pensions with the employers than with the politicians.

Not surprisingly, the upper-level white collar union, SACO, whose members are most affected by the ATP ceiling, wants to strengthen the connection between contributions and benefits. They are also critical of the fact that contributions are levied on income above the pension ceiling. However, SACO is reluctant to make changes within the framework of ATP. Following a proposal by its chief economist, the organization instead suggests that ATP should be gradually replaced by a new system based on defined contributions. Sweden's largest private insurance company, Scandia, is promoting a similar scheme with direct links between contributions and benefits.

The employers are very concerned about the present ATP program and they advocate a radical solution—the gradual abolition of the system. In SAF's model of a future pension system, earnings-related pensions are to be financed through compulsory but individual pension insurance premiums which are paid by employers. In the mean-time the ATP ceiling on earnings for contribution and benefit purposes should be maintained at its present level.

In the long run, such proposals would imply a remarkably increased scope for occupational and/or individual pension programs. Such alternative models evoke support among all of the bourgeois parties. Interestingly enough, the non-socialist motifs employed in the struggle over ATP three decades ago still have a strong bearing. But in contrast to that episode, the bourgeois parties are now more on the offensive, while the SAP has been taking a defensive stand. When in government the Social Democrats did not take any decision to cut back benefits—instead, as indicated above, it is precisely political "non-decisions" that will automatically lead to erosion of the ATP scheme and, simultaneously, to the growing importance of other pension forms. During the 1991 election campaign Social Democratic party leader Ingvar Carlsson, clearly declared that the party wants to maintain the present ATP-system, and raise the income ceiling if needed. But the views on this question are diffuse among the different ranks of the party. In fact the same is also true of the other parties.

In contrast to the Swedish situation, the Finnish TEL scheme enjoyed strong support from all major trade unions, although for differing and even contradictory reasons. The upper white-collar union AKAVA was most concerned about the possible implementation of pension ceilings and cuts in replacement levels. The reason is obvious: its members will be hit first. The white-collar workers fear that to be effective in cutting costs, a pension ceiling must be rather low, thereby threatening the pension security of TVK-members. The blue-collar unions (SAK) defended the present pension system since they were afraid that income ceilings would create complementary occupational programs which would disproportionately favor high-income earners and thus have undesirable distributional consequences.

The present design of the pension system is nevertheless a contested political issue in Finland. The Center Party in particular, following its traditional emphasis on basic pensions but with the addition of neo-liberal economic thinking, advocates pension ceilings and reductions in the TEL pension. This is justified by references to distributional justice and to deteriorating state finances. The former Communists are also in favor of fortifying basic security at the expense of income security. The possible expansion of occupational benefits to compensate for decreases in the legislated schemes are not mentioned in this discussion. Neither is the fact that TEL (operating in the private sector) has very little to do with the public finances discussed. These aspects of the question are emphasized by the Social Democrats, who are also most explicitly opposed to lowering the replacement rates. The Conservatives, previous supporters of TEL, are split on the issue. On the one hand, there is an employer-friendly faction insisting on considerable reductions in all social benefits. The conservative Minister of Finance, for example, insists on reducing the replacement levels in the earnings-related programs to 50%. This might enhance a shift towards a minimal welfare state where the state guarantees the basic security. Individuals can complete the minimum level by private initiatives. On the other hand, a number of conservative MPs representing the interests of the party's white-collar social constituency oppose such plans.

Interestingly enough, traditional cleavages between supporters of national basic pensions and the TEL scheme, previously "frozen" in the pension institutions, seem to reemerge in this context. However, there is one crucial difference compared to earlier pension debates. The employers are not as willing as previously to support TEL and complain about its high future costs, claiming it will cause serious problems for Finnish industry's international competitiveness.

Funding

Funding is not really a political issue in Finland. Pension funds, legislated or occupational, are managed by private insurance institutions. These collective funds are not seen as a socialist threat, which satisfies the political right, but are under some kind of collective control, which satisfies the political left. Thus, there are no grounds for a socialist/non-socialist divide as in Sweden. However, the present financial system is under pressure. First, the economic recession has implied severe losses since many companies that have used the option to relend their pension contributions have gone bankrupt. Secondly, among the employers there is a growing willingness to abandon the funded part of TEL in favor of a pure pay-as-you-go scheme. The reason is that, at least in a short run, it would reduce employers' social security contributions. That pension funds are sources for investment capital is subordinated to the goal of cutting indirect labor costs as much as possible.

Bureaucrats and experts are of the opposite opinion. They are convinced of the importance of pension funds for capital accumulation, as are many economists (e.g. Koskela, 1991). Since the TEL funds operate in the private sector, an increase in the funding has been regarded as an efficient way of increasing the rate of saving and accumulating capital for investments. Thus, the shift towards occupational schemes would make no difference in terms of capital formation.

In order to strengthen the financial basis of employment-related pensions, from the beginning of 1993 employees have been obliged to participate in scheme financing with gradually growing fees. (As a quid pro quo, employees' organizations are insisting that they be granted more administrative control over the pension funds.) Due to the present desperate economic situation in Finland, the enlarged employees' contributions will first be used to relieve the burden of employers. It is not clear whether there will subsequently be any decrease in the level of pension funding.

There are several reasons why funding has become a contested issue in Sweden. First is the traditional socialist/non-socialist conflict over the size and character of the pension funds in the ATP program. From time to time over the past 30 years, these funds have been subject to heated political discussion. The most recent debate came during the 1991 election after a Social Democratic proposal to let the funds buy company shares on the stock market. Even though the proposal have would have limited the funds' ownership share to 25% of any given company, and 25% of total stock market transaction volume, the proposal was heavily criticized by the bourgeois parties as a socialist threat.

A proposal was also made to merge wage-earner funds with pension funds, providing additional fuel for discussion. This has its roots in the intense political controversies over the wage-earner funds that have been going on in Sweden for more than a decade. Even though the size of the wage-earner funds has been smaller than expected, the issue has ideological connotations and tremendous symbolic weight. The debate is confined to the public funds whereas the occupational funds (ITP and STP) have not been considered problematic, despite the size and growing importance of this kind of collective ownership. Interviews with union leaders and employers' representatives confirm this impression. Neither side could give any examples of conflicts that have occurred over how to invest fund assets. Compared to insurance companies, the collective schemes have actually proved to be rather successful at management.

Costs

If funding is an issue in Sweden and not in Finland, the opposite is true when it comes to early retirement. The most acute and costly problem of Finnish pension policy is the extension of early retirement, which is taking place at a rate among the highest in the OECD area. Recent reforms have included an increase in the normal retirement age for public employees, in order to harmonize the scheme's rules with those governing TEL benefits. The accumulation rates of pension entitlements and the target levels for earnings replacement have been harmonized as well. This means that the occupational privileges which public employees have traditionally enjoyed are now abolished. These innovations indicate that, in addition to "pension diffusion" from civil servants to private sector employees, causal loops may also run in the other direction.

In Sweden, the generous rules for benefit calculation under ATP have caused problems. In the long run, the pension system is financially unstable: people get more than they pay in (Kruse, 1988). One way to control expenditures is to retain the ceiling at its present level. This would limit the growth of ATP expenditures in relation to GDP, even in the long run (SOU, 1990). Yet, if public pensions diminish in importance people will seek alternative ways of achieving income security—including the expansion of occupational benefits and individual insurance policies. Thus, the relative costs would shift from the public to the occupational schemes, but might still remain at the same overall level (Kangas and Palme, 1992).

However, in times of slower economic growth and harder competition in expanding international markets, employers will not accept the shift towards occupational benefits as easily as they did previously. For example, Swedish employers envision cost reductions by lowering the target replacement rates of the compulsory schemes, public and occupational, to about 50%, down from the 75% level of today.

Future Prospects

The "Scandinavian welfare model", with its heavy bias towards statist solutions, is facing new challenges and constraints. Different voices are calling for a change in the division of labor between public and private welfare institutions. This might, probably unintentionally, increase the scope for occupational welfare programs although such prospects are of clearly divergent character in our two countries.

Finland

The Finnish scenario implies that the tendency towards decreasingly important occupational pensions will persist. However, there are at least three factors that might reverse this trend. First, despite the fact that the construction of the Finnish TEL scheme is much more favorable to employers than the Swedish scheme—which the Finnish employers seem to be fully aware of—the STK still complains of the high indirect labor costs caused by the pension schemes. Recent measures taken by the Finnish parliament to partially relieve employers of this burden may, in the long run, result in a pure pay-as-you-go scheme. This might encourage expansion of funded occupational pensions in order to meet the need for capital accumulation.

A second factor that may give impetus to the growth of occupational schemes concerns the future levels of statutory pensions. At present, all major unions are satisfied with the replacement levels and the general framework of the existing pension schemes—consequently, further occupational arrangements are regarded as unnecessary. At the same time, they would all be willing to settle for occupational pension schemes in the event that the target pension level is reduced or a pension ceiling is introduced. Even though SAK, the blue-collar confederation, is concerned about the distributional consequences of such schemes, it would still feel obliged to negotiate on occupational pensions in order to achieve comparable conditions to salaried employees. This scenario, if realized, would have much in common with Swedish developments during the 1960s and 1970s. At first, certain employees in key positions are provided by extra pensions as fringe benefits, and then other groups also insist on similar pension rights (on this diffusion process, see Øverbye in this volume).

Thirdly, there has traditionally been a surplus of labor in Finland. The employers had no need of company-based welfare arrangements in order to attract employees. Consequently, occupational pensions have not been used as personnel management measures. But projected demographic changes foresee a gradual decrease in labor supply over the next few decades (Romppanen, 1991). Even if it is a little difficult to believe such forecasts with unemployment presently (during the fall of 1994) at 20%, demographic trends will in the long run intensify competition for labor between individual employers. This is true especially of employers of well-educated and skilled labor in expanding export sectors. If this competition coincides with the two above described prospective tendencies already hypothesized, a rapid expansion in occupational pensions may be anticipated.

Sweden

In the early 1990s the soil appeared to be more fertile for an expansion of occupational pensions in Sweden. With continued growth in real wages, it appeared that more people would have to rely on occupational benefits to obtain adequate income replacement. For white collar employees, occupational benefits would compensate more or less automatically for the loss of public provision, whereas blue-collar workers would have to negotiate for improvements because of the flatter character of their benefits. Adding to this momentum was the fact that all pension reforms tend to carry within them a historical legacy of coalition-building. Early in the decade the socialist/non-socialist divide that lay behind the ATP reform appeared to be reemerging. Several of the parties in the 1991-94 bourgeois government openly supported the notion that the state should provide only minimum income security. These parties were also concerned about Sweden's inadequate level of savings and the alleged "hazards" of state control over the funds in the ATP—additional reasons for their ambition to increase private savings, not least pension saving. One way to encourage this would have been to lower replacement levels and encourage compensatory private initiatives, for example by improving tax deductions. Although the intention was to promote individual insurance, occupational schemes could have proven to be the winner (even though our interviews suggested that this would have been an unintended consequence).

In 1994, however, the Swedish parliament took a decision about "guidelines" for the future of the public pension system which is likely to change the preconditions for the development of occupational programs (Palme, 1994). The decision concerned the principles for undertaking reform of the old-age pension system. It represented both continuity and change with respect to the old system. The continuity is to be found in the underlying goal that a universal publicly administered system should provide for both basic and income security (cf. Palme, 1990:86-87). The changes lay in the qualifying conditions, indexing of benefits, funding, and co-ordination between the basic and earnings-related benefits.

In the future, assuming that the new guidelines are implemented, earnings-related pensions will be shifted from a "defined benefit" to a "defined contributions" formula. However, it will continue to be a pay-as-you-go scheme, and the funding will be "fictitious". The system will be indexed to the development of real wages which means that the income ceiling for benefit purposes will be raised if real wages grow. This indicates that the present division of labor between the public and occupational programs will be maintained.

The basic pension will only be paid as a supplement for those with no or low earnings-related benefits. The coordination of the two kinds of benefits will in fact work in a fashion very similar to the Finnish system.

The earnings-related benefits will form the first-tier of the pension systems of both countries, and minimum pensions will only be used as supplements. This shift will be a relatively small step for the individual pension recipient but in terms of policy principles it represents a big step.[12]

A new element of the compulsory pension system is an individual and fully funded benefit to be based on contributions equivalent to 2% of the gross wage. Since each individual is supposed to be able take the decision about the placement and management of the funded contribution, this program implies a shift of the control of pension funding from the public to the private sector.

The new reform guidelines were established as a compromise between the bourgeois parties and the Social Democrats. This is reflected in their content. Each of the parties to some extent had to abandon old views. The political commitment to a "big state" in the provision of old-age pensions stands in clear contrast to the ideological preference of the bourgeois parties for a "small state". It is likely that the parties to the right were influenced by the fact that the old-system had generated interests and expectations among large segments of their own electorates. It simply made it difficult to abandon the public commitment to secure retirement incomes on purely ideological grounds. On the other hand, the Social Democrats also had to make certain concessions. They had, for example, to abandon "their" defined benefit plan (ATP) and introduce more market-oriented mechanisms into the system, such as the individual premium reserve program with its radical implications for the control of funding.

Conclusion

Class politics and institutional feedbacks are both crucial for explaining the development of occupational pensions in Finland and Sweden. It is evident that there was a strong impact from the class structure on the first pension institutions, which were the result of political coalition-building between workers and farmers. When we come to the earnings-related part of the programs, the class-political influences are also clear, but now the coalition was between the working and middle classes. Since the founding coalition was broader in Finland, income security was more extensive and support for the system was wider in class terms.

Differences in public schemes have clearly been important for the evolving differences between the two countries in occupational pensions. Given the level and structure of both the basic and earnings-related public programs in Sweden and Finland, one would certainly expect differences in the demand for additional occupational benefits. Lower replacement levels for earnings-related benefits in Finland would imply slightly greater pressure for occupational benefits. However, other institutional factors have undermined this dynamic. The lack of an income ceiling in Finland means less demand for occupational programs from high income-earners. The income testing of the supplementary amount of the national pension further weakens interest in occupational benefits in Finland. Moreover, the surplus in labor supply reduced the utility of occupational pensions as a means of personnel management. And last but not least, the existing occupational benefits were interwoven into the legislated TEL-scheme. At the same time, existing providers were offered the option of continuing as carriers of TEL insurance, this muted their resistance to the scheme.

Even though the public pension system has also crowded out occupational pensions in Sweden, it is interesting that there have been positive feedback loops as well. A good example is the rapid increase of ITP coverage following implementation of ATP legislation in Sweden. The legislation clearly stimulated the expansion of occupational pension coverage, at the same time as it restricted the relative importance of such benefits.

The development of public and occupational pensions in Finland and Sweden illustrates how political conflicts and differences in power resources, also structural differences, are built in to pension institutions. Once implemented, pension programs have turned out to be remarkably stable. They mature according to their own logic, and the ability of societal actors to change their structure is limited. However, the relative importance of structure and agency is not constant over time. During certain "liminal" or "transitional" periods (Turner, 1969; Alexander, 1988:37) social institutions are more open to fundamental restructuring. Although in each period in history contemporary observers have the propensity to overestimate the importance of their own times, we can safely argue that both Sweden and Finland currently find themselves in such a "transitional" period. The challenges and constraints facing their present pension institutions have enlarged the scope for intentional maneuvering by social actors.

Notes

1. During the two decades from 1945 to 1965, the Agrarians occupied an average of 26% of the seats in the Finnish Parliament, compared to 14% in Sweden. Over the same period, the Social Democrats held 25% of the seats in Finland but as much as 51% in Sweden, while the Communists held 23% and 3% respectively. The Conservative parties were equal in clout over these years, holding 15% of the seats in each country. In Sweden, the Liberal Party was the largest bourgeois party with 19% of the seats but it was the smallest in Finland with 5%. However, the Swedish People's Party in Finland, with its 11% of the parliamentary seats, should be counted as belonging to the liberal side. The locus of political hegemony is even clearer when we look at cabinet control. The Agrarian Party in Finland held almost half of the cabinet portfolios and most of the prime ministerial posts. In Sweden, the Social Democrats held more than 90% of the portfolios during the 1946-1965 period. It was only during the period of coalition rule with the Agrarian Party in the mid-1950s that the Social Democrats did not keep complete control over the cabinet.

2. "SSIB-data" is a data base that has been created at the Swedish Institute for Social Research, Stockholm University, as part of an ongoing comparative research project on the development of welfare state programs in 18 OECD countries.

3. TVK no longer exists. In the fall of 1992, the organization went bankrupt. Its assets had been invested in real estate and in the stock market. When there was a dramatic fall in real estate prices and in the stock market, TVK could no longer pay its bills.

4. In 1990 the TEL system covered 1.2 million employees. In the private sector, there are also separate schemes for seamen (12,000 members), for temporary employees (250,000 members), self-employed (165,000 members), farmers (175,000 members), and artists (7,000) (Social Insurance Institution 1991:33).

5. The Communists traditionally had a strong footing in the rural areas whereas support for the Social Democrats was more concentrated in urban areas and the industrial sector.

6. The relending option was a condition set by the employers when the TEL scheme was being developed. Relending relieves companies' liquidity problems and provides investment capital at comparatively reasonable prices, since the interest rate has been somewhat lower than that of the market. This is well in accordance with the traditional principles of the Finnish economic model, where the interests of capital have been of central importance and emphasis is laid upon the economic growth and profitability of the firms and their capacity for international competition (Kosonen, 1985:117).

7. In fact, there are two main schemes in the public sector, one for state employees (270,000 members in 1990), and one for the 450 000 local government employees. Benefit levels are the same in these programs. The main difference between them is that the former is financed directly through the state budget, while the latter is a partly funded scheme.

8. It is worth noting that the expenditure level is still lower than in many other OECD countries. This indicates that despite the universal coverage, the economic importance of the private schemes is still only marginal for the majority of recipients. In fact, almost 80% of the income package of people above normal retirement age is still coming from public transfers. In most of the OECD countries this share is notably lower. For example, the corresponding figures for the United States and Canada are below 40% (Hedström and Ringen, 1990:83).

9. Calculated as ITP (excluding relending to big companies) and STP funds as a share of ATP funds.

10. The severity of this problem varies dramatically. In Sweden, labor force participation rates for men aged 60-64 have fallen from 83% in 1960 to 63% in 1989. But the female activity rate in the same age group has increased from 22% to 51%. During the corresponding time period, participation rates for older Finnish males dropped from 79% to 28%, and from 36% to 22% for females. In fact, the decline in the Finnish activity rates is most rapid in the OECD-area (Jokelainen, 1991).

11. It is interesting to note that the director general of RFV, who was appointed by the Center Party, of which he also is a member, wants to maintain the income security offered by ATP by indexing benefits and ceiling to the development of wages—contrary to what the party works for. This suggests that the bureaucratic legacy in some instances may have more influence than party affiliations.

12. At the time of writing, in the spring of 1995, it is yet not clear whether occupational pensions will affect the size of the publicly provided minimum pensions in Sweden. Such reductions would affect the benefits of occupational programs for low paid workers.

9

Danish Occupational Pensions in the 1980s: From Social Security to Political Economy[1]

Fritz von Nordheim Nielsen

The multi-dimensional character of occupational pensions (OCP) is the key to the fascinating complexity of their political economy (von Nordheim Nielsen, 1986). At one and the same time OCP may represent an element in the remuneration of labor, a provision for income after retirement, and a pool of funds for investment. In their many functions occupational pensions thus span three terrains governed by distinct logics and populated by different protagonists: (1)labor processes and adjacent labor markets, (2)the welfare state, where markets for private pensions are shaped through policies of pension provision, taxation and regulation, and (3)financial markets. Though the three identities are but different sides to the same phenomenon and therefore should not be examined in isolation, they are seldom equally relevant or visible to the prime actors in the different terrains. In addition, we are faced not only with multiple actors but also with multiple and partly conflicting agendas. As a result, analysts face substantial uncertainty and contingency in the study of OCP.

Recent struggles about the future shape of pensions in Denmark may serve as a case that illustrates how difficult it is to reconcile the various elements and distinct dynamics in the political economy of OCP, and how these often interact to produce unintended outcomes. Beginning with an outline of the institutional heritage and political legacy from prior pension reforms and the feedback from these, this chapter will trace the dynamics at work in Danish pension politics in the second half of the 1980s.

The opening shot in a dramatic series of pension policy battles was fired in 1985, when the Danish association of blue and lower white-collar unions (LO) reversed its earlier, very critical stand on occupational pensions. The labor organization now launched an ambitious proposal for the mandatory extension of occupational pension rights to the large majority of wage-earners. This surprising opening towards a vastly increased role for private provision in Danish pensions and for pension funds in the national economy made a grand compromise on pension reform between the bourgeois government and the opposition Social Democratic Party (SD) seem imminent. Much to the displeasure of the LO and SD, however, their reform initiative was repeatedly blocked, until all hopes of a strategic agreement finally collapsed in the national rounds of collective bargaining in March of 1991.

From our perspective the 1985 proposal is particularly interesting because the LO quite deliberately sought to take all the multiple objectives of OCP into account. The labor organization's strategists were intensely aware of the capital formation aspects. They also recognized that as a substantial element in remuneration OCP contributions would have to be phased in over a long period and paid for by wage restraint in other areas. Furthermore, their design had clear social policy goals, being aimed at lowering income inequalities among future pensioners and modifying the divisive distinctions associated with existing OCP coverage. Thus, the planners had done their utmost to reconcile the various concerns of the labor movement in relation to the three faces of OCP. Their failure, as we shall see, can be traced to a range of unfavorable political circumstances.

Two important places to look for the politics of pension reform are the trade union movement and the state. This has been obvious to most observers so far as public pension systems are concerned (e.g. Korpi, 1983; Myles, 1984), but in relation to OCP the problem is more complicated. Union movements are strongly divided internally on this issue. European manual workers' unions have been rather persistent in their opposition to OCP. Usually they have only accepted or pursued OCP when other routes to pension provisions and pay raises have been blocked. In contrast, public sector and white-collar unions from their beginnings have had to cater to the interest of their constituents in selective forms of OCP. Nevertheless, the period since World War Two has everywhere witnessed expansion of occupational pensions (IPC,

1977-80; ISSA, 1980). As a form of social security, OCP has evolved from a functional alternative to public pensions open only to civil servants and higher white-collar employees, to a second or third-tier supplement to universal public provision.

Notwithstanding this generalization of status-group privileges, OCP has unquestionably been instrumental in the erection of a division between those wage-earners who thrive on tax deductions for their pension saving, and those dependent on schemes financed through direct taxes. Pension politics are thus a politics of stratification in which trade unions, political parties, and other actors in the political economy have considerable vested interests (Esping-Andersen, 1990).

The background: pensions and pension politics in Denmark[2]

As Øverbye has pointed out in an earlier chapter, the Danish pension system differs significantly from its counterparts elsewhere in Scandinavia. The first tier of the system, a flat-rate "people's pension", offers a similar level protection to its counterparts in the other Nordic countries. But this is decidedly not true of superannuation, the second tier of the public system, the magnitude of which is exceptionally small in the Danish case. Denmark shared with Sweden and Norway a common history of basic pension reform in the 1950s, capping the era of "red-green" alliances which propelled social democratic parties to power. But in the 1960s it failed to emulate the success of these parties (which was most notable in Sweden) in using the struggle for second-tier pensions (ATP) as the cornerstone for a renewed period of dominance (Esping-Andersen, 1985). By the mid-1980s ATP schemes, which accounted for 31% and 42% respectively of total pension payments in Finland and Sweden, contributed only a tiny fraction (less than 2%) of the Danish total. As partial compensation for this inadequacy, individual annuity schemes accounted for more than 8%, or between 4 and 16 times their share in the other Nordic states. The role of occupational pensions is harder to calculate, but if anything it has been more modest than elsewhere in Scandinavia, especially in the private sector (Perrin, 1972; Kangas and Palme, 1989).[3]

For most of the first two postwar decades, only public sector employees with civil servant status and white-collar staff in the private sector enjoyed occupational pension coverage. Company schemes offering defined benefit provisions predominated in the private sector. The public system has always left ample room for private provision, and in addition, pension savings have been generously subsidized through tax exemption of contributions and interest. Yet OCP failed to fully fill the vacuum in public provision. One of the reasons for this is that the issues of preserving and vesting pension rights in occupational schemes were settled very early on in Denmark, by legislation dating from 1936 and 1941. Consequently, individual employers did not face the same incentives as their counterparts in countries like Britain and the United States to employ OCP as a mechanism of personnel management (Hannah, 1986; Quadagno and Hardy, this volume). On the other hand, the scope for highly aggregated occupational pension schemes like those which constitute Sweden's third tier has been limited in Denmark by key institutional features of the labor market. The most salient of these are Denmark's comparatively low rate of unionization and decentralized system of collective bargaining.

During the 1960s the general expansion of white-collar employment augmented the number of workers covered by OCP. In addition, company-level provision was increasingly discontinued as obligations were moved to more comprehensive schemes run by the insurance sector, which began to resemble a real pension industry. However OCP growth occurred primarily in the public sector, driven largely by the specific character of expanding public employment. Since new entrants to the public sector were no longer employed as tenured civil servants, their proliferation initially threatened to undermine the rate of coverage by OCP. However, special alternative arrangements were developed for professional and semi-professional employees. These were offered employer contributions for occupational pensions provided they were organized as defined contribution multi-employer schemes. The result was a proliferation of member-run programs affiliated to the union representing the profession concerned (doctors, nurses, etc.). As public sector employment grew they rapidly expanded and accumulated funds. The general public came to see this organizational framework as very much the norm, even though OCP schemes in the private sector had for long been entirely employer-run or at least co-managed.

Nevertheless, in spite of the continuing absence of a second tier of earnings-related public or collective pensions, as late as the mid-1980s only a minority (about one third) of Denmark's employed labor force could expect to supplement public pensions with income from occupational provisions. Even in the public sector just half of the workforce, including civil servants, enjoyed OCP coverage—and this under a multitude of different schemes. In the private sector less than 20% of the labor force and a mere 5% of LO members were covered. Inequalities in prospective pension coverage between workers with and those without occupational pensions became far greater than in the other Nordic countries. The reforms of the 1960s in those countries had helped harmonize the pension interests of blue and white collar wage-earners, and reconcile these with the needs of the self-employed.

These elements of growth in OCP were important, but they did not negate the fact that most wage-earners—especially those represented by the LO—continued to suffer the absence of a full-scale second tier public scheme without any compensatory growth of OCP. Understanding why the public system was so limited is important in order to follow the later developments on which this paper focuses. Because of their largely flat-rate character, state pensions offered low replacement rates for people with above-average earnings. As noted earlier, this resulted from the failure of attempts at legislating a second tier of earnings-related pensions during the 1960s. Early in the decade the LO and the Danish employers' association (DA) had formulated a proposal for a general occupational scheme—although for different reasons, neither side wanted it to be earnings-related. In the 1963 round of wage bargaining the government decided to impose an incomes policy which incorporated elements of the proposed voluntary arrangement into a statutory ATP scheme. Since the purpose of this scheme was neither full-scale pension reform nor stimulation of savings, but simply to offer compensation for compulsory wage restraint, both worker and employer contributions were fixed at very modest levels.

Subsequently, neither the LO nor the Social Democrats were interested in expanding the magnitude of the ATP scheme, because they viewed it as no more than the prelude to a more ambitious reform. The prospects for such a reform quickly diminished, however, as a result of growing political polarization. Taking advantage of the leftwing majority produced by the 1966 elections, the SD abandoned its traditionally accommodative relations with the parties of the Center and Right and formed a minority government with the support of the Socialist People's Party. When this government attempted in 1967 to enlarge the ATP scheme along Swedish lines, it faced a newly united and radicalized opposition. For a variety of reasons, the plan also received only lukewarm support from the LO's constituent unions. Later reforms of the pension system, in the 1970s, were formulated under the impact of economic crisis, and focused exclusively on early retirement.

The conditions under which Danish pension policy entered the 1980s affected not only the substantive problems that new initiatives needed to address, but also the political scope for reform. The limited and uneven prevalence of OCP could not alter the fact that in the course of two decades of inertia in statutory pension policy, for those covered by occupational schemes they had developed from a temporary substitute into a permanent alternative to public superannuation. Occupational systems had become entrenched and their members had acquired definite interests in their preservation. Only at great political cost, if at all, could OCP now be demoted to a secondary role. The institution of wide and permanent cleavages between employees with and without occupational coverage also stands out as one of the lasting legacies of the abortive history of the 1960's. Interest divisions were exacerbated, which made it easy to use the pension issue to pit various groups of wage-earners against each other. The bourgeois parties soon recognized the new trend in pension relations, and they did their best to widen and exploit the growing cleavages between different strata in the labor market.

The origins of the LO's pension reform proposal

In 1978 a research unit within the labor movement published a position paper on "Private Pensions—Savings or Tax Shelter? A Study in Inequality". The rhetorical question in the title summed up the negative attitude towards occupational and individual pensions that prevailed in both the LO and the SD. The aggregate value of tax subsidies to private pensions had been estimated, and the message was that most of the cost of the nest eggs accumulating in non-statutory pension schemes was being borne by taxpayers. Since little additional savings of a genuinely private character was taking place, there was really no reason why the Exchequer should undertake to subsidize the pension aspirations of an already privileged minority—particularly not in a situation with scarce resources and inadequate public pensions. This position was reaffirmed when the SD-appointed Old Age Commission reported in 1981. Basic people's pensions only provided a level of living on the verge of poverty. The income drop at retirement was far too large. If the elderly were to live full lives as active, independent citizens the miserly levels of universal pensions had to be substantially increased. Moreover the Commission calculated that if the tax subsidies to non-statutory pensions were discontinued, basic pensions could be raised by a third.

In this phase political discourse about pensions focused on distributional justice and social needs. Labor movement spokespersons attacked special privileges for the few and demanded a fairer share for the old. The dedication of labor to social policy considerations and redistribution was further consolidated when the principal authors to the above-mentioned reports were soon after appointed to ministerial positions. Economic policy considerations in this period also created impetus for squeezing the OCP sector. In the wake of the second oil crisis interest rates on government bonds soared to unprecedented levels. As a majority of the bonds were held by institutional investors, including the totally tax-exempt pension funds, it was hardly surprising that the new Minister of Taxation in 1981 began to design a scheme to tax excessive real rates of return. At the same time, the new tax was an important element in a set of measures by which the social-democratic minority government hoped to curb the state deficit.

The pension industry was bound to protest, the Liberals and the Conservatives would object, the Center parties would be reluctant, and nobody expected the unions of professional and salaried white-collar employees to be jubilant. Still, the government was shocked by the vehemence of the reactions to which its tax proposal gave rise. Public sector unions joined in a coordinated campaign to block the scheme, and some of them used their connections with party and union leaders to try to topple the initiative. The government thus faced a paralyzing internal division in the labor movement, with both public sector and white-collar unions fiercely opposing the idea of taxing pension funds. It was also confronted by a solid block of bourgeois parties committed to the defense of tax exemptions for pension savings. When the Social Democrats realized that the scheme would be defeated, they drew a radical conclusion. Early in the fall of 1982 the government decided to resign. The background to this decision encompassed many problems other than pensions, and the resignation was tactical in intention. Yet as it happened, this development opened the way for the first stable bourgeois coalition government in more than a decade and resulted in a realignment which has managed ever since to relegate the Social Democrats to an increasingly frustrating role in opposition. In retrospect then, the pension issue has taken on an air of ominous political importance.

The Conservatives, who gained the premiership for the first time since 1901, and their closest coalition partner the Liberals, had learned the game of minority government survival from years of being outwitted by SD. They embraced two tactical objectives—to pit different groups of wage-earners against each other, and to separate the social democrats from the People's Socialists—that were especially well served by the pension issue. The opposition of the bourgeois parties to pension fund taxation lasted only so long as the issue was instrumental in straining relations between manual and white-collar unions. Faced once more with pressure to cut the state deficit and direct money to investments that would boost production and employment, the government could hardly allow private pension schemes to collect tax-free real rates of return on their government bonds of 10-15% when active investments subject to tax brought only 5-8%. After only a year in office the New Right-inspired government legislated a scheme of pension fund taxation similar to that which had been the downfall of their predecessors. To the displeasure of the Left, the social democrats supported the measure. The pension industry complained bitterly, but private business and bourgeois opinion at large generally recognized that continuation of Conservative rule had to take priority over sectional interests.

Not long after its volte-face on the tax privileges of private pensions, the government found a new opportunity to exploit the divisive potential of OCP. In the summer of 1984 prominent ministers suggested to the Metalworkers' Union that it opt for a funded occupational pension scheme for its members instead of the 35 hour week, a demand which LO—on behalf of all manual workers' unions—was about to make a top priority in the upcoming rounds of collective bargaining. The government's ploy succeeded to the point that the metalworkers, though deciding to stay in line in 1985, presented the LO with an ultimatum: either it would have to come up with a proposal for earnings-related supplementary pensions for all workers presently without coverage, or else in the next wage rounds in 1987 the metalworkers would negotiate their own scheme. These events convinced the leadership of the SD and the LO that something had to be done in order to avoid further splits on fundamental issues as well as to prevent large income differences in old age between wage-earners with and without adequate supplementary pension coverage.

The logic of the reform

The LO's 1985 proposal called for a comprehensive reform of the Danish pension system which, to the pleasant surprise of the bourgeois parties and the pension industry and the anger of the Left, included a general scheme of mandatory occupational pensions. The proposal comprised three main elements:

1. The nominal level of basic pensions was to be raised so that they could be made fully taxable without losing value. In addition, statutory pensions would be reduced for pensioners with exceptionally high incomes, while on the other hand, the income test in the general supplement was to be liberalized to allow for moderate occupational pensions.
2. Contributions to the existing ATP scheme were to be doubled and wage indexation introduced.
3. As earnings-related occupational scheme for the two-thirds of workers presently without occupational coverage would be introduced, to be financed by employer and employee contributions to a central pension fund under union movement control. In order not to jeopardize other union priorities and in recognition that it would have to be paid for partly by wage restraint, the new scheme was to be gradually introduced over a 10 year period.

The LO's plan was a carefully conceived package solution to a variety of problems. The labor organization tried to balance concerns for adequacy, equality, redistribution and equity in social policy, while taking due account of the dilemmas likely to confront Danish economic and collective bargaining policy during the coming decade. The ironic implication of the proposed blueprint was that after finally recognizing the necessity for earnings-related pensions, the LO had conceded that it was by now impossible to demote existing occupational schemes to a complementary role as a third tier on top of a general public scheme. The fate of the previous government's tax proposal had compelled the LO to conclude that earnings-related pensions in Denmark would have to take the form of occupational provision. Unable to negate the privilege of a minority, it tried instead to modify this privilege by extending it to everyone in the labor market.

A number of implications followed. LO was obliged to drop its longstanding opposition to tax subsidies for private pensions. If occupational pensions were to be attractive to LO members, the tax-deductibility of member and employer contributions had to be preserved. Furthermore, in order for the proposed arrangement to result in additional pension benefits for workers with average incomes, the provision in the existing first-tier system for income-tested supplements would have to be either changed or abolished. As for the extant occupational schemes, they were to be allowed to continue as before. Though the new scheme in time would modify some of the differences, the presently covered would thus retain a substantial part of their initial advantage and a significant measure of inequality would persist. Finally, to make sense of a general occupational scheme, LO had to relegate the universal people's pension to a junior role in the overall pension system, reducing redistribution in one sphere while raising it in another.

The details of the reform had been developed by the research unit of the labor movement in close consultation with LO's visionary chief economist. When it was presented to the union leaders the cleverly devised multi-functional character of the package was emphasized, and no doubt they accepted it as much for its potential macro-economic and macro-political consequences as for its effects on present and future pensioners. Some of the leaders saw the occupational scheme as particularly attractive because a giant pension fund under union control could serve as a substitute for a general scheme of wage-earner funds or profit-sharing—a long sought-after but elusive goal (Ohman, 1983). Handled in the right way, they expected that pension funds could be employed as a powerful tool in the struggle for economic democracy and worker co-ownership.

White-collar unions within the LO focused on the prospect of supplementary pensions for their members. The unskilled workers' unions, in contrast, remained skeptical about occupational provision. It would be difficult to ask the rank and file to forgo part of their comparatively low wages for supplementary pension credits. The establishment of adequate mechanisms of redistribution and solidarity which could safeguard the vulnerable interests of their members had been a condition for their acceptance of the package. To them it was therefore imperative that the occupational scheme be general and mandatory and inseparable from the suggested adjustments to the people's pension and ATP. The package had thus been carefully constructed to serve as a common denominator for the various interests in the LO. But their agreement was conditional. It depended on the balance and connections between the elements in the package. If these became undone, sectional interests were bound to come the fore.

The struggle over pension reform, 1985-1990[4]

In the fall of 1985 the LO presented its reform proposal to the government and organized employers (the DA) as an alternative to incomes policy and compulsory savings. The pension industry and the bourgeois parties complimented the labor organization on its policy reversal and welcomed the idea of vastly increased pension savings. But they were less enthusiastic about the format of the scheme and they were critical of the proposed changes to the universal people's pension. Though certainly in need of schemes by which to increase the national savings rate and continue a policy of wage restraint, the government was adamantly opposed to the idea of building a central investment fund under union control, and it was equally hostile to the idea of legislating a comprehensive mandatory scheme. Instead, cabinet ministers and DA leaders insisted that occupational pension coverage must result "voluntarily" from decentralized collective bargaining.

The Liberals were far more emphatic in their opposition to the plan than the Conservatives, who were looking for areas where they could strike a grand stabilizing deal with the SD. But the fact remained that both bourgeois parties had little strategic interest in occupational pensions if they did not reflect the varying market positions of different types of wage-earners. Neither the governing parties nor the employers' association were willing to allow the union movement control over the investment of the pension savings of their members in exchange for a little wage restraint and a higher rate of savings. Their implicit message to wage-earners was that workers would have to let their collective savings be handled by bankers, brokers and other money managers according to market criteria as usual, or else do without occupational pensions. Nevertheless, the government was careful not to dismiss LO's proposal entirely. Ministers kept indicating that if a sufficient number of unions demonstrated their willingness to trade part of their wages for occupational pension credits at the bargaining table, the government would back the results with a framework of legislation making occupational coverage of a certain standard mandatory. Meanwhile the plan came under increasing attack not just from the Left but also from within the labor movement.

Not surprisingly, the association of retired union members led by the former chairman of the LO objected to the reform on the grounds that it neglected the needs of present pensioners. Still more heated opposition was led by the SD's last Minister for Social Policy and former head of the Old Age Commission, Bent Rold-Andersen. Like other social policy experts and welfare economists in the party, Rold-Andersen had not been consulted when the LO proposal was developed, and saw it as contrary to his most fundamental beliefs about how a distributionally just and economically flexible pension system should be constructed. His critique caught the imagination of the general public with a theme of generational conflict which was picked up by the popular press and resounded for weeks. Many apparently agreed that the growth of private pensions signified that the baby boomers who had entered the labor market in the late sixties and early seventies were now a spoiled middle generation bent on penalizing both parents and children for their own excesses.

After the initial furor the LO managed to silence Rold-Andersen and secure the unreserved support of the party. The plan was adjusted in a few minor ways and the movement closed ranks behind it. However, FTF—the national peak organization of middle level white-collar employees—ended up being entirely negative towards the proposal. To the embarrassment of the LO and the Social Democrats, the FTF demanded compensation for its members if presently uncovered workers succeeded in securing OCP coverage through statutory intervention. Relations between the LO and the FTF deteriorated further during the 1987 wage round, when the LO and the DA agreed to rise the level of contributions to the second-tier ATP scheme by 50%. In the negotiations for the public sector that followed, the Minister of Finance dropped a bombshell by agreeing that public sector employees with occupational coverage could contract out of the proposed improvements to the ATP scheme. The result was a new dual structure that accentuated and consolidated interest cleavages between public and private employees. Solidarity in a unitary system in which all wage-earners shared the same conditions had been broken, and there was nothing the LO could do to prevent it.

Even at the LO's blue-collar base, support for its vision of pension reform was waning. In the spring of 1986 the labor organization launched a major campaign to convince union members and the general public of the urgency and ingenuity of its reform proposal. In spite of these efforts, surveys kept showing the rank and file to be anything but enthusiastic. Less than 20% were willing to forgo part of their current wages for better pensions in the future. In addition, the two largest unions of unskilled workers' unions decided to investigate the extent to which their members would benefit from a general occupational scheme.

It turned out that by and large they could not expect 40 years of savings in the occupational scheme to improve their aggregate pensions. Under the existing system of a universal allowance with income-tested supplements they were actually getting a post-tax replacement rate which was slightly higher than the one they would acquire when the proposed occupational benefits were added. The slender occupational pensions planned for the unskilled would simply be "taxed away".

The government had hinted that pension reform might follow if LO unions made it a high priority in the wage rounds for 1987, but the unions were still gambling on reform emanating from negotiations in parliament or as part of an imposed wage settlement. In the event, collective bargaining ended amicably after the shortest negotiating round ever. Employers simply conceded far larger pay raises than union leaders had counted on. Thus, reform was stymied in 1987 and postponed until the reopening of collective agreements two years hence.

At the opening of parliament in the fall of 1987 the Prime Minister declared pension reform a national priority in economic policy. Soon a tripartite committee to investigate the pros and cons of various pension scheme designs and the possible consequences of LO's proposal was set up under the auspices of the Department of Labor. A small army of civil servants assisted experts from the unions and the employers' association in a hurried attempt to complete the committee's work before the start of collective bargaining in January 1989. A ten-volume report which met with reluctant approval from most quarters was presented shortly before Christmas 1988. The public and certainly the unions now expected that negotiations about design and implementation would start early in the new year. But the Prime Minister stunned the entire nation—and even most of his inner cabinet—by announcing in his New Year's speech that pension reform had been dropped. Instead, he outlined a radical proposal for a 10% all-round wage reduction, arguing that this would offer far greater benefit to the economy.

This kind of proposal had not been voiced since the 1930's, and pension concerns were largely forgotten in the heated aftermath. It appeared that the Liberals and a recalcitrant but very influential section of the DA had imposed a veto on government negotiations with the unions about mandatory occupational pensions. The Liberals were hellbent on preventing LO unions from gaining control of large pension funds. It was their view that private pensions ought only to be encouraged in the framework of a broader strategy of popular capitalism. Only if occupational pensions were selective and individuals could influence the investment of their accruing savings, would they come to see their living standards in old age as a function of the market performance of their savings. Under collective control occupational pensions would be nothing but a source of power for union bosses.

The Social Democrats had a hard time arguing for the necessity of a single fund. Under pressure from the Liberals and the private pension industry they had already conceded that a number of separate schemes and funds would be possible so long as pension conditions were homogeneous and the contribution/benefit formula retained redistributive elements. Fund boards could be elected by members instead of being appointed by unions. And, if it could compete with union-operated pension institutes, the private pension industry would be allowed a share in the running of schemes. These concessions had been meant to patch up the odd and ailing alliance between the LO leadership, the pension industry and the financial sector at large concerning the necessity for a heavy emphasis on funded schemes in future provisions. They had also been intended to help pacify the Liberals. Now it seemed that none of these benefits was attainable. Whenever the SD and the unions retreated the Liberals responded by stepping up their attacks and augmenting their demands for concessions, while the private pension industry saw less and less reason to let the labor movement dictate the terms of its involvement in scheme management.

In the end, the LO found itself caught between the irreconcilable imperatives of internal and external politics. The premier's dramatic U-turn naturally made the unions lose all faith in the government, but there was nowhere else they could turn if they still hoped for enactment of even a watered-down version of their proposal. For internal reasons, reform was now more urgent than ever. The LO had originally believed that its proposal would stop the Metalworkers' Union from pursuing the struggle for occupational coverage on its own. However, in the winter of 1990 the metalworkers declared that they were fed up with waiting for a statutory reform. Consequently, they would attempt to negotiate a scheme exclusively for their members in the collective bargaining round of 1991. Clearly, sectional splits would result unless the labor organization somehow managed to extract binding commitments to common bargaining goals from individual unions. But the unions responded with only lukewarm agreement. In the unpredictable currents of nightly negotiations, inter-union solidarity had been subjected to greater pressures than it could withstand.

Why pension reform failed

The LO's reform proposal was a carefully drafted blueprint for the harmonization of union interests and a grand compromise with employers and the bourgeois government. From our analytical perspective, it represented a bold attempt to reconcile the three faces of OCP, with a primary view to the capital-formation dimension. Politically, its realization required that the protagonists in the conflict be governed by strategic concerns and be able to act as highly aggregated actors. However, apart from a few visionary leaders, the great majority of those affected had difficulty understanding or accepting the grand design and the resulting terms of a potential compromise. They tended to concentrate instead on the objectives that were crucial to their primary terrain. In the absence of the political conditions necessary for high level future-oriented bargaining, even a slightly altered version of the scheme could not materialize. Instead, the various aspects of the proposal took on a life of their own as actors in the three terrains pursued and fought over their little piece of the grand project and consequently tore it to shreds.

Social security concerns had marked the start of the struggle over pension policy, but from the moment LO presented its strategic design macro-economic and macro-political concerns came to dominate the discourse of pension politics. The traditional labor market context of OCP entered LO's proposal only at the aggregate level, in the notion that gradual increases in contributions would be offset by wage restraint. Since the design was supposed to be approved in a grand compromise with the bourgeois side, the interests of employers were neglected. The LO failed to recognize that even though OCP was sought primarily for its capital-formation and welfare potential, it would still have to be 'sold' as a form of deferred pay in order to be established.

Precisely because the LO tried to achieve so many potentially conflicting objectives with a single reform, the proposal became complex and abstruse. Its macro-level perspectives were too abstract to appeal to the majority of the rank and file in the unions, and in a choice between immediate and deferred wages only a small minority opted for the latter. Even local union officials had trouble believing in the implied promise of substantially better pensions in the distant future. They were more attracted to the prospect of using pension accumulations as a substitute for wage-earner funds in a renewed campaign for economic democracy.

The multiple objectives, the peculiar circumstances under which the proposal had been devised and its tactical implications in general politics quickly brought the LO on a collision course with significant actors and issues in all three of the terrains of OCP. The design and consequences of the scheme came under attack not just from employers, the bourgeois government, the pension industry and the financial sector, but also from the federation of public sector and white-collar unions, the socialist Left, present pensioners, and the social policy lobby. And the opposition was not only external. The LO leadership also had to lean heavily on some of its own unions to make them stay in line.

Ironically, the labor movement had entered the decade denouncing private pensions as parasitical and arguing that the huge tax expenditures devoted to additional pensions for the few ought to be diverted into making improvements to the universal people's pension. Yet when the 1980's drew to a close, the Social Democrats were engaged in an increasingly desperate fight for a watered-down version of LO's 1985 proposal for a mandated, general scheme of funded occupational pensions. By entertaining the idea that it must be financially worthwhile to forgo wages now for pensions later, the labor movement altered the terms of its own discourse. As the financial merits to the individual of wage deferral for pension insurance were pondered, traditional concerns about social adequacy and redistributional justice in pensions increasingly gave way to equity considerations—the question of value for money. At the same time, the political debate moved from a focus on public pensions for better living conditions and a fairer share for old people, to occupational pensions as an instrument of national economic recovery and a lighter burden on future cohorts of the gainfully employed.

From the moment that it became clear that the political road to pension reform would remain blocked, the macro-level implications of reform became secondary. Having waited more than five years in vain for a political breakthrough in pension reform, early in 1991 the LO felt compelled to inaugurate the extension of occupational provisions though collective bargaining in the labor market. With OCP converted into an issue in decentralized collective bargaining, its pay and pension aspects suddenly reasserted themselves. This unleashed a wave of inter-union rivalry that blew away all the grandiose hopes of acquiring the kind of pension fund control that could be employed in a gradual strategy of co-ownership and codetermination.

The OCP issue was left to labor market forces precisely in a period where the entire system of collective bargaining was being restructured and further decentralized. The LO was unable to control or even to foresee the outcome of negotiations, and Denmark ended up with exactly the inverse of what the labor movement had intended: a wide variety of very different schemes in both the private and the public sector, which left the least privileged third of the labor force without coverage. OCP provisions now constitute a larger but far more diverse set of schemes that vary greatly in size, conditions for entitlement, benefits, and member influence. This will further accentuate the thrust towards business unionism in the Danish labor movement.

In the political sphere, the 1980s can be seen as a period in which Denmark's long-frustrated need for earnings-related second tier pensions was turned into a vehicle for competing strategic projects of economic democracy and popular capitalism. Promises of pensions some time in the future are the sugar that is supposed to encourage wage-earners to swallow the bitter pill of compulsory savings through deferral of part of their current remuneration. Increased savings and wage restraint instead of better pensions are the dominant concerns of the Center parties in the bourgeois government. The Liberals view a voluntary expansion of occupational pension provisions as part of a move towards "popular capitalism". The labor movement, for its part, is increasingly indisposed to tying pension reform to a quest for economic democracy, or "fund socialism" as the bourgeois parties have labelled the project. The stage has thus been set for OCP as one of a number elements in a future of popular capitalism, while the high hopes of economic democracy disappear in the distance. The politics of pensions in Denmark have been turned into a struggle about the future contours of the Danish political economy, and the protagonists seem to have lost sight of the original purpose of pension reform: provision for income in old age.

Notes

1. This chapter is a revised version of previous papers which was prepared by the editor of this volume. It is based mainly on the Danish sections of a comparative study of all the Nordic states (von Nordheim Nielsen, 1990). That study was subsequently published in abbreviated form in *States, Labor Markets and the Future of Old Age Policy*, edited by Jill Quadagno and John Myles for Temple University Press (von Nordheim Nielsen, 1991). We

gratefully acknowledge the consent of the editors and publishers to reusing parts of this material here.

2. For fuller details see von Nordheim Nielsen (1990) and references cited therein, especially Nørby-Johansen (1986-87); Nelson (1984); Vesterø-Jensen (1984); and Henriksen, Rasmussen and Kampmann (1988).

3. For more complete numerical estimates see Table 1 of von Nordheim Nielsen (1990) and Table 6.2 in this volume.

4. The reconstruction which follows is based on both primary and secondary sources. The former include a wide selection of daily newspapers and other periodicals, including the main trade union and professional journals. The author also consulted a large body of professional commentary on pension reform proposals by economists and others, much of which has appeared in the *Nationaløkonomisk Tidskrift*.

Part 3

Canada and Japan

10

Between American Exceptionalism and Social Democracy: Public and Private Pensions in Canada[1]

Gregg M. Olsen and Robert J. Brym

Explaining the Canadian-American Difference

Canadians stand in the shadow of the world's most powerful country, and out of a slightly neurotic mixture of admiration and insecurity they often compare themselves to Americans, sometimes inventing differences when none springs immediately to mind. Europeans may be excused for not fully appreciating what all the fuss is about. From their point of view, the answer is plain: a large French minority and a certain sense of reserve—both legacies of British colonialism—seem the distinguishing features of Canada.

Students of the Canadian welfare state know better. The United States typifies the liberal, non-interventionist model of welfare state development; Canada only approximates it. That is evident, in the first place, from state expenditures on welfare effort as a percentage of GDP. In 1983, the US spent 11.7 percent of its GDP on public services, social security, and so forth. Canada spent 18.5 percent—58.1 percent more in proportionate terms. The welfare gap between Canada and the US, at least in terms of expenditure, is in fact greater than the corresponding disparity between Canada and Sweden. With 25.3 percent of its GDP allocated to welfare effort in 1983, Sweden spent 36.8 percent more than Canada in proportionate terms (O'Connor, 1989).[2]

Gross expenditures tell only part of the story, however. The Canadian welfare state is also more complete than its American counterpart. Canada's public health insurance program, for example, has served as a model internationally. Meanwhile, in the US, some 37 million Americans remain without health insurance, while many more lack adequate coverage. In addition, major social programs were introduced earlier in Canada and have emphasized universalism, prevention, and tax-financing to a somewhat greater degree (Gordon, 1990; Kudrle and Marmor, 1981; Olsen, 1994).

It is in terms of the nature and extent of private welfare that Canada is more like its giant southern neighbor, although even here there are differences. As opposed to Sweden, employer-sponsored welfare is prominent in both North American countries. In 1989, employee-benefit costs accounted for just over a third of Canadians', and nearly 40 percent of Americans', gross annual payroll.[3]

In this paper we offer a tentative explanation for the development, scope, and mix of occupational and public pensions in Canada.[4] Our perspective is comparative and historical. It is also aimed squarely at a prevailing wisdom in the comparative study of the Canadian welfare state: Seymour Martin Lipset's (1989:xiv) "stress...on the role of national values in affecting behavior and institutions." Lipset argues that certain divergent historical experiences in Canada and the US—notably the failure of the American Revolution to spread north of the 49th parallel—helped crystallize relatively unique cultures in the two countries. The US was founded on a heritage of individualistic rebellion against state authority, Canada on a heritage of respect for state authority. As a result, public welfare effort is greater in Canada, private welfare effort greater in the US. One country's constitution speaks of "life, liberty and the pursuit of happiness," the other's of "peace, order and good government." One does not have to know much North American history to guess which is which.

We lodge three charges against Lipset, all serious: ahistoricism, reification, and oversimplification (compare Brym with Fox, 1989). "Ahistoricism" because Lipset posits first causes as efficient causes. Said differently, events long past (for example, the American Revolution) are seen to influence today's behavior (for example, a certain level of spending on public and private pensions). In Lipset's work, proximate events seldom intervene as causal mechanisms of much importance.

"Reification" because Lipset regards values as almost changeless things. Once crystallized, they are, in his view, relatively fixed. "Oversimplification" because the actual relationship between values and behavior is unclear and may even be the opposite of what Lipset suggests. Many studies demonstrate that values are often poor predictors of behavior, many others that values often emerge to rationalize behavior (Cancian, 1975; Deutscher, 1973). In the case at hand, it is at least plausible that the constraints and opportunities afforded by historical change shaped behavior which, in turn, gave rise to values. There is no good reason to assume, as does Lipset, that values are independently important causes of welfare effort.

In contrast to Lipset, we stress three sets of forces in our analysis of the growth and mix of public and private pensions in Canada. We first examine the influence of the changing balance of class power (compare, for example, Myles, 1989 [1984]). Class power may be measured by the size, level of social organization, and access to resources of class members. From the late seventeenth century until the present, the effect of the ratio of power between capital and labor on Canadian pensions has been crystal clear. As we will see, when the power ratio has been comparatively high, capitalists have had a vastly predominant say in molding pensions to suit their interests; when the ratio has declined, labor has advanced its own cause to a degree.

That, however, is far from the whole story. Certain state structures have also influenced the character of the Canadian pension system. As the contrasting case of the US electoral system brings out sharply, during the twentieth century the Canadian parliamentary system has facilitated the emergence of a somewhat more progressive pension system than that in the US. Of course, state structures are themselves the institutional residues of past class and other social conflicts. But over time they take on lives of their own, and their independent influence must be given due weight in any analysis of the development of pensions in Canada.[5]

Finally, the historical record demonstrates that relations between Canada and other national states and economies have also played a vital role in the development of the Canadian pension system. Given its colonial status, British policies and programs were sometimes adopted in Canada. The northward incursion of American trade unions retarded developments in the pension field for decades while foreign investors, both British and American, promoted important Canadian pension innovations in the private sphere. Regional and global political-economies periodically placed vast competitive pressures on Canada;

these, in turn, caused the Canadian state to use the pension system as a defense mechanism.

None of this is to deny that there are relevant value differences between Canada and the US, although much research demonstrates that Lipset greatly exaggerates his case in this regard (for an excellent recent example, see Bowden, 1989). In the body of our article we simply demonstrate that a plausible explanation of variations in the pension systems of the two countries may be constructed without referring to value differences and using sturdier and more supple analytical materials than those offered by Lipset. Before turning to our analytical task, however, we require some historical background.

The Origins of the Canadian Pension System

In 1919 a Royal Commission on Industrial Relations (the "Mathers Commission"), appointed by the Conservative government of Robert Borden, noted that a wide range of employer-sponsored social welfare measures were already in place by the 1880s and had become increasingly common over the following three decades. These included a variety of benefit plans (pertaining to sickness, disability, accident, and death), pension programs, profit-sharing schemes, stock subscription plans, and other miscellaneous "fringe benefits," such as vacation pay, recreational programs, legal and financial advice, and plant cafeterias and libraries. Such corporate welfare measures did not usually require employees to contribute to their operation since they were for the most part designed to discipline and control labor in a variety of ways. There were some pension programs, even in the late nineteenth century, which did require employee contributions. However, they were primarily established for white-collar workers, who were generally not as militant as industrial workers and therefore did not require the harsh forms of labor discipline afforded by non-contributory pensions. Canadian firms such as McClary Manufacturing and Consumers' Gas Company, and American subsidiaries, such as Ford Canada and Canadian Kodak, often required that benefits be earned through punctuality, efficient production, and "decent living;" or they sought to ensure that their employees spent their leisure time in "healthy and moral pursuits" (see, for example, Naylor, 1991). Pension plans were among the most important and effective components of employer welfare packages.

The earliest forms of pension programs in Canada were not actually Canadian. For example, the Hudson Bay Company, a London-based enterprise which had been granted a Royal Charter to trap furs in Canada in 1659, provided its employees with retirement benefits as early as the late 1600s. Similarly, since 1681 the British government had furnished military pensions for its soldiers stationed in Canada. Since such employment entailed significant privations in an often harsh and hostile environment, old-age security was used by the former to attract trappers and by the latter to dissuade soldiers from migrating to the United States in search of an easier life.

The first truly Canadian pension system was introduced with the Superannuation Act of 1870, three years after Confederation, by the first Canadian government. This was a private, contributory, occupational plan for civil servants and other public workers modelled after a program introduced in Britain in 1834. Formally entitled "An Act for Increasing the Efficiency of the Civil Service of Canada," the plan, as Sir Francis Hincks, the Conservative Minister of Finance at the time, ungraciously explained, had been devised "not for the benefit of employees,...but to get rid of persons who had arrived at a time of life when they could no longer perform their work efficiently" (cited in Morton and McCallum, 1988:6). Thus the Preamble of the Act states that in order to ensure the "efficiency [of the] Civil Service of Canada, it is expedient to provide for the retirement...of persons, who, from age or infirmity cannot properly perform the duties assigned to them" (Statutes of Canada, 1870, cited in Stafford, 1987:129). In the following decades a number of contributory programs established by several large Canadian banks, including the Bank of Montreal (1885) and the Royal Bank of Canada (1904), served to tie workers to their employers and restrict labor turnover. In all of these cases, it was primarily the interests and actions of employers, public and private, rather than the demands of workers, which led to the creation of old-age security. Such plans often reflected Canada's colonial ties to Britain and commercial ties to the US.

By the last quarter of the nineteenth century, a few decades after Canada's industrial revolution began, a nascent labor movement emerged. Some of the unions that managed to gain a foothold began to set up systems of social welfare based on the mutuality principle, but they were few in number and could offer only modest protection for a tiny minority. The first genuine industrial pension plan in North America was a contributory scheme introduced in 1874 by the Grand Trunk Railway of Canada, a British-owned concern centered in Montreal. It had been set up by the company's conservative president, Richard Potter (father of Fabian socialist Beatrice Potter Webb). However, it covered only the clerical and "indoor" staff. American Express, a company closely linked to the railways, adopted a pension program for its employees in the US the following year. By the turn of the century, all of the major railroad companies in Canada and many in the United States had established pension plans for their employees. By 1908, when the Grand Trunk Railway adopted a non-contributory plan for all its employees, nearly 75 percent of railway workers in Canada and just under 40 percent of those in the US were covered by pension plans (Latimer, 1932).

As in the earlier cases of old-age security discussed above, occupational pensions in the railway industry were introduced almost unilaterally by employers. In a period of economic downturn and labor unrest, employers needed to achieve greater control over a workforce which was relatively large, highly skilled, and distributed across a vast expanse. Pensions, as well as a number of tactics employed by the military to discipline soldiers, such as the use of uniforms, hierarchies, and regulations, were thus adopted by the railway industry. Non-contributory pension systems predominated because they ensured complete employer discretion over all aspects of pension plans and were therefore a potent weapon that could be used to threaten or punish striking workers or employees who wished to sue the railway for injuries sustained at work. For example, striking workers' pension rights were withdrawn by the Canadian Pacific Railway in 1908 and by the Grand Trunk Railway in 1910 (Morton and McCallum, 1988; Stafford, 1986, 1987). During the first few decades of the twentieth century, non-contributory pension plans were implemented in other large Canadian- and American-controlled manufacturing industries as well, including Bell Telephone (1917), Massey-Harris (1919), and Eastman Kodak (1928) (Edwards, 1967; Industrial Relations Section, 1938; McCallum, 1990). Canada, it should not be forgotten, had and still has the highest level of foreign ownership of any industrialized country, and most of the direct investment in the country has been American. Many pension plans found their way into Canada as American companies set up branch plants north of the border.

With the onset of the Depression, the further growth of occupational welfare was stunted. The new plans that emerged during this period—such as those initiated by General Foods (1934), Campbell Soup (1938) and John Labatt (1938)—were almost exclusively contributory. A number of existing plans, such as those in place at Imperial Oil and Goodyear, were converted from non-contributory to contributory. Still other plans were eliminated altogether. During periods of economic downturn and high unemployment, labor recruitment and discipline presented much less of a problem to employers and non-contributory corporate welfare was thus viewed as an unnecessary expense. Canada's first public pension, implemented via the passage of the Old Age Pensions Act in 1927 (discussed below), was neither generous nor universal. It did, however, help to legitimize the decline of non-contributory private plans.

The Balance of Class Power, 1870-1939

The thumbnail sketch offered above permits us to conclude that, whether in the public or the private sphere, the industrial or the service sector, it was primarily the interests and actions of employers, not the demands of workers, that gave form to Canada's old-age security system before 1940.

Virtually complete employer control over pensions was in the first instance a function of the lopsided power ratio between capital and labor (compare Brym, 1986, 1989; Olsen, 1991, 1992). Why was capital so strong? Largely because during the early phases of development, capital was concentrated in only a few sectors—notably the iron, steel, woodworking, railway, banking, and insurance industries—and many captains of industry did not just massively influence state policy but quite literally ran the state.[6] Characteristically, nearly half the directors of the Grand Trunk Railroad were members of the legislature. The political strength and unity of the capitalist class was bolstered by the creation of the highly influential Canadian Manufacturers' Association in 1871. Thus, the unchallenged political and economic position of Canadian capitalists ensured that old-age security remained largely privately-controlled and non-contributory.

Why was labor so weak? Canada was a relatively late industrializer. While one usually dates the first phase of British industrialization from the middle of the eighteenth century and the first phase of American industrialization from the beginning of the nineteenth, Canadian industrialization did not begin in earnest until the middle of the nineteenth century. As a result, workers made up a comparatively small proportion of the labor force until well into the twentieth century.

Moreover, the working class was deeply divided. Apart from the old linguistic and religious division between English and French workers, it was difficult for working class immigrants of many ethnic backgrounds to form enduring ties of solidarity (see, however, Avery, 1979). Finally, workers were separated by vast distances and distinct regional identities.

Unions did grow quickly during the last decades of the nineteenth century. In the 1870s, the Knights of Labor set out to organize all workers in local and district trade assemblies, with little regard to differences in skill and industry. In 1883 the Knights were instrumental in forming the Trades and Labor Congress (TLC), a trade union central that had socialist leanings, wished to create an independent labor party, and, from 1905, pressed for the establishment of a public pension program like those in Germany, Denmark, and Great Britain.

These auspicious beginnings foundered, however, because of the northward incursion of the conservative American Federation of Labor (AFL) after 1898 (Babcock, 1974). Many Canadian workers joined the AFL. They were attracted by its size and affluence as well as the prospect it held out of free movement across the Canadian-US border in the search for work. As early as 1902, so-called "international" unions "far outnumbered and outweighed all the local, regional, national unions, and the Knights of Labor put together" (Forsey, 1985:12). By 1911, 82 percent of all Canadian trade unionists were organized by the so-called "internationals."

The rise of the AFL in Canada had grave consequences. First, the AFL delayed the formation of an independent labor party for decades. The American electoral system minimized the chances of third-party success (see below). For that reason, the AFL developed a strategy of rewarding its political friends and punishing its political enemies. It urged its members to support the establishment party that was more sympathetic to labor and oppose the other establishment party. Moreover, the AFL entrenched craft unionism. And it fostered resentment, disorganization, and deep cleavages in the Canadian union movement (Brodie and Jenson, 1980). The main fissures ran between the radical labor movement in the West, the AFL-dominated business unions in Ontario, and the even more conservative Catholic unions in Québéc.

We thus arrive at a first approximation of our explanation as to why the growth of Canadian public and private pension programs was stunted before 1940. Indeed, our explanation differs from the American version only in detail; parallel developments in the two countries were set in motion by similar social processes. In both countries the working class was rent by ethnic and organizational divisions and was left open to mobilization by conservative union leaders. In both countries the capitalist class was sufficiently cohesive and well organized to shape a pension system that helped control labor in major industries without incurring the massive costs required by a tax-based, universal old-age security scheme.[7]

We must emphasize, however, that this account is only a first approximation. Two additional analytical elements may be teased out of our brief historical overview. First, the Canadian pension system did not develop in national isolation. From its inception it was profoundly influenced by external factors, especially foreign capital (British and American) and foreign labor (American). Many colonial enterprises and, later, branch plants of transnational corporations, brought a host of innovative pension policies with them to Canada. Similarly, as the organized arm of the American labor movement swept into the northern half of the continent and recruited the overwhelming majority of Canadian trade unionists, it undermined the ability of the Canadian working class to fight for a more broadly-based public pension system.

The balance of class power and the foreign influences just mentioned were augmented by a third factor: state structures also held sway over the development of the Canadian pension system. Thus far, the influence of the state has been evident only in our references to various military and civil service initiatives in the pension arena. Below we will see that Canadian state structures actually had much broader implications for the growth and form of the country's pension system.

The Growth of Private Pensions in North America, 1940-80

After the outbreak of World War II, pension developments in Canada and the US continued to run parallel—but only up to a point. Private pensions proliferated in both countries. The number of private pension plans in Canada grew dramatically from 722 in 1937 to 3,545 a decade later. Between 1938 and 1947 the proportion of employees covered by occupational pensions increased from less than 8 percent to nearly 17 percent in Canada and from 11.3 percent to 19.4 percent in the US (Deaton, 1989; Edwards, 1967; Marsh, 1975 [1943]). How can these developments be explained?

The traditional explanation for the turn to private pension schemes in North America is that they provided an alternative to wage increases. With the outbreak of World War II, governments in Canada and the US sought to prevent inflation and raise funds for war mobilization by introducing wage controls and new taxes on excess profits. However, tax regulations in both countries allowed corporations to lower their costs and circumvent the wage freeze by making tax-deductible contributions to occupational welfare schemes. Such contributions also helped companies retain employees in a period of acute labor shortage. Favorable tax legislation in the 1950s encouraged further expansion of private plans.

Beth Stevens (this volume) has delineated the problem with this conventional view as it has been applied to the US. Private pensions were not just an alternative to wages. They also reflected labor's growing realization that the creation of a private alternative to public pensions was essential since the public option was effectively closed to American workers in the second half of the 1940s. Labor was shut out of federal policymaking, prevented by new campaign laws from organizing voters and backing candidates, limited in its ability to organize and retain workers by the 1947 Taft-Hartley Act, and encouraged by the federal government to campaign for fringe benefits.

As a result of these pressures, the pension strategy of the American labor movement shifted. Especially in the 1950s, labor began to push for an expansion of private welfare. The predominance of American branch plants and international unions in Canada ensured that Canadian workers would follow suit. Over the next few decades the number of private pension plans and the percentage of the labor force covered by them grew in lockstep in the two countries. In 1970 nearly 34 percent of Canadian workers were covered by private, employment-based pension plans, compared to almost 42 percent of workers in the US. A decade later, the corresponding figures were approximately 40 percent and 46 percent respectively.

Power, State Structures, and the Growth of Public Pensions, 1940-80

The postwar spread of occupational pensions in North America was accompanied in Canada by significant public welfare growth. With regard to pensions, two developments took place in 1951. The Old Age Assistance Act allowed those aged 66-69 to collect a means-tested benefit. More important, the Old Age Security Act introduced a universal, flat-rate demogrant payable to all Canadians over 70 years of age (65 as of 1970). In 1965, a second tier of old age protection was created with the enactment of the Canada Pension Plan and its counterpart in Québec (C/QPP). This was a national, wage-related program financed by contributions from workers and employers and covering virtually all members of the paid labor force. Other means-tested programs were later created to complement the C/QPP, such as the Guaranteed Income Supplement (1967) and the Spouse's Allowance (1975). While by no means generous or adequate, this package of programs ensured that elderly Canadians would be considerably more secure than their American counterparts. In Canada, private pensions would thus serve as a third tier of old-age security.

How can we explain the more robust expansion of relatively extensive and inclusive government-run pension schemes in Canada after the war? It is widely acknowledged that Canadians quite naturally demanded more security in the aftermath of the Depression. Moreover, the state gained legitimacy as a central planning agency during the war, while its personnel gained competence administering large-scale programs. What gave force to these demands and instrumentalities, however, was a steady rise in working class power combined with two features of state structure that facilitated the translation of class power into state policy.

Consider the power question first. As the size of the Canadian labor force increased from about four million to over twelve million between 1939 and 1980, the proportion of non-agricultural workers who belonged to unions rose from 17.3 to 37.6 percent and the real wages of workers grew by 119 percent (Brym, 1991 [1986]:687; Huxley, Kettler and Struthers, 1986:118). At the same time, the trade union movement consolidated, eventually forming a new trade union central, the Canadian Labor Congress, in 1956. And in the 1970s Canadian trade unions began a massive movement away from the conservative American-controlled internationals. Canadian unionists who were involved in protracted strikes were angered to watch their co-unionists in the USA work extra shifts to make up for lost production in Canadian plants. The feeling also grew that union funds were being drained from Canadian locals to head offices in the US. Combined with the general rise of nationalist feeling in Canada, these factors contributed to the so-called "breakaway movement": the resignation of Canadian members from international unions and the formation of independent Canadian unions. By 1977, for the first time in Canadian history, less than half of trade unionists were members of internationals. That number has now dropped to about a third.

The demands of the larger, better organized, more affluent, and more radical Canadian working class for better public pensions (and other accoutrements of the modern welfare state) were facilitated by two features of the Canadian state. First, the Canadian electoral system encourages the emergence of third parties, and especially labor parties, to a greater degree than does its American counterpart (compare Lipset, 1976). In Canada there is only one elective political arena at the federal and provincial levels—the legislatures—and seats in the legislatures are filled on a constituency-by-constituency basis. In the US, separate elections are held for the legislative and executive branches of government. These elections are state- or nation-wide. Thus in a Canadian constituency in which radicals are highly concentrated, a vote for a radical candidate is more likely to "pay" since he or she stands a reasonable chance of winning and therefore influencing government policy in the legislature. In voting for state governors or the President, however, Americans must take into account the political complexion of a very large social unit that inevitably contains diverse interests, so that a vote for a third-party candidate is almost bound to be perceived as wasted. In the US case, therefore, electors tend to vote for the presidential or gubernatorial candidate who offers the platform closest to the voter's interests and who is among the more likely winners. Thus the separation of legislative from executive authority in the US militates against the success of third parties, while Canada's centralized parliamentary government is more conducive to their success.

Electoral systems also affect third-party strength in Canada through the principle of party loyalty. In state legislatures and the US Congress representatives vote according to their individual views as they are shaped by the interests of the people who support and elect them. This in no way endangers the tenure of the administration. In Canada, intraparty disputes are resolved in caucus, and once representatives enter the legislature they are obliged to vote as a bloc. If representatives of the ruling party fail to do so they can cause the downfall of the government. In Canada, interests that are not satisfied with the policies of the existing parties thus have little alternative to forming a third party, while in the US diverse interests can be accommodated inside existing parties without major difficulty.

The effect of the Canadian electoral system on the development of public pensions was evident by 1921, although at first it was negative because of the preponderant role played by farmers in protest politics. Western and Ontario farmers were long upset over steep tariffs on the import of manufactured goods, high interest rates, exorbitant transportation costs, and price-setting on wheat by monopsonistic Eastern buyers. They were unable to influence the establishment parties on these issues and consequently decided to form the Progressive Party.

The Progressives first ran in the 1921 election and won 65 seats—a quarter of the total. The Liberals needed their support in order to form a government. But the Liberals also relied on the votes of organized labor and the backing of the two Labor MPs elected to Parliament; and the labor movement was at odds with the farmers on a number of economic and social issues. For instance, tariffs protected manufacturing jobs and raised the price of farm machinery. Consequently, labor favored tariffs while farmers opposed them. Similarly, unemployment insurance offered to protect workers against the worst vagaries of the market but to make it more difficult for farmers to attract cheap, unskilled, seasonal labor from the East.

The Liberals clearly needed to effect a compromise between workers and farmers in order to maintain parliamentary control. As far as pension proposals were concerned, it soon emerged that a minimal, means-tested pension program would not create many problems for farmers. Moreover, it would allow the Liberals to gain the electoral support of labor as well as progressive elements in the middle class (Orloff and Parker, 1990a). And it could do so without challenging the type of corporate welfare system favored by urban capitalists. Thus Canada's parliamentary political system facilitated the formation of a minority government and a set of party alliances that gave rise to the first public pension in Canada in 1927.[8]

In the late 1920s and the 1930s, the radical and moderate wings of the farmers movement split, and an alliance was struck between radical farmers and organized labor. Out of this union, the Cooperative Commonwealth Federation (CCF) was born in Saskatchewan in 1933. Twelve years later the CCF became the first social-democratic government in North America when it was elected Saskatchewan's ruling party. In 1961 the CCF was dissolved and replaced by the more urban and labor-oriented New Democratic Party (NDP).

The NDP has grown substantially since the first half of the 1990s, it formed governments in the provinces of British Columbia, Saskatchewan and Ontario, which together contain over half of Canada's population. Occasionally the NDP has held the balance of power in Parliament, using the opportunity to win concessions from minority governments. But even when not so conveniently poised to influence policy, it has represented a constituency whose demands cannot be ignored. It is almost a platitude of Canadian political science that many governments have remained popular and prevented the further strengthening of social-democratic forces by implementing policies first proposed by the CCF and the NDP.

For six decades the CCF and the NDP have struggled to improve the quality of public pensions and other elements of the modern welfare state and to help the trade union movement grow in size and influence.[9] In turn, welfare state reforms have helped the Canadian working class resist making concessions to employers. In contrast, there is no independent labor party in the US. Union density in the US reached its peak in 1954, declining from nearly 35 percent of the nonagricultural labor force to less than 17 percent today (Galenson, 1986:60; Huxley, Kettler and Struthers, 1986:118). And the absence of a national, universal health care system, family benefits, and adequate, all-inclusive compensation for the unemployed has weakened American labor's ability to resist making concessions. Much of this cross-national difference can be attributed to the distinctive electoral systems of the two countries.

A second feature of the Canadian state that makes the country's welfare system more generous than that in the US is a response to what David Cameron (1986) has called the "openness" of the Canadian economy. Compared to most other industrialized countries, the Canadian economy is characterized by a relatively high value of exports relative to GNP. Through spending, government has sought to mitigate the consequences of troughs in the business cycle and secular increases in unemployment, both of which are related to Canada's vulnerability to the volatile and deteriorating American economy. More generally, the Canadian state has always played a more prominent role in economic affairs than the American state because of the threat from the south. As H.G.J. Aitken (1967 [1959]:221) put it more than 30 years ago:

[Economic] expansionism in Canada has been largely induced rather than autonomous. It has been contingent on state action... Throughout Canadian development expansionism has been defensive in character. It has been part of a general strategy of containing the expansionism of the stronger and more aggressive economy of the United States and preserving a distinct political sovereignty over the territory north of the present international boundary. Each phase of expansionism in Canada has been a tactical move designed to forestall, counteract, or restrain the northward extension of American economic and political influence. Primary responsibility for maintaining and strengthening this policy of defensive expansionism has fallen on the state.

Said differently, the circumstances of Canada's political economy have led to the adoption of state policies that defend the population against the vagaries of an unusually high-amplitude business cycle in the short term, a trend towards deteriorating demand for Canadian products in the medium term, and recurrent political and economic threats from the south in the long term. One result is a public pension system that is more highly developed than that in the US.

Recent Developments, 1960-90

Thus far we have emphasized divergences between the Canadian and US pension systems. But parallel developments could also be observed in the two countries after 1980. Specifically, it became clear that the augmentation of old-age security in the foreseeable future would occur only in the private sphere, and mainly among full-time, highly-paid, unionized employees. As with other Canadian welfare state programs, public pension growth outpaced its American counterpart, but reached an upper limit that now seems impervious.

We believe that the apparent upper limit to Canadian public pension reform is constituted by capitalist class power. That was evident as early as the 1960s. Predictably, the powerful insurance industry was alarmed and dissatisfied with the introduction of the C/QPP. Therefore, the Canadian government deliberately set low maximum benefit levels so that even the average worker had to seek additional coverage in the private sphere. Despite the introduction of supplementary, means-tested programs in the 1960s and 1970s, the overall picture changed little (Myles, 1988; National Council of Welfare, 1989).

The efforts of organized labor and other lobbying groups to expand the public pension system in the 1970s foundered when powerful business interests, especially the insurance and trust companies of Ontario, formed an opposition alliance and sought to promote occupational pensions as an alternative (Banting, 1987). The relative decline in corporate savings between 1963-67 and 1978-82 meant that personal savings, and private pension systems in particular, would become a principal source of industrial and commercial investment. Indeed, net private pension saving (contributions plus investment income minus benefits paid and administrative costs) as a percentage of gross private domestic business investment more than doubled between 1960 and 1980, increasing from 6.8 to 15.7 percent. The primary purpose of private pension savings, from the corporate perspective, is not the provision of old-age security. Rather, it represents an increasingly important source of capital that would be seriously threatened by further expansion of the public program. Business leaders also feared that an expanded public pension system would provide the state with tremendous economic power and threaten the survival of the entire business community (Deaton, 1989).[10]

In the 1980s and 1990s the state proved unable to sustain the levels of spending reached in the 1970s. Together with the heightened international competition of the era, this significantly weakened labor while augmenting capital's blocking power. More generous public pensions could hardly be won while state budgets were under attack and demands for international competitiveness legitimized a lower social wage. But these developments overdetermined what was already clear by 1980: the further development of old-age security would occur at the workplace, if at all.[11] It was also obvious that income security would continue to be unevenly distributed. In 1988, over 4.8 million Canadian workers participated in some 21,239 employment-based pension plans (Statistics Canada, 1990), but 63 percent of Canadian workers still relied exclusively on the modest and inadequate public system.

The prospect of private pension coverage is much greater in the primary than in the secondary segment of the labor market and is thus associated with unionization, gender, and sector of employment (whether monopoly or competitive, public or private). As in most other capitalist countries, private pension plans in Canada are much more likely to be found among highly-paid, unionized men working full-time in large firms and among full-time, public sector employees. Thus in 1978 expenditures on a variety of occupational welfare programs were much higher among unionized employees than among the non-unionized. In particular, 74 percent of the total spent on occupational pensions went to unionized workers (Statistics Canada, 1978:27). Similarly, in 1986 almost 75 percent of unionized workers, but only 37 percent of the total labor force, participated in employment-based pension plans (Statistics Canada, 1990).

If employment-based pensions reinforce the division between unionized and non-unionized workers, it should not be assumed that such divisions are absent within the ranks of the unionized. At least in the

Canadian context, enterprise-level welfare programs foster corporate, not class, loyalty. They lead employees to seek further welfare reform at the workplace level rather than through the state. In Canada, private pension plans discourage opportunities for the type of society-wide welfare bargaining found in Sweden.

Conclusion: Canadian Pensions in Comparative Perspective

In our brief survey we have sought to explain the evolution of Canadian pension programs and differences between the Canadian and American systems. Substantively, we have focused on the use of the Canadian pension system before 1940 as a means of worker control; the emergence of the first public pension system in 1927, eight years before parallel developments in the US; the development, between 1940 and 1980, of a more universal, contributory, public pension system that is in some important respects superior to the US variant; the growth of private pension schemes since the 1940s; and the limits placed on public pension reform since the 1970s.[12]

Analytically, we have emphasized the following points:

♦ The distribution of power between labor and capital has always been a chief cause of the development, size, and mix of the Canadian pension system. Most students of comparative political economy are content to analyze the impact of working class power alone on a variety of state policies. In contrast, we have emphasized that we are dealing with a power *ratio*; capitalist class power is also a key determinant of state policy (for an elaboration of this point, see especially Olsen, 1991, 1992).

♦ While relatively powerful capitalist classes and weak working classes in the US and Canada have kept public pensions underdeveloped compared to the Swedish system, there are important divergences between Canada and the US that may be attributed to differences in state structure. In particular, the Canadian parliamentary system has encouraged the development of a social democratic party that has pushed the growth of public pensions beyond US levels. The US has no counterpart to the NDP. Moreover, as a defense against the threat of US expansionism, the Canadian state has been relatively interventionist. This too has had a salutary impact on the growth of public pensions.

♦ The Canadian case brings out particularly sharply the need to examine the international context of changes in public policy. For 300 years Canadian pension programs have carried the stamp of foreign influence. As a colony of Britain, the major source of American foreign direct investment, and an important appendage of the US labor movement until recently, Canada has been especially vulnerable to influence by outside forces. This is certainly evident in the pension field, where many progressive innovations—and stumbling blocks to further growth—have originated outside the country.

Values, it will be noted, are absent from our account. Canadians may be more "collectivity-oriented" than Americans, as Lipset suggests. But if so, these value differences are firmly rooted in the political economies of the two countries, as are differences in their pension systems.

Notes

1. We thank Michael Shalev for his invaluable comments on drafts of this paper.
2. For a comparison of Swedish and Canadian approaches to unemployment and labor market policy, see Olsen (1988).
3. In both countries that percentage increased since 1984, while the gap between the two countries grew. The 1984 Canadian and US figures were, respectively, 32.5 and 36.7 percent. The corresponding 1989 figures were 33.5 and 39.0 percent (Courchene, 1989:44; Kumar, Coates, and Arrowsmith, 1986:473).
4. We will not discuss "fiscal welfare" (tax benefits) and retirement savings plans due to space limitations.
5. Lipset ignores the balance of class forces entirely but does mention some of the other forces we discuss, for the most part in passing. See especially Lipset (1976). On the class bases of state structures, see Denis (1989) and Esping-Andersen (1976).
6. Indeed, even today, the economy is comparatively highly oligopolized and corporate interlocking among top capitalists is relatively dense (Ornstein, 1989).
7. It should be noted that the 1935 Old Age Insurance program in the US, although earnings-related and far from generous, made the American pension system more generous than its Canadian counterpart for a period. On the

special circumstances surrounding the implementation of New Deal pension plans, see especially Anglim and Gratton (1987), Jenkins and Brents (1989), Orloff and Parker (1990b), Quadagno (1984) and Skocpol and Ikenberry (1983).

8. The political circumstances that allowed the implementation of the New Deal in the US in 1935 were somewhat different. While they never achieved power, the emergence of a string of third-party challengers and a sustained wave of protest and demands by the unemployed, veterans, farmers and striking workers, produced a crisis which provided the impetus for welfare reform. The disunity of the American capitalist class in terms of its support for New Deal proposals—reflected in the diverse counterproposals put forth by various blocs of capital—created the political opportunity for reform (Jenkins and Brents, 1989).

9. Since 1976 the Parti Québécois has performed a functionally equivalent role in Québec, although less consistently than the NDP. Of course both NDP and PQ governments have been somewhat hampered by their "sub-national" status, and tensions between the labor movement and the NDP have been exacerbated recently in Ontario. For a brief but critical account of the fortunes of the incumbent NDP governments in Ontario, British Columbia and Saskatchewan, see Watkins (1994), Cohen (1994) and Hansen (1994) respectively. In the 1995 Ontario election, the NDP not only lost office but placed third in the polls. The national NDP has not fared well recently either. The dramatic decline in the number of NDP seats in the 1993 federal election lost the NDP its "official party" status.

10. This was, at least, the case in English-speaking Canada. In Québec a nationalistic political environment caused public pensions to be viewed as an instrument of state-building and a means of stimulating the growth of a local capitalist class (Brym, 1992). The Québec public pension fund (the Caisse de dépôt et placement du Québec), with assets of over 42 billion dollars, is now the largest institutional investor in Canada, and the companies it controls account for fully 10 percent of the trading activity on the Montreal Stock Exchange.)

11. The rate of growth of occupational pension plans declined somewhat in the 1970s in both Canada and the US, suggesting that the "upper limit" of voluntary employer-based pensions has perhaps been reached (Deaton, 1989).

12. During the late 1980s and early 1990s, Canada's Conservative government implemented policies to further encourage private alternatives to the public pension system such as retirement savings plans and occupational pensions. Moreover, it effectively eliminated the universal character of the OAS by introducing a "clawback" mechanism.

11

Occupational Welfare and the Japanese Experience

Toshimitsu Shinkawa and T.J. Pempel

Japan is a frustratingly uncooperative case when it comes to comparative studies of industrialized democracies. Analyses of various contributors to economic performance have long been confounded by Japan's systematically superlative experience. Examinations of corporatism make highly accurate predictions of national behavior, but only to the extent that they either ignore or treat in theoretically idiosyncratic ways the experience of Japan (Shalev, 1990:64-65). When virtually every incumbent government in North America and Western Europe was toppled in the wake of the oil shocks of the early 1970s, Japan's ruling Liberal Democratic Party (LDP) remained tenaciously in power. (Inoguchi, 1990). Favorable government policies toward unemployment are highly correlated with the strength of the political left in virtually all countries; however, Japan (along with the peculiar case of Switzerland) is a noteworthy exception (Therborn, 1986). Crime rates have been rising in most industrialized democracies; in Japan they have been dropping for two decades. It is the rare social, political or economic study that finds the Japanese experience to be at or near the median of the cases studied; Japan seems to defy categorization as "average." The resultant temptation, of course, is to accept the notion, advanced by many Japan specialists, and an even larger proportion of Japanese, that Japan is unique, and hence defiant of "normal," i.e. "Western-oriented" theories. This is certainly the case with regard to Japan's experience with occupational welfare.

In the area of occupational welfare, Japan is definitely something of an oddity. Many Japanese firms spend considerable sums to create, if not cradle-to-grave socialism, at least its hiring-to-retirement equivalent. They provide subsidized housing, housing allowances, and/or downpayment loans for new homes; transportation allowances; medical facilities for employees and their families; in-plant canteens, barber shops, nurseries, and discount shopping centers; organized company vacation spots at ski centers or hot springs; child care allowances and often on-site nurseries; as well as company picnics, athletic clubs, marriage brokerage facilities, cultural clubs and libraries. In addition, the best programs provide generous insurance schemes and retirement plans. One extensive survey of Japanese firms indicated that the costs of such occupational-welfare programs added 18 percent to an employee's monthly compensation for all firms, and as much as 21 percent more at firms of over 5000 employees (Hall, 1988:13). Those who work under such conditions have little personal or political interest in the development of state-generated nationwide social benefits. For the most part, a large segment of their most basic needs are met by their employers.

This pattern has given rise to an extensive cottage industry extolling the merits of the Japanese employment system, Japan as a classless society, and the beneficence of the Japanese manager. Yet, while such benefits are common in many Japanese firms, they generally remain less costly than comparable benefits in other industrialized countries. (Hall, 1988:25-26; see also Table 11.3—all tables and figures are located at the end of the chapter.) Furthermore, far more Japanese employers provide few, and in some cases, almost none of these amenities, a fact conveniently ignored by those lauding the alleged cultural inexorability of Japan's presumed proclivity toward generous workplace welfare schemes. (See Table 11.2 and Figure 11.1).

In this unevenness of benefits provided by employers, Japan is by no means alone. Like most countries, such as the United States, which do not have elaborately developed state welfare systems, Japan displays an unevenness in the delivery and availability of social benefits that correlates positively with the size of the firm for which one works and the sophistication of the occupational tasks one performs. Employment-related perks become a crucial salary supplement for those whose skills are in high demand, while others in the workforce receive far fewer benefits. Thus, Japan, like the United States, seems an apparent antithesis to the social democratic and corporatist forms of welfare society that prevail in Scandinavia.

If this were all there were to the Japanese experience, standard notions of dualism would suffice to provide an adequate explanation: Japan has a small welfare state; most "welfare" benefits come through the employment system; these are provided unevenly to those in different locations within the labor market. (Goldthorpe, 1984). Indeed, dualism does offer a useful analytic starting point in understanding much of Japan's historical development in the areas of labor relations and occupationally-based welfare. But there are far greater anomalies in the Japanese case that make it more analytically interesting. For example, most dualistic systems are marked by high levels of unemployment during economic downturns, by the creation of a relatively permanent underclass near the bottom rungs of the skills' ladder, and by widespread differentials in income throughout the citizenry. They are, in effect, highly stratified, overtly class-based societies. Yet, in the Japanese case, particularly over the postwar decades, unemployment has consistently been among the lowest in the industrialized world. Meanwhile, Gini index measurements of income equality show Japan to be about as egalitarian as Sweden, Norway, the Netherlands and Denmark—all countries with well-elaborated systems of state-provided social welfare (Sawyer, 1976; Bronfenbrenner and Yasuba, 1987; Verba et al., 1987; Kosai and Ogino, 1984, Cameron, 1988).

Nor is such equality an unusual artifact just of income statistics. In areas such as education, infant mortality, crime, health care, and so forth, Japanese citizens enjoy widely similar, and generally positive, opportunities to live wholesome and fulfilling lives. This is also the case in areas such as the distribution of capital goods such as cars, telephones, washing machines, video recorders, and the like. Given such relative comparability in access to material benefits, it is little wonder that 90 percent of Japanese citizens identify themselves as "middle class" (Murakami, 1982). In this sense, Japan hardly fits the standard profile of a politically conservative, dualistic system in which widely differentiated benefits are unevenly delivered to systematically unequal citizens. In these ways, Japan stands distinctive and apart from other dualist countries such as Canada, Australia, the United States, or Britain.

This overall picture of a Japan whose "welfare mix" does not comply with standard portraits is made even more complicated when one searches for theoretically-satisfactory explanations for the development of different types of social welfare system. Three major models compete for explanatory predominance: the class, or social sectors model; the bureaucratic model; and the economic/demographic model. Most contemporary class models of social welfare offer close corollaries to notions of dualism. Scholars such as Stephens (1979), Korpi (1983), Esping-Andersen (1985, 1990) and others, have suggested that comprehensive state-sponsored social welfare systems will emerge in response to a highly mobilized working class and/or to the ability of leftist political parties to capture government positions for long periods of time. According to this logic, the driving force behind a particular nation's mix of public and private services in social welfare will be a function of class or social sectoral politics, most notably the interactions of business and labor, but secondarily the interactions of these two classes with agriculture and the white collar middle class. Under such a logic business is inherently resistant to government spending of large sums for programs that will benefit workers. Capitalist governments respond to such business preferences, keeping state spending for social welfare low, unless workers can command sufficient resources to take control—directly, or through their elected representatives—of state organs. They may then redirect toward labor, the lower classes and/or the general populace, the policy preferences of state organs that would otherwise serve exclusively as the "executive committee of the bourgeoisie." The specific character of welfare regimes is thus a function of the relative power levels of the various social sectors and the types of compromises which they make over time.

The Japanese case reflects important aspects of this class-based model. Japan has had a politically weak and divided labor movement. Until a socialist-led coalition was formed in 1994, the Japanese left never held cabinet positions (except for a brief few months during the US Occupation, when Japanese government powers were subject to military oversight). Weakness of the working class and the left are certainly congruent with the historically and comparatively low levels of social welfare spending by the Japanese government. Yet they fail to deal with two important and contradictory sets of facts. First, as noted above, Japan is far more egalitarian than is predicted by such class-based models. And second, Japan went through a major programmatic expansion of social welfare programs and government spending for social welfare during the 1970s, despite the fact that labor movement strength was at a historical low: unionization rates were at about 28 percent, strike rates had withered and no socialist, democratic socialist, or communist held national office. Why then, in class-terms, should the government have expanded its social welfare commitment?

Given such puzzles, interpretations rooted in class and dualism must confront two different sets of explanations. From the standpoint of bureaucratic models, such as those offered by Heclo (1974), social welfare programs frequently expand as the consequence of initiatives by state bureaucrats anxious to solve social problems while at the same time expanding their budgets and spheres of political influence. Unlike the class model in which the prime movers of social welfare programs are social sectors, in the bureaucratic model, the prime movers are state elites. Social welfare programs will thus be heavily reflective of the relative success or failure of bureaucratic innovators and elite interactions.

Such elite-driven models are separate from, but congruent with demographically-ratcheted analyses such as those of Wilensky (1975, 1985) and Pryor (1968) who contend that high levels of social spending for welfare will be largely the consequence of three things: rising levels of GNP, changing demographics, and (along with the bureaucratic models) the longevity of social welfare programs.

From these latter two perspectives, and quite unlike the class-driven models of social welfare, the richer a country gets, the more needy its citizens, and the more imperialistic its social welfare bureaucrats, the more redistributive programs it will institute for its citizens; and the longer these programs are in effect the larger they will grow, the more benefits they will deliver, and the greater, consequently, will be the overall level of government spending for, and comprehensiveness of coverage by, social welfare. In short, welfare spending is linked more to supply and demand than to class forces.

The expansion of Japan's social welfare spending programs during the 1970s would appear to be congruent with explanations rooted in such factors and hard to interpret in terms of the balance of class power. By the early 1970s, Japan's GNP had been expanding for nearly two decades at annual rates of about 11 percent; this rate was completely without precedent among the industrialized democracies and was one which allowed Japan to leap from being merely one of many middle-sized economies to being the third (and subsequently the second) largest economy in the world. Furthermore, Japan's population distribution had begun to change, with far more elderly citizens per capita than had been the case at the end of the war. Finally, there was a certain maturing effect taking place within the limited pension programs that had been in place since the later 1950s that would also account for portions of the government's spending increase (Campbell, 1992).

This combination of wealth, demographics and program maturation certainly offers a prima facie explanation for why Japanese government expenditures for social welfare jumped so rapidly in the 1970s and early 1980s. What it does not explain at all are two complicating facts: first, completely new programs were instituted on a scale so widespread as to defy explanations rooted in either bureaucratic or economic incrementalism; and second, these programs were suddenly cut back and government spending for social welfare was dramatically curtailed by the mid-1980s, making Japan one of the few, if not the only, major industrialized countries in the world actually to make a serious dent in spending for established entitlement programs.

Thus, neither the dualistic-class based model, nor the bureaucratic-demographic models offer completely convincing explanations over time for the various ebbs and flows of the Japanese welfare mix. It is our argument that the unusual mixture of state plus occupational welfare in Japan, along with the dynamic changes in this mixture over time, can best be understood in the context of a political-economic model. Such a model requires sensitivity, on the one hand, to the quite separate economic needs of different segments of business. In effect, the broadbrush label "capital" is far too comprehensive a varnish, obscuring critically dissimilar orientations toward "labor" by large, highly sophisticated firms on the one extreme, and smaller, far less sophisticated shops on the other. Even more complicating in any oversimplified notions of "business" are the orientations of the self-employed, the farmer and the government ministry to name but a few. In effect, understanding the complexities of the Japanese case requires a sensitivity to such gapingly disparate needs of the many different types of Japanese employers.

Secondly, the Japanese case requires a sensitivity to electoral and political considerations. Clearly, the "power resources" of the working class and their organized political parties are not immaterial to such matters. The strength of left-wing political parties and their representation in government are often important determinants of a nation's social welfare posture. Prewar labor weakness is critical in understanding the political reluctance of the Japanese government to create and/or expand nationwide programs of social welfare. So is labor's weakness at various junctures in the postwar period. But at least two additional factors must be considered.

First, what is the socio-economic composition of the left's major opponent(s)? In the Japanese case, for the bulk of the postwar period this was the long-ruling Liberal Democratic Party (LDP). As we will attempt to show, for most of the thirty-eight years of its reign (1955-93), the LDP followed social welfare strategies that reflected its composition as a party drawing important support from organized agriculture, as well as both small and large businesses. These support groups complicated the conservative government's approach to occupational welfare and to state-sponsored welfare programs, making a simple dualistic approach politically untenable.

And second, a politically sensitive model must be cognizant of what might be thought of as the anticipatory dynamics of electoral politics. Electoral politics was far less critical in prewar Japan than it became in the postwar period. For most of its long rule, the LDP was a party keenly attuned to the changing currents of public opinion, even if it sometimes chose to ignore them. The same seems to be true of its successor governments. Consequently, in contemporary Japan, as in most electoral democracies, a mere threat to government can often be as significant a catalyst for policy formation or change as is actual governance by an opposition. Astute governments make policies designed to deflect perceived threats rather than allow them to build until they are overwhelming, irresistible and beyond malleability. Moreover, such political astuteness often makes ruling politicians quite aggressive in readjusting their coalitional base by attempting to "recruit" new socio-economic sectors and/or to "replace" diminishing socio-economic sectors (Pempel, 1990).

It is our argument that this political-economic dynamic was critical to understanding first, the overall reliance on occupationally-based welfare among Japan's largest and most internationally competitive firms; and second, the expansion and then the diminution of state-sponsored social welfare programs in the 1970s and 1980s, and Japan's return to a more occupationally-determined welfare system by the end of the 1980s and the beginning of the 1990s.

This chapter is divided into five sections. The first details the links between Japan's late industrialization, its heavy reliance on occupationally-based welfare programs, and its early congruence with dualist and class-based interpretations of a nation's social welfare mix. The second section explores the rise in the power of organized labor during the early postwar period; the early debates over how best to create a mix of state and enterprise welfare schemes; and the very limited development of state-led social welfare programs that occurred at that time. It shows how Japan might well have moved in any one of several directions, but how the direction that emerged structured many subsequent choices. The third section explores the actual mix that prevailed from the mid-1950s until the early 1970s, a system with some small programs run by the government but with the nation's primary reliance being on well-institutionalized, occupationally-based welfare schemes. This combination left Japan during that period as the industrialized world's most conspicuous 'welfare laggard.' The fourth section examines the relative explosion of governmental programs and spending for social welfare during the 1970s, focusing on the mixture of economic and political factors that contributed to this expansion, and then the political economy of Japanese government cutbacks starting in the mid-1980s on its embryonic efforts at expansion and the return to a balance in which occupationally-based welfare remained preeminent. Finally, the fifth section examines the socio-economic causes and consequences of Japan's heavy reliance on occupationally-based welfare systems, and seeks to unravel the puzzle of relative equality among citizens without heavy state intervention for the provision of social welfare.

Industrialization, Labor and Enterprise Welfare in Prewar Japan

The prewar Japanese experience replicates many of the classic traits of dualist and class-based interpretations of welfare development. Japan's industrialization began in the last third of the 19th century under a state vigorously committed to creating "a rich country and a strong army." An economically strong and politically well-positioned business sector confronted a much weaker and late-developing labor movement. A succession of conservative governments, most of them independent of electoral politics, were committed to rapid national industrialization and to economic and ideological policies which rejected any major public expenditures for social welfare. Instead, state powers were used principally to enforce tight labor market discipline and to oppose any organizations committed to a class-based strategy of politics. The primary government orientation to social problems and poverty was to encourage reliance on non-governmental agencies such as the family and the firm. About the only significant government welfare effort nationwide was a minimalist poor-relief plan, modelled on the Poor Laws of England, which was introduced in 1874 and revised in 1931 (Okamoto, 1991).

The government's only involvement with pensions, for example, was to offer lump-sum payments to officials, soldiers, and other citizens who had been of noteworthy service to the state. Thus, naval and army pension plans were enacted in 1875 and 1876 respectively while a civil service pension plan was introduced in 1884. These three were integrated in 1923. This system of onkyu, or gratitude payment, to selected government employees was not terribly dissimilar from the Civil War pensions paid by the US government to veterans and widows (Amenta and Skocpol, 1989). Well into the 1920s such onkyu payments were the largest single government expenditure (Anderson, 1993:68) and as late as 1923 when a variety of expenditures for health insurance, pensions and disaster relief rose by a factor of twenty-five, social spending had still not reached one percent of Japan's net domestic product (Anderson, 1993:68).

Virtually any welfare benefits enjoyed by non-government employees was occupationally-generated and was administered primarily through the factory. Both government and business sought to promote a version of labor-management harmony linked to Japan's allegedly historical "beautiful customs" (bifu) involving close, paternalistic relations between worker and employer. As Shoda Heigoro, the director of the Mitsubishi Shipyard stated in opposing a proposed factory law:

Since ancient times, Japan has possessed the beautiful custom of master-servant relations based firmly on a spirit of sacrifice and compassion, a custom not seen in the many other countries of the world... [This relationship] has its roots in our family system...and [because] of this relationship, the employer loves the employee and the employee respects the master. Interdependent and helping each other, the two preserve industrial peace... Today, there exist no evils and we feel no necessity [for a factory law]...which will destroy the beautiful custom of master-servant relations and wreak havoc on our industrial peace. (Gordon, 1985:66-67)

Japan's earliest efforts at industrialization involved light industry, most notably textiles, where the principal workers were young females, typically recruited from the country's rural areas. Thus, paternalism at the workplace was initially an easily justified, and economically rational, policy. Since young women typically stayed in the labor market for only several years before returning to their villages to get married, the labor supply was plentiful and the owners' economic incentives to promote special benefits were few. Meanwhile, factory-run dormitories provided a convenient way for managers to oversee both the morality and more importantly the hours of their female employees. With the dormitory system in place, the young women were isolated from the outside world and widely available for overtime work at the owner's behest. They were also kept away from the organizers of the embryonic union movement. As one additional consequence, Japanese unionism was particularly slow to start in this initial area of industrial production.

Not until 1914, as heavy industry began to replace light industry as the locomotive of the Japanese economy, did male workers constitute a majority of industrial workers (Shirai, 1983:45). Only at that point was skilled labor in short supply. Large firms in shipbuilding and iron and steel therefore introduced various techniques to secure stable supplies of skilled labor: so-called lifetime employment, seniority-based wages, and enterprise welfare. Moreover, retirement allowances and mutual-aid credit systems were developed. So too were industry-wide blacklists of workers who quit one firm in search of a better job elsewhere or those who were otherwise troublesome. All of these measures were begun as means to keep workers tied closely to their employers.

Retirement allowances in particular became a core starting point for enterprise welfare as the Japanese economy suffered a prolonged recession in the 1920s. These recessionary conditions had encouraged the emerging labor unions to call, among other things, for the institution of government-sponsored unemployment insurance. Both the government and big business, fearful that any such program might be viewed as creating a right for labor and fearful of anything that might strengthen the sense of class solidarity at the expense of firm loyalty, rejected the idea of unemployment insurance. Instead they opted for a revision of the 1911 Factory Law.

That 1922 revision (enforced in 1926) required management to give a dismissed employee fourteen days' notice or else to pay an allowance equivalent to fourteen days' wages. This hardly constituted a satisfactory response from the standpoint of labor's demand for unemployment insurance; but it did reconfirm the longstanding links between employment and welfare. In this way, firm-based retirement allowances were introduced, first as a means of securing skilled labor, and then as a substitute for a national program of unemployment insurance.

Reflecting their separate labor markets, however, there were huge differentials in the benefits offered by firms of different size. As of 1926,

89 percent of Japan's establishments with 1,000 employees or more had retirement allowance programs while only one percent of those with fewer than 50 employees did (Yamazaki, 1988:21). Moreover, larger firms (200 or more employees) paid a lump sum dismissal fee equal to between 542-714 days wages for employees with 20-25 years' service, while smaller firms (fewer than 200 employees) paid less than half that amount, i.e. 291-377 days' wages (Yamazaki, 1988:30).

Finally, retirement allowances were typically treated as a gratuity from management rather than as a worker's right. Thus, when an employee left the job of his own volition, he would receive only about half the amount given to one dismissed by management. Moreover, allowances were often not paid at all when employees quit "against the will of the management," moved to rival companies, or started competing businesses (Yamazaki, 1988:32-33).

In addition to providing lump sum retirement payments, large factories began to set comparatively young ages for retirements. This helped management to get rid of aging and more highly paid workers and to replace them with younger, cheaper labor. As early as 1919, the nation's largest iron factory set a policy of dismissing operatives at the age of 55. By the mid-1920s over 50 percent of Japan's factories had some form of mandatory retirement age for skilled and semiskilled workers. (It should be noted, however, that most Japanese were self-employed or worked in small family type manufacturing industries and that such mandatory retirement ages did not reach the bulk of Japan's work force) (Kii, 1991:269). Finally, to mix paternalism with maximum control over scarce capital, employers usually preferred lump-sum retirement payments to long-term pensions.

For the most part, government strongly supported such occupationally-based forms of providing social benefits. In the absence of major government programs for social welfare, taxes on business could be kept relatively low; scarce capital could be allocated to other programs, including the massive military buildup; organized labor could be kept weakened; and the prevailing ideology of hierarchy and deference to authority could be reinforced. There were, however, two important exceptions to the limited state involvement in citizen welfare during this period, namely the passage of the National Health Insurance Law in 1938 (Sudo, 1991) and the Employee Pension System Law in 1941.

Both pieces of legislation emerged primarily as the result of elite initiative, but lest it be thought that the Japanese government was gradually undergoing an ideological metamorphosis in favor of broad social welfare provisions, it is essential to note that the first law was passed largely to deal with the deleterious effects of tuberculosis among Japanese soldiers. The latter law, meanwhile, sought to generate funds for munitions and the military through obligatory contributions to a program which would not mature and provide benefits until decades after the war was to be over. At the same time, it should be recognized that such efforts were important in the long-term democratization of the country's benefits' programs and served as a basis for subsequent expansions during the period following the war. In sum, however, throughout the prewar period, there was little systematic recognition by state authorities of some generalized obligation to provide widely and generously for its citizens. In this case, benefits were clearly linked and limited to the national military mission.

Occupationally-based welfare schemes allowed a relatively small number of employers to attract and hold the cream of Japanese labor while most of the remaining workforce had few cushions against the harshness of the labor market. Labor unions provided little collective help. Under the Police Regulations of 1900 the government banned any actions to "instigate" or "incite" workers to participate in collective actions related to working conditions and wages. Subsequently, the Peace Preservation Law of 1925 prohibited any activities that challenged private ownership. It was consequently difficult for labor to become organized in prewar Japan; the highest unionization ratio remained only 7.9 percent in 1931 (cf. Garon, 1987; Kinzley, 1991).

Moreover, even the small segment of labor that was organized was ideologically divided. Class-based Marxist unions were numerous. But much stronger were unions that accepted the underlying paternalistic ideology of a plant-level harmony between the interests of business and labor. As Garon (1987:192) has put it, such "Japanist" unions "came the closest to constituting a truly fascist movement in the sense of a vehemently antisocialist, mass-based front." Rejecting the confrontational images of business-labor relations so closely linked to class models of social welfare, and also rejecting any hostility (and most demands) toward the state, this new orientation came to dominate the labor movement during the mid- to late-1930s and further inculcated the principles of "sound trade unionism" and "industrial cooperation" that had been so much a part of the prevailing occupational welfare system and that were to play an important role in postwar labor organization.

The cumulative picture that emerges is one in which organized labor was weak and systematically excluded from the inner circles of Japanese power—both at the governmental and at the plant level. At the same time, a well-differentiated system of occupationally-linked benefits began to emerge in those Japanese firms that were anxious to ensure stable supplies of skilled labor. This was especially true in heavy industry and larger firms. By providing a host of benefits, some involving deferred payments (in the form of bonuses and retirement allowances) that were linked to long-term employment, Japan's most advanced firms ensured themselves stable supplies of skilled labor and also laid the groundwork for the subsequent evolution of approaches to occupationally-linked welfare. Meanwhile, the Japanese government, eschewing major commitments to costly national programs of welfare, was able to keep the state small and also to delay any major bureaucratic impetus toward escalation and expansion of the social welfare state over time. Despite some important changes politically in the 1940s and 1950s, this basic pattern held until the early-to mid-1970s. In short, a class-based, dualistic model provides a good approximation of the prewar Japanese welfare mix, particularly when one recognizes Japan's highly differentiated labor markets: the one that prevailed in the relatively few big industries and sophisticated manufacturing firms which were in the vanguard of providing various occupationally-based welfare programs on the one hand; and the far less competitive market that prevailed for the country's more numerous smaller shops and factories on the other, most of which provided few if any significant benefits beyond basic wages.

Power Realignment in the Early Postwar Period

In its first two years, the Allied Occupation created an environment that demonstrably favored organized labor in Japan. Under the influence of New Deal policies from Washington, and attempting to eliminate what were seen to have been the socio-economic roots of Japan's wartime expansion, SCAP (Supreme Commander of the Allied Powers) dismantled Japan's largest business conglomerates (zaibatsu). It also purged numerous top business, political, journalistic and academic leaders deemed to have been closely tied to the wartime regime. Meanwhile, modelling Japanese legislation on the US Wagner Act, it imposed labor laws which established minimum working conditions, favored unionization, and legitimized collective negotiations of labor disputes. As a result, the business-labor power balance in Japan shifted dramatically in favor of labor. As early as December 1945, 509 trade unions had already organized 380,000 workers. The unionization ratio reached 55 percent in 1949, the highest in the history of the Japanese labor movement.

This massive organizational success might have provided a major boost to efforts at transferring the welfare burden from the firm to the state, had Japanese unions followed the precedents of European unions. However, in two critical ways, the Japanese movement was different. First, at the national level, it was highly fragmented, particularly in the split between Marxian unions and social democratic unions. The former favored unrelenting class-based confrontations with business and the conservative government; the latter was far more open to economic compromises at the factory level. In the early postwar years, the Marxian strand dominated the union movement, making collective political action by the union movement as a whole exceptionally difficult. It also virtually ruled out any national level cooperation between management and labor.

But second, at the plant level, Japanese unions were organized not along trade or industrial lines as was the pattern in most union movements that had been important policy welfare catalysts in other countries; rather, Japanese unions were formed largely along enterprise lines. The end result was to complicate the links between labor strength and pressures for comprehensive national welfare programs. What was in the best organizational interests of the enterprise unions was not always compatible with national welfare programs.

In the enterprise union, all workers in a particular firm, regardless of skill or position in the hierarchy became members of a single organization. In its earliest stages, this pattern had highly egalitarian underpinnings. The guiding union philosophy seemed to be: all of us have suffered equally during the war; we should all be part of the same organization. But fundamentally, enterprise unionism involved a pattern inherently hostile to political or economic organization along class lines, and in turn was hostile toward action aimed at prying benefits, such as an extensive social welfare system, from the institutions of state. Rather the enterprise union was highly compatible with the prewar occupationally-based welfare system and its highly differentiated benefit structure. As such, it was strongly promoted by both government and larger Japanese businesses as the preferred organizational form.

294 Toshimitsu Shinkawa and T.J. Pempel

Largely as the result of the enterprise union system, workers in an enterprise tended to identify their welfare with that of the firm, an identification which management could enhance through firm-specific benefits. The overall result was a defusing of state-oriented, or class-based, political actions. Managers were systematic for example in pointing out that Toyota workers had interests inherently hostile to those at Nissan, and/or that if Matsushita profited as a company so would its workers. Competition with Toshiba and NEC was made far more important than seeking from the Japanese government benefits for all electronics workers (let alone all workers generally).

Japanese management immediately after the war was far from a replica of its prewar predecessors. The dismantling of the prewar conglomerates facilitated the rise of rather liberal employers who advocated a so-called revised capitalism. Anticipating a far more powerful labor movement—and hence greater difficulties in securing stable labor supplies—a group of business leaders sought to promote economic reconstruction through voluntary co-operation between labor and management. To do this, they established the Economic Reconstruction Council (ERC) in July 1947. Principally concerned with providing factory level cooperation between labor and management, much along lines that would have been compatible with the prewar occupational welfare system, the ERC was also open to prospects of corporatist-like cooperation with organized labor.

However, largely because of its ideological orientation, and the organizational form of the enterprise union, Japanese labor did not take advantage of the ERC as a means toward creating a social democratic contract. The moderate union federation, Sodomei, with 850,000 members, supported the basic idea of a revised capitalism; however, the largest confederation, Sanbetsu, which had 1,630,000 workers, held stubbornly to Marxist doctrine and rejected any compromise with capital, including any that might have involved cooperative and/or corporatist arrangements such as were beginning to prevail in much of Western Europe (Otake, 1987; Zushi, 1982). In addition, as the Cold War broke out, Sanbetsu and other unions on the ideological left devoted the bulk of their policy attention to matters of defense, foreign policy, protecting Japan's so-called "peace constitution," and broadscale attacks on the evils of capitalist economics. Bread and butter unionism, or the introduction of national social benefits, were not high on their political agenda. Eventually, Sanbetsu was to loose out in the intramural struggles within the labor movement, but at this historical juncture, its power served primarily to marginalize organize labor and to prevent the development of any form of social democratic, cross-class cooperation that might have led to state-generated and/or nation-wide benefits for labor.

The failure of the ERC came at about the same time as the US Occupation began its "reverse course." In the face of increasing West-East tensions throughout Europe, the establishment of a Communist regime in China, the increased conservatism of US domestic politics, and radicalism in the Japanese labor movement, by 1947-48 American policy began shifting toward the right. Many organized labor leaders were subjected to an anti-communist purge; public sector strikes were subjected to new and stricter regulations; many unions were dismantled; the pro-labor legislation of the early Occupation was replaced by far more conservative regulations modelled on America's Taft-Hartley Act.

In addition, Occupation authorities began to encourage conservative business and political leaders to return to leadership positions. As an important consequence of these efforts, Nikkeiren (the Japan Federation of Employers' Associations) was established in 1948 as management's organization for dealing with labor affairs. Militantly ideological, it warmed to its self-description as "fighting Nikkeiren," and vigorously encouraged employers to confront, rather than cooperate with, the leftist labor movement. The economic recession of the early 1950s made Nikkeiren's belligerent policy particularly effective and helped it to overcome both the strength of the Marxist oriented unions and to enhance the influence of the more moderate factions within individual enterprise unions. In addition, Nikkeiren's emergence as the main voice of employers served to quiet the more moderate voices within the business community. During the early postwar years, therefore, the relationship between business and labor was highly charged ideologically, leaving little room for pragmatic compromise.

One of the more important strategies devised by Nikkeiren was to encourage employers to circumvent union radicalism by assisting their more moderate workers to create "second unions," i.e. unions within their plants that were opposed to the existing, more radical unions, and hence more pliant to management's demands and to identification of workers' welfare with that of the firm. Many of these came to form the core of the more conservative enterprise unions that began to prevail within the private sector labor movement by the mid-1960s. (Public sector unions, anchored in the federation, Sohyo, continued to be far more radical into the late 1980s).

Also as part of the American "reverse course," from 1949 to 1950, the Japanese government conducted a policy of strict aggregate-demand restraints. This program, called the "Dodge Line" after Detroit banker Joseph Dodge who headed the investigation committee that made the various proposals, called among other things for tight budgetary controls to stem the hyperinflation caused by the breakdown of the wartime economy. The resultant government policies brought on a serious recession, which in turn undermined labor's bargaining power in the labor market. Many companies, small and medium-sized firms in particular, went bankrupt, or were forced to streamline their businesses, creating massive labor layoffs. Of those firms which underwent such streamlining, 87.4 percent had fewer than 200 employees. In addition, there were massive layoffs of public sector employees who had been among the most militant members of the new union movement (Pempel, 1987).

As a consequence of such bankruptcy, business reorganization, overt government and business hostility, as well as the dramatic declines in total employment opportunities, the number of labor unions decreased from 34,688 in 1949 to 29,144 in 1950. Among dissolved unions, those in establishments with fewer than 200 employees accounted for 82.5 percent (Yamashita, 1991:95). The result was that while larger Japanese plants remained heavily unionized, the union movement virtually disappeared from Japan's smaller firms. And as noted, the unions that remained were heavily of the enterprise variety. Well over 90 percent of all unionized workers at this time were members of enterprise unions.

The redundant labor force created by the recession allowed major enterprises to reorganize the national labor market in a fundamental way. The result was a sharply differentiated and separately-tiered set of markets. At the top of the new hierarchy were the large firms oriented toward recruiting Japan's "best and brightest" as part of their permanent, core, workforce. These firms were often unionized, but almost always along enterprise lines. Management was usually willing to provide good salaries and occupationally-linked benefits able to attract and hold the most desirable workers from the national employment pool. Included in this group, with minor variations, were workers in the national and local government bureaucracies and many national public corporations. Further down in the pecking order were workers in smaller, typically, subcontracting, firms. Most of these firms were unable to attract the best talent and in many cases were less concerned with such workers than with keeping down labor costs. Hence, such firms rarely competed for the same workers as did the firms at the top of the hierarchy. Workers in smaller sub-contracting firms were rarely unionized and hence would typically take what they could get in individual negotiations with management. At the bottom of the order were temporary and part-time workers, often though by no means always women and/or older, less skilled men. Again, such workers were drawn from an almost totally separate pool from those in the first two spheres. In some cases, these workers might operate side-by-side with unionized and better paid workers in Japan's "best" firms (Wood, 1980). But in almost all instances, these workers enjoyed few if any of the employment-linked benefits of those at the top of the hierarchy.

With the rearrangement of the employment order came a reorganization of labor-management relations. The Japan Productivity Center (JPC) was created in 1955 to pursue productivity improvement through labor-management co-operation. In retrospect, the JPC referred to its own establishment as representing a shift in industrial relations from confrontation to co-operation. The central principle around which this was to occur was "increased productivity."

According to the JPC, co-operation would be based on an agreement between labor and management under which labor would respect the rights of management while management would not dismiss employees simply to improve productivity (JPC, 1985:5-7). So long as this cooperation occurred, both sides could focus less on redistributive battles about how the economic pie would be divided, and more on how jointly to increase the size of the pie.

JPC's orientation may seem quite similar to that of the earlier ERC in that both advocated productivity improvement through labor-management harmony. However, they really emerged from a set of political-economic conditions that were virtually the opposite. The ERC had tried to achieve labor-capital harmony through a social democratic contract at the national level, largely in recognition of the overwhelming power of organized labor in the immediate postwar years and the corresponding weakness of employers. In contrast, what the JPC aimed at was the division and co-optation of labor along enterprise lines. It had emerged out of the newly recovered power of business and organized labor's diminished capabilities.

In this sense, JPC's initiative was possible mainly because organized labor was not unified, was facing a declining unionization ratio in the 1950s and was organized primarily along enterprise lines. But it is also critical to recognize that the Japanese labor federations at the national level, as well as the Japan Socialist Party and the Japan Communist Party, had little in their respective programs that was designed to promote the expansion of state welfare programs. As noted above, the parties and the national labor federations were far more animated by questions of foreign policy, security arrangements with the United States, and with preventing what they feared would be a new Japanese militarism, than they were with increasing governmental spending on welfare programs. Moreover, at the plant level, many union leaders were far more concerned with the specific benefits they could accrue for their members than they were with staging campaigns for nationally distributed benefits that would help both union members and non-union members alike. In this context, a good deal of union political pressure was either not focused on issues of social welfare, or when it was, served heavily to complement the already existing bias toward occupationally-based welfare.

Thus, by the early 1950s, Japanese employers had succeeded in re-establishing their unshakable managerial rights. As a consequence, occupational welfare emerged again as an effective instrument of labor market management largely under the initiative and influence of business.

This reconsolidation of the strength of management at the plant level was bolstered in the political arena by the unification of the country's two conservative parties into the Liberal Democratic Party (LDP) in 1955. Although the LDP had to confront a united Japan Socialist Party (JSP) for several years, and although electoral statistics and numerous pundits suggested that the JSP would quickly gain control of the parliament and the cabinet sometime in the mid-1960s, in fact the JSP split in 1964 while the LDP continued to outdraw it electorally by a nearly 2:1 margin. The result was that by the early to mid-1960s, the chances for a labor-based government in Japan seemed almost nil. As a consequence of such an unshakable control over the instruments of state, in whatever battles took place between business and labor, Japanese government policies were almost invariably biased in favor of business.

This was critical since the politics of the 1950s had involved a vicious two-tiered battle between left and right. At the national political level, the conservative LDP battled the Marxian JSP on a range of ideologically charged issues, including (albeit at the margins of the debate) social welfare. On the economic front, a series of major labor-management disputes, high strike rates and numerous lockouts characterized relations between business and labor throughout the manufacturing, mining and public sectors. Naturally, these two levels were frequently interwoven on specific matters, including issues related to occupationally-based welfare.

These early postwar years were charged with high levels of political volatility. At various historical junctures, outside analysts might well have predicted the logical emergence of strongly labor-based governments pressing for the institutionalization of massive state-led welfare programs such as were developing in Scandinavia. At other points, certainly important segments of the business community seemed amenable to corporatist arrangements with organized labor, with or without state involvement. But by the first decade after Japan's surrender, the major components of dualism that had prevailed in the prewar period were again coming back into place: a powerful, but widely segmented business community broadly committed to increased productivity through differentiated treatment of their respective labor markets; a shrinking and fragmented labor movement, large segments of which identified their interests with those of the firms in which they worked; and a government clearly aligned with business and hostile to organized labor. This set of structures played itself out in fairly predictable ways in shaping the balance between state and enterprise in the provision of social welfare until well into the 1970s.

The Roots of the State-Enterprise Mix in Japanese Welfare

By the late-1950s, individual firms at the top of the employment pyramid, heavily influenced by the philosophy of the JPC, and by the realization that politically there would be no major governmental initiatives toward a social welfare state, began increasing company welfare benefits and expanding intrafirm training programs (Shinkawa, 1993; Shirai, 1983). Smaller firms, less pressed to make generous offers to draw workers from the large and expanding labor pool, were strongly resistant to any taxes for government programs and themselves resisted developing "excessively generous" occupationally-based welfare schemes in their own plants. Farmers and small shopkeepers, meanwhile, who still formed an extremely large segment of the Japanese workforce, and an important voting constituency of the ruling LDP, were similarly reluctant to pay for any major new government programs in social welfare. The result was a return to a welfare mix in which occupationally-rooted benefits played the most significant part, and in which the larger firms were the most generous in the benefits provided.

The government was, however, not a passive bystander on matters of occupationally based welfare. Official government policies on the one hand involved the explicit rejection of any new national level programs; in addition, the government directly encouraged businesses which took the initiative in creating worksite programs to improve the social wellbeing of their workers. Government assistance to encourage enterprise-welfare took several forms, the most notable of which involved allowing employer contributions to private pension plans to be treated as tax deductions.

It was Nikkeiren that most strongly demanded the tax law change. The 1952 tax law had allowed employers to claim certain portions of retirement allowances as a non-taxable business expense.[1] Consequently, retirement allowance plans diffused quickly; by the mid 1950s, two thirds of the nation's establishments with 30 employees or more had adopted some kind of retirement plan. In 1959 small and medium-sized companies were encouraged to adopt retirement allowance plans through a mutual-aid corporation which would manage and invest the funds contributed by such employers. Contributions to the funds were also to be non-taxable.

The 1952 tax code change soon turned out to be insufficient. Business claimed that expenses for retirement allowances would become unbearable for employers as life expectancy increased and lifetime employment became more common. Thus, in the late 1950s, Nikkeiren proposed a shift from lump-sum payments to a pension system. Although some major companies had introduced their own enterprise pension plans in the 1950s, these did not spread primarily because contributions to the pension fund were not granted non-taxable status.

Nikkeiren, together with the associations of credit banks and life insurance companies—who would be the most immediate beneficiaries of any large expansion in such programs—called on the government to introduce a qualified pension plan with preferential tax treatment to replace the lump-sum retirement allowances that had hitherto prevailed. In addition to helping firms level off their annual expenses for retirement allowances through non-taxable pension funds, enterprise pensions also fostered a spirit of mutuality among employees, helped to maintain long-term labor-management harmony, and provided reliable resources for capital formation (Daiichi Seimei Hoken ed., 1982:23; Yamazaki, 1988:82).

In 1954, the government responded by creating an Employee Pension System (EPS). This reformed earlier plans and affected all firms employing more than five employees. Five years later in 1959, a safety-net National Pension System (NPS) was added to provide coverage for those not covered by the EPS, including farmers, those in firms with fewer than five employees, and others not eligible for EPS. (Although small, this program was somewhat innovative internationally with only eleven similar programs throughout the world at the time.)

Central to the EPS system, and highly congruent with the principles of occupationally-based welfare, was the fact that pension benefits were explicitly linked to employment. Even more importantly, establishing this link was the opportunity for individual firms to "contract out" of the plan. Within the EPS system, an employer who employs more than a certain number of workers (currently 500) can contract out of the earnings-related part of the EPS if the majority of insurants (employees) and the trade unions support the idea (cf. Fisher, 1973).[2] In effect, the retirement plans were firm-specific and occupationally-linked.

The most popular form of contracting out involves a firm's pension fund paying a substitute benefit, at least 30 percent higher, compared to that obtainable under state-managed plans. By the end of 1966, there were 142 employee-pension funds, of which such substitute plans accounted for 75.4 percent (Yamazaki, 1988:196).[3] Such programs also enjoyed better preferential tax treatment with special corporate taxes levied only on those portions of the pension fund which go over 2.7 times the substitute benefits. As a result, most contracted out pension funds are completely non-taxable. These also provide better benefits to their employees than the minimums available through the NPS or the EPS.

Smaller firms must adopt what are called "qualified pension plans." In these, insurance companies can accept small plans with 15 and more insurants; trust banks are eligible to accept only plans with more than 200 insurants. Hence, larger firms can choose freely between insurance companies or trust banks, considering the specific advantages and disadvantages provided by each. Table 11.1 shows that the larger firms (1,000 employees or more) play only a minor role in terms of the absolute number of qualified pensions. However, Table 11.2 indicates that, in percentage terms, qualified pensions spread even more among larger firms than smaller ones. Despite this, the bigger enterprises are most sharply distinguished by their reliance on Employee Pension Funds, either alone or in combination with qualified plans.

The point here is that occupationally-linked pensions involved more than simply private firm behavior. By creating the EPS (and also the NPS), the government became a direct structurer and overseer of occupationally-linked pensions. Moreover, by allowing tax deductibility to firms making retirement contributions, the government explicitly encouraged businesses to take such measures and, in the case of the largest firms, to make contributions that were more generous than those of smaller firms. The level of one's retirement pension was thus quite directly linked to the size and profitability of one's employer, and this was done through official government sanctions.

Much the same system prevailed in regard to health insurance. The government had in place a National Health Insurance (NHI) system, originally established in 1938. In 1958 NHI was modified to make it mandatory for municipalities to organize health care associations for groups (farmers, the self-employed, the employees of tiny businesses) that are not covered by occupational plans. The latter, known as the Employee Health Insurance (EHI) system, are differentiated along the familiar lines of sector, occupation, and firm size. The EHI system thus allowed and even encouraged larger firms to provide greater benefits to their employees than the minimalist programs run by the state and/or required of smaller businesses. What is most striking about all of these programs in combination, therefore, are their links to the employment system and the low and widely differentiated benefits that resulted to potential recipients. There was clearly little sense of either health care or retirement benefits as "rights of citizenship," except insofar as a minimalist safety net, linked to means testing, was held up for the most extreme cases. Essentially, at this point in time, the public programs (NHI and NPS) remained small and residual, providing low benefits, and in the case of the pensions system, requiring a long period of contributions before one became eligible for regular benefits.

It is worth noting that this employment-linked system was not put into place over the violent protests of Japanese organized labor. For example, labor originally opposed the opportunities for firms to contract out of the pension system, but it eventually supported the move once it was linked to higher benefits for those whose employers opted out and once control over pension funds was taken away from the employers themselves and given to insurance companies and banks. In short, once organized labor could see that its members could benefit differentially from the new system, it accepted it without challenge. In short, just as was the case in the period immediately following World War II, the unions were, at best, lukewarm supporters of national welfare schemes; far more frequently, they were positive supporters of occupationally-based welfare schemes under which union members did quite well.

Furthermore, labor did not press hard for the introduction of a tax based national program of health care or pensions. For the most part, unions favored a pay-as-you go system, wanting immediate benefits involving low contributions; and, as relatively well-paid members of the work force, they also wanted benefits proportional to their actual incomes rather than flat-rate payouts that would be equal nationwide. Most opposed any system of retirement or health benefits that would be paid out of general taxes, preferring the kinds of differentiated benefits that could be provided through an employment based welfare system and that would be of greatest benefit to union members. The Seamen's union was particularly strong in resisting any changes that would sweep existing seamen's benefits into a broader national scheme. Thus, the government-business collaboration took place in a context of vaguely positive support from important segments of the union movement as well (Campbell, 1992).

Finally it should be noted that government programs and actions were intimately collaborative with the competing labor market and employment demands of very different types of Japanese businesses, and also of Japanese farmers. The LDP, which ruled until 1993 as a conservative but catch-all party, faced a diversity of constituent demands from such groups. Large businesses, e.g. must compete for Japan's best educated and most well-positioned workers. As such this competition can well take place through differentially-structured occupational benefits. From the employer's perspective, the immediate payoff is much more direct and immediate than would be the case from, say, a national welfare scheme for which they would be heavily taxed, and whose beneficiaries would include not just their firm's workers but workers throughout the entire country.

Smaller and medium sized firms have traditionally faced more favorable labor markets and have been able to offer lower wages and fewer benefits than their larger counterparts competing in more competitive labor markets. Minimal, tax deductible contributions to retirement and health care schemes over which they have some say, provide an attractive alternative.

Finally, farmers and self-employed Japanese were given a system under which they would be able to make small contributions toward their eventual retirement and health needs, but with no major tax burdens to pay for national pension or health care schemes that in their eyes would be needlessly costly and from which they would derive few if any specific benefits.

In short, various segments of the Japanese workforce, as well as different types of employers, all rallied around a system that was heavily rooted in occupationally-distinct contributions and entitlements that were relatively divorced from state actions on a nationwide and universalistic basis. Japan's orientation was completely the opposite of that of most Scandinavian countries, for example. Indeed in a 1973 publication, the Japan Productivity Center noted that since public welfare was confined largely to poor-relief, enterprise welfare in fact provided a substitute for social consumption and for Japan's relatively underdeveloped public welfare programs (JPC, 1973:19). This was compatible with the JPC contention that profits from productivity improvement would be distributed fairly (JPC, 1985:5).

The Japanese government, meanwhile, had strongly emphasized that rapid economic growth would resolve the dual structure of the Japanese economy (EPA, 1957).

How accurate were these expectations? Public welfare, which might have modified the inequalities inherent in the occupationally-based welfare system to a certain degree remained underdeveloped throughout the era of rapid economic growth. Public welfare expenditure in Japan during the early 1960s accounted for only 7.0 percent of GDP, while the figure was 17.0 percent in France, 16.5 percent in Germany, 13.6 percent in Italy and Sweden, 12.6 percent in the UK, and 10.3 percent in the US, respectively (OECD, 1978:25). Income maintenance expenditure, which is a major item in social security expenditure, also shows no substantial change throughout the 1960s. Japan spent 2.1 percent of GDP for income maintenance programs in 1962 and 2.8 percent in 1972, both of which were only a third of the OECD average (OECD, 1976:36).

In this context, retirement pensions for the non-contributing elderly were minuscule even into the early 1970s with only 3.7 million people over 70 who could pass a means test being eligible for pensions of about ¥2300 (roughly $14 per month). This covered about three-fourths of that age group (Campbell, 1992:153). Because of the long period of contributions required before becoming eligible for full benefits, the contributory pensions served an even smaller group. Only about 3.4 million Japanese were eligible for such benefits as recently as the early

1970s, although their benefits, linked as they were to salary-based contributions, were larger once received.

Even though total Japanese government spending was far less than other industrialized countries, it is also worth noting that what was spent was directed heavily to health care (with its clear links to the maintenance of a healthy workforce); meanwhile, public assistance, child care and retirement benefits were all dramatically lower than in the other OECD countries. Again the link between employment and welfare was unmistakably clear. Welfare was by and large not a government function.

Furthermore, it is worth noting that during this era of exceptionally high growth, Japan's overall productivity improvements vastly outstripped improvements in wages. Thus, between 1955 and 1970, productivity rose approximately 3.6 times while real wages rose only about 2.3 times, a lag greater than in other industrial countries (Pempel, 1989:170). Even those workers who were presumably the greatest beneficiaries of occupationally-based welfare were putting in more than they were getting back out. In short, the entire occupationally-based welfare system delivered highly differentiated benefits to a select portion of the labor force, namely those in larger, unionized and usually highly competitive, firms. The remainder of the Japanese population received very limited benefits in most areas of social welfare. As Japan moved into the 1970s, it was clearly the industrial democracies' most conspicuous "welfare laggard."

Japan's Brief Flirtation with State Welfare Programs

Just about the time of the 1971 breakdown in exchange rates among world currencies and just before the 1973 oil crisis, Japan seemed ready to embark on a new era of welfare. Two decades of rapid economic growth had brought about new social problems, such as urbanization, environmental pollution and congestion, and more pervasively, a broadening national sense that growth should somehow lead to improvements in the quality of one's own life, not simply that of unborn future generations. In addition, as health care improved and birth control reduced the size of the average family, Japan began to face an "elderly problem."

Japan had an unusually young population for its level of industrialization with only about 5 percent of its population aged 65 or more in the 1950s and only 7 percent in the 1970s. Both figures were well below those for other industrialized countries. But Japan could anticipate a rapid aging, catching up to the rest of the industrialized world early in the 2000s. (Keizai Koho Center, 1992:9). Thus, in the middle of the 1970s there were about seven people of productive age to support every dependent old person, but by the year 2000 this ratio will have fallen to just over 4:1 and by 2015 to less than 3:1 (Collick, 1988:217).

Such problems of pollution, urban overcrowding and the elderly were all resistant to solutions at the plant level. Welfare could no longer be exclusively occupationally-based; governmental action seemed necessary.

Furthermore, such action had become politically expedient, although not particularly as a result of increased power by organized labor. In numerous local areas, citizens rights movements, most of them devoid of links to any established political parties or interest associations, had begun to challenge governmental authority on pollution while the several opposition parties (including the non-labor based Clean Government Party) had begun to forge coalitions strong enough to allow them to dominate many local and prefectural legislatures. It seemed politically, as well as socially, clear that the dominant conservative government would be well-advised to take preemptive actions if it was to remain in power. Even the larger businesses, whose beneficial position through occupationally-based welfare would be partially undercut by new government programs, shared this viewpoint, and urged government action to ward off potential electoral defeat.

One of the major steps taken in this regard involved a bid to coopt and outflank its opponents through the expansion of welfare benefits. Left-of-center governments had taken control of numerous of Japan's larger cities and prefectures, typically introducing various forms of social welfare, including medical and retirement plans. The success of the left with such programs led the conservatives to give a top priority to social welfare in the drafting of the 1973 national budget, and 1973 was called the "first year of the welfare era." Free medical care for the elderly, which had been initiated by progressive local governments, was introduced at the national level. Moreover, the proportion of medical expenses paid by the two existing insurance programs was also increased. All of this pushed the average increase in medical costs upward, from 17.2 percent between 1966 and 1972 to 27.3 percent between 1973 and 1975.

In addition, pension payouts in both the EPS and the NPS were greatly enhanced with the average increase in pension costs between 1973 and 1975 reaching 54 percent, while that between 1966 and 1972 had been 25.3 percent (Fujita, 1984:30). The employees pension benefit was almost doubled to a level equivalent to about 45 percent of the average employee's income, and the national pensions were increased proportionately. More importantly still, indexation was introduced into both systems.

It is worth noting, however, that the introduction of these national measures came primarily from a conservative government anxious to forestall electoral challenges, rather than from a socialist government anxious to institutionalize them. And in heading off any massive national level electoral changes, the government was quite selective and conservatively-biased in the types of programs it brought about.

With such changes in place, spending on social welfare measures, both as a proportion of the national budget and as a percent of GNP, increased steadily from 1973 until the early 1980s. Even in 1980, however, social security transfers in Japan remained relatively low compared to the other OECD countries at 10.9 percent of GNP, compared to 22.9 percent in France, 15.3 percent in Germany and 15.8 percent in Italy (Noguchi, 1987:188)

In addition to national level policy changes, there were shifts at the plant level. Most fundamentally, the more moderate of Japan's private sector unions agreed in 1975 to moderate their wage demands in exchange for job security from employers and low taxes and anti-inflationary policies from the government. This "de facto incomes policy" allowed Japanese manufacturers to regain control over labor costs; helped to reduce labor-management tensions and strike rates; and also helped the national government to contain the rampant inflation that had followed the oil shock of 1973 (e.g. Shimada, 1983; Shinkawa, 1984; Tsujinaka, 1986; Kume, 1988). Furthermore, it refocused a good deal of the policy energy that had been directed at the national government back to the level of employment and occupation.

If the "era of welfare" had lasted at least for a decade or so, Japan's welfare mix might have moved decisively toward a more institutionalized system of high state spending on welfare benefits. It might even have begun to create an "institutional" welfare state based on social citizenship rights, and the de-commodification of welfare. In such a case, occupational welfare might have been reduced in its overall significance and given way to more fully institutionalized benefits to all Japanese citizens as a matter of right, rather than as a matter of one's position in the workplace. This, in turn, might well have weakened management's control over employees and the wide differentials in the availability of social welfare to different groups of employees.

However, the oil crisis took place in the very first year of the welfare era. Japan's twenty years of dramatic economic growth, which were to be the basis for funding the new programs, were suddenly reduced to more normal proportions. This, coupled with a weak conservative party's reluctance to increase taxes on a fragile electorate, stimulated funding the new social welfare programs (as well as pollution control) largely though deficit spending. Japan's deficit dependency ratio had been just over 4 percent in 1970, but rose rapidly to the 11-16 percent range for 1971-74, then to just below 30 percent in 1976 and 1977, and finally up to 37 percent in 1978. In the next year it hovered near 40 percent. (Yamamura, 1985:497-98). (This method of financing did have the advantage of being far less visible to the general public than had it been based on major hikes in taxes or employee contributions.)

As these public deficits rapidly mounted, the idea of emulating the Western-style welfare state began to come under withering attack particularly from the business sector. Furthermore, the preemption of the opposition's opportunities to exploit the welfare issue and to topple the LDP had also been accomplished even during the relatively short period of flirtation with larger social welfare spending. During the middle of the 1970s, the LDP and the combined opposition parties had shared almost equal numbers of seats in the parliament. But in the famous 'double election' of 1980, the LDP reversed its seemingly inexorable decline; instead it was the opposition parties that were whisked to the sidelines.

As a consequence of the conservatives' new electoral strength, the marginalization of the opposition parties, and the reintroduction of a close affinity between private sector unions and management at the employment level, Japan was poised politically and occupationally for a rollback in the minimalist welfare state that had been created.

The major nail in the coffin of the Western style welfare state was administrative reform. During the early 1980s, this became a nationwide movement with major impact on the size and orientation of the Japanese state. A paramount goal of administrative reform was to retrench the escalating government expenditures and to ease the rapidly rising levels of deficit finance. Privatization of certain semi-public corporations such as the national railroads and Nippon Telephone and Telegraph were a central target of the rollback. So too were welfare expenditures, including the hitherto unchallenged, and generally quite generous, pensions to public servants.

Conservative intellectuals developed an extensive campaign against the welfare state by contending that excessive welfare service led to outbreaks of the "advanced-country disease," or the "English disease." The expansion of public service, it was contended, encouraged people to depend excessively upon the state, discouraged the desire to work, and weakened the incentive to invest and improve productivity. Such conservatives warned that Japan, which was going to undergo rapid aging, would become a big spender and, sooner or later, would begin to suffer from the advanced-country disease unless steps were taken immediately to reverse past trends (Koyama, 1978; Kanbara, 1986:118-143).

Thus, returning to the basic theme that Japan was different from other advanced democracies and that welfare should be largely left to the family and the firm, Japanese conservatives advanced the notion of building a "welfare *society* with vitality," or of creating a "Japanese-style welfare *society.*"

The attitude of the LDP government towards social welfare had clearly changed by the mid-1970s. The Policy Affairs Council of the LDP released the "Lifetime Welfare Plan," which stressed welfare based on self-help and embraced the negative views about the expansion of public spending on social welfare. The ideas presented in the plan were subsequently reflected in a government report, the "Economic Plan for the Late 1970s" issued in 1976. In such formulations, the enterprise, as well as the individual, family, and local community, were all expected to play an essential role in improving the nation's overall welfare.

The Economic Planning Agency released a report in 1977 which employed the catchword, "Japanese-style welfare society" (JSWS) officially for the first time.[4] Prime Minister Ohira argued for just such a "Japanese-style welfare society" in his January, 1979 Policy Speech to Diet. The goal was made official in August of that year with the publication of the government's New Economic and Social Seven Year Plan.

The major goals of this ideological shift were achieved through administrative reform begun under the Suzuki cabinet in the early 1980s. Contending that the free medical care for the elderly had turned hospitals into "old people's salons" (Asahi Nenkan, 1983:440), the government passed an Old People's Health Bill in 1982 which abolished free medical care for the elderly, introduced co-payment by users, and pressured local governments to reduce their initiatives in improving medical care for elderly patients.

In addition, the Employees Pension Plan was revised so as to curb increases in benefits and raise contributions. In effect, the pension system was integrated into a two-tiered system, with a base pension for all topped by a wage-linked pension tied to one's occupation, i.e. to employment level and salary. The first level was based on a combination of flat-rate contributions by the self-employed, employer contributions and government tax monies. Moreover, one would have to contribute for a period of 40 years and retire at 65 to be eligible for the basic pension of ¥50,000 (approximately $400 per month). The second level was financed completely by employer and employee contributions with no government subsidies. In effect, it made one's ultimate pension a direct function of wage levels during employment. But it was neither managed by, nor specifically linked to, individual firms. These reforms involved major cuts in the NPS benefits, reducing them to ¥50,000 instead of the ¥70,000 which would have been given after 40 years of participation. Meanwhile, a single EPS participant would be cut from ¥197,600 to ¥126,200 per month and couples would see their benefits shrink from ¥212,600 to ¥176,200 (Campbell, 1992:337-8). Pensions to government employees were similarly slashed.

Thus, government contributions were slowed, or actually reduced, from the pattern that had begun in the 1970s. Moreover, this change institutionalized the wide differentials that prevailed in the retirement benefits of those in larger and those in smaller firms.

The end result of these changes was an effective capping of the previously geometrically rising expenditures for social security and medical care at about 27 percent of the national budget for the decade of the 1980s and an actual reduction in spending for health and income security from 18 percent in 1982 to 16.3 percent in 1990 (Keizai Koho Center, 1992:80). Nonetheless, elements of the public programs remained in place; the rollbacks did not put a complete end to public programs and their replacement with purely occupational plans. Rather, the subsequent system was one in which pieces of each remained in place, but with the occupational programs having received a major reinforcement as a result of the rollback in spending for government programs. Any zero-sum trade off between "public" and "private" welfare was adulterated and a mixture with a heavy dose of reliance on private sector programs was given substantial reinforcement.

Corresponding to the state plan for a "Japanese-style social welfare" system, businesses also started to review their welfare plans. Plans for "lifetime comprehensive welfare" (LCW) were released one after another in such industries as distribution, food, textiles, electric machinery, and metal refining (JPC, 1983:160-164). The concept of LCW presumes that the enterprise will provide regular employees with comprehensive physical and mental benefits during their productive employment as well as after their retirement. LCW goes far beyond conventional enterprise welfare by including items concerning employment security, personnel management and training and education (JPC, 1983:178; JPC, 1987:194). It aims at integrating occupational welfare with personnel management in such a comprehensive way as to involve every aspect of employees' lives (cf. Fujita, 1983).

Japanese business through the JPC asserts that LCW, unlike traditional enterprise welfare, does not aim specifically at raising corporate identity/loyalty, maintaining labor-management harmony, and improving productivity. On the other hand, however, the center confesses its hope that labor-management harmony and productivity improvement will be achieved as spillover effects of LCW. Moreover, it points out that LCW is a plan to distribute the benefits of productivity improvement. Since LCW will be developed in conjunction with improvements in productivity, it will reinforce employees' greater commitment to the enterprise in order to enjoy the "enriched" life that is promised (JPC, 1983:176-180).

LCW is thus, after all, a mechanism through which Japan's longstanding dualism is reproduced on an enlarged scale. Figure 11.1 and additional data for other years show that the gap between large and small firms in terms of non-statutory welfare is particularly noteworthy, and that it widened considerably between 1973 and 1975. Subsequently the tendency towards further divergence continued. By 1985 the cost of non-statutory welfare in medium-sized firms (with between 100 and 300 workers) was only a fourth of its counterpart in firms with 5,000 employees or more.

Large firms also tried to restrain the costs of occupational welfare in the face of recession, despite their commitment, in principle, to LCW. In the process of business reorganization, the elasticity of non-statutory welfare expenditures with respect to productivity (value-added) in large firms decreased from 0.944 between 1963 and 1973 to 0.828 between 1975 and 1980. In short, large firms kept making most of their welfare payments even when they were not required to do so by law, and even as corporate profits fell. In contrast, there was a sharp fall in such payments within small firms, from 0.959 to 0.173 (MOL, 1984:140). Since occupational welfare is, after all, subject to an employer's discretion, it most precisely reflects differences in productivity by firm size, especially when the employer faces a management crisis.

In all of these ways, it is clear that for highly political reasons, linked principally to electoral preemption of potentially appealing programs from opposition parties, the ruling LDP in the 1970s moved away from a heavy reliance on the longstanding orientation toward occupationally-based welfare and began to institute a series of state programs involving such things as medical care, child allowances and pensions. However, once the catalytic electoral pressures had receded, and once the magnitude of the costs of long-term deficit financing became apparent, particularly to potential taxpaying and contributing firms, the government was quick to back off its earlier commitments and to return to a greater reliance on occupationally-based welfare programs.

The Political Economy of the Japanese System

The central argument of this paper has been that while dualism, demographic models, and even bureaucratically-driven expansionism provide various insights into the Japanese welfare mixture at different times, none captures the totality as effectively as does a political economic model which simultaneously directs our attention to Japan's changing electoral configurations in Japan as well as to changes in big social sectors such as "business" and "labor". Nowhere is this more clear than in Japan's anomalous position as a relatively egalitarian economy. This section attempts to underscore how the peculiar mixture of public and private welfare in Japan maintains both its political and economic viability within the country. Who benefits, and in which ways? And more importantly, how does the entire system cohere to stimulate both high economic growth and yet relatively low levels of entrenched poverty?

As noted in the introduction, many aspects of the Japanese system of heavy reliance on occupationally-based welfare would appear to be the simple outgrowth of dualism. The total picture however, is complicated by the fact that on balance, Japan is a country with high income equality and with almost no permanent underclass—an anomaly not anticipated by dualist arguments.

How is this accomplished? How has Japan, with its widely differentiated system of welfare benefits, linked intimately to one's occupation and job status, managed to achieve levels of income equality comparable to those of Scandinavia? Why does Japan not have the skewed income profile of Britain, France, Canada, or the United States? Essentially, three features are critical. First, Japan has rather consistently had relatively full employment, and employment has been among the most critical factors in reducing the size of any permanent underclass. Secondly, the longstanding ties of Japan's farmers and small shopkeepers have made them the beneficiaries of a wide variety of income-equalizing government subsidies totally divorced from what is traditionally thought of as "social welfare." Yet through such subsidies, many do indeed become economic wards of the state treasury. But thirdly, Japan's widely differentiated salary and welfare benefits are masked by that country's family structure. In effect, Japanese occupational discrimination, and the differentiated salary and welfare benefits that accompany this discrimination, are primarily intra-familial, rather than between one family and other.

Beginning with this last point, it is helpful to examine how different segments of the Japanese employment picture help to sustain the current system. An important first consideration in this regard concerns the general public, the family system and the reliance on lump-sum payments.

The Japanese Mass Public

In the Japanese employment structure, discrimination is most extreme against women, the elderly and the young, (and is linked to subcontract and part-time labor, but this too frequently falls most heavily among these groups). Yet income statistics are kept by family, not by individual, and a not-untypical Japanese family might have a husband in his mid-40s working in a well-paid firm with extensive occupationally-based welfare programs; a wife working only part-time and enjoying few if any occupationally-linked perks; a 69 year old father who is technically "retired" but who is in fact working for a reduced salary in a small service sector shop, and two children, a son working part-time while in college and a daughter working full time in a department store. All members would have both widely differentiated base salaries and also very different occupationally-related welfare benefits. But the money of all is pooled, and in most instances, many of the husband's relatively generous benefits from work—health care, spas, canteens, etc.—would be available for the entire family unit. The result is that the overall life styles of large segments of the Japanese population take place within a narrower band of differences than in most "dualist" economies.

Another element of the Japanese system that needs to be examined for the general and mass public is the question of the relationship between income maintenance and labor market maintenance. The recent diffusion of pension funds may seem to indicate that the retirement allowance now works primarily for income maintenance and social protection for the broad sector of Japanese labor after retirement, rather than for labor market management in the interests of business. This, however, is not necessarily the case. Most occupational-pension schemes   provide employees a choice between a pension and a lump-sum payment, and the majority of retired employees choose a lump sum. In the case of qualified pensions (those that prevail in smaller firms), more than 90 percent of the retired choose a lump-sum payment (Murakami, 1991:53).

There are various reasons why the employee tends to prefer a lump-sum. First, a lump-sum payment is more privileged than a pension in terms of taxation. An employee with 30 years' service can enjoy a tax-free lump sum up to 10 million yen. Moreover, only half of the portion which goes beyond 10 million yen is taxed. On the contrary, pension benefits are taxed as a sundry income (they used to be taxed as a salary income). Overall, a person who receives a pension must pay more tax than one who receives a lump sum. Second, in Japan, the retirement allowance is used to cover not only the costs of living after retirement but also such items as housing and the education of children (Yamazaki, 1988:227). Third, since most occupational pensions prior to the 1985 reforms are not indexed, they are vulnerable to inflation.

It should also be noted that most occupational pensions are not lifetime pensions. For example, 98 percent of the qualified pensions have the limited term of payment from five years to ten years (Arai and Goto, 1991:88). This fact indicates that a qualified pension is actually payment of a lump sum in installments. This is not surprising when we consider that occupational pensions have been introduced only on management's terms. According to a poll in 1985, the top three reasons why the employer had introduced the qualified pension plan were: (1) to enjoy preferential tax treatment (77.8 percent), (2) to level off each year's retirement expenses (75.1 percent), and (3) to give employees a sense of security by outside funding (57.3 percent). This order is the same in the case of EPFs (Arai and Goto, 1991:76). Since the "pension funds" are established to pay a lump-sum money, life security after retirement is not considered to be a major reason for the introduction of outside funding.

The Employers

Building from the last point, it should become clear that some elements of the system that seem on the surface to be highly beneficial to the Japanese mass public, are at a minimum, not at all in conflict with the dominant economic interests of business. Business represents the most significant single stimulus to the broad mixture of occupationally-based and state-based welfare in Japan. As noted throughout, most of the occupationally-based programs were particularly beneficial in allowing Japan's larger and more sophisticated firms to attract the best educated and potentially most appealing segments of the labor pool. In contrast, the far less well-endowed smaller and medium sized firms typically offered much smaller occupationally-based programs. These firms continue to employ a far larger proportion of the national work force (29 percent) than most other industrialized countries (cf. France, 17 percent; Germany, 14 percent; the United States, 9 percent; and the UK, 8 percent) (Patrick and Rohlen, 1987:335). As a result, what happens in these small Japanese firms has a much greater impact on the nation's total welfare mix than it does in most other industrialized countries. Dualism thus remains prevalent throughout the Japanese employment system but it is far more complicated than notions of simple bipolarity imply.

Businesses have also managed to make a number of changes in their specific calculations of, and hence contributions to, and payments for, retirement benefits. Again, it is helpful to see how different sized businesses have dealt with this problem. Most notably, over time there have been important decouplings between a worker's base salary and the salary used to compute retirement benefits. During the 1950s and early 1960s, preferential tax treatment for pension funds was designed to prevent increases in costs for retirement allowances from hampering capital accumulation. However, the ratio of the cost of retirement allowances to total labor costs steadily increased from 3.5 percent between 1955 and 1959 to 4.5 percent between 1965 and 1969 (Yamazaki, 1988:127). Against this background, individual businesses started in the late 1960s to break the conventional connection between wage raises and retirement-allowance increases. A common strategy was to introduce the "second basic salary," which would only partly reflect annual wage raises, in order to calculate the total amount of an employee's retirement allowance. Naturally, trade unions strongly opposed the idea at the outset. However, enterprise-based unions, which do not have such power as to protect their own interests against the will of management, have gradually accepted the idea of restraints over retirement-allowance increases in exchange for straight wage raises. This leads, then, to an examination of labor's broader involvement with the Japanese welfare mixture.

After the 1973 oil crisis, retirement-allowance increases slowed or stopped. The ratio of retirement-allowance increases to wage hikes was 62.8 percent in 1969; this fell to 49.6 percent in 1974. Nikkeiren consistently contended that the issue of retirement allowances should be treated separately from that of wages (Nikkeiren, 1974:7). In 1974, 70.3 percent of employers calculated retirement allowances using an employee's total basic salary at retirement. By 1981 this had decreased to 58.1 percent in 1981 and in 1989 to 42.0 percent. Larger establishments (1,000 or more employees) were particularly more likely to have two separate systems for calculating retirement benefits and hence the ratio among these firms is much lower: 51.6 percent in 1974, 38.1 percent in 1981, and 27.7 percent in 1989 (Yamazaki, 1988:113; Arai and Goto, 1991:19).

Thus, restraints of retirement-allowance increases have been more common among larger firms than among smaller ones. Retirement-allowance increases are more threatening to larger firms since they naturally have to spend more for such allowances due to higher salaries and longer-term employment. Recent research shows that the model retirement allowance in small firms (30-99 employees) accounts for only about half of its counterpart in firms with 1,000 employees or more (Arai and Goto, 1991:25)

The revision of the retirement-allowance scheme is sometimes also triggered by a rise in the retirement age. Forty-eight percent of larger firms raised the retirement age between 1973 and 1982. Among them, 50 percent of the largest companies (5,000 employees or more) revised retirement-allowance schemes at the same time (Yamazaki, 1988:276-

277). Lest the rise in the retirement age damage flexibility over the inner labor market, it is often coupled with the introduction of an early retirement plan. Although only 6.4 percent of Japanese firms had early retirement plans as a whole in 1990, among the largest firms (5,000 employees or more) those which had the early retirement plan reached 59.3 percent (Arai and Goto, 1991:47). Smaller firms usually do not need such plans due to the high turnover in their work forces.

How complementary was occupational welfare to Japan's underdeveloped public welfare? Table 11.3 demonstrates that employer contributions to both spheres of welfare—their overall "non-cash labor costs"—are lower in both Japan and the US than in Continental countries such as West Germany and France. However, Japanese and American firms spent more on non-statutory welfare and retirement allowances, whereas West Germany and France did considerably more for statutory welfare. In these contrasting systems, customary and statutory provision clearly function as substitutes (see Martin Rein's chapter in this volume).

To be sure, occupational welfare plays an important role of complementing public welfare in "residual" welfare states, but only in the direction of reinforcing dualism in the labor market. Rapid economic growth in Japan never resolved such inequalities, as the 1957 economic white paper had predicted. Figure 11.1 makes clear that there has been no convergence in wages and other cash costs between large and small firms, not only between 1965 and 1973 (the period of rapid economic growth) but throughout the years 1965-85. These data also show that differentials in occupational (non-statutory or "customary") welfare are more explicit than wage differentials; and they have enlarged over time. Thus, occupational welfare amplifies dualism and inequalities, instead of modifying them.

Overall, it is clear that numerous benefits accrue to the varying segments of the Japanese business community as a result of the mixture of state-welfare and occupational-welfare. And most of these are directly tied to the differentiated labor markets that prevail in different segments of Japanese employment.

Yet, just as different segments of Japanese business operate with quite different occupationally-based welfare, so too Japanese labor benefits, or loses, proportionally. And it must be noted that the organized segment of Japanese labor has, for the most part, been quite supportive of many aspects of the occupationally-based welfare system.

Labor

Japanese labor has always been somewhat ambivalent concerning issues of social welfare. Historically weak, both at the factory and the political levels, labor has rarely been in a powerful position to demand national state-run welfare programs. With the bulk of the organized labor movement working for large employers, the differentiated system of benefits has typically accorded well with individual unions' basic interest in advancing the welfare of their specific members rather than of the working class as a whole.

This point is especially noteworthy in the context of the links between retirement-allowances and wages, noted above. Japanese unionization rates are almost directly proportional to the size of a firm. And firm size is directly proportional to the occupationally-linked welfare benefits. Thus, Japanese unions historically have been quite reticent in pressing for state-led programs that would benefit the entire Japanese population. Far more central to union pressures have been programs that would be of direct benefit to their members, and these have frequently been benefits that have been provided by the firm, rather than by the state.

It is worth noting that Japan's unions, most particularly its moderate labor federations, such as Domei and IMF-JC (International Metal Federation-Japan Council) promoted Japanese-style welfare and "lifetime comprehensive welfare" plans in conjunction with management. Moderate labor had collaborated in the management of the economic crisis which had accompanied the 1973 oil crisis and this in turn reinforced labor-management harmony. The leftist federation, Sohyo, was overwhelmed by the unified front formed among the state, capital, and moderate labor. Finally, it too, by the early 1980s, had accepted the restraints on public welfare expenditures and the increasing role played by enterprise welfare.

Moderate labor succeeded in establishing a loose alliance of private-sector unions across national confederations (Zenmin Rokyo) in 1982. This developed into Rengo (Confederation of Japan Private-Sector Trade Unions) in 1987, and the new Rengo (Japan Trade Unions Confederation) in 1989. However, such national level integration of Japan's unions has been paralleled by systematic declines in the unionization ratio since the mid-1970s: 34.4 percent in 1975, 30.8 percent in 1980, 28.9 percent in 1985, and 25. 9 percent in 1989 (JSY, 1990:114; cf. Shinkawa ,1993).

One last anomaly concerns public sector workers. As was noted in the first section, it was public officials who were the first targets of governmental health and retirement programs. In general, Japanese public sector workers have been among the most militant unionists in the postwar period and also among the most generously compensated by government programs. Along with the employees in large private firms, government employees were heavily recruited from among the talent pool of "the best and brightest." And like their private sector counterparts, they were heavily unionized and they received disproportionately better occupationally-related benefits than private sector workers in small firms.

In 1961, for example, the average amount of yearly benefits to a retiree from the national government was almost three times greater than that to a retiree under the EPS. In 1970 it was still about twice as large. (Yokoyama and Tada, 1991:188-89, 214-15, 302-3). Yet, the retrenchment of the 1980s that took place under the aegis of "administrative reform" dealt a sharp blow to the public sector workforce. Public sector unions were broken or badly weakened in areas such as the public railways (Kokuro). Other public sector unions, such as those in the telecommunications industry and the Tobacco and Salt Monopoly were forced to compromise with notions of privatization. Furthermore, public sector pensions were capped and/or reduced as a result of the various administrative reform measures. By 1985 they represented only a 30 percent bonus over EPS. Thus, at present, public sector pensions remain better than most in the private sector, but employee contributions are up sharply and by the retirement of those currently paying into the system, benefits will not be significantly different (and in some instances quite a bit lower) from those for the private sector.

Overall, therefore, it is clear that organized labor has failed to unify the interests of the vulnerable parts of the labor market, such as employees in small firms, temporary workers, and part-time workers (cf. Ishikawa, 1981). It has also been slow to move into the emerging service sector. Meanwhile, one of the most powerful segments of the labor movement, namely public sector workers, have been sharply constrained, if not permanently crippled, by the official government policies of retrenchment that prevailed during the mid-1980s. The end result has been a restrengthening of Japan's occupationally-based welfare at the expense of any broadening of state-led welfare. But perhaps more importantly, with the pressure from organized labor for improved state-led social welfare programs being so minimal, it is highly improbable that any future changes in the welfare mix will be the result of labor-led demands.

The Japanese State, the Ruling Party and Capital

Finally, it is important to note the political benefits that the conservative government and private finance capital have derived from the mixture as well. Perhaps most important for the government has been the ability to run a low-cost administration. As noted above, Japan has continued to rank at or near the bottom of the OECD countries in proportion of GNP spent by government, in total social welfare spending by government, and in the extensiveness of various social programs. Moreover, through the late 1960s, the government managed to operate with almost constantly balanced budgets, and following the introduction of administrative reform in the mid-1980s, Japan also went a long way toward reversing its dependence on deficit financing for its annual budgets. The amount of public debt issued annually fell rather steadily over the subsequent decade. The 1991 level was less than one-half that of 1981 (Keizai Koho Center, 1992:81).[5] In turn, this allowed far more capital to be directed toward productive investments.

In this light, it is also important to recognize the fact that pension contributions from the private sector have been of great benefit to government investment programs. The funds which enjoyed preferential tax treatment for business have also provided important resources for capital accumulation and contributed to the growth of the Japanese economy through the government. Individual employers have no discretionary power to manage the funds. The 1962 tax code change simply allows the employer to claim his contributions to the pension funds as a non-taxable expense when the funds are invested in trust banks or insurance companies. Since the management of the funds is strictly regulated by law, it is impossible for individual employers to receive privileges through investment from trust banks or insurance companies. (Although the contributions to the funds are non-taxable, one percent of the funds is charged as a special corporate tax.)

Yet, the funds invested through trust banks and insurance companies eventually entered the government's Fiscal Investment and Loan Program (FILP) and in turn provided, for a sustained period, relatively low cost investment capital in line with governmental economic programs. The FILP was in effect the government's second budget and was funded heavily with money that had been contributed to employee retirement plans and health insurance plans. And in the long run, these monies were utilized by the government for a variety of investment programs that benefited important (and targeted) segments of Japanese industry.

This situation is gradually changing with Japan's greater internationalization. As the funds have expanded, demands for a liberalization of the pension market have grown stronger as well. As Table 11.1 shows, by 1990 the accumulations of the qualified-pension funds had reached nearly 12 billion yen, while those of EPFs stood at 22.5 billion yen (in 1989). Based on a study of the management and investment of enterprise pensions in the United States, the Association of EPFs released a report in May 1983, which leveled harsh criticisms at the existing monopoly system of 8 trust banks and 20 insurance companies that dominate investment of pension funds. Since there is no competition under this monopoly system, it contends, the trustees collaborate to maintain similar interest rates without making competitive efforts for efficient management of the funds. In order to introduce a more efficient and competitive system, disclosure of information and liberalization of management, including inhouse management, have been proposed. After this report, the Association of EPFs directed an active campaign towards in-house management throughout the 1980s (Daiichi Seimei Hoken, ed. 1988:101-105).

Securities companies and local/urban banks have also pressed for liberalization of the pension market. Detonated by an attempt by Nomura Securities to establish a joint trust company with the Morgan Guaranty Trust in 1983, various actors in finance have tried to enter the pension market by establishing joint trust or investment counselling companies. Since liberalization of the financial market was a prearranged program of the 1980s, the Ministry of Finance (MOF) was unable flatly to refuse liberalization of the pension market. In December 1984, the MOF declared that foreign banks would be able to start trust businesses in Japan with its authorization. By March 1985, six American banks, two Swiss banks, and a British bank were authorized (Daiichi Seimei Hoken ed., 1988:101-110; Migiya, 1984). Eventually, the Law of Employees' Pension Insurance was revised in 1988 and 1989 so that in-house management and management by the investment consultant could be authorized by the MHW up to a third of the funds (Shoji, 1990:56). It remains to be seen whether such funds will eventually revert in some form or other to the actual employers and become for them an important and additional source of capital investment. But again, these changes are hardly likely to lead to any substantial recalibration of the balance between state-led and occupationally-based welfare.

In all of these ways, it is clear that a more finely grained political economic treatment of Japanese "labor" and Japanese "business" reveals numerous interesting interstices within the broader struggles between these two major economic sectors. Furthermore, such a differentiated treatment allows one to see why at different times, these segments have taken political positions that would seem at odds with a strictly class interpretation. Moreover, this analysis also sheds light on the ways in which the Japanese welfare mixture has resulted in relatively high overall employment and generally egalitarian distributions of income, at least as across families, if not individuals.

Conclusions

Thanks to stable conservative governance and weak organized labor, Japan's diversified business sector has enjoyed the benefits of a segmented system of occupationally-based welfare. This has been of particular value in regard to both labor market management and capital formation. And the balance between labor and business in government has been relevant at various junctures from 1950s through the 1990s. Most notably, when the ruling LDP ran into electoral troubles during the 1970s, widespread changes were made in national level welfare programs as one means of keeping the pro-business LDP in power. Yet, these revisions took place rapidly, not incrementally, and were carried out without any labor-based political party gaining so much as one cabinet seat. Preemptive electoral politics was the prevalent motivation.

This became clear when by the early 1980s, the end of rapid economic growth forced the state to review its welfare policy and the reversal in the electoral fortunes of the LDP made it feasible to do so. Japan's then-ruling conservatives deliberately chose to avoid any path that put the country on track to create a Western-style welfare state. Instead, it returned to form and reinforced the importance of an occupationally-based system of Japanese-style welfare. Under this scheme, while certain government programs remained as a stronger ultimate safety net than had prevailed in any earlier period, the primary role of occupational welfare was substantially reinforced in Japan's welfare mix.

Overall, however, even though large segments of the Japanese population enjoy far fewer social benefits than some of their more occupationally-privileged peers, it is also important to recognize that in some respects, there is a much higher level of equality in Japan than in most dualist economies. A widely differentiated workforce, receiving widely differentiated occupationally-linked benefits, clearly serves the interests of Japanese employers and the conservative Japanese government. But by keeping total employment high, and by providing benefits that are widely differentiated in ways compatible with Japan's extended family structure, these "conservative" policies have highly egalitarian economic consequences for most segments of the Japanese workforce.

It is also worth noting that the occupationally-based retirement system has generated a substantial pool of valuable investment capital that, funneled through the Japanese government, has been vital to long-term national economic growth. In this regard, it might be worth speculating that the reliance on occupationally-based welfare may have contributed in some measure not only to Japan's economic success, but also to the wellbeing of important segments of its workforce. To date, Japan's workers have been relatively secure in the expectation of employment, and many have benefitted from the kinds of job retraining that is available only in the kind of labor markets that ensure long-term stability of a company's workforce. Despite Japan's recent moves to invest heavily abroad, few Japanese at home have lost jobs as a result, even following the bursting of the "economic bubble" in the early 1990s and the severe recession that followed. Instead, most have been able to move into more skill-intensive and high paying positions, unlike their peers in many other dualist economies.

Notes

1. One hundred percent of retirement-allowance expenses were non-taxable for a while. The 1956 revision reduced a non-taxable expense to 50 percent. The 1980 revision again reduced it to 40 percent.

2. An enterprise group with more than 1,000 employees, and an association formed by companies in the same industry/local area with more than 3,000 employees, are also able to contract out.

3. Subsequently, approval for the substitute type of contracting-out was withdrawn. As a result the additional type is now predominant. In 1990, the additional type accounted for 74.5 percent of 1,025 EPFs (Arai and Goto, 1991:102).

4. The EPA pointed to the importance of enterprise welfare, although at the time it also expected that its importance would diminish as the life styles and values of the Japanese people began to change. (cf. Hyodo, 1990). Subsequently, apparently in response to the government's desire to relieve the public budget of responsibilities for welfare, the EPA embraced enterprise welfare without reservations.

5 Public debt rose again with the onset of recession after 1992.

TABLE 11.1: *The Growth of Occupational Pensions*

	Qualified Pensions			
	Number of Firms		Insurants	Funds
	Total	1,000+	(thousands)	(billion yen)
1965	2,472	66	452	130
1981	61,437	488	5,837	3,052
1990	82,793	943	9,045	11,859

	Employee Pension Funds		
	Number of Firms	Insurants	Funds
		(thousands)	(billion yen)
1975	929	5,340	1,438
1985	1,091	7,058	12,596
1989	1,358	9,034	22,488

Sources: Yamazaki (1988:161); Arai and Goto (1991:87,102); Shoji (1990:57).

TABLE 11.2: *Percentage of Firms with Occupational Pensions*

		Qualified Pensions	Employee Funds	Hybrid Plans	Other Plans	Total
All Firms	1975	27.4	1.6	1.5	2.4	32.9
	1990	33.0	4.4	7.0	6.3	50.7
30-99	1989	29.5	3.4	5.1	5.0	44.3
1,000+	1975	27.7	23.5	2.5	6.2	59.9
	1990	39.5	25.8	15.6	5.5	86.4

Sources: Yamazaki (1988:163); Arai and Goto (1991:74).

TABLE 11.3: *Components of Total Labor Costs* (Percentages)

	Statutory Welfare	Customary (non-Statutory) Welfare		Other Welfare	Total Non-Cash
		Total	Retirement & pensions		
Japan (1978)	6.8	8.1	4.7	1.2	16.1
USA (1977)	6.6	10.6	4.9		17.4
W. Ger. (1978)	16.2	3.4	3.2	2.0	21.5
France (1978)	19.0	6.5	3.7	4.5	30.0

Note: "Other welfare" includes payment in kind and training costs.

Source: Ministry of Labor (1984:135)

FIGURE 11.1: *The Impact of Firm Size on Labor Costs*
Medium-sized firms [100-299] as % of large firms [5,000+]

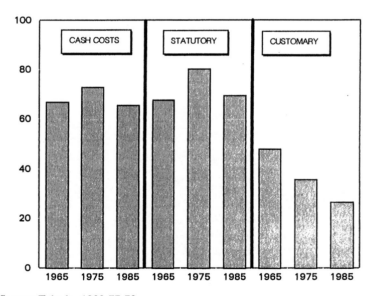

Source: Takada, 1989:77-78

Conclusion: Occupational Welfare in the Social Policy Nexus

Gøsta Esping-Andersen

The meaning of occupational welfare depends on one's chosen perspective. To the individual worker, occupational benefits are likely to be regarded positively; as a welcome, perhaps even necessary, supplement to living standards and income security, or as just remuneration for effort and loyalty. In some cases our worker may, of course, also be negatively disposed: inequities in the allocation of fringe benefits may arouse jealousies; if they do not meet expectations, frustration. The point, however, is that occupational welfare is, more likely than not, a positive good at the level of the individual. Why, then, does occupational welfare invoke such widespread scepticism in the social policy literature?

Possibly the best answer lies in its potential for a severe dissynchrony between individual and collective utility. Where trade unions are national in scope and representation, their power depends on minimizing intra-membership inequities and divisions. Occupational plans tend to foster exactly this. Where large portions of the more privileged labor force enjoy private social protection, broad solidarity behind the public social security system is likely to diminish. Hence, occupational welfare may be more than a mere supplement to the welfare state; under certain conditions it may contribute actively to its erosion.

Most students of social policy, at least in the Anglo-Saxon tradition, tend to be prejudiced against occupational welfare for two reasons: One, that employment-based pensions and allied programs hardly provide the kind of guaranteed citizens' rights that state programs do; the other, that there is assumed to exist a direct trade-off between occupational and public systems of protection, with the welfare state being the preferred alternative.

In answer to the first claim, as von Nordheim Nielsen's chapter makes clear, occupational welfare serves two important objectives in addition to worker welfare: it is an often important element in labor market management and collective bargaining; and it plays a decisive role in generating savings, investment, and capital formation.

That these identities are not mutually exclusive comes out in several chapters in this book, perhaps most clearly in Jacoby's study of Folsom's pioneering initiatives in the Kodak company. Folsom played a vital role in bringing about social security for American workers because this, at the same time, helped Kodak consolidate its competitive market position and its quest for internal labor peace. Quadagno and Hardy's chapter shows similarly how management rationalization strategies and union social security concerns came together in promoting private pension solutions to early retirement. Seen from yet another angle, the Scandinavian studies also elucidate how intertwined are the different faces of occupational welfare. Its growth is now favored by many of the better-off employee strata, dissatisfied with what they perceive as too modest public benefits; by employers interested in shifting the control of savings and investment capital towards the private market; and by governments desperate to diminish the threatening fiscal overload caused by revenue shortages and population aging.

Even when treated exclusively as an issue of social protection, the studies presented in this volume suggest that occupational welfare is a much more complex phenomenon than most existing welfare state research has acknowledged. Following in the footsteps of Richard Titmuss (1974), scholarship has typically interpreted private plans as a symptom of welfare state residualism and, by implication, of labor movement political failure. The social democratic model of the welfare state assumes, and occasionally also documents, that labor movements would systematically disfavor occupational plans because of their divisive and inegalitarian properties, because they do not extend the kind of inviolable social rights that do legislation, and because they are too easily a potential weapon of managerial power and.

Clearly, this theoretical perspective will define the relationship between private and public social protection in zero-sum terms: collective social welfare is inversely related to the relative dominance of private occupational welfare. We still await a thorough study of how differences in the public-private welfare mix affect equality and the distribution of social welfare, but there is substantial evidence to suggest that the zero-sum view enjoys some empirical support. Studies on the redistributive impact of pension systems unequivocally conclude that private plans are substantially more inegalitarian than public.[1]

The contributions to this volume confirm the widespread argument that private occupational plans are—with the possible exception of Sweden—quite unevenly distributed among the population: typically concentrated in the unionized sector, within the large corporations, and within the public sector, and rare in smaller companies, or within the lower-end of the service sector. In addition, they are much less likely to cater to women than men because of often long vesting and job tenure stipulations. And, as many (including our contributors) have documented, management has for more than a century installed occupational welfare programs to attract, retain, and reward its most cherished employees, thus contributing to the emergence of insider-outsider labor markets, cleavages, rivalries and differentiation within the labor force. It is safe to assume that management frequently succeeded. Certainly, in the early days of occupational welfare, employer plans were usually discretionary and reserved for top-level staff only. The ideological campaign for welfare capitalism in the early decades of the 20th Century did very little to bring occupational welfare to a broader clientele. This is as true for social democratic Denmark as it is for liberal United States and conservative Japan.

Yet, the zero-sum view may be contested. It may be held that private sector welfare is not so much a substitute for public as it is complementary. The two may grow in tandem and even nurture each other's expansion. There is evidence in favor of this view. Hippe and Pedersen show that under the favorable conditions prevailing over much of the postwar era, the growth of occupational welfare in Norway followed this kind of "positive dialectic". Dobbin and Boychuk's chapter suggests that in the United States, private employers responded to benefit hikes in the Social Security program by further extending private benefits, one reason being that the marginal cost became more advantageous.

The mechanism of complementarity clearly works in other ways. Here I shall mention but two. The first might be called the leap-frogging model, perhaps best illustrated by Swedish postwar developments: after World War Two, white collar employees were increasingly covered under private supplementary pensions to compensate for the relatively modest flat-rate peoples' pension.[2] As their private coverage grew, so did manual workers' demand for equal treatment, leading eventually to the legislation of a universal second-tier pension. In its wake followed a new spurt of occupational pension growth among the upper-level white collar employees in the form of a third-tier pension, and subsequently the LO fought successfully to have it extended across the entire unionized labor force (which, in Sweden, means virtually everybody). Leap-frogging, in short, favors a complementary evolution, instead of either the public or the private sector crowding out the other.

The second model involves fusion of private and public schemes. The proto-typical example is when occupational benefits are made mandatory through government intervention. In some cases, an existing framework of private plans is subjected to regulation and made mandatory for all: private becomes semi-public. This is the case of the Dutch second-tier industrial pensions. In Finland, legislation for a second-tier earnings related pension, inspired by the Swedish ATP system, provided for private administration and insurance; and, in the UK, legislation permitted contracting-out: public becomes private.

The Search for Theoretical Explanation

This volume has been deliberately cast at a fairly low level of theoretical ambition. A grand (or even middling) theory of occupational welfare is clearly not possible when our empirical knowledge of the phenomenon is still quite rudimentary. But there are other reasons why we should fear to tread into the terrain of theory. To begin with, the multi-faceted roles that occupational plans occupy imply that there are different dependent variables. It is likely that explanations will differ, depending on which facet is being discussed. The motives which propelled actors to pursue occupational welfare might diverge even if the outcome is convergent. Alternatively, as von Nordheim Nielsen stresses, different actors might have similar motives, but the results might be quite variable.

Much of the material presented in this book confirms that it is easy to become trapped in a causal labyrinth. On the employer side, occupational welfare has been shown to serve firms' investment objectives (the deferred wage allows an accumulation of savings at the employer's disposal). In other cases, the employer's principal motive seems to have been better labor force management with little direct regard for the issue of capital formation (the Kodak company, for example). In Japan, the two appear completely inseparable. In still other instances, the most plausible interpretation is that employers cede to pressures from the trade unions.

On the union side, there is less ambiguity in terms of the overriding motive: unions seek better benefits and conditions for their members, and the urge to bargain for occupational welfare is obviously strengthened where welfare state programs are considered inadequate. Still, even here we find ambiguity. As Stevens' chapter shows, American unions (especially the pre-war AFL) were hardly even interested in social security legislation. Their strategy seems, indeed, to have converged beautifully with the ideologists of welfare capitalism.

We would need much more research in order to answer the tempting hypothesis that union demands for occupational welfare depend not only on public benefit adequacy, but also on trade union structure. It is very possible that craft unions, representing largely a labor aristocracy, possibly with monopolistic powers of entry, will favor occupational solutions to a much greater extent than will industrial unions, representing easily replaceable mass workers. Craft unions invoke, almost by definition, narrow occupational solidarities and have, by virtue of the master-journeyman tradition, a more weakly developed sense of the universal, naked, and polarized class struggle. As we shall discuss below, the recent surge of occupational welfare across Europe may very well mirror the emergence of new kinds of crafts-like identities, professional upgrading, and occupational differentiation (Piore and Sabel, 1984; Boyer, 1988; Regini, 1991).

A second reason why it is difficult to theorize is that the causes behind occupational welfare growth (or decline) differ from one historical period to the next. If we step back from the comparative historical evidence provided in this book, a pattern of three rather distinct phases can be discerned. There is, firstly, the formative period when usually states and occasionally vanguard corporations (like American Express and Kodak, Krupp and Siemens, and Cadbury, Lever and Rowntree) introduced welfare plans for their most valued employees. They acted on a logic that was, in a sense, preindustrial; the employer adopting the role of a gratuitous feudal lord, paternalistically dispensing benefits in order to reward or secure unwavering loyalty. Pressure from below was, in this period, mainly notable for its absence.

The emergence of high industrialism marks the beginnings of a second phase; World War Two its end. With high industrialism emerged the phenomenon of the mass worker and strong trade unions. In tandem evolved also intense pressures on governments to address the "social question". Trade unions and labor parties typically formed their own friendly societies and welfare associations (which, in the 1920's United States, were as large as corporate welfare plans), and states began deliberately to pave the way for welfare capitalism with tax inducements, regulatory acts and ideological encouragement (Esping- Andersen, 1990: Chapter 4). In this second phase we therefore see the makings of a much more complex structure of actors and objectives. In Europe as in America, occupational welfare plans grew in fits and bursts but nowhere did they become a dominant or even important source of social protection for the majority of workers.

We can cite many reasons for the relatively aborted move towards occupational welfare in this period. In Europe, almost all the principal actors directed their claims towards the state. Across the industrialized world, the business cycle remained untamed and, culminating with the Great Depression, huge numbers of corporate and trade union welfare plans simply bankrupted, defaulted, or were pirated for other purposes. But we should also not forget that the principle of retirement had not yet been institutionalized effectively before the War. Thus, the largest and most important element in contemporary bargained welfare remained still a residual (Graebner, 1980; Myles, 1984). Before the war, private welfare plans for the non-elite were largely preoccupied with burial costs or protection against sickness or widowhood. Pensions were very undeveloped.

A third—we could call it the "fordist"—phase of occupational welfare development opened after World War II, when each of the elements which had been decisive during the interwar phase was dramatically transformed. Firstly, be it in the form of the New Deal, the Beveridge Plan, or the Nordic Peoples' Home, most advanced nations took a major leap towards the notion of social citizenship rights; the idea of universal retirement was born. Secondly, the war had altered both the structure and balance of power between the social classes. As Stevens shows, the ups-and-downs of trade union power played a major role in the cycles of postwar American occupational welfare expansion. Correspondingly, the strength of the labor parties came, in Europe, to be a major condition for new waves of welfare state reform. Thirdly, the most distinctive characteristic of the postwar political economy was the embrace of Keynesian stabilization policies which, coupled to the Bretton Woods and GATT agreements, secured steady non-inflationary growth. Unemployment and economic crisis appeared to have been relegated to a distant past. This went hand in hand with industrial stabilization: the consolidation of the fordist model of mass consumption and mass production under conditions of market expansion. The fordist corporation needed social stability and was prepared to pay for it.

It was in this context that postwar Europe, North America, and eventually also Japan, set off in different directions. Across Europe, the centrality of state solutions to social welfare demands was doubly strengthened: firstly, because of the construction of a practically universal and comprehensive welfare state apparatus; secondly, because privately bargained plans were, with few exceptions, incorporated into the state; thirdly, and perhaps most importantly, because governments in the 1960s and 1970s reconstructed public pensions around the "adequacy principle", thereby guaranteeing retirees full income maintenance in accordance with previous earnings.[3]

Our volume has centered on the Northern European countries, but the conclusions are generally valid for Western Europe. In the United States, it is sometimes held, occupational welfare plans mushroomed after the war because public social security stagnated. The contributions of Stevens, as well as Dobbin and Boychuk, suggest that we should question this simple causal relationship. It would be more correct to say that they stagnated and exploded in tandem. Still, it is doubtful that occupational welfare would have grown so large in the United States had government introduced universal national health care, sickness pay, family benefits, and pension adequacy for higher income earners. Also, recent trends in the United States point towards a sharp decline (8 percent during the 1980s) in coverage under the traditional defined-benefit model of occupational pensions (Mishel and Bernstein, 1993). Corporations eager to shed themselves of burdensome labor costs are shifting their emphasis to more individualized and actuarial benefit plans, such as the 401K schemes (Myles, 1995).

At first glance, the Japanese model seems to resemble the American with its welfare state residualism: modest public pension coverage combined with a huge system of occupational plans in the corporate sector, the outcome of which is to accentuate dualisms. Yet, as Shinkawa and Pempel also show, the principal characteristics of the Japanese welfare mix have a different structural interpretation. Firstly, Japanese pension policy has, until now, refrained from any major social security improvements by invoking the Confucian tradition of familial solidarity and the three-generation household. Hashimoto (1992) shows that 65 percent of the elderly in Japan live with their children—down from 77 percent in 1970. In Japan, then, the family may still constitute the dominant partner in the public-private pension nexus. Secondly, in Japan the primary corporate sector and the secondary flexible sector are syncopated and interdependent. And, the occupational welfare schemes in the former are decisive in this syncopation. State social policy seems to serve primarily the quest of diminishing the social costs of perpetuating flexibility in the secondary sector. In Japan, the relationship between private and public is surely complementary, but in an entirely different way than in the case of the United States.

If it is clear that the postwar era gave rise to international divergence, the ultimate root causes of this are less evident. There is certainly a strong case to be made from a working class power mobilization perspective. In Europe, it was the heyday of labor movement power, a circumstance which favored the emergence of neo corporatist types of political exchange (for an overview of this large literature, see Esping-Andersen and van Kersbergen, 1992). In contrast, labor in the United States was strong only within the labor market or, more precisely, only within the primary sector labor market. Finally, the Japanese model of "corporatism without labor" has been attributed to the absence of labor movement power at either level (Pempel, 1989).

But, since occupational welfare has multiple identities, it may very well be the case that postwar divergences should be ascribed to entirely different forces. As a system of savings, finance and capital formation, occupational plans could have evolved in divergent ways because crucial actors and institutions differed in their approach. We are still very far away from any systematic comparative analysis of this side of the occupational welfare coin, and must therefore leave the issue to future scholars. In the material presented in this book, we are, however, provided with small glimpses of why we cannot simply transpose the explanation of occupational plans as welfare to the explanation of occupational plans as capital formation. In their analysis of Scandinavia, Hippe and Pedersen as well as Kangas and Palme, suggest that the recent government initiatives to encourage more occupational pension development is motivated by the inability of public pension schemes to assure adequate savings and available private sector investment capital.

The Emergence of a Fourth Phase?

There are numerous indications that the world of occupational welfare is in flux. In the United States, the forces that have always been dominant in its expansion and consolidation are now in the vanguard for change. The large corporation, in particular, has emerged in favor of national health care legislation. At the same time, it has been active in dismantling existing occupational schemes; indeed, the corporate merger movement has often been motivated by the prospects of raiding over-funded plans. Clearly, the occupational welfare model is perceived as increasingly incompatible with corporate interests. The other main driving force, namely the trade unions, has in the recent decade been emasculated and has, in particular, difficulty asserting itself within the new service economy.

In the United States, structural change combined with recast interests and power relations among the principal actors is therefore likely to have substantial effects on the future of private pensions. The shift from defined-benefit to more individualized plans is one indication; the notable decline in coverage, another. Collectively bargained welfare benefits were part-and-parcel of the "middle class" status that American workers achieved in the postwar era. Today, American workers find themselves losing the middle class dream as low-wage employment grows and the labor market polarizes.

Paradoxically, within Europe we see a significant thrust in the opposite direction. Privatization as an explicit and desirable goal may be limited to Britain, yet there are unmistakable tendencies at work in both Scandinavia and on the Continent. Individual retirement accounts (similar to the American IRAs) are mushrooming everywhere. In an immediate sense, their growth has been fueled by government tax concessions, but behind this lies a more complex change. Governments, be they of conservative, liberal or socialist persuasion, are keen to shift the financial responsibilities for welfare into the market. With population aging, public sector deficits and heightened fiscal strain, even the most robust welfare state faces the specter of financial crisis. Except for Germany, the fiscal imbalance of public pension funds has deteriorated. In Belgium, the deficit in 1991 was more than three percent of GDP; in Italy, 4.3 percent. Indeed, subsidies to the pension insurance funds in Italy account for almost a third of the annual government deficit.[4] Employers, in turn, view the problem primarily from the point of view of labor costs and financial markets and see funded, private plans as hugely preferable to state controlled savings.

Contemporary European trends suggest, nonetheless, that American-style, defined benefit plans are unlikely to grow much. In essence, the burden of employers' fixed labor costs is already regarded as far too heavy. More likely is a trend towards actuarially-based, individualized savings schemes akin to the American 401K plans.

Finally, the consensus that seems to be emerging between employers and governments on the finance-side is strengthened more than weakened by the recast nature of employee and union demands on the welfare-side. Structural economic change over the past decades has radically altered labor markets. Industrial rationalization has sharply diminished the size and clout of the traditional fordist mass workers; skill upgrading and flexibilization have changed the interests, composition and collective identities of the new core workforce in manufacturing. The fordist-type mass worker may, as a result, be splintering into a dualism akin to Japan: a core work-force of skilled employees, and a periphery of flexible workers. Further, the process of multi-nationalization of production is creating an ever-expanding labor force that is divorced from national welfare schemes. As an example, the Airbus industries—because they have operations across a multitude of EEC nations—have been conceded the right to offer their own corporate welfare state.

As Regini (1991) suggests, these trends are accompanied by a shift towards "micro-concertation" within the fabric of collective bargaining: negotiations become increasingly tied to individual firm-performance. The drift towards individualization, differentiation and narrower guild-like, or company-based, welfare bargaining is complemented by the pervasive growth of narrower professional and semi- professional cadres, demanding tailor-made rather than universal mass-packaged welfare schemes. Hence, even in Sweden the social democratic labor movement is being called upon to reverse its egalitarian wages and welfare policies.

The possible decay of occupational welfare in the United States, the almost certain push towards social security in Japan, and the rise of private pensions in Europe, seem in combination to suggest the coming of a new era of international convergence. Still, there are discernable forces that point away from this kind of scenario. The debate on "post-fordism" has begun to identify a variety of likely developmental trajectories that, moreover, are nationally or at least regionally anchored. Some nations, like Germany and Japan, favor an industrial strategy that emphasizes upgraded, quality mass production; others, notably the

United States, rely heavily on lowering wage costs for industrial flexibility needs; and still others (at the regional level at least) encourage decentralized, smaller-scale flexible production units (for an overview, see Boyer, 1988). These trajectories are sharply at odds with one another, not solely in terms of their implications for international competitiveness, but also for the future of collective bargaining and the role of social welfare in the public-private nexus. One possibility, much discussed in connection with the debate on the European Community Social Charter, is that national welfare differentials may narrow while regional diversity may heighten (Streeck, 1990). We may, indeed, see a generalization of the Italian case: despite the existence of a unified national welfare state, vanguard welfare-regions (such as Emiglia Romagna) coexist with laggard welfare-regions (such as Calabria) because, increasingly, the decisive welfare margin derives from the interplay of the regional polity and local firms.

With such cataclysmic changes taking place everywhere one might consider our preoccupation with occupational welfare to be quite pedestrian. But this would be a huge mistake. The welfare state was one of the single most important institutions in the architecture of postwar capitalism. As we have tried to show, its functioning was linked to private sector welfare and the two were intimately intertwined. The institutional matrix that is presently unfolding will almost certainly look very different, and one day we may even have a name for it, but it is almost impossible to imagine that its core will be without a recast public-private welfare nexus.

Notes

1. For a recent overview, see A. West Pedersen (1994).

2. See also Einar Øverbye's chapter in this volume.

3. Thus, pension benefits as a percent of previous earnings hover around 80-90 percent in Belgium, France, Germany, and Italy. In Spain, at close to 100 percent. The notable exceptions are Denmark and the United Kingdom, both countries without a fully developed earnings-related superannuation scheme.

4. Calculated from OECD (1993). The deficit problem is augmented by a host of concurrent problems: the use of early retirement as a means to manage industrial conversion; often widespread cheating on social contribution payments; and the shift in favor of employment relations exempt from

contributions, including part-time work, temporary contracts, self employment and, of course, irregular undeclared employment.

References

Achenbaum, W.A. 1986. *Social Security: Visions and Revisions.* Cambridge: Cambridge University Press.

Ackerman, C.W. 1930. *George Eastman.* Boston: Houghton Mifflin.

Ahtokari, R. 1988. *Tuntematon Vaikuttaja.* Juva: Wsoy.

Aitken, H.G.J. 1967. "Defensive Expansionism: The State and Economic Growth in Canada." Pp. 183-221 in W. Easterbrook and M. Watkins eds., *Approaches to Canadian Economic History.* Toronto: McClelland and Stewart.

Alber, J. 1987. "Germany." Pp. 1-154 in P. Flora ed., *Growth to Limits: The Western European Welfare States since World War II.* Vol. 2. Berlin: de Gruyter.

Alestalo, M. 1986. *Structural Change, Classes and the Welfare State: Finland in an Historical and Comparative Perspective. Research Reports No. 33.* Helsinki: Research Group for Comparative Sociology, University of Helsinki.

Alestalo, M., P. Flora and H. Uusitalo. 1985. "Structure and Politics in the Making of the Welfare State." Pp. 188-210 in R. Alapuro, E. Haavio-Mannila and R. Väyrynen eds., *Small States in Comparative Perspective.* Oslo: Norwegian University Press.

Alestalo, M. and S. Kuhnle. 1987. "The Scandinavian Route. Economic, Social and Political Developments in Denmark, Finland, Norway, and Sweden." Pp. 3-47 in R. Erikson, E.J. Hansen, S. Ringen and H. Uusitalo eds., *The Scandinavian Model: Welfare States and Welfare Research.* Armonk NY: M.E. Sharpe.

Alexander, J. 1989. *Action and Its Environments: Towards a New Synthesis.* New York: Columbia University Press.

Allen, D. 1969. *Fringe Benefits: Wages or Social Obligation?* Ithaca NY: Cornell University Press.

Alsop, J. 1955. "He Sparked A Revolution." *Saturday Evening Post* 228:19, 132-36.

Altmeyer, A.J. 1968. *The Formative Years of Social Security.* Madison: University of Wisconsin Press.

Amenta, E. 1989. "Taking Exception: Explaining the Distinctiveness of American Public Policies in the Last Century." Pp. 292-333 in F.G. Castles ed., *The Comparative History of Public Policy.* Cambridge: Polity Press.

Amenta, E. and S. Parikh. 1991. "Capitalists Did Not Want the Social Security Act: A Critique of the Capitalist Dominance Thesis." *American Sociological Review* 56:124-29.

Amenta, E. and T. Skocpol. 1986. "States and Social Policies." *Annual Review of Sociology* 12:131-57.

Amenta, E. and Y. Zylan. 1991. "It Happened Here: Political Opportunity, the New Institutionalism, and the Townsend Movement." *American Sociological Review* 56:250-65.

American Council of Life Insurance. Various Years. *Life Insurance Fact Book*. Washington DC: American Council of Life Insurance.

American Management Association. 1929. *Retirement Annuity Plans*. New York: AMA.

———. 1935. *Economic Security: Pensions and Health Insurance*. New York: AMA.

Ames, C.B. 1935. "Listening in as Business Speaks." *Nation's Business* 23:18-22.

Anderson, S.J. 1993. *Welfare Policy and Politics in Japan*. New York: Paragon House.

Anglim, C. and B. Gratton. 1987. "Organized Labor and Old Age Pensions." *International Journal of Aging and Human Development* 25:91-107.

Arai, K. and A. Goto. 1991. *Taishokukin, Nenkin Seido no Sekkei to Unyo*. Tokyo: Keiei Shoin.

Asahi Shimbunsha. Annual. *Asahi Nenkan*. Tokyo: Asahi Shimbunsha.

Avery, D. 1979. *'Dangerous Foreigners': European Workers and Labour Radicalism in Canada, 1896-1932*. Toronto: McClelland and Stewart.

Babcock, R.H. 1974. *Gompers in Canada: A Study in American Continentalism before the First World War*. Toronto: University of Toronto Press.

Baker, H. 1940. *Current Policies in Personnel Relations in Banks*. Princeton, NJ: Industrial Relations Section, Princeton University.

Baker, H. and D. Dahl. 1945. *Group Health Insurance and Sickness Benefits and Collective Bargaining*. Report No. 72. Princeton NJ: Princeton University, Industrial Relations Section.

Baldwin, P. 1990. *The Politics of Social Solidarity*. Cambridge: Cambridge University Press.

Bankers Trust Company. 1960. *A Study of Industrial Retirement Plans*. New York: Bankers Trust Company.

Banting, K.G. 1987. "Institutional Conservatism: Federalism and Pension Reform." Pp. 48-74 in J.S. Ismael ed., *Canadian Social Welfare Policy: Federal and Provincial Dimensions.* Kingston Ont.: McGill-Queen's University Press.

Barfield, R. and J. Morgan. 1969. *Early Retirement, The Decision and the Experience.* Ann Arbor: University of Michigan Press.

Barnard, J. 1943. *Walter Reuther and the Rise of the Autoworkers.* Boston: Little Brown.

Baron, J.N., F.R. Dobbin and P.D. Jennings. 1986. "War and Peace: The Evolution of Modern Personnel Administration in US Industry." *American Journal of Sociology* 92:350-83.

Baron, J.N., P.D. Jennings and F.R. Dobbin. 1988. "Mission Control: The Development of Personnel Systems in US Industry." *American Sociological Review* 53:497-514.

Bastiansen, H. 1988. "Tanker i Forbindelsen Med KLPs 40-Års Jubileum." In Kommunal Landspensjonskasse (KLP) ed., *Årsberetning (Annual Report) for 1988.* Oslo: KLP.

Bell, D.R. 1975. "Prevalence of Private Retirement Plans." *Monthly Labor Review* 98:17-20.

Bergh, T. 1987. *Storhetstid, Vol. 5: Arbeiderbevegelsens historie i Norge.* Oslo: Tiden Norsk Forlag.

Berkowitz, E.D. 1987. "The First Advisory Council and the 1939 Amendments." Pp. 55-78 in E.D. Berkowitz ed., *Social Security After 50.* Westport: Greenwood Press.

Berkowitz, E.D. and D. Fox. 1989. "The Politics of Social Security Expansion: Social Security Disability Insurance, 1935-1986." *Journal of Policy History* 1:233-60.

Berkowitz, E.D. and K. McQuaid. 1980. *Creating the Welfare State: The Political Economy of Twentieth-century Reform.* New York: Praeger.

———. 1988. *Creating the Welfare State: The Political Economy of Twentieth-century Reform* 2nd ed. New York: Praeger.

Bernstein, A. 1990. "In Search of the Vanishing Nest Egg." *Business Week* July 30, 46.

Bernstein, B. 1965. "The Truman Administration and Its Reconversion Wage Policy." *Labor History* 6:214-31.

Bernstein, I. 1960. *The Lean Years: A History of the American Worker, 1920-1933.* Boston: Houghton Mifflin.

———. 1970. *The Turbulent Years: A History of the American Worker, 1933-1941.* Boston: Houghton Mifflin.

342   *References*

————. 1985. *A Caring Society: The New Deal, the Worker, and the Great Depression*. Boston: Houghton Mifflin.

Bernstein, M.A. 1987. *The Great Depression: Delayed Recovery and Economic Change in America, 1929-1939*. Cambridge UK: Cambridge University Press.

Bernstein, M.C. 1964. *The Future of Private Pensions*. New York: The Free Press.

Bessey, B. and S. Ananda. 1991. "Age Discrimination in Employment: An Interdisciplinary Review of the ADEA." *Research on Aging* 13:413-57.

Bixby, A.K. 1986. "Social Welfare Expenditures, 1963-83." *Social Security Bulletin* 49:12-24.

Bloom, D.E. and R.B. Freeman. 1992. "The Fall in Private Pension Coverage in the United States," *American Economic Review* 82:539-545.

Boaz, R.F. 1987. "The 1983 Amendments to the Social Security Act: Will They Delay Retirement? Summary of the Evidence." *The Gerontologist* 27:149-52.

Bowden, G. 1989. "Labour Unions in the Public Mind: The Canadian Case." *Canadian Review of Sociology and Anthropology* 26:723-42.

Boyer, R., ed. 1988. *The Search For Labor Market Flexibility*. Oxford: Clarendon Press.

Braden, B.R. 1988. "Increases in Employer Costs for Employee Benefits Dampen Dramatically." *Monthly Labor Review* 111:3-7.

Brandes, S.D. 1976. *American Welfare Capitalism, 1880-1940*. Chicago: University of Chicago Press.

Brinkley, A. 1982. *Voices of Protest: Huey Long, Father Coughlin, and the Great Depression*. New York: Knopf.

Brodie, J. and J. Jenson. 1980. *Crisis, Challenge and Change: Party and Class in Canada*. Toronto: Methuen.

Brody, D. 1968. "The Rise and Decline of Welfare Capitalism." Pp. 174-78 in J. Braeman, R. Bremner and D. Brody eds., *Change and Continuity in Twentieth Century America: The 1920's*. Columbus: Ohio State University Press.

————. 1980. *Workers in Industrial America*. New York: Oxford University Press.

Bronfenbrenner, M. and Y. Yasuba. 1988. "Economic Welfare." Pp. 93-136 in K. Yamamura and Y. Yasuba eds., *The Political Economy of Japan, Vol. 1: The Domestic Transformation*. Stanford CA: Stanford University Press.

Brown, E.C. 1949. "The NLRB-Wagner Act Through Taft-Hartley Law." Pp. 179-214 in C.E. Warne ed., *Labor in Postwar America*. Brooklyn: Remsen Press.

Brown, E.R. 1991. "Health Coverage in California." UCLA School of Public Health, Los Angeles, June.

Brown, J.D. 1969. *The Genesis of Social Security in America.* Princeton NJ: Princeton University Industrial Relations Section.

Brym, R.J. 1986. "Incorporation Versus Power Models of Working Class Radicalism: With Special Reference to North America." *Canadian Journal of Sociology* 11:227-51.

————. 1989. "Canada." Pp. 177-206 in T. Bottomore and R. Brym eds., *The Capitalist Class: An International Study.* New York: New York University Press.

————. 1991. "Social Movements." Pp. 670-99 in L. Tepperman and J. Richardson eds., *The Social World: An Introduction to Sociology* 2nd edn. Toronto: McGraw-Hill Ryerson.

————. 1992. "Some Advantages of Canadian Disunity: How Quebec Sovereignty Might Aid Economic Development in English-Speaking Canada." *Canadian Review of Sociology and Anthropology* 29:210-26.

Brym, R.J. with B. Fox. 1989. *From Culture to Power: The Sociology of English Canada.* Toronto: Oxford University Press.

Bureau of Economic Analysis. 1986. *The National Income and Product Accounts of the United States, 1929-1982.* Washington DC: GPO.

Bureau of Labor Statistics. 1928. *Beneficial Activities of American Trade Unions.* Washington DC: BLS.

————. 1929. *Care of Aged Persons in the United States (Bulletin 465).* Washington DC: BLS.

————. 1934. "Benefits Payments By Standard National and International Unions 1933." *Monthly Labor Review* 38:1365-69.

————. 1935. "Insurance and Benefit Plans." *Monthly Labor Review* 39:53-56.

————. 1948. *Union Health and Welfare Plans—1947.* Bulletin 900. Washington DC: BLS.

————. 1950. *Problems and Policies of Dispute Settlement and Wage Stabilization During World War II.* Bulletin 1009. Washington DC: BLS.

————. 1951. *Employee Benefits Plans Under Collective Bargaining; Mid-1950.* Bulletin 1017. Washington DC: BLS.

————. 1989. *Employment, Hours and Earnings.* Bulletin 1312-12, Vol. 1-2. Washington DC: GPO.

Bureau of The Census. 1975. *Historical Statistics of the United States: Colonial Times to 1970.* Washington DC: The Bureau.

Burk, R.F. 1990. *The Corporate State and the Broker State: The Du Ponts and American National Politics.* Cambridge: Harvard University Press.

Burns, R.K. 1949. "Industrial Relations in Printing." Pp. 419-29 in C.E. Warne ed., *Labor in Postwar America*. Brooklyn NY: Remsen Press.

Burstein, P. 1985. *Discrimination, Jobs and Politics, The Struggle for Equal Employment Opportunity in the United States since the New Deal*. Chicago: University of Chicago Press.

Cameron, D.R. 1984. "Social Democracy, Corporatism, Labour Quiescense, and the Representation of Economic Interest in Advanced Capitalist Society." Pp. 143-78 in J.H. Goldthorpe ed., *Order and Conflict in Contemporary Capitalism*. Oxford: Oxford University Press.

———— 1986. "The Growth of Government Spending: The Canadian Experience in Comparative Perspective." Pp. 21-51 in Keith Banting ed., *State and Society: Canada in Comparative Perspective*. Toronto: University of Toronto Press.

Campbell, J.C. 1992. *How Policies Change: The Japanese Government and the Aging Society*. Princeton NJ: Princeton University Press.

Cancian, F. 1975. *What are Norms? A Study of Beliefs and Action in a Maya Community*. Cambridge UK: Cambridge University Press.

Castles, F. 1978. *The Social Democratic Image of Society*. London: Routledge and Kegan Paul.

Castles F.G. and D. Mitchell. 1991. "Three Worlds of Welfare Capitalism or Four? Discussion Paper No. 21, Australian National University Graduate Program in Public Policy, June.

Cates, J. 1983. *Insuring Inequality: Administrative Leadership in Social Security, 1934-54*. Ann Arbor: University of Michigan Press.

Causey, M. 1995. "Pension Reform Outlook." *Washington Post* January 25, D2:118.

Chandler, A.D.J. 1990. *Scale and Scope: The Dynamics of Industrial Capitalism*. Cambridge: Harvard University Press.

Civilian Production Administration. 1947. *Industrial Mobilization for War*. Washington DC: GPO.

Clark, R. 1990. "Income Maintenance Policies in the United States." Pp. 382-97 in R. Binstock and L. George eds., *Handbook of Aging and the Social Sciences*. New York: Academic Press.

Clark, R.and A. McDermed. 1991. *The Choice of Pension Plans in a Changing Regulatory Environment*. Washington DC: AEI Press.

Collick, M. 1988. "Social Policy: Pressures and Responses." Pp. 206-36 in J.A.A. Stockwin ed., *Dynamic and Immobilist Politics in Japan*. Honolulu: University of Hawaii Press.

Cornfield, D. 1986. "Declining Union Membership in the Post-World War II Era: The United Furniture Workers of America, 1939-1982." *American Journal of Sociology* 91:1112-53.

Courchene, M. 1989. *The Current Industrial Relations Scene in Canada 1989: Wages, Productivity and Labour Costs.* Kingston Ont.: Industrial Relations Center, Queen's University.

Daiichi Seimei Hoken, ed. 1982. *Nenkin Hakusho.* Tokyo: Shakai Hoken Kohosha.

————, ed. 1988. *Kigyo Nenkin Saishin Joho.* Tokyo: Toyo Keizai Shinposha.

Dailey, L.M. and J.A. Turner. 1992. "US Private Pensions in World Perspective: 1970-1989." Pp. 11-33 in J.A. Turner and D.J. Beller eds., *Trends in Pensions 1992.* Washington DC: GPO.

Davey, P.J. 1978. *Current Directions in Pension Fund Management.* Conference Board Information Bulletin #39. New York: The Conference Board.

Dearing, C. 1954. *Industrial Pensions.* Washington DC: The Brookings Institution.

Deaton, R.L. 1989. *The Political Economy of Pensions.* Vancouver: University of British Columbia Press.

Denis, C. 1989. "The Genesis of American Capitalism: An Historical Enquiry into State Theory." *Journal of Historical Sociology* 2:328-56.

Department of Health and Social Services (DHSS). 1987. "Note 1." Washington DC: DHSS Office of Research and Statistics, January.

Derthick, M. 1979. *Policymaking for Social Security.* Washington DC: The Brookings Institution.

Deutscher, I. 1973. *What We Say/What We Do: Sentiments and Acts.* Glenview IL: Scott Foresman.

DeVyver, F. 1949. "Collective Bargaining in Steel." Pp. 387-98 in C.E. Warne ed., *Labor in Postwar America.* Brooklyn: Remsen Press.

Dobbin, F. 1992. "The Origins of Private Social Insurance: Public Policy and Fringe Benefits in America, 1920-1950." *American Journal of Sociology* 97:1416-50.

Dore, R. 1989. "Where We Are Now: Musings of an Evolutionist." *Work, Employment & Society* 3:425-46.

Dvorsky R. 1956. "The Development of Negotiated Health Insurance and Sickness Benefit Plans of the Steel, Automobile, and Electrical Equipment Industries." Unpublished Ph.D. Dissertation, University of Pittsburgh.

Dyer, J.K. 1977a. "Coordination of Private and Public Pension Plans: An International Summary." Pp. 29-40 in D. McGill ed., *Social Security and Private Pension Plans: Competitive or Complementary?* Homewood IL: Richard D. Irwin.

――――. 1977b. "Appendix A. Concept of Pension-Social Security Integration." Pp. 123-33 in D. McGill ed., *Social Security and Private Pension Plans: Competitive or Complementary?* Homewood IL: Richard D. Irwin.

Economic Planning Agency (EPA). 1957. "Keizai Hakusho" (Economic White Paper). Tokyo: EPA.

Edebalk, P.G. and E. Wadensjö. 1987. *"Contractually Determined Insurance Schemes for Manual Workers."* Working Paper No. 15/1987. Stockholm: Swedish Institute for Social Research, Stockholm University.

Edwards, A.C. 1967. "Canadian Private Pension Plans: A Study of Their History, Trends, Taxation, and Investments." Unpublished Ph.D. thesis, Department of Business Administration, Ohio State University.

Edwards, R. 1979. *Contested Terrain.* New York: Basic.

Elmstedt, E. 1985. *"Hur avtalsparter och lagstiftare reglerat arbetsvillkoren."* Pp. 180-238 in Fred eller fejd. Stockholm: SAF.

Elmér, Å 1960. *Folkpensioneringen i Sverige med särskild hänsyn till ålderspensioneringen.* Lund: CWK Gleerup.

Epland, J. 1990. "Høgreparti og Velferdsstatsekspansjon i Norge og Sverige 1945-1965." Pp. 213-41 in S. Kuhnle and P. Selle eds., *Frivillig organisert velferd - alternativ til offentlig?* Bergen: Alma Ater.

Epstein, A. 1933. *Insecurity, A Challenge to America.* New York: Smith and Haas.

Epstein, L. and E. Snyder. 1949. "Urban Price Trends." Pp. 137-76 in C.E. Warne ed., *Labor in Postwar America.* Brooklyn: Remsen Press.

Eriksen, T. and E. Palmer. 1992. "The Detoriation of the Swedish Pension Model." Paper presented at the SPRU Conference "Social Security 50 years after Beveridge", York, September 27-30.

Erikson, R., E.J. Hansen, S. Ringen and H. Uusitalo, eds. 1987. *The Scandinavian Model: Welfare States and Welfare Research.* Armonk NY: M.E. Sharpe.

Esping-Andersen, G. 1978. "Social Class, Social Democracy, and the State: Party Policy and Party Decomposition in Denmark and Sweden." *Comparative Politics* 11:42-58.

――――. 1985. *Politics against Markets.* Princeton NJ: Princeton University Press.

————. 1987. "State and Market in the Formation of Social Security Regimes: A Political Economy Approach." Working Paper No. 87/281, European University Institute (Florence).

————. 1990. *The Three Worlds of Welfare Capitalism.* Oxford: Polity Press.

Esping-Andersen, G., R. Friedland and E.O. Wright. 1976. "Modes of Class Struggle and the Capitalist State." *Kapitalistate* 4-5:186-220.

Esping-Andersen, G. and W. Korpi. 1987. "From Poor Relief to Institutional Welfare States: The Development of Scandinavian Social Policy." Pp. 39-74 in R. Erikson, E.J. Hansen, S. Ringen and H. Uusitalo eds., *The Scandinavian Model.* New York: M.E. Sharpe.

Esping-Andersen, G., M. Rein and L. Rainwater. 1988. "Institutional and Political Factors Affecting the Well-Being of the Elderly." Pp. 39-74 in J.L. Palmer, T.M. Smeeding and B.B. Torrey eds., *The Vulnerable.* Washington DC: The Urban Institute Press.

Esping-Andersen, G. and K. van Kersbergen. 1992. "Contemporary Research on Social Democracy." *Annual Review of Sociology* 18:187-208.

Eurostat. 1987. *Labour Costs in Industries and Services.* Population and Social Conditions Rapid Reports, No. 2. Luxembourg: Statistical Office of the EC (Eurostat).

————. 1988. *Social Protection: Current Expenditure and Receipts 1970-1985.* Population and Social Conditions Rapid Reports, Provisional Version, June 16. Luxembourg: Statistical Office of the EC (Eurostat).

————. 1991. *Labor Costs Survey 1988: Initial Results.* Population and Social Conditions-Accounts, Surveys and Statistics. Luxembourg: Statistical Office of the EC (Eurostat).

Feldman, R. and M. Betzold. 1988. *End of the Line: Autoworkers and the American Dream.* New York: Weidenfeld and Nicolson Press.

Feldstein, M. 1974. "Social Security, Induced Retirement and Aggregate Capital Accumulation." *Journal of Political Economy* 82:905-26.

Ferguson, T. 1989. "Industrial Development and the Coming of the New Deal." Pp. 3-31 in S. Fraser and G. Gerstle eds., *The Rise and Fall of the New Deal Order, 1930-1980.* Princeton NJ: Princeton University Press.

Fisher, P. 1973. "Major Social Security Issues: Japan, 1972." *Social Security Bulletin* 36:26-38.

Fitzgerald, R. 1988. *British Labor Management and Industrial Welfare, 1846-1939.* London: Croom Helm.

Flora, P. and J. Alber. 1981. "Modernization, Democratization, and the Development of Welfare States in Western Europe." Pp. 37-80 in P. Flora and A. Heidenheimer eds., *The Development of Welfare States in Europe and America.* New Brunswick and London: Transaction.

Folsom, M.B. 1928. "Industrial Pensions and Group Life Insurance." Kodak Archives, Rochester NY, 28 June.

————. 1930. "Program of Stabilized Production and Employment." Speeches, vol. 1, Folsom Papers, University of Rochester, December.

————. 1934. "Future Protection of the Jobless." *Nation's Business* 22:64-68.

————. 1936. "Company Annuity Plans and the Federal Old Age Benefit Plan." *Harvard Business Review* 14:414-24.

————. 1962. *Executive Decision Making: Observations and Experience in Business and Government*. New York: McGraw-Hill.

————. 1967. "Interview with Columbia University Oral History Project."

Forbes Magazine. 1963. "Eastman Kodak What Makes It Click?" *Forbes* 91:23-24.

Forsey, E. 1985. "The History of the Canadian Labour Movement." Pp. 7-22 in W.J.C. Cherwinski and G. Kealey eds., *Lectures in Canadian Labour History*. St. John's NF: Memorial University Committee on Canadian Labour History.

Foster, D. 1989. "Post Yuppie America." *Mother Jones* February:17.

Foster, J. 1975. *The Union Politic: The CIO Political Action Committee*. Columbia, MO: University of Missouri Press.

Fujita, S. 1984. *Fukushi Seisaku to Zaisei*. Tokyo: Nihon Keizai Shinbunsha.

Fujita, Y. 1983. *Shogai Fukushi to Zaisei*. Tokyo: Sangyo Rodo Chosajo.

Galenson, W. 1986. "The Historical Role of American Trade Unions." Pp. 39-73 in Seymour M. Lipset ed., *Unions in Transition: Entering the Second Century*. San Francisco: ICS Press.

Gallup, G. 1972. *The Gallup Poll: Public Opinion, 1935-1971*. Connecticut: Greenwood Press.

Garon, S. 1987. *The State and Labor in Modern Japan*. Berkeley: University of California Press.

Goldman, E. 1960. *The Crucial Decade - and After: America 1945-1960*. New York: Vintage.

Goldmann, F. 1948. "Labor's Attitude Toward Health Insurance." *Industrial and Labor Relations Review* 2:90-98.

Goldthorpe, J.H. 1984. "The End of Convergence: Corporatist and Dualist Tendencies in Modern Western Societies." Pp. 315-43 in J.H. Goldthorpe ed., *Order and Conflict in Contemporary Capitalism*. Oxford: Oxford University Press.

Goodman, P.S. 1977. "Social Comparison Processes in Organizations." Pp. 97-132 in B.M. Staw and R. Sulancik eds., *New Directions in Organizational Behavior*. Chicago: University of Chicago Press.

Gordon, A.W. 1985. *The Evolution of Labor Relations in Japan: Heavy Industry, 1853-1955*. Princeton NJ: Princeton University Press.

Gordon, C. 1991. "New Deal, Old Deck: Business and the Origins of Social Security, 1920-1935." *Politics and Society* 19:165-207.

Gordon, D.M., R. Edwards and M. Reich. 1982. *Segmented Work, Divided Workers*. London: Cambridge University Press.

Gordon, M.S. 1990. *Social Security Policies in Industrial Countries: A Comparative Analysis*. Cambridge UK: Cambridge University Press.

Gordus, J.P. 1980. *Leaving Early: Perspectives and Problems in Current Retirement Practice and Policy*. Kalamazoo MI: W.E. Upjohn Institute for Employment Research.

Graebner, W. 1980. *A History of Retirement, The Meaning and Function of an American Institution*. New Haven: Yale University Press.

Greenough, W. and F. King. 1976. *Pension Plans and Public Policy*. New York: Columbia University Press.

Gross, J.A. 1981. *The Reshaping of the National Labor Relations Board: National Labor Policy in Transition 1937-1947*. Albany NY: State University of New York Press.

Hagen, K. 1988. "Finansieringsproblemer Som Privatiseringsargument." Pp. 16-49 in H. Bogen and O. Langeland eds., *Offentlig eller Privat?* Oslo: FAFO Research Report 078.

Hagen, K. and J.M. Hippe, eds. 1989. *Svar skyldig?* Oslo: FAFO.

Hakala, D.R. and K.M. Huggins. 1976. "ERISA: Impact on Business Financial Management." *Michigan Business Review* 28:19-23.

Hall, R. 1988. "Enterprise Welfare in Japan: Its Development and Role." Discussion Paper WSP/31, Welfare State Program, Suntory-Toyota International Center for Economics and Related Disciplines, London School of Economics.

Hannah, L. 1986. *Inventing Retirement: The Development of Occupational Pensions in Britain*. Cambridge: Cambridge University Press.

———. 1991. "Similarities and Differences in the Growth and Structure of Private Pensions in OECD Countries." Paper presented at the OECD Conference of National Experts on Private Pensions and Public Policy, Paris, July 1-3.

Hansen, P. 1994. "Saskatchewan: The Failure of Political Imagination." *Studies in Political Economy* No. 43:161-67.

Harbrecht, P. 1959. *Pension Funds and Economic Power*. New York: The Twentieth Century Fund.

Harrington, M. and M. Levinson. 1988. "The Perils of a Dual Economy." Pp. 333-41 in F. Hearn ed., *The Transformation of Industrial Organization.* Belmont CA: Wadsworth.

Harris, H. 1982. *The Right to Manage: Industrial Relations Policies of American Business in the 1940's.* Madison: University of Wisconsin Press.

Hart, R.A. 1980. *The Economics of Non-Wage Labour Costs.* London: Allen and Unwin.

Hashimoto, A. 1992. "Ageing in Japan." In D. Phillips ed., *Ageing in East and South East Asia.* London: Edward Arnold.

Hatland, A. 1982. "Folketrygdens finansiering." INAS Working Paper no 15, Oslo.

————. 1984. *Folketrygdens framtid.* Oslo: Universitetsforlaget.

————. 1986. *The Future of Norwegian Social Security.* Oslo: Universitetsforlaget.

Haydu, J. 1988. *Between Craft and Class: Skilled Workers and Factory Politics in the US and Britain, 1890-1922.* Berkeley: University of California Press.

Heclo, H. 1974. *Modern Social Politics in Britain and Sweden: From Relief to Income Maintainance.* New Haven: Yale University Press.

Hedström, P. and S. Ringen. 1990. "Age and Income in Contemporary Society." Pp. 77-104 in T. Smeeding, M. O'Higgins and L. Rainwater eds., *Poverty, Inequality and Income Distribution in Comparative Perspective.* Smeeding, Michael O'Higgins & Lee Rainwater New York: Harvester.

Hem, P. 1991. "Sammenhengen Mellom Valg av Organisatorisk Design og Føringer Som Legges På Den Politiske Beslutningsprosessen: En Studie av Norsk Pensjonspolitikk 1967-1989." Unpublished MA (Hovedoppgave) Thesis, Institute of Political Science, University of Oslo.

Henriksen, J., J. Rasmussen and P. Kampmann. 1988. *Fordelingen af Private Pensioner.* Copenhagen: Institute of Sociology, University of Copenhagen.

Himmelberg, R. 1976. *The Origins of the National Recovery Administration.* New York: Fordham University Press.

Hippe, J.M. 1988. *Sosialpolitisk kalender.* Oslo: FAFO.

Hippe, J.M. and A.W. Pedersen. 1988. "For lang og tro tjeneste: Pensjoner i arbeidsmarkedet." Report no 084. Oslo: FAFO.

————. 1991. *Førtidspensjonering i private bedrifter.* Oslo: FAFO.

————. 1992. *Arbeidsplassen som velferdsarena.* Oslo: FAFO.

Holler, K. 1958. "Tariffoppgjøret." *Fri Fagbevegelse* (Oslo) 51:69-71.

Horowitz, R. 1978. *Political Ideologies of Organized Labor.* New Brunswick NJ: Transaction Books.

Hoskins, C. 1931. "Will the 'Rochester Plan' Solve Unemployment?" *Forbes* 27:13-14.

Huxley, C., D. Kettler and J. Struthers. 1986. "Is Canada's Experience 'Especially Instructive'?" Pp. 113-49 in Seymour M. Lipset ed., *Unions in Transition: Entering the Second Century*. San Francisco: ICS Press.

Hyman, J. and T. Schuller. 1984. "Occupational Pension Schemes and Collective Bargaining." *British Journal of Industrial Relations* 22:289-310.

Hyodo, T. 1990. "Tenkanki niokeru Shakai Seisaku Shiso." Pp. 135-57 in Shakai Seisaku Sosho Henshu Iinkai ed., *Sengo Shakai Seisaku no Kiseki*. Tokyo: Keibunsha.

Ilse, L. 1953. *Group Insurance and Employee Retirement Plans*. New York: Prentice-Hall.

Industrial Relations Section. 1938. *Industrial Retirement Plans in Canada, 1938*. Kingston Ont.: Queen's University.

Inoguchi, T. 1990. "The Political Economy of Conservative Resurgence Under Recession: Public Policies and Political Support in Japan, 1977-1983." Pp. 189-225 in T.J. Pempel ed., *Uncommon Democracies: The One-Party Dominant Regimes*. Ithaca NY: Cornell University Press.

Institute of Life Insurance. Various Years. *Pension Facts*. New York: Institute of Life Insurance.

International Pension Consultants (IPC). 1977-80. *State Pension Systems and Private Pension Practice - An International Survey*. Wiesbaden: Arbeit und Alter.

International Social Security Association (ISSA). 1980. *Occupational Pension Schemes. European Series No. 10*. Geneva: ISSA.

———. 1987. *Conjugating Public and Private: The Case of Pensions*. Geneva: ISSA, *Studies and Research* No. 24.

Ippolito, R.A. 1986a. *Pensions, Economics and Public Policy*. Homewood IL: Dow Jones-Irwin.

———. 1986b. "A Study of the Regulatory Impact of the Employee Retirement Income Security Act." *Journal of Law and Economics* 31:85-126.

Ishikawa, M. 1981. "Soshikiritsu Teika ni Nayamu Rodo Kumiai." *Ekonomisuto* Feb 10, 45-49.

Jackson, P. 1977. "Philosophical Basis of Private Pension Movement." Pp. 14-28 in D. McGill ed., *Social Security and Private Pension Plans: Competitive or Complementary?* Homewood IL: Richard D. Irwin.

Jacoby, S.M. 1984. "The Development of Internal Labor Markets." Pp. 23-69 in P. Osterman ed., *American Manufacturing Firms Internal Labor Markets*. Cambridge MA: MIT Press.

————. 1985. *Employing Bureaucracy: Managers, Unions, and the Transformation of Work in American Industry, 1900-1945*. New York: Columbia University Press.

————. 1993. "Pacific Ties: Employment Systems in Japan and the United States." Pp. 206-48 in H. Harris and N. Lichtenstein eds., *Industrial Democracy in the Twentieth Century*. Cambridge: Cambridge University Press.

James, M. 1947. *The Metropolitan Life: A Study in Business Growth*. New York: Viking.

Japan Productivity Center (JPC). Various years. "Roshi Kankei Hakusho." (White Paper on Labor Relations). Tokyo: JPC.

Jenkins, J.C. and B.G. Brents. 1989. "Social Protest, Hegemonic Competition, and Social Reform: A Political Struggle Interpretation of the Origins of the American Welfare State." *American Sociological Review* 54:891-909.

Jokelainen, M. 1991. "Työvoiman osuus 55-64 -vuotiaasta väestöstä OECD-maissa vuosina 1950-1989." *Kansaneläkelaitoksen julkaisuja* 9:40.

Jones, H. 1983. "Employers' Welfare Schemes and Industrial Relations in Inter-War Britain." *Business History* 25:61-75.

Josephson, M. 1952. *Sidney Hillman: Statesman of American Labor*. New York: Doubleday.

Kanbara, M. 1986. *Tenkanki no Seiji Katei*. Tokyo: Sogo Rodo Kenkyusha.

Kangas, O. 1988. "Politik och Ekonomi i Pensionsforsäkringen. Det Finska Pensionssystemet i ett Jämförande Perspektiv." Meddelande (Report) No. 5, University of Stockholm, Institute of Social Research.

————. 1991. *The Politics of Social Rights*. Stockholm: Swedish Institute for Social Research, Stockholm University.

Kangas, O. and J. Palme. 1989. "Public and Private Pensions: The Scandinavian Countries in a Comparative Perspective." Working Paper No. 3/1989, Swedish Institute for Social Research, University of Stockholm, April.

Karl, B.D. 1983. *The Uneasy State: The United States from 1915 to 1945*. Chicago: University of Chicago Press.

Katz, H. 1985. *Shifting Gears: Changing Labor Relations in the US Automobile Industry*. Cambridge, MA: The MIT Press.

Katzenstein, P.J. 1984. *Corporatism and Change: Austria, Switzerland, and the Politics of Industry*. Ithaca: Cornell University Press.

Keizai Koho Center. 1992. *Japan, 1992: An International Comparison*. Tokyo: Keizai Koho Center.

Kennedy, J.B. 1908. *Beneficiary Features of American Trade Unions*. Baltimore: Johns Hopkins Press.

Kerns, W. and M. Glanz. 1988. "Private Social Welfare Expenditures, 1972-1985." *Social Security Bulletin* 51:3-11.

Kerry, T. 1980. *Workers, Bosses, and Bureaucrats: A Socialist View of Labor Struggles Since the 1930s*. New York: Pathfinder.

Kii, T. 1991. "Retirement in Japan." Pp. 268-89 in J. Myles and J. Quadagno eds., *States, Labor Markets, and the Future of Old-Age Policy*. Philadelphia: Temple University Press.

Kinzley, W.D. 1991. *Industrial Harmony in Modern Japan: The Invention of a Tradition*. London: Routledge.

Kjellberg, A. 1983. *Facklig organisering i tolv länder*. Lund: Arkiv.

Klein, M.F.J. and R.H. Moses. 1974. "Pension Plans: What's At the End of the Rainbow." *Price Waterhouse & Company Review* 19:10-17.

Kohl, J. 1981. "Trends and Problems in Postwar Public Expenditure Development in Western Europe and North America." Pp. 307-44 in P. Flora and A.J. Heidenheimer eds., *The Development of Welfare States in Europe and America*. New Brunswick NJ: Transaction.

Kommittébetänkande. 1991a. "Betänkande av Pensionskommitté 1990." *Kommittébetänkande No. 41*. Helsinki: Statenstryckericentral.

——. 1991b. "Betänkande av Kommissionen för Arbetspensionsfonder." *Kommittébetänkande No. 44*. Helsinki: Statenstryckericentral.

Könberg, B. 1994. Ett pensionssystem för framtiden. Hovuddragen i pensionsarbetsgruppens förslag. Stockholm.

Korpi, W. 1978. *The Working Class in Welfare Capitalism: Work, Unions and Politics in Sweden*. London: Routledge & Kegan Paul.

——. 1983. *The Democratic Class Struggle*. London: Routledge and Kegan Paul.

——. 1985. "Power Resources Approach vs. Action and Conflict: on Causal and Intentional Explanations in the Study of Power." *Sociological Theory* 3:31-45.

——. 1989. "Power, Politics and State Autonomy in the Development of Social Citizenship: Social Rights During Sickness in 18 OECD-Countries Since 1930." *American Sociological Review* 54:309-28.

Kosai, Y. and Y. Ogino. 1984. *The Contemporary Japanese Economy*. Armonk NY: M.E. Sharpe.

Koskela, E. 1991. "Näkokohtia Yksityisen Sektorin Työeläkejärjestelmästä Suomessa." *Kansantaloudellinen aikakauskirja* 87:349-55.

Kosonen, P. 1985. "Public Expenditure in the Nordic Nation-States—The Source of Prosperity or Crisis?" Pp. 108-23 in R. Alapuro, E. Haavio-Mannila and R. Väyrynen eds., *Small States in Comparative Perspective*. Oslo: Norwegian University Press.

Koyama, K. 1978. *Eikokubyo no Kyokun*. Kyoto: PHP Kenkyujo.

Könberg, B. 1994. *Ett pensionssystem för framtiden*. Stockholm: Hovuddragen i pensionsarbetsgruppens förslag.

Kroll, J. 1946. "Why Labor is in Politics." *New York Times Sunday Magazine* October 27.

Krooss, H.E. 1970. *Executive Opinion: What Business Leaders Said and Thought on Economics Issues*. Garden City: Doubleday.

Kruse, A. 1988. *Pensionssystemets stabilitet*. Rapport till pensionsutredningen, Socialdepartementet. Stockholm: Allmänna Förlaget.

Kudrle, R.T. and T.R. Marmor. 1984. "The Development of Welfare States in North America." Pp. 81-121 in Peter Flora and Arnold J. Heidenheimer ed., *The Development of Welfare States in Europe and America*. New Brunswick NJ: Transaction Books.

Kuhnle, S. 1981. "The Growth of Social Insurance Programs in Scandinavia: Outside Influences and Internal Forces." Pp. 125-50 in Peter Flora.and A. Heidenheimer ed., *The Development of Welfare States in Europe and America*. New Brunswick and London: Transaction.

———. 1983. *Velferdsstatens utvickling—Norge i komparativt perspektiv*. Bergen: Universitetsforlaget.

Kuhnle, S. and L. Solheim. 1981. *Party Programs and the Welfare State: Consensus and Conflict in Norway 1945-1977*. Bergen: Institute of Comparative Politics.

Kumar, P., M.L. Coates and D. Arrowsmith. 1986. *The Current Industrial Relations Scene in Canada, 1986*. Kingston Ont.: Industrial Relations Section, Queen's University.

Kume, I. 1988. "Changing Relations Among the Government, Labor and Business in Japan After the Oil Crisis." *International Organization* 42:659-87.

Latimer, M. 1932. *Industrial Pension Systems in the United States and Canada*, 2 vols. New York: Industrial Relations Counselors Incorporated.

Leff, M.H. 1983. "Taxing the 'Forgotten Man': The Politics of Social Security Finance in the New Deal." *Journal of American History* 70:359-81.

———. 1987. "Historical Perspectives on Old-Age Insurance: The State of the Art on the Art of the State." Pp. 29-54 in E.D. Berkowitz ed., *Social Security After 50: Successes and Failures*. New York: Greenwood Press.

Levy, F. 1988. *Dollars and Dreams*. Russell Sage: New York.

Lewin, L. 1992. *Samhället och de organiserade intressena.* Stockholm: Norstedts.

Lichtenstein, N. 1982. *Labor's War at Home: The CIO in World War II.* New York: Cambridge University Press.

———. 1989. "From Corporatism to Collective Bargaining: Organized Labor and the Eclipse of Social Democracy in the Postwar Era." Pp. 122-52 in S. Fraser and G. Gerstle eds., *The Rise and Fall of the New Deal Order 1930-1980.* Princeton NJ: Princeton University Press.

Lipset, S.M. 1976. "Radicalism in North America: A Comparative View of the Party Systems in Canada and the United States." *Transactions of the Royal Society of Canada, IV* 14:19-55.

———. 1989. *Continental Divide: The Values and Institutions of the United States and Canada.* Toronto and Washington DC: Canadian-American Committee, sponsored by the C. D. Howe Institute and the National Planning Association.

Lipset, S.M. and W. Schneider. 1983. *The Confidence Gap: Business, Labor and Government in the Public Mind.* New York: The Free Press.

Macaulay, H. 1959. *Fringe Benefits and their Federal Tax Treatment.* New York: Columbia University Press.

Maier, C.S. 1970. "Between Taylorism and Technocracy: European Ideologies and the Vision of Industrial Productivity in the 1920s." *Journal of Contemporary History* 5:27-61.

Marsh, L. 1975. *Report on Social Security for Canada.* Toronto: University of Toronto Press.

McCallum, M.E. 1990. "Corporate Welfarism in Canada, 1919-39." *Canadian Historical Review* 71:46-79.

McGill, D.M., ed. 1977. *Social Security and Private Pension Plans: Competitive or Complementary?* Homewood IL: Irwin.

McGrady, E. 1930. "Old Age Pensions." *American Federationist* May.

McQuaid, K. 1978. "Corporate Liberalism in the American Business Community." *Business History Review* 52:342-68.

Meier, E. 1986. *Early Retirement Incentive Programs: Trends and Implications.* Washington DC: AARP.

Melling, J. 1991. "Industrial Capitalism and the Welfare of the State: The Role of Employers." *Sociology* 25:219-39.

Metcalf, E.B. 1972. "Economic Stabilization By American Business in the Twentieth Century." Unpublished Ph.D. dissertation, University of Wisconsin.

Meyer, M. 1981. *Profile of Employee Benefits: 1981 Edition*. New York: The Conference Board.

Meyer, M. and H. Fox. 1974. *Profile of Employee Benefits*. New York: The Conference Board.

Michanek, Å. 1959. *De Nya Pensionerna*. Stockholm: Tiden Forlag.

Migiya, R. 1984. *Kigyo Nenkin Star Wars*. Tokyo: Shakai Hoken Kohosha.

Mills, C.W. 1971. *The New Men of Power: America's Labor Leaders*. New York: Augustus M. Kelley.

Ministry of Labor (MOL). 1984. "Rodo Hakusho." (White Paper on Labor). Tokyo: MOL.

Minkoff, N. 1948. "Trade Union Welfare Programs." *Union Health and Welfare Plans, 1947*. Bulletin 900. Washington DC: Bureau of Labor Statistics.

Mishel, L. and J. Bernstein. 1993. *The State of Working America*. New York: M.E. Sharpe.

Molin, B. 1965. *Tjänstepensionsfrågan: En studie i svensk partipolitikk*. Göteborg: Akademiförlaget.

Morton, D. and M.E. McCallum. 1988. "Superannuation to Indexation: Employment Pensions in the Public and Private Sector in Canada, 1870-1970." Pp. 3-41 in *Task Force on Inflation Protection for Employment Pension Plans, Research Studies Vol. 1*. Toronto: Queen's Printer for Ontario.

Morton, W. 1933. "The Aims of Unemployment Insurance With Especial Reference to the Wisconsin Act." *American Economic Review* 23:395-412.

Mosley, H. 1981. "Corporate Social Benefits and the Underdevelopment of the American Welfare State." *Contemporary Crises* 5:139-54.

Munnell, A. 1982. *The Economics of Private Pensions*. Washington DC: The Brookings Institution.

Munts, R. 1967. *Bargaining For Health: Labor Unions, Health Insurance, and Medical Care*. Madison, WI: University of Wisconsin Press.

Murakami, K. 1991. *Kigyo Nenkin no Chishiki*. Tokyo: Nihon Keizaisha.

Murakami, Y. 1982. "The Age of New Middle Mass Politics: The Case of Japan." *Journal of Japanese Studies* 8:29-72.

Murray, R.F. 1968. *Economic Aspects of Pensions: A Summary Report*. New York: National Bureau of Economic Research.

Myles, J. 1984. *Old Age in the Welfare State: The Political Economy of Public Pensions*. Boston: Little Brown.

———. 1988. "Social Policy in Canada." Pp. 37-53 in Eloise Rathbone-McCuan and Betty Havens ed., *North American Elders: United States and Canadian Perspectives*. New York: Greenwood Press.

———. 1989. *Old Age in the Welfare State: The Political Economy of Public Pensions*, revised ed. Lawrence Kansas: University Press of Kansas.

———.1995. "Social welfare in North America: Adapting to a low wage economy." UNRISD project paper on the future of the Welfare State in connection with the 1995 United Nations World Summit Meeting, Copenhagen, March 8.

National Council of Welfare. 1989. *A Pension Primer*. Ottawa: Minister of Supply and Services Canada.

———. 1990. *Pension Reform*. Ottawa: Minister of Supply and Services Canada.

National Industrial Conference Board (NICB). 1925. *Industrial Pensions in the United States*. New York: NICB.

———. 1929. *Industrial Relations in Small Plants*. New York: NICB.

———. 1934. *Recent Developments in Industrial Group Insurance*. New York: NICB.

———. 1936. *What Employers are Doing for Employees*. New York: NICB.

———. 1937. *Personnel Practices Governing Factory and Office Administration*. New York: NICB.

———. 1939. *Company Pension Plans and the Social Security Act*. New York: NICB.

———. 1940. *Personnel Activities in American Business*. New York: NICB.

———. 1944. *Trends in Company Pension Plans*. New York: NICB.

———. 1947. *Personnel Activities in American Business (Revised)*. New York: NICB.

———. 1949. *The Social Security Almanac*. New York: NICB.

———. 1950. *Handbook on Pensions*. New York: NICB.

———. 1954. *Personnel Practices in Factory and Office*. New York: NICB.

———. 1955. *Pension Plans and their Administration*. New York: NICB.

———. 1964. *Personnel Practices in Factory and Office: Manufacturing*. New York: NICB.

———. 1965. *Office Personnel Practices: Nonmanufacturing*. New York: NICB.

National Labor Relations Board. 1948. *Legislative History of the Labor Management Relations Act, 1947*. Washington DC: Government Printing Office.

National Personnel Association. 1922. *Pensions for Industrial and Commercial Employees*. New York: National Personnel Association.

Naylor, J. 1991. *The New Democracy: Challenging the Social Order in Industrial Ontario, 1914-25*. Toronto: University of Toronto Press.

Nelson, D. 1969. *Unemployment Insurance, The American Experience, 1915-1935*. Madison: University of Wisconsin Press.

———. 1975. *Managers and Workers*. Madison: University of Wisconsin Press.

———. 1982. "The Company Union Movement, 1900-1937: A Reexamination." *Business History Review* 56:335-57.

Nelson, G.R. 1984. *ATP's Historie 1964-83 i Hovedtraek*. Hillerod (Denmark): ATP.

New York Times. 1923. "Eastman Tells About His Plan of Profit Sharing." *New York Times*, 4 Feb.

———. 1928. "Eastman Employees in Huge Insurance." *New York Times*, 21 Dec.

Niemelä, H. and K. Salminen. 1994. *State or Corporations: Trends of Pension Policy in Scandinavia*. Mimeo, Finnish Social Insurance Institute, Helsinki, January.

Nikkeiren. 1974. *Korekarano Taishokukin Kanri-Sono Mondaiten to Taisaku*. Tokyo: Nikkeiren.

Noguchi, Y. 1988. "Public Finance." Pp. 186-222 in K. Yamamura and Y. Yasuba eds., *The Political Economy of Japan, Vol. 1: The Domestic Transformation*. Stanford CA: Stanford University Press.

Nordisk Socialstatistisk Komite. 1992. *Social Tryghed i de Nordiske Lande*. Copenhagen: Nordic Statistical Secretariat.

Nørby-Johansen, L. 1986-87. "Denmark." Pp. 363-81 (Vol.1) and 191-246 (Vol.4) in P. Flora ed., *Growth to Limits: The Western European Welfare States since WWII*. Berlin and New York: de Gruyter.

O'Connor, J.S. 1989. "Welfare Expenditure and Policy Orientation in Canada in Comparative Perspective." *Canadian Review of Sociology and Anthropology* 26:127-50.

OECD. 1976. *Public Expenditure on Income Maintenance Programmes*. Paris: OECD.

———. 1978. *Public Expenditure Trends*. Paris: OECD.

———. 1988. *The Future of Social Protection*. Paris: OECD.

———. 1992. *Private Pensions and Public Policy*. Paris: OECD.

———. 1993. *National Accounts: Detailed Tables*. Paris: OECD.

Ohman, B. 1983. "The Debate on Wage-Earner Funds in Scandinavia." Pp. 35-52 in C. Crouch and F. Heller eds., *International Yearbook of Organizational Democracy, Vol. 1: Organizational Democracy & Political Processes*. London: John Wiley & Sons.

Okamoto, T. 1991. "Kyuhin Seido no Hensen." Pp. 20-41 in K. Yokoyama and H. Tada eds., *Nihon Shakai Hosho no Rekishi*. Tokyo: Gakubunsha.

Olsen, G.M., ed. 1988. *Industrial Change and Labour Adjustment in Sweden and Canada.* Toronto: Garamond Press.

———. 1991. "Labour Mobilization and the Strength of Capital: The Rise and Stall of Economic Democracy in Sweden." *Studies in Political Economy* 34:109-45.

———. 1992. *The Struggle for Economic Democracy in Sweden.* Aldershot: Avebury Press.

———. 1994. "Locating the Canadian Welfare State: Family Policy and Health Care in Canada, Sweden and the United States." *Canadian Journal of Sociology* 19:1-20.

Olsen, L.K. 1982. *The Political Economy of Aging: The State, Private Power and Social Welfare.* New York: Columbia University Press.

Olson, C. A. 1995. "Health Benefits Coverage Among Male Workers." *Monthly Labor Review* 118:55-60.

Olsson, S.E. 1990. *Social Policy and Welfare State in Sweden.* Lund: Arkiv.

O'Rand, A.M. 1986. "The Hidden Payroll: Employee Benefits and the Structure of Workplace Inequality." *Sociological Forum* 1:657-83.

Orloff, A.S. and E. Parker. 1990a. "Agrarian politics in the emergence of the North American welfare states, 1920-1940." paper presented at the Annual Meeting of the American Sociological Association, Washington DC.

———. 1990b. "Business and Social Policy in Canada and the United States, 1920-1940." *Comparative Social Research* 12:295-339.

Orloff, A.S. and T. Skocpol. 1984. "Why Not Equal Protection? Explaining the Politics of Public Social Spending in Britain, 1900-1911, and the United States, 1880's-1920." *American Sociological Review* 49:726-51.

Ornstein, M. 1989. "The Social Organization of the Canadian Capitalist Class in Comparative Perspective." *Canadian Review of Sociology and Anthropology* 26:151-77.

Osterman, P. 1990. "The Dynamics of Change in the US Welfare State: The Public-Private Interaction." Mimeo, Department of Sociology, MIT, October.

Otake, H. 1987. "Keiei Kyogikai No Seiritsu to Henyo." Pp. 349-84 in Y. Sakamoto and R.E. Ward eds., *Nihon Senryo no Kenkyu.* Tokyo: Tokyo Daigaku Shuppankai.

Øverbye, E. 1991. "Offentlige og private pensjoner i Norden." Report to the Nordic Ministry Council/INAS-report 91:10.

———. 1988. "Jakten På Det Private. Spenningen Mellom Privat og Offentlig Styring i Pensjonssektorenn." Pp. 311-44 in H. Bogen and O. Ove Langeland eds., *Offentlig Eller Privat.* Oslo: FAFO.

360   *References*

————. 1990. *God tjenestepensjon eller høy lønn?* Oslo: INAS.

Palme, J. 1990. *Pension Rights in Welfare Capitalism. The Development of Old-Age Pensions in 18 OECD Countries 1930 to 1985.* Stockholm: Swedish Institute for Social Research, Stockholm University.

————. 1994. "Recent Trends in Income Transfer Systems in Sweden." Pp. 39-59 in N. Ploug and J. Kvist eds., *Recent Trends in Cash Benefits in Europe.* Copenhagen: Danish National Institute for Social Research.

Papadakis, E. and P Taylor-Gooby. 1987. *The Private Provision of Public Welfare: State, Market and Community.* New York: St. Martin's Press.

Parks, D.S. 1936. "1936 Personnel Trends." *Factory Management and Maintenance* 94:39-40.

Pedersen, A.W. 1994. "What makes the difference? Cross-national variations in pension systems and their distributional outcome." Paper presented at the Workshop on Convergence and Divergence, Soro, Denmark, June 9-11.

————. 1990. *Fagbevegelsen og Folketrygden: LOs målsetninger, strategi og innflytelse i pensjonspolitikken 1945-1966.* Oslo: FAFO.

Pempel, T.J. 1987. "The Tar Baby Target: 'Reform' of the Japanese Bureaucracy." Pp. 157-87 in R.A. Ward and Y. Sakamoto eds., *Democratizing Japan.* Honolulu: University of Hawaii Press.

————. 1989. "Japan's Creative Conservatism: Continuity Under Challenge." Pp. 149-91 in F.G. Castles ed., *The Comparative History of Public Policy.* Cambridge: Polity Press.

————. 1990. *Uncommon Democracies: The One-Party Dominant Regimes.* Ithaca NY: Cornell University Press.

Pentikäinen, T. 1987. "Arbetspensionssystemet i Finland 25 År." *Nordisk Forsikringstidsskrift* 75:25-37.

Pestieau, P. 1992. "How Fair is the Distribution of Private Pension Benefits?" Luxembourg Income Study (LIS) Working Papers, No. 72, April.

Perrin, G. 1972. "Supplementary Pension Schemes in the Nordic Countries." *International Social Security Review* 25:357-75.

Petersen, E. 1975. *Norsk Arbeidsgiverforening 1950-75.* Oslo: NAF.

Petersen, J. 1990. "The Danish 1981 Act on Old Age Relief: A Response to Agrarian Demand and Pressure." *Journal of Social Policy* 19:69-91.

Pettersen, P.A. 1982. *Linjer i norsk sosialpolitikk.* Oslo: Universitetsforlaget.

Phillips, S.M. and L.P. Fletcher. 1977. "The Future of the Portable Pension Concept." *Industrial and Labor Relations Review* 30:197-204.

Piore, M. and C. Sabel. 1984. *The Second Industrial Divide.* New York: Basic Books.

Piven, F.F. and R.A. Cloward. 1971. *Regulating the Poor: The Functions of Public Welfare*. New York: Vintage.

———. 1977. *Poor People's Movements: Why They Succeed, How They Fail*. New York: Pantheon.

Ploug, N. and J. Kvist, eds. 1994. *Recent Trends in Cash Benefits in Europe* Volume 4 of *Social Security in Europe*. Copenhagen: Danish National Institute for Social Research.

Pryor, F.L. 1968. *Public Expenditures in Communist and Capitalist Nations*. London: George Allen and Unwin.

Quadagno, J. 1984. "Welfare Capitalism and the Social Security Act of 1935." *American Sociological Review* 49:632-47.

———. 1988. *The Transformation of Old Age Security: Class and Politics in the American Welfare State*. Chicago: University of Chicago Press.

Quinn, J. and R. Burkhauser. 1990. "Work and Retirement." Pp. 307-23 in R. Binstock and L. George eds., *Handbook of Aging and the Social Sciences*. New York: Academic Press.

Raff, D. 1991. "Ford Welfare Capitalism in Its Economic Context." Pp. 90-105 in S.M. Jacoby ed., *Masters to Managers: Historical and Comparative Perspectives on American Employers*. New York: Columbia University Press.

Rasmussen, E. 1985. "Arbeiderbevægelsen og pensionssystem i Sverige 1913 til 1983." Working Paper, University of Copenhagen, Institute of Sociology.

Regini, M. 1991. *Confini Mobili: La Costruzione dell'Economia fra Politica e Societa*. Bologna: Il Mulino.

Rein, M. 1982. "The Social Policy of the Firm." *Policy Sciences* 14:117-35.

Rein, M. and L. Rainwater, eds. 1986a. *Public/Private Interplay in Social Protection: A Comparative Study*. New York: M.E. Sharpe.

———. 1986b. "The Public/Private Mix." Pp. 3-24 in M. Rein and L. Rainwater eds., *Public/Private Interplay in Social Protection*. Armonk NY: M.E. Sharpe.

———. 1986c. "The Institutions of Social Protection." Pp. 25-56 in M. Rein and L. Rainwater eds., *Public/Private Interplay in Social Protection: A Comparative Study*. Armonk NY: M.E. Sharpe.

Rein, M. and E. Wadensjö. forthcoming. *The Emerging Role of the Enterprise in Social Policy*. Cheltenham UK: Edward Elgar.

Ringen, S. 1987. "Mål og Motiv i Velferdspolitikken." *Norsk Statsvitenskapelig Tidsskrift* 4:63-76.

Ringen, S. and H. Uusitalo. 1992. "Income Distribution in the Nordic Welfare States." in J.E. Kolberg ed., *The Study of Welfare State Regimes*. Armonk NY: M.E. Sharpe.

Robertson, D.B. 1989. "The Bias of American Federalism: The Limits of Welfare-State Development in the Progressive Era." *Journal of Policy History* 1:261-91.

Rokkan, S. 1981. "The Growth and Structuring of Mass Politics." Pp. 53-79 in E. Allardt ed., *Nordic Democracy*. Copenhagen: Det Danske Selskab.

————. 1966. "Norway: Numerical Democracy and Corporate Pluralism." Pp. 70-166 in R.A. Dahl ed., *Political Oppositions in Western Democracies*. New Haven NY: Yale University Press.

Romppanen, A., ed. 1991. *Finland 1990-2005, a Time of Challenge and Preparation*. Helsinki: Government Institute for Economic Research.

Ross, D. 1991. *The Origins of American Social Science*. Cambridge, UK: .

Rowe, E.K. 1951. "Employee Benefit Plans Under Collective Bargaining, Mid-1950." *Monthly Labor Review* 61:156.

Ruben, G. 1990. "Collective Bargaining in 1989: Old Problems, New Issues." *Monthly Labor Review* 113:19-30.

Salminen, K. 1993. *Pension Schemes in the Making: A Comparative Study of the Scandinavian Countries*. Helsinki: Central Pension Security Institute.

Sawyer, M. 1976. *Income Distribution in OECD Countries*. Paris: OECD.

Scheinberg, S. 1966. "The Development of Corporation Labor Policy, 1900-1940." Unpublished Ph.D. dissertation, University of Wisconsin.

Scheuer, S. 1990. "LO's Strukturdebat." *Politica* (Copenhagen) 22:470-87.

Schieber, S.J. 1982. *Social Security*. Washington DC: Employee Benefit Research Institute.

Schmahl, W. 1990. "On the Future Development of Retirement in Europe, especially of Supplementary Pension Schemes", Paper presented at the International Seminar on "The Future of Basic and Supplementary Pension Schemes in the European Community—1992 and Beyond." Bremen, January 29-30.

Schmidt, F. 1974. *Almänna och private pensioner: Mål och medel*. Copenhagen: P. A. Nordstedt and Söners.

Schulz, J. 1985. *The Economics of Aging*. New York: Van Nostrand Reinhold.

Schulz, J., A. Borowski and W.H. Crown. 1991. *Economics of Population Aging*. New York: Auburn House.

Schwartz, D.and H. Grundmann. 1991. "Social Insurance Programs: Old Age, Survivors and Disability Insurance." *Social Security Bulletin* 54:5-19.

Seidman, J. 1953. *American Labor From Defense to Reconversion*. Chicago: University of Chicago Press.

Shalev, M. 1983. "The Social Democratic Model and Beyond: Two 'Generations' of Comparative Research on the Welfare State." *Comparative Social Research* 6:315-51.

———. 1988. "The Political Economy of Employment-Based Social Protection: An Approach and an Illustration." Paper presented at the ISA Workshop on Comparative Research in Social Policy, Labor Markets, Inequality, and Distributive Conflict.

———. 1990. "Class Conflict, Corporatism and Comparison: The Japanese Enigma." Pp. 60-93 in S.N. Eisenstadt and E. Ben-Ari eds., *Japanese Models of Conflict Resolution*. London and New York: Kegan-Paul International.

Sheppard, H. 1991. "The United States: The Privatization of Exit." Pp. 252-83 in M. Kohli, M. Rein, Anne-M. Guillemard and H. van Gunsteren eds., *A Time for Retirement*. Cambridge: Cambridge University Press.

Shimada, H. 1983. "Japanese Industrial Relations—A New General Model?" Pp. 3-27 in T. Shirai ed., *Contemporary Industrial Relations in Japan*. Madison WI: University of Wisconsin Press.

Shinkawa, T. 1984. "Senkyuhyaku Nanajugonen Shunto to Keisai Kiki Kanri." Pp. 189-232 in O. Hideo ed., *Nihon Seiji no Shoten*. Tokyo: San-ichi Shobo.

———. 1993. *Nihongata Fukushi no Seiji Keizaigaku*. Tokyo: San-ichi Shobo.

Shirai, T., ed. 1983. *Contemporary Industrial Relations in Japan*. Madison WI: University of Wisconsin Press.

Shoji, H. 1990. "Kosei Nenkin Kikin-Kigyo Nenkin-Unyo no Kaizen nimo Kadai." *Chingin to Shakai Hosho* 1041/42:56-57.

Skocpol, T. 1980. "Political Response to Capitalist Crisis: Neo-Marxist Theories of the State and the Case of the New Deal." *Politics and Society* 10:155-201.

Skocpol, T. and E. Amenta. 1985. "Did Capitalists Shape Social Security?" *American Sociological Review* 50:572-75.

Skocpol, T. and J. Ikenberry. 1983. "The Political Formation of the American Welfare State in Historical and Comparative Perspective." *Comparative Social Research* 6:87-148.

Skolnik, A.M. 1976a. "Private Pension Plans, 1950-1974." *Social Security Bulletin* 39(6):3-17.

———. 1976b. "Twenty-Five Years of Employee-Benefit Plans." *Social Security Bulletin* 39(9):3-22.

Skånland, H. 1989. "Samfunnsøkonomiske perspektiver i trygdepolitikken." Lecture notes 10/10. Oslo:Norwegian National Bank.

Slavick, F. 1953. "The Provision of Disability and Medical Care Insurance Through Collective Bargaining: An Analysis of Ten Programs." Unpublished Ph.D. Dissertation, Princeton University.

Slichter, S. 1961. *Potentials of the American Economy: Selected Essays of Sumner H. Slichter.* Cambridge, MA: Harvard University Press.

Social Insurance Institution. 1991. *Statistical Yearbook of the Social Insurance Institution 1990.* Helsinki: Social Insurance Institution.

Social Security Administration. 1985. *Social Security Bulletin: Annual Statistical Supplement, 1984-85.* Washington DC: GPO.

SOU. 1990. *Statens offentliga utredningar 76/1990.* Stockholm: Allmänna Förlaget.

Spencer, R. 1994. "State Health Reform Hits ERISA Law: Pension Act Restricts Innovation." *Washington Post* December 1, A10:117.

Stafford, J. 1986. "Retirement Pensions: Reinforced Exploitation." Pp. 285-308 in James Dickinson and Bob Russell ed., *Family, Economy and State: The Social Reproduction Process Under Capitalism.* Toronto: Garamond Press.

————. 1987. "The Rise of Pensions in Canada." Pp. 124-36 in R. Argue, C. Gannage and D.W. Livingstone eds., *Working People and Hard Times.* Toronto: Garamond Press.

Stark, H. 1989. "1988 World Vehicle Production Sets New Record." Pp. 75-76 in *Ward's Automotive Yearbook.* Detroit MI: Ward's Communication Inc.

Starr, P. 1982. *The Social Transformation of American Medicine.* New York: Basic Books.

Statistics Canada. 1978. *Employee Compensation in Canada, All Industries.* Ottawa: Minister of Supply and Services Canada.

————. 1990. *Pension Plans in Canada, 1988.* Ottawa: Minister of Supply and Services Canada.

Stein, B. 1957. "Labor's Role in Government Agencies During World War II." *Journal of Economic History* 17:389-408.

Stein, L. 1977. *Out of the Sweatshop: The Struggle for Industrial Democracy.* New York: Quadrangle.

Stephens, J.D. 1979. *The Transition from Capitalism to Socialism.* London: Macmillan.

Stevens, B. 1988. "Blurring the Boundaries: How the Federal Government Has Influenced Welfare Benefits in the Private Sector." Pp. 123-48 in M. Weir, A.S. Orloff and T. Skocpol eds., *The Politics of Social Policy in the United States.* Princeton NJ: Princeton University Press.

Stokke, T.A. 1994. "Organisasjonsgraden i Norge 1956-1993: Oppdaterte beregninger." Unpublished paper. Oslo: FAFO.

Stone, M. 1957. *Since 1845: A History of the Mutual Benefit Life Insurance Company.* New Brunswick NJ: Rutgers University Press.

Streeck, W. 1990. "La Dimensione Sociale Del Mercato Unico Europeo: Verso Un'economia Non Regolata?" *Stato e Mercato* 10:29-68.

Ståhlberg, Ann-C. 1988. *Pensionssystemets inverkan på hushållens sparande. Expertrapport till Spardelegationens sparutredning.* Stockholm: Almänna förlaget.

Sudo, M. 1991. "Shakai Hosho Seido No Ayumi." Pp. 42-63 in K. Yokoyama and H. Tada eds., *Nihon Shakai Hosho no Rekishi.* Tokyo: Gakubunsha.

Therborn, G. 1986. *Why Some Peoples Are More Unemployed Than Others.* London: Verso.

Thulin, E. 1946. *Samanställning av bestämmelser inom det statliga pensionsväsendet.* Stockholm: Statens Pensionsvärk.

Tilove, R. 1960. "Social and Economic Implementation of Private Pensions." *Industrial and Labor Relations Review* 14:24-34.

———. 1968. "The Impact of Social Insurance on the Development of Private Benefit Plans." Pp. 187-209 in W.G. Bowen, F.H. Harbison, R.A. Lester and H.M. Somers eds., *The American System of Social Insurance.* New York: McGraw-Hill.

Titmuss, R.M. 1974. *Social Policy.* London: Allen & Unwin.

———. 1958. *Essays on 'The Welfare State'.* London: George Allen & Unwin.

———. 1959. "The Social Division of Welfare: Some Reflections on the Search for Equity." Pp. 34-55 in R.M. Titmuss ed., *Essays on 'The Welfare State'.* New Haven: Yale University Press.

Tomlins, C. 1985. *The State and the Unions: Labor Relations, Law, and the Organized Labor Movement in America, 1880-1960.* New York: Cambridge University Press.

Tsujinaka Yutaka. 1986. "Rodo Dantai." Pp. 223-62 in M. Nakano ed., *Nihongata Seisaku Katai no Henyo.* Tokyo: Toyo Keizai Shimposha.

Turner, J.A. and L.M. Dailey. 1990. *Pension Policy: An International Perspective.* Washington DC: GPO.

Turner, J.A. and N. Watanabe. 1995. *Private Pension Policies in Industrialized Countries.* Kalamazoo MI: W.E. Upjohn Institute.

Turner, V. 1969. *The Ritual Process: Structure and Antistructure.* New York: de Gruyter.

US Congress (House Ways and Means). 1934. "Hearings Before a Subcommittee on Unemployment Insurance." (73rd Congress, 2nd Session).

———. 1939. "Hearings Relative to the Social Security Act Amendments of 1939 (Vol. 2)." (76th Congress, 1st Session).

US Congress (Senate). 1935. "Statement of Marion B. Folsom." Hearings before the Committee on Finance (74th Congress, 1st Session).

Valen, H. and S. Rokkan. 1974. "Norway: Conflict Structure and Mass Politics in a European Periphery." Pp. 315-70 in R. Rose ed., *Electoral Behavior: A Comparative Handbook*. New York: Free Press.

van Gunsteren, H. and M. Rein. 1985. "The Dialectic of Public and Private Pensions." *Journal of Social Policy* 14:129-49.

Verba, S.et al. 1987. *Elites and the Idea of Equality*. Cambridge MA: Harvard University Press.

Vesterø-Jensen, C. 1984. *Det Tvedelte Pensionssystem*. Roskilde (Denmark): Roskilde University Centre.

Vise, D.A. 1994. "Senate Passes Pension Reform Measures: Bill Requires Companies to Put More Money in Underfunded Plans." *Washington Post* December 2, D3:117.

Vogel, J. 1991. *Statistical Reports of the Nordic Countries. Social Reports for the Nordic Countries: Living conditions and Inequality in the Late 1980's*. Stockholm: Nordic Statistical Secretariat.

von Nordheim Nielsen, F. 1986. "Occupational Pensions in Northern Europe." Working Paper No. 1, University of Copenhagen, Department of Sociology.

———. 1990. "The Long Shadows of the Past: Scandinavian Pensions Politics in the 1980s." Paper presented at the 12th World Congress of Sociology, Madrid, June 9-13.

———. 1991. "The Politics of Aging in Scandinavian Countries." Pp. 127-74 in J. Quadagno and J. Myles eds., *States, Labor Markets and the Future of Old age Policy*. Philadelphia: Temple University Press.

Vroman, W. 1990. *Unemployment Insurance Trust Fund Adequacy in the 1990s*. Kalamazoo: W.E. Upjohn Institute for Employment Research.

Waldo, D., K. Levit and H. Lazenby. 1986. "National Health Expenditures, 1985." *Health Care Financing Review* 8:1-22.

Ward's. 1989. *Ward's Automotive Yearbook*. Detroit MI: Ward's Reports Inc.

Warne, C. 1949. "Industrial Relations in Coal." Pp. 367-86 in C.E. Warne ed., *Labor in Postwar America*. Brooklyn: Remsen Press.

Watkins, M. 1994. "Ontario: Discrediting Social Democracy." *Studies in Political Economy* No. 43:139-48.

Webber, J.E. 1924. "Making Kodaks and Contentment." *American Industries* 25:28-30.

Whiteside, N. 1980. "Welfare Legislation and the Unions During the First World War." *The Historical Journal* 23:857-74.

Whitney, A. 1934. "Operation of Unemployment Benefit Plans in the United States Up To 1934." *Monthly Labor Review* 38:1305-17.

Wiebe, R. 1967. *The Search for Order, 1877-1920*. New York: Hill and Wang.

Wilensky, H. 1975. *The Welfare State and Equality: Structural and Ideological Roots of Public Expenditures.* Berkeley CA: University of California Press.

Wilson, W.H. 1962. "How the Chamber of Commerce Viewed the NRA." *Mid America* 44:95-108.

Witte, E. 1948. "The Taft-Hartley Act in Operation." *Industrial and Labor Relations Review* 2:403-7.

———. 1963. *The Development of the Social Security Act.* Madison: University of Wisconsin Press.

Woods, J.R. 1994. "Pension Coverage Among the Baby Boomers: Initial Findings from a 1993 Survey." *Social Security Bulletin* 57:19-25.

Wolfskill, G. 1962. *The Revolt of the Conservatives: A History of the American Liberty League.* Boston: Houghton Mifflin.

Yamamura, K. 1985. "The Cost of Rapid Growth and Capitalist Democracy in Japan." Pp. 467-508 in L. Lindberg and C. Maier eds., *The Politics of Inflation and Economic Stagnation.* Washington DC: The Brookings Institution.

Yamamura, K. and Y. Yasuba, eds. 1987. *The Political Economy of Japan, Vol. 1: The Domestic Transformation.* Stanford CA: Stanford University Press.

Yamashita, T. 1991. *Nihonteki Keiei no Tenkai.* Kyoto: Horitsu Bunkasha.

Yamazaki, H. 1988. "Kosei Nenkin Seido no 'Bappon Kaitei'." Pp. 79-169 in Tokyo Daigaku Shakai Kagaku Kenkyujo ed., *Tenkanki no Fukushi Kokka 2.* Tokyo: Tokyo Daigaku Shuppankai.

Yokoyama, K. and H. Tada, eds. 1991. *Shakai Hosho no Rekishi.* Tokyo: Gakubunsha.

Zushi, S. 1982. "Jiban Chinka Ichijirushii Keizai Doyukai." *Kokumin no Dokusen Hakusho* 6:95-108.

Author Index

Subject Index and Glossary

This index includes laws, programs, organizations, and economic branches; countries other than those analyzed in the study; and references to individuals not covered by the Author Index. Institutions or programs with no stated or implied location are based in the USA.

—W—

Wage-earner funds (Sweden), 233, 255
Wagner Act (1935), 76, 110-11, 114-5, 117-8, 129, 292
Wagner-Lewis bill (1934), 56-8
Wagner-Murray-Dingell National Health Bill, 84, 99
Walker, Elmer, 100
War Labor Board, 117
War Labor Disputes Act (1943), 80
War Production Board, 117
West Germany, *see* Germany
Western Europe, 104, 279, 294, 333
West-Nordic countries, 18, 159
White House, 46
Williamson, W. Rulon, 100
Woll, Matthew, 101, 102
World War II, 17, 75, 78, 195, 212-3, 215, 217, 225, 269-70, 302, 329, 331

—Y—

YEL (pension scheme for the non-farm self-employed, Finland), 172
YMCA Silver Bay Conference, 46